Dr. William Gibson MA PhD
F.R. Hist.S. F.R.S.A.

'Good and Proper Men'

Lord Palmerston and
the Bench of Bishops

Nigel Scotland

James Clarke & Co

First Published in 2000 by:
James Clarke & Co
P.O. Box 60
Cambridge
CB1 2NT
England

e-mail: **publishing@jamesclarke.co.uk**
website: **http://www.jamesclarke.co.uk**

ISBN 0 227 67946 6 hardback
ISBN 0 227 67947 4 paperback

British Library Cataloguing in Publication Data:
A catalogue record is available from the British Library.

Contents

Illustrations

Preface

Lord Palmerston could best be described as a nominal Anglican. He was an irregular attender at the Sunday worship of his parish church in Romsey. He believed religion had a role to play in upholding values and encouraging a sense of duty. In his early Tory days in 1824 he spoke in the House of Commons of the importance of preventing the falling off in the congregations of the Church of England in view of the role which the establishment performed in upholding the social structures of England. Palmerston had a general hostility to High Churchmen linking them with Roman Catholicism and popish doctrines for which he had a particular dislike and even fear. This paranoia may have stemmed from his Irish upbringing.

In the summer of 1829 Palmerston's step-daughter, Lady Emily Cowper, met a young evangelical Tory aristocrat, Anthony Ashley, whom she married in June the following year. Although neither Palmerston nor his wife shared the fervent personal faith of their daughter and son-in-law, their relationship was deep and affectionate.

In 1855 Palmerston was appointed Prime Minister, an office which he held until his death in 1865 except for a period of fifteen months in 1858-1859. Ashley who had by this time become the seventh Earl of Shaftesbury possibly exaggerated Palmerston's ignorance of things biblical and ecclesiastical when he declared: ' He does not know, in theology, Moses from Sydney Smith.'[1]

Nevertheless the fact of the matter was that Palmerston clearly lacked the confidence to make high ecclesiastical appointments off his own back. Shaftesbury later recalled that his father-in-law only ever made one appointment, that of Blakesley, Canon of Canterbury, without bringing him into the matter. When Shaftesbury told Palmerston that he had better consult the other bishops he was told, 'No no, you are quite enough; I had rather take your advice than that of all the bishops put together.' Palmerston did take note of the opinions of others but Shaftesbury, 'the bishop-maker' as he came to be called, was clearly the most influential voice.

During his premiership Palmerston made appointments to twenty-one English bishoprics and a number of Irish Sees in addition. When he died more than half the bishops of England were his appointees and they marked a significant change in the nature of English episcopacy. The Palmerstonian prelates were not without their critics. Samuel Wilberforce, the leader of the High-Church party described them as 'wicked' and the *Saturday Review* even suggested that they couldn't read Greek! This book, which is based on a detailed scrutiny of primary sources, aims to provide a balanced assessment of Lord Palmerston's English prelates. It compares them with the generation who preceded them as well as with their successors. Contrary to popular Victorian opinions the Palmerstonian bishops were not only good pastors but there were also able scholars among them.

My debts are various. I am grateful to David Bebbington for stimulating my interest in this topic, to Meg Davies, and to the school of Theology and Religious Studies for a semester's leave to facilitate study and writing. Adrian Brink gave me helpful and constructive advice on the first draft of the manuscript. I am also indebted to Joanna Warnerand Christine Preston for their help in word-processing the text.

Nigel Scotland
Cheltenham

I

Bishops in the Early Nineteenth Century

The Church of England's Book of Common Prayer in its preface to 'The Form and Manner of Making, Ordaining, and Consecrating Bishops, Priests and Deacons' declares that there have been bishops since the apostles' time. The service for 'Ordaining or consecrating of an Archbishop or Bishop' prays that all Bishops 'may diligently preach thy Word, and duly administer the godly Discipline thereof.' Early nineteenth-century Church of England Bishops were, however, very far removed from their New Testament counterparts, and most fell very short of ideals set out in the Prayer Book Service.

In the early Christian centuries there were many bishops, some of whom had charge of only one or two churches, or very small geographical areas. In contrast, the early nineteenth-century bishops of the Established Church were few and far between. In the year 1800 twenty-six bishops had an average of 412 parishes in their several dioceses. Put another way, they had to fulfil the role of fathers-in-God to a population of sixteen million souls. What made matters worse was the fact that the burgeoning towns and cities of the Industrial Revolution, such as Liverpool, Birmingham, Manchester, Sheffield and Newcastle, were often a long way from the residence of their chief pastor. Each bishop had a seat in the House of Lords, and this meant that if they were concerned about this responsibility they were often away from the diocese during parliamentary sessions. It was not surprising, therefore, that visitations and visitation addresses were comparatively rare occurrences, and that confirmations were infrequent, large and badly organised. For instance, Bishop Sparke confirmed 8,000 children in Manchester in one day between 8.00 a.m. and 8.30 p.m.[1] When Bishop Bathurst died in 1837 at the age of ninety-three, his Norwich diocese contained 900 parishes. He held confirmations once every seven years.[2]

A number of the early nineteenth century bishops still lived in the manner and style of medieval princely prelates such as William Warham and Thomas Wolsey. Richard Soloway pointed out that only thirty-eight of a hundred bishops already installed in 1783, or appointed over the next sixty-nine years, lacked any direct familial relationships with the aristocracy.[3]

Among the more prominent aristocratic prelates of the early nineteenth century were Shute Barrington (1734-1826), Bishop of Durham from 1791-1826, who was the son of the first Lord Barrington. Another was Charles

Manners-Sutton (1755-1828), Primate of All England from 1805-1828, who was brother to the first Baron Manners. Others included Brownlow North (1741-1820) successively Bishop of Lichfield, Worcester and Winchester, whose father was Francis North, first Earl of Guildford, and Edward Harcourt (1757-1847), Archbishop of York from 1807-1847, the son of Lord Vernon. Inevitably, therefore, these prelates were identified with the peers of the realm and were, generally speaking, aligned with the landed and commercial interests of the upper echelons of society. Most had little time to grapple with the Church, which, in the words of Owen Chadwick, 'had a parochial system adapted to ministry in villages, its clergy gentlemen, its legal framework inflexible and unable to meet new circumstances'. He continued that 'the clergy were learned, well-connected, socially acceptable, and influential as magistrates are influential'.[4]

The more prominent sees commanded a considerable income. At the turn of the century the archbishop of Canterbury and the bishop of Durham both received more than £19,000 per year, and the Archbishop of York and the bishops of London and Winchester received about £12,000 a year.[5] Bishop Sparke of Ely not only commanded a stipend of £12,000 per annum, but went on to appoint his two sons and his son-in-law to benefices worth a total of £12,000. It was said that Bishop Sparke was pleased when he succeeded in obtaining a prebendal stall for his eldest son, but when he managed to get another for his second son he was so delighted that he gave a ball at his palace to celebrate the occasion.[6] Archbishop Charles Manners-Sutton (1755-1828) saw his son-in-law obtain an archdeaconry, a chancellorship, two prebends, two rectories and a curacy, together yielding an income which was estimated to be £10,000. Brownlow North (1741-1820), whose brother Lord North was Prime Minister, began his episcopate at the young age of thirty when he was appointed to the See of Lichfield in 1771. He was translated to Worcester in 1774 and Winchester in 1781, where he remained for nearly forty years. He was known as an 'honourable English gentleman' who was dignified and courteous, amiable and generous. He was also frequently absent from his diocese for long periods of continental travel.[7] Richard Hurd (1720-1808), who was Bishop of Worcester from 1781-1808, was renowned as 'a great stickler for the external dignities of his office'. To outward observers he seemed 'ostentatious, vain and fond of state'. He also liked to move from place to place with 'a certain pomp of retinue'.[8] William Van Mildert (1756-1836) was literally a prince bishop, receiving with his translation to the See of Durham the County Palatine of Durham and the County of Sadberge. Pomp and ceremonial marked Van Mildert's new palatinate. His entry into the diocese on 14 July 1826 was 'a masterpiece of traditional pageantry'. When he crossed over the Croft-on-Tees Bridge into County Durham, he was greeted by 'about forty other carriages besides a large cavalcade of horsemen, and some hundreds of people on foot'. He was then escorted by a guard of honour of some thirty or forty men to the Castle Gate.[9] When Van Mildert entertained the Duke of Wellington, over one hundred distinguished guests were entertained in the Great Hall of Auckland Castle to a sumptuous banquet with a private entertainment. The floors were covered with crimson drugget and no expense was spared. Amongst other items it was noted that there were bills for 27 pounds of Cheshire Cheese and an 'intolerable deal of alcohol'.[10]

William Howley (1766-1848), who was Archbishop of Canterbury from 1828-1848, was another prelate who was noted for his ostentatious behaviour and general extravagance. When he drove from Westminster to Lambeth he rode in a coach flanked by outriders. Whenever he crossed the courtyard of Lambeth Palace to Mrs. Howley's lodgings, he was preceded by men carrying flaming torches. On one day each week Howley kept open house. The invitation to dine was open to anyone who wore court dress. The food was served by thirty flunkeys clad in livery.[11]

Numbers of the early nineteenth century bishops were party to pluralism. For instance when Van Mildert was Rector of St. Mary-le-Bow, Cheapside in London, he thought it perfectly acceptable to ask for the living of Farningham, near Sevenoaks, 'as an agreeable retreat within a convenient distance from the town'. The Archbishop of Canterbury, to whom he had applied, Charles Manners-Sutton (1755-1828), 'thought it quite right to give it to him for this purpose'.[12] While holding the See of Exeter, Henry Courtenay (1741-1803) held the living of St. George's, Hanover Square with a population of 43,396, George Pelham (1766-1827) had a living in Sussex, and Christopher Bethell (1773-1859) an incumbency in Yorkshire.[13]

With many bishops conducting their episcopates in these kinds of way it was no surprise that the spiritual life of many dioceses was at a low ebb. Indeed, even if bishops had genuinely wanted to improve the situation, the legal system offered little means of redress. The first thirty years of the nineteenth century were therefore marked by apathy, indifference and low levels of spirituality. Ordination examinations were often at best perfunctory, and at other times scandalously lacking in integrity. J.H. Overton wrote: 'We hear of strange tales of one bishop examining his candidates for ordination in a tent on a cricket field, he himself being one of the players; of another sending a message by his butler, to the candidate, to write an essay; of another performing the difficult process of examining a man while shaving'.[14] Even as late as 1830, thirteen bishops voted, probably out of party loyalty, with the government against a proposal by the Duke of Richmond to establish a Select Committee 'to enquire into the condition of the working-classes'.[15] An inhabitant of Norwich stated: 'In 1837 I saw from my windows nine parishes, of which only one contained a resident clergyman'. In another deanery in the same city only five churches out of twenty-eight held two services every Sunday.[16] In 1834 it was reported that in the Oxford diocese there were only 7,000 communicants out of a total of 152,000 souls.[17] Richard Bagot (1782-1854) who held the See from 1829 to 1845 was eventually eased out of Oxford by Peel, who wanted a stronger resident bishop to deal with the growing influence of the Tractarians. Bagot was therefore translated to Bath and Wells, where he was very shortly afterwards incapacitated and never completely recovered. During most of that time his diocese was administered by the Bishop of Gloucester and Bristol.[18] When Charles Blomfield (1786-1857) first arrived as Bishop of Chester in 1828 he discovered that no episcopal returns had been sent out since 1788, and that during the previous hundred years no bishop had made more than one perfunctory visit of each parish.[19] John Stoughton, who wrote at the end of the Victorian era, summed up the bishops in the early years of century as inaccessible and neglectful.

> People in general who favoured reform were alienated from the prelates because they opposed liberal measures. They had almost all been appointed by Conservative governments during a long lease of political power. For the most part they continued to adopt aristocratic habits, and lived apart from the commonalty. The revenues of certain Sees were enormous, very different from what they are now; and there was a display of wealth and state of splendour such as could not fail to alienate the humble class. Neglect of spiritual duties, absence of religious zeal, immense nepotism, and the toleration of abuses and scandals in clerical life, had been for many years increasing public disfavour.[20]

All this meant that bishops were generally speaking uncritical both of the Church, the Establishment and the Nation. The result of this enforced apathy was that bishops in the early nineteenth century were the subject of general abuse and personal attacks. The 1820s and 1830s were noted as a period of hostility to clergy. On 5 November 1830 there were some particularly anxious moments. All over the countryside the local bishop and, in some cases the Pope, replaced Guy Fawkes for the ceremonial burning. At Clerkenwell all twenty-one bishops were consumed in a holocaust. Archbishop Howley received word that a mob was due to descend on Lambeth Palace and asked the Home Secretary for an armed guard. Elsewhere the Bishop of Winchester's castle in Farnham had to be barricaded, and twenty-five constables were employed to disperse a menacing mob from the episcopal residence at Worcester. On 7 August, when Archbishop Howley arrived at Canterbury to give his primary visitation address, he was met by jeering crowds. Various missiles including hats, caps, brickbats and cabbage stalks were thrown at his carriage. One of the windows was smashed, although the Archbishop himself was unharmed.[21] John Stoughton commented that Church of England bishops in the early nineteenth century had incurred odium from their opposition to reform.[22]

The Beginnings of Reform

The majority of bishops who held office or were appointed to the Bench in the early years of the nineteenth century were never really faced with the full implications of industrial change. It was not until the eighteen twenties and thirties that the full extent of the disruption of agrarian society became apparent. It manifested itself in bread riots, rick burning and campaigns in the name of Captain Swing. The year 1825 saw the Repeal of the Combination Acts and the emergence of the first trade unions followed shortly in its wake. This in turn generated a growing working class consciousness in many of the manufacturing centres where the Industrial Revolution had taken root. Additionally, by the beginning of the third decade an aggressive middle-class radicalism was strongly in evidence, and ready to throw its weight behind campaigns for parliamentary reform, Chartism and the repeal of the Corn Laws. All this meant that the generation of bishops who were raised to the episcopate in the 1820s and 1830s, as well as those who were responsible for their elevations, were much more acutely aware of the need for reform in both Church and State. Although some of the men who were appointed still appeared to reflect the views of the previous generation of bishops, they were relatively few in number and their influence insufficient to halt the moves for change.

The new breed of reforming bishops, whether they were high or low churchmen, were men of spiritual purpose, possessed of a determination to improve the situation in both diocese and nation. Evangelicals such as Henry Ryder, Charles Sumner and his older brother John, as well as high churchmen such as Charles Blomfield, John Kaye (1783-1853), Christopher Bethell and Henry Phillpotts, were enthusiastic at the prospect of the Established Church becoming an effective spiritual institution. Blomfield, for example, was as strong on sabbatarian and moral issues as most evangelicals, and in 1830 he joined in the campaign for tighter licensing laws. He also urged that much sterner measures were needed to counteract bastardy, and supported his own clergy who refused to 'church' women who had given birth to children outside wedlock.

In contrast to the majority of earlier prelates, Charles Sumner (1790-1874) endeavoured to explain to the clergy of Winchester in 1829 that they needed to develop a much greater concern for the poor of their parishes. He was strongly of the opinion that unless this matter was properly attended to, their prayer and preaching would have little or no effect. Twenty-five years later Sumner was reiterating the same message with more emphasis and a broadened scope. Speaking in 1854 he declared: 'The Church as never before, must enter the field of adult education – support institutes, reading rooms, libraries, lectures and local displays of nature and art – and be primarily concerned about sanitation, the improvement of living and working conditions, as well as the further reduction in working hours'.[23]

Thomas Musgrave (1788-1860), the evangelical Archbishop of York from 1847 to 1860, stressed to his clergy that improving their miserable living conditions 'will make the poor more receptive to us'.[24] He was strongly of the view that if the Church was to succeed as a national institution, it must promote the temporal as well as the religious good of the poor. When still bishop of the rural diocese of Hereford, Musgrave had declared that it 'is idle to expect that persons depressed by severe poverty and wretchedness will always be so well conducted, or so accessible to the pastor's warnings and advice, as those who are in easier or more comfortable circumstances'. Focusing on his own diocese and its agricultural needs Musgrave wrote:

> without entering on the question whether the manufacturing and mining or purely agricultural labourers are in the better condition, our lot is cast almost exclusively among the latter, with the exception of a very few parishes. And we cannot shut our eyes to the fact that their social state admits of amendment. Their dwellings are often dark and confined, sordid and cheerless, with little or no space for profitable employment on their own account, or for recreation. The natural tendency of this privation is to degrade and demoralise the character of the inmates.[2]

Musgrave went on to urge clergy to use their good offices with local landowners in a way which 'would elevate the honest and industrious poor in the social scale'. Such action would 'at the same time contribute to the security and happiness of all'.[26]

The high church Samuel Wilberforce (1805-1873), who had become Bishop of Oxford in 1845, made pleas to his diocesan clergy which resonated with Musgrave's charges. Speaking in 1848 he urged his clergy to become social reformers, to fight prostitution, oppose blood sports, support prison reform, endorse sanitary health measures, improve and humanise the Poor Law, and in general, endorse any proposal that would increase the comfort and well-being of the labouring population.[27]

In general terms the reforming prelates of the 1830s and 1840s who preceded mid-century Palmerstonian bishops were of two kinds. There were those who might be termed ecclesiastical and social reformers, and those whose emphasis was predominantly diocesan and pastoral. Typical of the former group were Charles James Blomfield, John Bird Sumner and John Kaye (1783-1853). Prime examples of the latter group include Edward Stanley, who was Bishop of Norwich from 1837 until 1848, Walter Kerr Hamilton (1808-1869), the saintly Tractarian Bishop of Salisbury from 1854 until 1869, and John Jackson, who was Bishop of Lincoln from 1853 until 1868, when he moved on to London. Samuel Wilberforce came to be influential in both spheres, particularly in the later 1850s when he was prominent in the revival of Convocation.

The Ecclesiastical Commission

By the early 1830s 'reform' was in the air in almost every aspect of the nation's life and the Church was no exception. Prelates such as Charles Blomfield and John Bird Sumner were keenly aware that something much more than charity and biblical explanations of poverty were going to be necessary if the working-classes were ever to be touched by the Christian message. It was also clear to them that the Church's ecclesiastical organisations and structures were in need of a radical overhaul if there was to be any hope of providing adequate pastoral care for the unchurched masses of the expanding towns and cities in industrial areas. The problem was that the Church of England was essentially a rural Church, and its parochial system was primarily geared to the small agrarian village presided over by the local squire and parson. In the rapidly growing and densely populated manufacturing areas the parish system broke down. It was in Lord Shaftesbury's words 'a shadow of a name'. To put it starkly, there were simply too many people in a confined geographical space for one clergyman to have any hope of even supplying the occasional offices, let alone engaging in any systematic visiting, catechising and regular teaching. Both Sumner and Blomfield recognised that in the new urban areas parishes must be broken down in size, district churches erected and new parishes established. Up until the 1843 Act new Church of England parishes could not be created without a separate bill being put through Parliament, although daughter churches and proprietary chapels could be established.

There was, however, a further problem – that of money. How were the much-needed churches to be financed? More importantly, how were their clergy's housing and salaries to be paid for? Reforming bishops such as Sumner and Blomfield were well aware that the Church had considerable financial reserves, but the problem was that much of it was tied to cathedral chapters and particular episcopal estates. What was needed was a mechanism with legal powers sufficient to compel the redistribution of the Church's wealth. Such a body was the Ecclesiastical Commission, which was created in 1836. The Commission, which had been operating on a temporary basis since 1831, was set up by the government in conjunction with Archbishop William Howley. As a corporate body it had authority to establish ecclesiastical schemes and then to receive episcopal and capitular income and redirect it to finance them. When these decisions were ratified by the Commission's council they had the full force of law. At the time it was first established the number of commissioners were few in number and could be removed by the Crown as Head of the Church, but in 1840 all bishops became ex officio members.

The Reforming of the Whig government and the Church's reforming Ecclesiastical Commission worked well together. Charles Blomfield, who was a permanent member, proved to be the most influential episcopal member of the Commission. 'Till Blomfield comes,' said the Archbishop of York, 'we all sit and mend our pens and talk about the weather.'[28] Blomfield proved a master of information and statistics and was readily able to illustrate the huge differences of provision between the less populous districts and the densely packed industrial areas. He was, for example, able to demonstrate that in certain districts of north-east London the ratio of churches to population was one to nineteen thousand and that of clergy one to fourteen thousand. This kind of information impressed itself deeply on Bishop John Kaye, whom Blomfield had persuaded to become a member of the Commission.[29] Whilst helping to compile the second report with the Ecclesiastical Commission, Kaye was shocked to discover in 1836 that in a part of the Diocese of Lichfield and Coventry there were only church sittings for 29,000 people in sixteen parishes with a population of 235,000 people.[30] It was this kind of information which led to his endorsing, along with James Monk, another high-church bishop, the proposal to reduce the number of cathedral stalls and redirect the income for use in the urban parishes. In total the commission proposed to remove the revenues of some three hundred and sixty prebends and use them for clerical stipends in crowded areas. Blomfield was criticised by high churchmen, who saw the Commission as a secular body laying unholy hands on the church's finances. But he was hard to argue against. He said on one occasion:

> I pass the magnificent church which crowns the metropolis, and is consecrated to the noblest of objects, the glory of God, and I ask myself in what degree it answers the object. I see there a Dean, and three residentiaries, with incomes amounting in the aggregate to between £10,000 and £12,000 a year. I see, too, connected with the Cathedral twenty-nine clergymen whose offices are all but sinecures, with an annual income of about £12,000 at the present moment, and likely to be very much larger after the lapse of a few years. I proceed a mile or two to the east and north east, and find myself in the midst of an immense population, in the most wretched state of destitution and neglect, artisans, mechanics, labourers, beggars, thieves to the number of at least 300,000. I find there upon an average, about one church and one clergyman for every 8,000 or 10,000 souls; in some districts a much smaller amount of spiritual provision; in one parish, for instance, only one church and one clergyman for 40,000 people . . . the opponents of this measure assert, not a farthing must be taken from these splendid endowments, for which so little duty is performed, to furnish spiritual food to some of the thousands of miserable destitute souls that are perishing of famine in the neighbourhood of this abundance.[31]

To Blomfield the equalisation of bishops' salaries and the use of capitular income for the needs of industrial parishes were an absolute necessity. As

he saw it, an unreformed Church had not, and would not, make any in-
roads towards meeting the temporal needs of the poor. Until such moves
were initiated there would be little prospect of addressing their spiritual
needs. Blomfield viewed the suppression of ten Irish bishoprics as an inevitable and right step forward. For how could so many small dioceses be
justified, particularly in the south of the Province, when so few of the
population belonged to the United Church of England and Ireland? With
the passing of time Blomfield was able to convince the majority of his
colleagues on the Bench, that these new sources of wealth should be used
to provide for the spiritual welfare of the poor in the new manufacturing
centres which had been created by the Industrial Revolution. Between 1840
and 1855 The Ecclesiastical Commission endowed or supplemented the
income of 5,300 parishes with the money which it derived from positions
and offices which were brought to an end by the Cathedrals Act of 1840.[32]
In addition the new dioceses of Ripon and Manchester were created, with
St Alban's coming a little later.

Although Blomfield was understandably not appreciated by Pusey and
other high churchmen, he certainly could not be regarded as a mere puppet of the Whig government (in fact he was a Tory), nor could he be seen
as a mere servant of the State. In his own diocese of London he worked
assiduously, making an appeal for fifty new churches. Although his proposal was met with a certain amount of hostility on the part of *The Times*,
by 1846 forty-four churches had been completed, ten were in the process
of building and nine were scheduled to begin. Blomfield himself gave
generously to his scheme which, as the churchwardens of Bethnal Green
later testified, resulted in 'the improved moral and religious habits of the
people'.[33] He was also active in the field of education, and here, too, he
was supportive of a certain amount of government intervention. For instance, he was happy that there should be some kind of state inspection of
Church primary schools. In 1839 he founded The London Diocesan Board
of Education as an auxiliary of the National Society. This organisation
helped some of his own diocesan schools to earn grants, and in addition
established some schools for children of the middle-classes. Blomfield
was also influential in the establishment of an agreement by which clergy
should have a recognised place on the boards of Church School managers.
In summary, Blomfield was essentially an orthodox churchman who built
new churches, endowed poor livings and worked to reform the structures
of the national institution. Nevertheless, his enlightened ways helped the
Church to struggle through a time of crisis and to prepare itself for the
challenges of the mid-Victorian years.

Blomfield's episcopate was in some ways echoed by that of John Bird
Sumner. Although the latter's churchmanship was low and Protestant, he
nevertheless shared Blomfield's political and reforming interests. Both
played an important role in the reform of the Poor Law system, which

eventually took place in 1834. At the end of the Napoleonic wars, with the return of demobilised soldiers, the expense of the Poor Law supplement to those without work or sufficient income reached the staggeringly large total of £5,072,028. This sum was nearly three times the amount paid out in relief immediately before the war. The result of this increasingly large commitment was that both clergy and laity began to question whether this system of relief was the best way to continue.[34] Early in 1832 the Government appointed a special commission to study the question. Sumner and Blomfield were the only two clerical members of the Commission. Both Blomfield, who was Chairman, and Sumner were decided opponents of the existing system of relief measures. They agreed that poverty was the God-ordained lot of many, but they were unhappy that such individuals were not motivated to work because full or supplementary relief would be paid by the parish. They were both therefore strong advocates of the 1834 Poor Law Act which brought in a series of workhouses, where the unemployed and those without income had to go instead of the previous arrangements of being paid a cash sum to allow them to stay in their own cottages. The workhouses, which separated husband and wife, were specifically designed as unwelcoming places, in order to persuade labourers to remain in work or actively seek a new position when their contracts came to an end. However, with the passing of time, when it became clear that the market could no longer sustain full employment for the whole population, Sumner in particular began to alter his views on the matter.

Neither Blomfield nor Sumner neglected their dioceses on account of their public work. Sumner was widely known as a man of enormous energy, and during his twenty-year episcopate in Chester he consecrated 244 churches. This was more than any of his contemporaries.[35] In addition some 700 schools were opened in the diocese during the same period.[36] Sumner was something of a visionary in that he saw a school building as a higher priority than a church, because the former could also be licensed as a place of worship.[37] Sir Robert Peel paid tribute to J. B. Sumner's achievements in a speech in the House of Commons in May 1843. Among other things he said: '. . . it would not be just, were I not to express in strong terms, my admiration of the Bishop of Chester who has effected so much improvement in that diocese'.[38]

If Blomfield and Sumner are held to be political reforming bishops, a number of their contemporaries who can justly be regarded as pastoral reforming bishops were appointed in the years before Palmerston became Prime Minister. They included Edward Stanley (1779-1849), appointed Bishop of Norwich in succession to Lord Bathurst in 1837, Samuel Wilberforce (1805-1873) who became Bishop of Oxford in 1845, James Prince Lee (1804-1869), Bishop of Manchester in 1848 and John Jackson (1811-1885) who became Bishop of Lincoln in 1853. Walter Kerr Hamilton (1808-1869), who was raised to the See of Salisbury in 1854 shortly before Palmerston took office, upheld the Tractarian pastoral ideals. Of these Wilberforce was undoubtedly the most energetic and dynamic.

Samuel Wilberforce was the son of the evangelical reformer, William Wilberforce. He owed his appointment to royal favour[39] and to the confidence which Peel had in him that he could control the Tractarian controversy which was raging in Oxford and beyond. Whilst he was a powerful figure on the Bench, Wilberforce's contribution to the Church was made in his diocesan administration. He was a great traveller and each year spent ninety days, if the weather permitted, journeying through his diocese meeting personally with his clergy and getting matters to rights. It was his custom from time to time to bring together small groups of clergy and to urge them to raise the quality, and in some cases the frequency, of parish worship. He was particularly keen that incumbents should give full attention to their preaching. He devoted a large section of his 1863 visitation address to the importance of proper preparation. He underlined the maxim that 'the sermon which has cost little is worth just what it cost'. He urged prayer and patient labour.[40]

Although he was numbered among high churchmen, Wilberforce's evangelical upbringing left a strong mark on his spirituality. He set himself a disciplined rule of life resolving to guard against 'secularity' by 'self-examination, and above all by living in prayer'. He also determined 'when not hindered by illness, or some impossibility, to secure at least one hour before breakfast for devotional exercises'.[41] Wilberforce gave detailed and careful attention to the examination of candidates for ordination, something, as was noted, which in earlier times was often treated by bishops in a perfunctory or even casual way. He took particular care with his ordination addresses to invite his prospective candidates to reflect carefully on whether or not they had been misled by empty emotion to seek Holy Orders. Wilberforce was a man of strong feelings, and he was sometimes deeply pained at having to tell his ordinands that their examination papers or their interviews were unsatisfactory.

Wilberforce often combined an ordination with a mission to a group of parishes. The ordination would take place on a Sunday morning. In the afternoon he would preach a mission sermon and then come back towards the end of the week to give a concluding address. In 1864 for example, he held a mission at Brampton which embraced twenty-six other churches in the locality. The week also included seven confirmations and a series of morning conferences.

Integrally related to Wilberforce's concern over ordinations was his interest in theological education. He became the leading inspiration behind the founding of Cuddesdon Theological College, which was opened in 1854. It was by no means the first such institution, for Sumner had been involved in the opening of St Aidan's College, Birkenhead in 1846, and had taken an active interest in a much earlier institution which had been established at St. Bees in the Lake District.[42] Cuddesdon commenced its work with the threefold aim of fostering devotion, parochial work and theological reading. The College began with his aspirations but unfortunately ran into difficulties fairly early on, when accusations of Romanism were made of the Vice-Principal, Henry Liddon. When two men, one a former and the other a present student, went over to Rome, Liddon resigned. Notwithstanding this early set-back, incumbents who employed Cuddesdon students as curates testified to their usefulness. The college also became a centre for diocesan retreats and conferences, and Wilberforce delighted in its atmosphere and teaching.

As Sumner before him, Wilberforce was a great promoter of diocesan organisations and institutions. He created societies for church building, spiritual help and the education of the poor. He was an active free trader and opposed the corn laws because he saw that this would improve the cost of bread for those on low incomes. Following Sumner, although not on the same scale, Wilberforce actively promoted the building of churches. Whilst during the period 1820-1845 only twenty-two new churches were built, during Wilberforce's twenty-four year Oxford episcopate, one hundred and six new churches were built, fifteen rebuilt and two hundred and fifty were restored.[43]

Undoubtedly Wilberforce's great contribution to the Church was made in his diocesan administration. Like his relative John Bird Sumner before him, he proved himself a pastor, church builder, preacher and educationalist. Along with Sumner and Blomfield he was also much concerned about the state of the Church as a national institution. Yet his later desire to free the Establishment from the clutches of the State and to recall Convocation, rather than rely on parliament to continue to deal with church business, ran him into conflict with the Court and prime ministers such as Lord John Russell. However, his persistence eventually led Lord Derby to advise the Crown in 1852 to authorise Convocation to resume its former functions. Strangely perhaps, despite Wilberforce's insistence on the necessity of the Church having its own voice, it was left to the Palmerstonian appointees to establish the first diocesan conferences.

Other reforming prelates of the 1830s, 1840s and early 1850s are worthy of mention. Edward Stanley who came to Norwich in 1837 was described by J.H. Overton as a man of 'enlightened views and unselfish exertions in the matter of the education of the poor'.[44] He was, according to Lord Shaftesbury, the first bishop to take up the cause of the ragged schools. He was a pastor through and through, and used on occasion to say that 'a bishop should always be at his post in the chief city of his diocese'.[45] For this reason he refused the offer of a pleasant retreat a few miles from Norwich and was frequently to be found among the schools and the city's working classes. James Prince Lee, who was consecrated the first Bishop of Manchester in 1848 was viewed as 'a somewhat despotic individual'.

He nevertheless proved himself to be an admirable diocesan organiser. In his charge to clergy in November 1851 he showed his qualities as a reforming strategist. He urged his incumbents to give high priority to education, and in particular make every effort to retain the services of 'superior teachers'.[46] He was also adamant that 'education to be useful . . . cannot exist without religious instruction'. Prince Lee was also a strong advocate of the Sunday School, which he viewed as an important means by which clergy can make contact with 'a number of young parishioners'.[47]

John Jackson was appointed by Lord Aberdeen to the See of Lincoln in 1853. Jackson remained in post until 1868 when he was translated to London. During that time twenty-four new churches and seven mission houses were built. Sixty-one churches were rebuilt and more than two hundred restored at a cost in excess of four hundred thousand pounds. He overhauled the ruri-decanal system and welded together the counties of Lincolnshire and Nottinghamshire. It was observed that the clergy took much greater care in the preparation and conduct of Sunday Services, and that there were very few churches which did not have two acts of worship on the Lord's Day. Jackson was particularly gladdened by the increased frequency with which Holy Communion was celebrated. He took a great interest in education and the building of schools. He was also a great supporter of the Teacher Training Institution which provided a steady supply of 'well-taught and well-principled mistresses'. Clearly, on any showing, Jackson ranked among the earlier reforming bishops.

One other who was representative of the pastoral reforming bishops was Walter Kerr Hamilton, who was promoted to the See of Salisbury in 1854. His appointment appears to have been due to the fact that when his predecessor, Bishop Denison, lay dying, he penned a letter to Lord Aberdeen urging that Hamilton was the most fitted to carry forward the work of Christ in the diocese. Like Edward Stanley he believed a bishop should reside in his cathedral city. He never left Salisbury unless it was for a short holiday or to attend to urgent business. He seldom attended the House of Lords unless there was a debate in which the interests of religion and morals appeared to be at stake. Like his Archbishop John Bird Sumner, he wanted to shed the episcopate of its aristocratic and lordly image. For this reason he gave up his carriage soon after his consecration to office. He was regarded by those who knew him as 'the bishop of the poor', and he considered that it was they who had first claim on the servants of Christ.[48] Each year on a day near to Epiphany about a hundred poor people were invited to share dinner with the bishop and his family. The bishop looked forward with delight to these occasions. In later years he joined with the Palmerstonian appointees to the bench in opposing *Essay and Reviews*, a collection of writings published in 1860 which embraced liberal approaches to Scripture.

Although much had changed in episcopal attitudes by 1850, most, if not all, who sat on the Bench still believed in a fixed, divinely ordered hierarchical society which left the poor permanently at the bottom of the social pile. Some, such as Henry Phillpotts, Bishop of Exeter since 1830, had an in-built fear of socialism. In a speech during the second reading of the 1832 Reform Bill he justified the retention of Rotten and Pocket boroughs, declaring that they 'ought not to be got rid of ' because they provided 'checks' and 'corrections' to the constitution.[49] He expressed himself in more fulsome terms when he declared: 'the socialist may be doing philanthropic works, but his community is illegal, his writings are revolutionary, blasphemous and obscene. A government which refuses to condemn him is guilty of treason to God'.[50] Samuel Wilberforce when Archdeacon of Surrey stated in 1842 that 'diversity of rank and station do exist among us, they are evidently part of God's appointment for maintaining quick and real mutual charity'.[51]

It was not until the last quarter of the nineteenth century that any members of the episcopal bench offered different understandings of either the class structure or socialism. Even then they were the largely isolated voices of a Westcott or a Gore. The majority of bishops in the 1850s were Tories, and all were solidly orthodox defenders of the creedal faith. Some of the old 'Greek play' academic bishops, such as Edward Maltby (1770-1859) of Durham and James Henry Monk (1784-1856) of Bristol and Gloucester, survived into the Palmerston era, and the incompetent Richard Bagot (1782-1854) lingered on, first at Oxford and then at Bath and Wells, until 1854. Nevertheless there was clearly a changed attitude on the part of the episcopal Bench as a whole by the 1840s and 1850s. There was a growing concern for the poor and a determination to make an effort on their behalf to build schools and provide new places of worship. Bishops such as the Sumner brothers, Samuel Wilberforce and Walter Kerr Hamilton were building relationships with their clergy and seeking to raise the standards of the clerical office. Bishops were also beginning to look seriously at the structures of their dioceses and to make the rite of Confirmation a more spiritual and personal occasion.

It was against this background that Lord Palmerston came to office in 1855. High churchmen such as Samuel Wilberforce were keenly aware that the new Prime Minister's presence signalled ecclesiastical change. Wilberforce noted in his diary for 7 February, 'Palmerston will be aware of Lord Shaftesbury'.[52] However it was not until the following year that a new appointment to the Bench was made.

II

Lord Palmerston and his Bishops

Anthony Trollope's novel *Barchester Towers* begins with the upper-class and worldly Archdeacon Grantly earnestly pacing the hallways and anxiously waiting to see if his father, the bishop of Barchester, will die before the political crisis compels the Government to resign. The archdeacon had recently stayed with the head of his Oxford College when the Prime Minister was there, and it was arranged that he should be the next bishop. However, his hopes were dashed with the government falling before the bishop died. The new Prime Minister had a decided preference for the low-church party and appointed the enthusiastic Dr. Proudie with his staff and legalistic chaplain, Mr. Slope. *Barchester Towers* was published in 1857[1] and all Trollope's readers knew the political controversies and the leaders to whom he was referring. The outgoing Prime Minister was the Tory, Lord Derby, who appointed high-church clergymen over glasses of port in Oxford Colleges. The incoming Prime Minister was Lord Palmerston, who revealed a decided liking for middle-class evangelical pastors whom Trollope unkindly misrepresented as 'Slopes' and 'Proudies'.

On the surface of things this championing of a church party not altogether popular with the aristocracy appears to be yet another anomaly in Palmerston's long political career. The underlying reason, however, was the influence over him of his step son-in-law, Lord Shaftesbury, who was not only an ardent evangelical leader but a staunch opponent of the Oxford Movement and all things ritualistic.

Palmerston's Politics

Lord Palmerston was born at his father's English home on 20th October 1784. He was christened Harry John Temple in the 'House of Commons church' St Margaret's, Westminster. It was an appropriate beginning, since 'Harry' Temple was to be a member of the Lower Chamber from 1807 until the day of his death on the eve of his eighty-first birthday. He was sent to Harrow at the young age of ten, and proceeded to Edinburgh University in November, 1800.

In 1802 he succeeded to his father's title, becoming the 3rd Viscount Palmerston and inheriting the family estates at Broadlands in Hampshire and in County Sligo. He entered St. John's College, Cambridge, in 1803 and graduated MA in 1806. While still an undergraduate, he contested the university seat left vacant by the death of William Pitt. He lost on that occasion and was again unsuccessful in the general election of 1807. He did, however, represent the University of Cambridge from 1811 to 1831.

His political life began when he was made a Junior Lord at the Admiralty in the Tory administration of 1807. Palmerston was then asked to enter Parliament as a candidate for the pocket borough of Newport, Isle of Wight. He declined Prime Minister, Spencer Perceval's offer of the post of Chancellor of the Exchequer in 1809, taking instead the office of Secretary at War. Palmerston, who was strikingly handsome, enjoyed London society to the full and was particularly enamoured by the delights of Almack's Club, whose three principal hostesses were Lady Jersey, the Princess Lieven and Lady Cowper, whom he married in 1839 after she was widowed. It is probable that all three were his mistresses, which may account for his being widely ribbed as 'Lord Cupid'.

In 1827 Palmerston was appointed Secretary at War in the Tory Government of George Canning. He also served in that same office under Viscount Goderich and the Duke of Wellington. In his early days Palmerston was recognised as a strong supporter of Pitt, who was hostile to increasing civil liberties in the post war years. However, as the century's third decade progressed, Palmerston found himself making a gradual move towards 'Liberal Toryism' and subsequently he applauded 'the great strides which public opinion has made in the last few years'. In 1826 he owed his return to the Cambridge parliamentary seat to the support of the Whigs. He declared his liking for his Whig colleagues in cabinet, stating that he preferred them to the Tories with whom he seemed to have much less in common. In 1830 he not only expressed his satisfaction as to the Paris revolution, but he was also appointed Foreign Secretary in the Whig-Canning coalition under Earl Grey.

From 1849 to 1865 Palmerston came to represent the opposition of many landed gentry and middle-class people to the enfranchisement of trade unionists. He also stood out against the many legislative assaults on landed property. This said, Palmerston was strongly of the view that the Great Reform Act of 1832 had prevented social revolution and produced a climate of peace. This made him proud of his country and of the opinion that foreign autocrats, and Britain's allies in particular, ought to conduct themselves like sensible Whigs. Yet Palmerston was no advanced democrat or republican, but rather a British Nationalist. He urged that the country had 'no permanent allies only permanent interests'.

Palmerston first became Prime Minister in 1855, when Russell resigned as Leader of the House of Commons on account of his refusal to oppose a motion for inquiry into the misconduct of the Crimean war. With public support behind him Palmerston took the reigns of the premiership from Lord Aberdeen. His first ministry lasted until February 1858, when he was defeated following his failure to sufficiently condemn French attacks on Britain for harbouring French refugees who were conspiring to murder Napoleon III.

Palmerston's second ministry followed the election of 1859. During this term of office he continued to be held in high esteem at home. He greatly increased the Liberal Majority in the election of 1865 with a hustings' slogan of 'Leave it to Pam'. Parliament was dissolved on 6 July 1865 and Palmerston went down to his constituency and won his seat. He died at his wife's estate at Brocket Hall in Hertfordshire on 18 October, shortly before Parliament re-convened.

Palmerston and Lord Shaftesbury

Palmerston's links with Shaftesbury came about when, at the age of fifty-four, he married Lady Emily Cowper in 1839 after she had been widowed. She had probably become Palmerston's mistress as early as 1809. Only when her husband, the Fifth Earl Cowper, died was it possible for her to marry Palmerston. Three of Emily's children, Emily (Minnie), William and Frances were in all probability Palmerston's, although Emily was believed to have had several other lovers, including Francis Conyngham, the son of George IV's mistress, Lady Conyngham.[2]

The young Anthony Ashley first met Lady Emily (Minnie) in the summer of 1829 and at once found himself strongly attracted to her. 'She is', he wrote, 'lovely, accomplished, clever, lady-like, of modest demeanour, with an air of virgin indifference towards all admirers'.[3] The chief worry for the youthful Tory suitor was the Whiggishness of her mother's family. Lady Emily senior was the daughter of the First Viscountess Melbourne. Minnie, who was not yet twenty, was widely regarded as 'one of the belles of the season, a bright new star in the central constellation of Whig aristocracy'.[4] Love proved stronger than politics, and within a matter of weeks Shaftesbury found separation from her unbearable. Whatever the nature of her religion it was quite more than sufficient to satisfy his forthright evangelical convictions. He believed her to be the answer to his many prayers that God would give him a wife who would share his faith and be sufficient to keep him from temptation. After their marriage they read the Bible together and made prayer a central aspect of their relationship. They taught their children in the tenets of the Christian faith on a carefully structured plan. In later years Minnie revealed her 'Recordite' evangelical convictions, when she sought to console her dying son Francis with the fact that 'Dr Cumming and others were of the opinion that the close of the present dispensation was nearer than was ordinarily calculated by one hundred and sixty years'.[5]

Despite her flirtatious nature, of which the puritanical Ashley can have had no doubts, he found in her that which was truly 'estimable and loveable'. Whereas his own parents were cold and indifferent, he found his in-laws warm and welcoming. Their home was a place of refuge where it was his delight to take his young clutch of growing children for week-end visits and holiday periods. With the passing of the years the Seventh Earl was to find in Lady Palmerston a valuable friend, whose warm-hearted kindness brought him comfort and encouragement.

When Lady Palmerston died in September 1869 Shaftesbury wrote:

> Poor, dear, kind mum. How can I ever forget – nay how can I ever fully remember – all her unbroken, invariable, tender, considerate goodness towards me? Turn her very inmost heart unto Thyself, O God, for Christ's blessed sake![6]

Following her funeral service on 22 September Shaftesbury noted in his diary:

> To my dying hour I shall remember her perpetual sunshine of ex-pression and affectionate grace, the outward sign of inward sin-cerity, of kindness, generosity and love. . . . Forty years have I been her son-in-law, and during all that long time she has been a well-spring of tender friendship and affectionate service.[7]

There seems to be little doubt that Lady Emily was able to draw Shaftesbury into an equally close relationship with her second husband. Palmerston came to admire, to love and esteem Shaftesbury above all others, but it was a reciprocal relationship. When 'Pam' died Shaftesbury wrote:

> Ah but to none will the loss be as it is to myself. I lose a man who, I knew, esteemed and loved me far beyond every other man living. He showed it in every action of his heart, in every expression of his lips, in private and in public as a man, as a relative, and as a Minister. His society was infinitely agreeable to me and I admired, every day more, his patriotism, his simplicity of purpose, his inde-fatigable spirit of labour, his unfailing good humour, his kindness of heart, and his prompt, tender, and active considerateness for others in the midst of his heaviest toils and anxieties.[8]

The development of such a close relationship between step-father and step-son-in-law inevitably led to the latter becoming a confidante. Shaftesbury's advice was to prove more and more influential with the pass-ing of the years, but never more so than in the last decade of Palmerston's life, when he held the premiership. Shaftesbury reflected in 1865 that 'applicants, in abundant instances, approached the Prime Minister through me as their channel, and, as I never undertook any but deserving cases, so I never met with anything but ready acquiescence'.[9] He recalled his ear-nest entreaties for Baxter of Dundee and Crossley of Halifax to be given baronetcies, and for McClintock and Harry Parkes, both overlooked by Lord Russell, to be rewarded for their 'great services'.[10] Shaftsbury's in-fluence over his step-father was further extended by the fact that his son, Evelyn Ashley, (1836-1907), was Palmerston's private secretary during the years 1858-1865. Evelyn in fact completed Lord Dalling's unfinished *Life of Palmerston* in 1876.

Palmerston and Religion

Palmerston had long upheld the Established Church as an institution. In his Tory days he had stressed to the House of Commons the importance of counteracting the decline of Church of England congregations which had, in his view, an important role in upholding the social structure of society.[11] He recognised the growing strength of Non-conformists in the country, but was always somewhat suspicious of 'dissenters' as he called them, particularly in the early years of the century. As to Roman Catholics, Palmerston was constant in his views that they had no right to hold any political or other positions in a Protestant country, and were entitled to do this only as a privilege granted to them at the discretion of the State.

On a personal level Palmerston had no religious enthusiasm. His own Sunday church attendance was spasmodic at best. When he became Prime Minister, Shaftesbury penned the following lines to his son, Evelyn, on 25 February 1855:

> He does not know in theology, Moses from Sydney Smith. The Vicar of Romsey, where he goes to church, is the only clergyman he ever spoke to; and as for the wants, the feelings, the views, the hopes and fears, of the country, and particularly the religious part of it, they are as strange to him as the interior of Japan. Why it was only a short time ago that he heard, for the first time, of the grand heresy of Puseyites and Tractarians.[12]

For these reasons, despite his warm and affectionate close relationship with his step-father, Shaftesbury feared the worst in so far as his prime ministerial church appointments were concerned. However, he was soon to change his mind on the matter. Palmerston came to an almost total reliance on Shaftesbury in the matter of ecclesiastical preferment. He sought his advice about all the five archbishops and the twenty bishops he appointed or translated in England and Ireland. Shaftesbury later wrote in 1865: 'He oftentimes thanked me, in the warmest language, for the advice I gave him, and showed his appreciation of it by never making but one appointment, as far as I can recollect (that of Blakesley, Canon of Canterbury), without consulting me on the matter'.[13] It was small wonder that Shaftesbury was soon justly dubbed the 'Bishop Maker'.

Palmerston on Bishops

In addition to his step-son-in-law's counsel, a number of principles came to govern Palmerston's ecclesiastical appointments. Perhaps most obvious was his fear of Roman Catholicism. Gladstone, whom Palmerston wrongly suspected of being almost a Roman Catholic himself, wrote that Palmerston was absurdly suspicious of Roman Catholics.[14] Associated with this phobia was Palmerston's intense dislike for Tractarians, whom he regarded as all-of-a-piece with Romanism. Shaftesbury himself wrote approvingly that Palmerston 'regarded any approximation to popery, popish doctrines, and popish practices, with special dislike and even fear'.[15] It is very probable that Palmerston's forthright anti-Roman stance stemmed from his background as an Anglo-Irish Protestant landlord.

Whilst Palmerston never feared high churchmen in the way that he did ritualists and Romanists, he nevertheless had a general dislike for them and avoided putting promotions in their direction. His observation was that high churchmen had an inbuilt capacity to arouse the suspicions and antagonisms of Non-conformists, who were growing steadily in numbers and influence. Shaftesbury wrote that a part of Palmerston's definition of a 'good and proper man' for the episcopal bench, was 'one who would go on well with the Non-conformists'. His step father-in-law, he continued, 'had a very special dislike of every form of clerical presumption'.[16] Although Palmerston's early appointments to the bench provoked the ire of Bishop Wilberforce and the high church party who regarded them as 'an insult to the church', they won him the thanks and support of many in Yorkshire and Lancashire. After returning from a tour of the north, Palmerston was particularly heartened by the response he received from the 'manufacturers, clothier-workmen, Methodists and dissenters' of the Diocese of Ripon who were gratified by the appointment, as bishop, of the low church evangelical Robert Bickersteth.[17] It was Palmerston's considered opinion that 'the intolerant maxims of the high-church bishops have exasperated the dissenters who form a large portion of the nation, and have given offence to many good churchmen'. 'The People of this country', he continued, 'are essentially Protestant, they feel deepest aversion to Catholicism, and they see that the High Church, Tractarian and Puseyite doctrines lead men to the Church of Rome'.[18]

In his ecclesiastical promotions Palmerston also avoided men with theological learning. He had nothing against those who were at home in the world of biblical criticism and drank deeply from the latest scholarship, but he didn't feel their place was on the Bench. He wrote concerning the matter:

> Professors, tutors and dons of colleges are by no means, on an average, men fitted for episcopal duty. The knowledge of mankind, and experience of parochial life, are not acquired in musty libraries and easy chairs. Practical divinity is one thing, speculative divinity another, and the accomplishments that make an active bishop, are purchased at the cost of that learning which would make him a theological champion, armed at all points, and ready on all occasions.[9]

In a letter written to Queen Victoria on 2 December 1860, Palmerston defended his practice of not selecting theological bishops. First he submitted that diocesan duties will take up the bulk of their time. 'Much mischief', he suggested, 'has been done by "theological bishops" and if the Bench were to be filled with men like the bishops of Oxford and Exeter 'there would be no religious peace in the land'. He underlined the fact that the theological learning of the Bishop of Exeter has caused 'much mischief to the established church'.[20] He also contended that some of those bishops notable for their theological attainments did not make a strong impression on their dioceses: 'Thirlwall, Bishop of St. David's, and Blomfield, the late Bishop of London, were chosen on account of their learning; the former is acknowledged to be insufficient and the latter greatly mismanaged his diocese'.[21]

It should not, however, be imagined that Palmerston chose men of weak academic attainment. Of the fourteen individuals whom he either appointed or translated to nineteen Sees, six of their number, Charles Baring, Archibald Tait, Charles Longley, Samuel Waldegrave, Henry Philpott and Francis Jeune, all achieved first-class honours at either Cambridge or Oxford. In addition, Henry Philpott, William Thomson and Harold Browne all proceeded to the degree BD, while Thomson and Jeune were also awarded doctoral degrees by research. Philpott was appointed Master of St. Catherine's College, Cambridge in 1845 and elected Vice-Chancellor of the University in 1846, 1856 and 1857. Charles Ellicott went on to become Professor of New Testament at King's College, London in 1858 and Hulsean Professor of Divinity at Cambridge in 1860. Harold Browne was appointed Norissian Professor of Divinity at Cambridge in 1854, while Francis Jeune became Master of Pembroke College, Oxford and Vice-Chancellor of the University from 1858-1862. William Jacobson, who was Palmerston's last appointment, had become Vice Principal of Magdalen College, Oxford and Regius Professor of Divinity in 1848. In addition William Thomson was Bampton Lecturer in 1853, and Samuel Waldegrave in 1854. Several of them also produced publications and scholarly work of high distinction. Harold Browne authored what became a standard nineteenth-century text on the 'Thirty Nine Articles of Religion', and Charles Ellicott chaired the group of New Testament scholars who were responsible for the publication of the Revised Version of the Bible which was published in 1885.

Palmerston's preference was men who were distinguished in learning other than theology. In defence of his appointees he wrote to Queen Victoria that 'several of the bishops whom he has had the honour of recommending to your Majesty had distinguished themselves by their classical and academic attainments, and he may mention in this respect the names of Baring, Longley, Tait, Wigram and Waldegrave.'[22] Clearly it is not only unjust but also incorrect to suggest, as Sabine Baring-Gould did in the words of Puck, that they were 'hempen homespuns'. By the standards of their day, and of bishops in general, they were above the level of their fellows.

Palmerston recognised the growing strength of Non-conformity in the middle years of the nineteenth century. It had doubtless been impressed on him by the growing number of bills brought forward in the Commons for the abolition of church rates and to allow Free Church ministers to conduct their own burial services in parish churchyards. He therefore deemed it essential that those chosen to sit on the Bench of Bishops should be men who would not antagonise the Free Churches. He noted that 'High Church bishops have exasperated the Dissenters who form a large portion of the nation, and have given offence to many good churchmen'. As examples, he singled out Bishop Phillpotts of Exeter, the late Bishop of Carlisle and the Bishop of Rochester, George Murray. The latter two individuals were, he submitted, 'kind-hearted and good natured men, but both refused to consecrate burial grounds unless a wall of separation divided the portion allotted to dissenters'.[23] It is noteworthy that several of Palmerston's earlier appointees enjoyed particularly good relationships with Non-conformists. Montagu Villiers, the first Palmerstonian bishop, worked vigorously with dissenters, some of whom were members of the vestry of his London parish of St. George's Bloomsbury.[24] It was apparently Villiers' custom on Sunday mornings when he passed William Brock, the Pastor of Bloomsbury Baptist Chapel, to offer the ancient greeting: 'The Lord be with you'. Brock would respond with the customary response 'And with Thy Spirit'.[25] Robert Bickersteth, who was appointed to Ripon in 1857, was greatly loved by many of the Methodists and Free Churchmen of the diocese. Large numbers of them were enthusiastic supporters of his plain straightforward preaching and his diocesan missions in Leeds and elsewhere. John Thomas Pelham of Norwich invited Non-conformist leaders of the city to come to his palace for informal discussions on some of the major issues of the day. Harold Browne had enjoyed cordial relationships with the Methodists in his Cornish parish of the St. Kenwyn-cum-Kea.[26] Other Palmerstonian appointees had rather more natural sympathies, having come from Non-conformist backgrounds themselves. Archibald Tait, for example, had been brought up in a Presbyterian home and attended Glasgow University[27] and William Jacobson had attended Mr. Brewer's Baptist School in Norwich and Homerton Non-conformist College in London.[28]

Perhaps the most important qualification for a bishop in Palmerston's mind was that he should be a good pastor to the clergy of his diocese. For this reason he was intent on selecting men for office who had wide and successful parish experience. Thirteen out of the fourteen men whom Palmerston chose had parochial experience as incumbents. In the case of Villiers, Baring, Bickersteth, Wigram and Browne, their experience was substantial in a variety of demanding situations. Only Philpott of Worcester appears to have lacked a benefice, but his long and distinguished university career must have given him considerable pastoral opportunities. Palmerston's opinion was that bishops are in the Church what generals of districts are in the army.[29] He regarded their chief duties 'as watching over the clergy of their diocese, seeing that they perform their parochial duties properly, and preserving harmony between the clergy and the laity'.[30] There is no doubt, as the subsequent chapters of this study make plain, that Palmerston's English bishops devoted much of their time to helping to encourage and support their clergy. They gave particular attention to salaries, the condition of parsonage houses, and the way in which worship and pastoral duties were attended to.

One thing is clear. Palmerston was rarely motivated by political considerations in his dispensing of ecclesiastical patronage. In a letter to Lord Carlisle, then Lord Lieutenant of Ireland, he wrote:

> I have never considered ecclesiastical appointments as patronage to be given away for grace and favour, and for personal or political objects. . . . I have always endeavoured, to choose the best man I could find, without any regard to the wishes of those who may have recommended candidates for choice.[31]

In a remarkable letter Lord Shaftesbury testified to the disinterested nature of his step father-in-law's appointments: 'He ever sought for good and proper men; and he discarded, in the search, all considerations of mere politics or attention to personal requests'.[32] He quoted Palmerston's own words:

> If the man is a good man, I don't care what his political opinions are. Certainly I had rather not name a bishop who would make party speeches and attacks on the Government in the House of Lords; but, short of that, let him do as he likes.[33]

Palmerston's only episcopal appointment that was possibly coloured by political considerations was his last, that of William Jacobson to Chester in July 1865. Shaftesbury suggested, and Palmerston accepted, the name of Archdeacon Prest of Durham. However, shortly afterwards Palmerston received a letter from Gladstone in which he stated that Jacobson was the chairman of his election committee. The nomination of this professor 'would be very encouraging and greatly strengthen his interests'. Palmerston remarked to Shaftesbury: 'I should be glad to aid Gladstone to keep his seat for Oxford, because, small though it be, it tends to check him, and save him running into wild courses. But I will not do it unless you assure me that the Doctor is a proper man'.[34] Shaftesbury commented: 'this is the only nomination that had a taint of politics in it'. It was also, he observed, the only appointment where the bishop openly and speedily gave offence, which he did by refusing to give his sanction to the Bible Society in both Chester and Liverpool.[35]

Among the Palmerston papers deposited at Southampton University is a memorandum, which deals with the qualities necessary in a bishop.[36] It is undated but must have been written at some point in 1856, since it makes reference to the vacant sees of London and Durham and the kind of men which are needed to supply them. Palmerston also proffers a general comment regarding the ability of bishops to take part in House of Lords debates.

> Very great evils have arisen from the inability of the majority on the Bench to take part in the Ecclesiastical Debates in the House of Lords. One or two in consequence, practised and eloquent speakers, govern and silence the rest, and mislead a number of lay peers attached to Episcopal and Church interests, who would be oftener of another mind were the true opinions of the Bishops known to them. But these not liking to take part, as they otherwise would feel themselves obliged to do, in the debates, do not attend, and their absence and silence is regarded either as assent or indifference, and acts most injuriously on public opinion towards them both amongst inferior clergy and laity.[37]

In summary, Palmerston's appointments were, in Shaftesbury's words, 'conspicuous for justice, propriety, impartiality, and freedom from merely political views'.[38]

Palmerston's Appointees

Palmerston's first ministry extended from 1855 to February 1858, when his Whig party was defeated on an amendment to the Conspiracy to Murder Bill. This led to Lord Derby forming an administration which only lasted a matter of a few months, following his defeat in the snap election of 1859 which left the Conservatives in a minority of about fifty.

In his first ministry Palmerston chose almost exclusively evangelicals. In this he was strongly influenced by the suggestions of his son-in-law. Shaftesbury commented in his diary:

> The first bishops were decidedly of the Evangelical School; and my recommendations were made with that intention. I could not forsee the duration of his power, and I was resolved to put forward men who would preach the truth, be active in their dioceses, be acceptable to working people, and not offensive to the Nonconformists. He accepted my suggestions on these very grounds, and heartily approved of them.[39]

The appointees of the first ministry were not, however, all as 'decidedly evangelical' as Shaftesbury's comments might suggest. Of the six bishops, Montagu Villiers, who was appointed to Carlisle, Charles Baring who went to Gloucester and Bristol, and Robert Bickersteth and John Pelham who were given Ripon and Norwich respectively, were all pronounced members of the evangelical party. Charles Longley, who was translated from Ripon to Durham, and Archibald Tait who was promoted to London, could not be considered as members of the evangelical party. Longley was a moderate High Churchman[40] while Tait was later described by Shaftesbury as the mildest of Broad Churchmen.[41]

In his second ministry Palmerston began to adopt a slightly broader policy and Shaftesbury, while still pressing the claims of socially orientated evangelical men, concurred with his objectives. Indeed, on occasion, he put forward the names of those who were representatives of other parties within the Church of England. Both Palmerston and Shaftesbury in particular were greatly perturbed at the publication of *Essays and Reviews* in 1860. This volume contained contributions from seven liberal Anglicans, who in varying degrees supported modern critical ideas which undermined the authority and inspiration of the Bible. Shaftesbury in particular was resolved that those who had made a determined defence of the orthodox Christian faith in opposition to 'the Seven against Christ' should be rewarded. In 1861 William Thomson, who was Provost of Queen's College, Oxford, began to edit a series of essays under the title *Aids to Faith*. This counterblast to *Essays and Reviews* was not published until after his elevation to the Bishopric of Gloucester and Bristol, but his forthcoming endeavours were doubtless communicated to Shaftesbury. Two others of his fellow contributors, Charles Ellicott and Harold Browne, owed their elevations to their roles as defenders of the faith. Reflecting on the second ministry appointments, Shaftesbury later wrote that it was 'my own feeling that honour should be done to every one (wherever occasion offered) connected with the answers to *Essays and Reviews*'.[42]

When Palmerston somewhat unexpectedly succeeded in being elected for a second term, Shaftesbury appears to have relaxed his earlier insistence on evangelical appointments to the Bench. Perhaps, as he reflected on his early success in getting four sound men to the Bench, he was more ready to look beyond the confines of his own party. At any rate he penned a letter to his step-father-in-law on 18 November 1862:

St Giles House,
18 November 1862

Dear Palmerston,

On my return here last night I found your letter. I fuly concur with you that the Church holding various shades of opinion, should have its several representations.

Surely you have observed your own rules – pray consider this list.

1. Villiers to Carlisle   - called Low church
2. Waldegrave to do   - do.
3. Baring to Durham   - do.
4. Pelham to Norwich   - do.
5. Bickersteth to Ripon   - do.

Of the *ultra* High Church, there are none, but of the moderate High Church there are

1. Longley, successively to Durham, York, Canterbury
2. Philpott to Worcester
3. Wigram to Rochester

Of the Broad Church

    4. Tait to London

    5. Thomson to Gloucester and now to York. . . .

Ellicott whom you think of for the Bishopric of Gloucester, is a very moderate and judicious man formerly Hulsean Professor of Divinity, and now Dean of Exeter by your appointment – He would be linked with the moderate High Churchmen – And the same may be said of Broderick of whom everyone speaks well.[43]

What is interesting in Shaftesbury's letter is his designation of Wigram as 'moderate high church' and Thomson as of 'the Broad Church'. Both were quite clearly of the evangelical party and designated as such by the church press. Was Shaftesbury trying to use a little worldly subterfuge with a man who probably had very little personal knowledge of his appointees' churchmanship? It is hard to conceive that Shaftesbury really saw Wigram and Thomson as not belonging to his own party.

Shaftesbury's Influences on Palmerston's Appointments

In December 1856 Shaftesbury wrote to Palmerston that 'the Country will, no longer, submit to the old type of Bishops'. What was needed, he suggested, was 'men drawn from the larger parishes; men of great activity and experience; men with the disposition to live on friendly terms with their clergy'.[44] Shaftesbury went on to stress that this new breed of bishop should be those who will be busy in all things 'relating to the temporal and spiritual influences of the working classes'. He looked for bishops, not as scholars, but as those who would work as vigorously in their dioceses as they did as priests in their parishes.[45] The years which were immediately to follow this letter demonstrated the high measure of success which Shaftesbury was to achieve in securing his objectives. The entries in his diary in 1855 and 1856 contain a number of his comments on vacant bishoprics, and his intercourse with the Prime Minister concerning them. On 29 June 1856 Shaftesbury reported, 'Again successful (to God be all the glory) in obtaining from Palmerston, a blessed appointment to a Bishopric, C. Baring is elevated to Gloucester! Grant that we may have many such!'[46] Two months later Shaftesbury made an entry which revealed his great concern: 'Hear evil report that Palmerston will appoint Dr. Waddington, Dean of Durham, to be Bishop of London'. He continued, 'Oh what anxiety these appointments give me; yet blessed be God, twice have I succeeded in obtaining Bishoprics'.[47]

There is no further mention of London in the diary, but several entries in October and November are concerned with the vacant see of Ripon. The entry for 14 October included the following lines:

Ripon is still vacant, and he will fill it (I cannot blame him) with a Cambridge man. He is beset on all sides for his many Oxford appointments – No fit men in Cambridge of any note – Have commended Selwyn, not that he is absolutely good, but relatively the best.[48]

There is no other reference to the matter for another month and then on 22 November we find the following sentence: 'Urged, strongly urged P to the appointment of Robert Bickersteth to the see of Ripon!'[49] The matter was evidently of deep concern to Shaftesbury for the following day there is a lengthy entry in which he wrote of his 'fear that my success of Friday evening (for such it was) is fallen back; and that he has conceived something against Bickersteth!' Shaftesbury even significantly reveals that his reason for pressing the cause of the evangelical Bickersteth so strongly was, quite simply, that he feared that Palmerston might either die or be hounded out of office.

I trouble with eagerness of solicitude – It seems humanly speaking, the best and only hope for the Church – Palmerston is old; he may die, be turned out. No one who succeeds him would give us anything good; nay he would give us anything bad – I would I had helped lay such a foundation that might *hereafter* stand a few shocks of vicious appointments. If he fail us, all is lost; I recognise the hand of a justly indignant God.[50]

As it turned out, Shaftesbury's anxieties were short-lived. Just four days later he recorded his 'deep, humble, hearty and everlasting gratitude to Almighty God for his unspeakable goodness, mercy and graciousness in inclining the heart of Palmerston towards Bickersteth'. He concluded his entry in forthright mode: 'We have now some Bishops, we thank thee O Lord, who will declare and exalt the name of Christ'.[51]

The matter of the vacant See of London does, however, appear in an undated seven page memorandum in the Broadlands Papers. In it Shaftesbury proposes Archdeacon Sinclair, who is Vicar of Kensington and 'has great knowledge of the diocese'. He inclines, Shaftesbury noted, to the 'High Church' but in his favour, he added 'he is very anti-Puseyite, and a firm opponent of the Bishop of Oxford'.[52] Although Shaftesbury's proposal was not accepted, he cannot have been altogether disappointed, since Tait, who was given the post, was his nomination for a proposed new See of Hexham. Shaftesbury reported: 'He is a worthy man and has worked in his Deanery as in a Parish – no doubt there are men fitter to be Bishops than he is; but he represents a section of the Church of England, which will claim to be heard and have its share'.[53] Shaftesbury did write a few months later, that his own wish had been that 'Mr Pelham should be nominated to London and Dean Tait to Norwich or elsewhere'.

Whilst it is true that Shaftesbury certainly championed the cause of evangelical appointments to the Bench, it needs to be recognised that he also, on occasion, supported the claims of those from other parties. In January 1864, for example, Shaftesbury penned a hasty note to Palmerston

'The Bishop of Ely is dead. You have a man made to your hands, as his successor, the Revd. Harold Browne DD, Norissian Professor of Divinity in Cambridge. Everyone would, I think, look to him'.[54] Although Browne was a mild-high churchman, Shaftesbury was gratified at his appointment and wrote to Palmerston in the most positive frame about the public's response to him.[55] A year later when Chester became vacant, Shaftesbury urged that 'Dr. William Jacobson, Regius Professor of Divinity at Oxford, is a good man, and *at present* belongs to no extreme School of Theology'. He continued that Jacobson 'is learned being deep in books. He can, of course, have but little parochial experience . . . and I am not aware that he has any power of preaching'.[56] All this seems to reveal a very different approach on Shaftesbury's part. It's certainly a far cry from his early insistence in 1855 that men who were effective pastors and preachers in their parishes were what was wanted. It suggests that Shaftesbury had become sensitive to the needs of the wider Church of England. Perhaps also, following the publication of *Essays and Reviews*, he had recognised the need to have at least some bishops who could make a reasoned theological defence of the orthodox creedal faith. It was also probably for this reason that Shaftesbury pressed the claims of Francis Jeune, who was of his own evangelical persuasion. On 12 December 1863 he wrote to Palmerston that 'Jeune is a very good man. I had always looked to him, as one you might consider for the Bishopric of Exeter'.[57] A week later he followed it with a brief note which stated 'The enclosed letter from the Bishop of Gloucester should have been given to you. It bears strong testimony to Dr Jeune'.[58] It wasn't until the following summer just a few months after Jeune had made a firm stand on the authority of the Bible and the doctrine of the atonement, that he was offered the vacant See of Peterborough. Shaftesbury wrote to Palmerston in April in glowing approbation of Jeune. His letter also reveals his anxieties about the growing influence of Dean Stanley over Queen Victoria.

> Dr. Stanley has determined, aided by his "better half" to have the appointment of all preferment in the Kingdom; and unless you resist him, he will carry thro [sic] our most *unconstitutional* Queen all matters just as he pleases.
>
> The objection to Dr Jeune is neither more nor less than that he is personally objectionable (I knew that before) to Dr. Stanley. . . .
>
> The theological and ecclesiastical learning of Dr. Jeune; his bigness of mind and experience of business, make him a man of special importance at the present day for the service of the House of Lords. . . . Dr. Jeune, as a theologian, is first rate; as a man of business the same – His aid . . . as effecting University Reform at Oxford, was invaluable.[59]

The Record described his elevation as 'one of the most significant and telling of all Lord Palmerston's appointments'.[60]

Although Palmerston valued Shaftesbury's counsel and sought his advice on every ecclesiastical appointment save one,[61] he by no means followed it slavishly. In November 1860, for example, Shaftesbury wrote to Palmerston that the Bishop of Worcester is 'in extremis'. He continued: 'pray be on your guard against Claughton of Kidderminster. He is of the very ultra School, and would be a most ready and effective supplicator of the Bishop of Oxford on the Episcopal Bench'. Shaftesbury commended in his stead William Broderick, a former Rector of Bath and now Canon of Wells.[62] Palmerston chose rather a high churchman in Henry Philpott, Master of St. Catherine's College, Oxford.

Two years later when Archbishop Sumner died, Shaftesbury recommended that Dr. Baring, Bishop of Durham, should be translated to Canterbury, but Dr. Longley, Archbishop of York, and a high Church favourite, was preferred.[63] A struggle then ensued as Gladstone and others made a real push to obtain York for Samuel Wilberforce. The candidate proposed by Palmerston and Shaftesbury was Samuel Waldegrave, Bishop of Carlisle. Shaftesbury wrote of him as 'that good man Waldegrave', whose appointment 'would defy all objections, and be highly popular'.[64] The Queen vetoed the appointment, and to the great indignation of her Prime Minister insisted on the translation of the new Bishop of Gloucester and Bristol, William Thomson. It was remarked to Bishop Wilberforce, who was doubtless very disappointed: 'It is a curious thing, but whenever Mrs Thomson presents her husband with a baby the Archbishop has got preferment'.[65] The Bishop replied: 'Mrs Thomson had better be very careful, because there are only Canterbury and Heaven before him'.[66] Ethel Thomson wrongly stated that Shaftesbury's influence over Palmerston's ecclesiastical appointments ceased at this point. The preceding discussion shows him to have been influential in the subsequent appointments of Browne, Jeune and Jacobson.

Denouement

Clearly it is correct, as several writers have asserted, to describe Shaftesbury as 'the bishop maker'. Although his wishes were by no means always acceded to, he was without doubt the power behind the throne. Shaftesbury's diary and correspondence reveal that he constantly put forward the names of worthy men and offered advice, often unsolicited. Significantly, neither Shaftesbury not Palmerston sought solely to appoint those who were evangelicals. Particularly during the second ministry, Shaftesbury was ready to support the claims of scholars and moderate churchmen.

Despite Shaftesbury's strong influence on Palmerston, it was not the case that he slavishly followed his step-son-in-law's advice at every turn. There clearly were some occasions when he sought wider opinion and made decisions which were not altogether to Shaftesbury's liking. Palmerston's overriding aim was to do what he perceived to be in the best interests of the established Church. *The Record* asserted that 'his great object' was that the Church of England might 'be officered by sound and orthodox Churchmen'. Its leader continued that these were men who 'would neither countenance the pernicious views of sacerdotal ritualism, nor yet sap the foundations of the faith by adopting speculative and sceptical opinions in religion'.[67]

There is no doubt that the Palmerstonian bishops were the 'bête noire' of the high-church party, and the ritualists in particular. In a letter to William Gladstone, Bishop Samuel Wilberforce spoke of the 'Shaftesbury Bishops' as 'wicked appointments'[68] and others unjustly denounced them as ignoramuses who had little theology and were narrow minded. On the other hand, as *The Christian Observer* noted, Palmerston had showed himself 'ready to assert the great principles of the English Reformation'.[69]

In the complex interaction between Shaftesbury, Palmerston and the Queen strange things sometimes happened. For example, when Palmerston expressed his great surprise at how young the new Bishop of Ripon was, it was rumoured that he had thought that he was appointing Robert's uncle, Edward Bickersteth, and had got confused. A little later it was said by William Thomson's wife, Zoe, that when the Archbishopric of York fell vacant, Palmerston suggested one name after another. The Queen rejected each in turn. Eventually the frustrated Prime Minister said: 'Here madam is an entire list of the bishops from the oldest to the youngest!' Queen Victoria responded: 'I'll take the youngest'.[70] And so, Thomson was elevated to the Archbishopric of York.

All things considered, there is no doubt that Palmerston's English bishops were popular with the great majority of the British public, and particularly with dissenters and the working classes with whom, by and large, they enjoyed good relationships. *The Record* commented on one occasion that Palmerston's appointments were popular even among the Tories, and helped to sway the electorate in 1857, in 1859 and 1865.[71] Whatever else could be said of the bishops, there is no doubt that they brought a lasting change of emphasis to English episcopacy. It is this change and this new emphasis which the succeeding chapters will endeavour to examine.

III

Bishops in the Making

Birth and Parentage

The criticism was often made, and with good reason, that the majority of the Palmerston bishops were appointed, as a result of Lord Shaftesbury's influence, on account of their evangelical convictions. A case might, however, also be made that their promotions were given on the grounds of their family connections. It is significant that four of Palmerston's evangelical bishops were from aristocratic Whig families. Montagu Villiers (1831-1861) was the fifth son of the Hon. George Villiers and younger brother of George William Villiers (1800-1870), the fourth Earl of Clarendon, Foreign Secretary 1853-1858 and 1868-1870.[1] Charles Baring (1807-1879) was the fourth son of Sir Thomas Baring, Second Baronet, and of the eminent banking firm of Baring brothers. His brother, Thomas Baring (1799-1873), was M.P. for Huntingdon 1844-1873.[2] John Thomas Pelham (1811-1894) was the fourth son of Thomas Pelham (1756-1826) who was the second Earl of Chichester. His mother, Lady Mary, was also well-connected being the eldest daughter of Francis Godolphin, fifth Duke of Leeds. John's elder brother, Henry Pelham (1804-1866), third Earl of Chichester, was a Whig in politics and also held pronounced evangelical views. He was appointed an ecclesiastical commissioner on 22 February 1841 and in 1850 became head of the Church of England's Estates' Committee with the title of 'First Church Estates Commissioner'. For more than half a century he was President of the Church Missionary Society as well as being active in the Evangelical Alliance and the British and Foreign Bible Society.[3] Even without the influence of Shaftesbury, it is difficult to imagine Thomas Pelham not being marked out for promotion. Samuel Waldegrave (1817-1869), who was appointed Bishop of Carlisle in 1860, was the second son of William, the eighth Earl of Waldegrave.[4]

In addition to the aristocratic birthrights of Villiers, Baring, Pelham and Waldegrave, several other Palmerston bishops came from influential and landed families. Archibald Tait's father, Crauford Tait, was a Scottish landowner who for a time commanded the Clackmannanshire Yeomanry.[5] Joseph Cotton Wigram was the fifteenth child of Sir Robert Wigram, (1744-1830), who was an eminent Irish merchant and ship owner of London and Wexford. At one time he owned more than thirty ships based on the river Thames. He was returned as Member of Parliament for Fowey in Cornwall in 1797 and later for his home town of Wexford. His eldest brother, Robert (b.1773) was also Member of Parliament for Fowey and one of the directors of the Bank of England. Another brother, James (1793-1866), was elected Tory M.P. for Leominster in 1841.[6]

Robert Bickersteth (1816-1884) was described by Frederick Arnold as belonging to a family 'that of late times has made itself eminently distinguished in Church and State'.[7] One of his uncles, Henry Bickersteth, was senior wrangler at Cambridge who was subsequently called to the Bar and later became Master of the Rolls. He was created Baron Langdale and died in 1851.[8] William Thomson (1819-1890) was the eldest son of John Thomson of Kelswick House, near Kelswick in Cumbria. He was a director of the Bank of Whitehaven from its establishment in 1837, and of The Cleator Moor Hematite Iron Company, as well as a Justice of the Peace, and was involved as a Liberal in local politics. His mother, Isabella, was a descendant through her mother of Patrick Home of Polwarth and related to the Earl of Marchmont.[9]

Thus eight of Palmerston's fourteen English bishops were either from the aristocracy or from well-connected, influential families who had varying degrees of wealth, land and political influence. Of the other six: Longley, Philpott, Ellicott, Browne and Jeune came from solid middle-class families, most of whom had been of sufficient means to afford a public school education for their sons. John Longley, the father of Charles Longley (1794-1868), was a widely read political writer, Recorder of Rochester and one of the magistrates at the Thames Police Court.[10] In 1831 Longley married the Hon. Caroline Parnell, the eldest daughter of Sir Henry Brooke Parnell, whom he had met at Cobham Hall. His father-in-law, who later became Lord Congleton, suggested his name to Lord Melbourne as a suitable candidate for a bishopric. This led to Longley's departure from the head-mastership of Harrow in 1836 to the See of Ripon. Ellicott (1798-1869), who was Vicar of Whitwell in county Rutland and later at Clifton near Bristol, was a respected rural cleric who had graduated from Trinity Hall in 1821 with an LLB degree.[11] Harold Browne (1811-1891) was the son of Colonel Robert Browne of Morton House in Buckinghamshire.[12] Francis Jeune (1806-1868) came of a French Huguenot family established in Jersey since 1565. His father, also Francis, was a prosperous miller with premises at St. Aubyn.[13] William Jacobson (1803-1884) was the only one among Palmerston's appointments with an unlikely upbringing for a Victorian prelate. He was the son of William Jacobson, who was a clerk in a Great Yarmouth firm of ship owners. He died of a fever later in the year of his son's birth, leaving his wife a widow for eight years. When Judith Jacobson re-married, it was to a dissenter and young William was therefore brought up a Non-conformist.

Schooling and University

As one would expect of Victorian bishops, Palmerston's appointees all received a sound education in preparation for either Oxford or Cambridge. Several were educated privately: Robert Bickersteth was tutored at home with other pupils by his father, the Reverend John Bickersteth, who was an old fashioned classical scholar;[14] Charles Baring was also privately educated up until the time he entered Christ Church, Oxford in 1825; as was Joseph Cotton Wigram, prior to his going up to Trinity College in 1816.[15] John Pelham, Charles Longley, Henry Philpott, William Thomson and Harold Browne were all educated at public schools: Longley and Pelham both attended Westminster School, Longley going first to a private school before being elected a King's scholar at Westminster in 1808; Philpott attended Chichester Cathedral School, Thomson and Browne, Shrewsbury and Eton respectively.

Thomson was sent initially to a small school at Whitehaven in the charge of a dissenting minister, Archibald Jack. When he reached the age of eleven he went on to Shrewsbury, which was then under the headmastership of Dr. Samuel Butler, an able scholar, who succeeded in making the school a distinguished centre of classical excellence. Young William was no great scholar and took no prizes. His main interests were scientific projects and logic. In his holidays he would dabble with chemistry experiments.[16] Some snippets of information of Thomson's Shrewsbury days remain. We know for example that his journey home by coach always cost £5. He immensely enjoyed the experience of travelling by coach, which in later years he often drove, sometimes in the bitterest weather.[17]

Harold Browne attended Eton for only four years, and then was sent to the Rev. R. Holt who prepared one or two pupils for university at Postford House, near Albury on the South Downs. Whilst under the care of Mr. Holt, Browne, along with the other pupils, attended Sunday services at Albury parish church, where the Rev. Hugh McNeile was Rector. There he came under the influence of evangelical preaching which was to remain with him all his life.[18] His mother was apprehensive about the situation and wrote to a friend: 'I am afraid Harry so much admires Mr. McNeil's manner, that he will endeavour to follow it'.[19] As things turned out he survived the experience without 'giving his dear head a rest' as his mother wished.[20]

Archibald Tait was admitted to the celebrated Edinburgh High School in October 1821. At the time most of the best-known Scottish families sent their sons to be educated at this institution. Here he made rapid progress and developed a penchant for Latin translation. In 1824 'Archie' was removed to the newly founded 'Edinburgh Academy' where he was placed in the highest class. At the end of the year the name of Archibald Tait was placed third in order in the school despite his age being considerably below that of the average age of the boys in the upper class. In his second and third years he obtained, in each case, the gold medal as 'Dux' of the whole school. In his final year, 1827, Tait's success was remarkable; he secured no less than six of major prizes. Lord Cockburn who was the speaker on that occasion, addressed him with these words: 'Go forth, young man, and remember that wherever you go, the eyes of your country are upon you'.[21] Months later Archibald Tait matriculated as a student at Glasgow University, which was to be followed by a scholarship to Balliol College.

Charles Ellicott was educated at grammar schools in Oakham and Stamford, which were presumably chosen because they were sufficiently close to his father's parish of Whitwell. William Jacobson was first educated under the tuition of the Reverend William Walford, who was minister of the 'New Meeting' in Great Yarmouth. When he was about nine he was sent to a school at Norwich kept by Mr Brewer, a Baptist. Then at sixteen he moved on to another Non-conformist institution, Homerton College in London. Like Tait he subsequently had a spell at Glasgow University before going up to St. Edmund Hall.

One of the strange ironies regarding Palmerston's bishops is the accusation brought against them that they were ignoramuses who lacked scholarship and academic finesse.[22] The criticism was probably laid at their feet on account of their straight-forward evangelical preaching and their united hostility to critical scholarship as reflected in the publication of *Essays and Reviews*. In reality nothing could be further from the truth: seven of the fourteen achieved a first-class honours degree at either Oxford or Cambridge, and two had the distinction of achieving a double first. Of the remaining seven, four went on to take higher degrees and to hold distinguished university positions. Only Villiers, Pelham and Bickersteth were undistinguished in terms of academia. It should not, however, be supposed that they were academically inadequate. All three were concerned to raise the level of their ordination examinations, and to recruit as many university graduates as they were able to supply the parishes in their respective dioceses. Bickersteth stated that if clergy 'are really to influence society . . . there should be a breadth and depth in their education which the contracted sphere of a Theological college does not permit'.[23] Pelham insisted that his clergy have a knowledge of Greek and Latin.[24] Villiers also gave much attention to improving the quality of his parish clergy. He achieved this in part by raising the academic standards of the newly ordained prospective entrants into the diocese.[25]

Those of Palmerston's bishops who achieved first-class honours degrees were Baring, Longley, Tait, Waldegrave, Philpott and Jeune, each of them achieving their distinctions in classics. Baring and Waldegrave took double firsts in classics and mathematics. In addition, Joseph Cotton Wigram graduated sixth wrangler at Cambridge in 1819. Of his pleasing result, Archibald Tait remarked: 'I do not know how much this success was due to my viva voce examination in Aristotle which was conducted by William

Sewell but I know that Sewell . . . always had a friendly feeling toward me through his long, chequered and sadly overclouded life'.[26] When Francis Jeune went in for the final honours school of Literae Humaniores in 1827, he performed below expectations in the examination, which was mainly oral. However, the flexible system that prevailed at the time enabled him to sit a demanding paper on Aristotle's *Ethics* and so gain his First. Significantly, Jeune showed little further interest in the subject and proceeded to both the degree BCL and DCL in 1834.

By a strange quirk it was the four of Palmerston's bench who did not obtain first-class degrees who went on to achieve considerable distinction within the university setting. William Thomson gained only a third-class honours degree, although it proved enough to enable him to obtain a College Fellowship. Following his tutor's advice he apparently presented only sufficient books to secure his moderate classification. The truth of the matter was, according to his biographer, that he found his tutor's advice to his liking. At the beginning of his university career he had, in fact, been so lazy that he had failed his preliminaries. Thomson also won the distinction, claimed by no other bishops in the nineteenth century, of being rusticated for the remainder of a term for knocking down a fellow student, C.H. Angell, whom he felt had been ungentlemanly in his conduct.[27]

Despite having only a third-class honours to his name, Thomson had received the honour of having written and published an erudite text book on logic while still only an undergraduate. Entitled *An Outline of the Necessary Laws of Thought* it was based on broad reading, was well-written and concise in style and, perhaps most important, it was full of illustrations. The *Outline* soon passed through several editions and was widely acclaimed among undergraduates as the book to read if you wanted to obtain a second class in Moderations. Indeed, as a result of conversations in his room, many of Thomson's fellow students professed to have their first experiences of what was later referred to as culture.

Even before he had completed his undergraduate work, Thomson had developed an undiminished love of books that was to remain with him until the end of his days. Despite his pastoral work at Guildford and elsewhere he continued to write, producing an important article on Thomas Carlyle's *Heroes, Hero-Worship, and the Heroic in History* in August 1843 and *Crime and its Excuses* which appeared in 1855. He proceeded to his MA in January 1844 and BD and DD in 1856.[28] He became first a tutor in his own college and then, after a spell of parish work he returned to Queen's in 1845, serving as Tutor, Dean and Bursar. He tightened up on college disciplinary procedures and put his mathematical brain to work to overhaul the college's properties, mortgages and repair work. As Thomson perceived it, the issue for the university was not about the admission of dissenters, but its system of closed fellowships. Out of 542 teaching fellowships in the university, only 22 were by open examinations in which anyone could compete. Most colleges awarded their positions only to their own graduates. In 1850 a Royal Commission was approved to examine the state of the universities. The Provost of Queen's, Dr. Fox, proved to be a reactionary defender of the old order and refused even to give any information to the Commissioners. In opposition Thomson published an able pamphlet entitled *An Open College Best For All* and at the same time communicated his views to William Gladstone who was then Chancellor of the Exchequer. In 1855 Provost John Fox died and Thomson was elected in his place, his own vote as a Fellow being decisive in his favour.

Still a young man at only thirty-six, Thomson set about with vigour to reform the college in accordance with the provisions of The Oxford University Act of 1854. His preaching gifts were also recognised by the university authorities and he was twice appointed Select Preacher in 1848 and 1856, with large congregations coming to listen to his address. Thomson's reputation was further enhanced by his Bampton Lectures of 1853. He took as his subject *The Atoning Work of Christ* and examined the difficulties which prevented people from accepting it. He considered with seriousness the arguments of those who deny the resurrection and maintain that Jesus' teaching about his own death was an afterthought. His view was that the new scientific discoveries and critical biblical studies were not only to be reconciled with religion, but to serve it. As Thomson saw it, the Bible as it stands, meets the highest human wants. He dealt with the nature of sin and its reality and demonstrated that it needs a remedy. In contrast he argued that it is exactly at this point that Buddhism falls short as a religion. 'It was', he asserted, 'a scheme of metaphysics rather than moral law; and taught that God was all in all, and that the human spirit must strive to become absorbed in Him, without attending to the barrier which sin had thrown across the path'. 'Thus', he concluded, 'Buddhism stands out as a religion without sacrifice'.[29]

Charles Ellicott, who took his undergraduate degree the year after Thomson, followed a somewhat different path into academia. He graduated with a second-class honours in classics but his abilities were estimated to have been much higher than his degree result suggested. Perhaps his attaining the very difficult distinction of a fellowship at St. John's College demonstrated his true capabilities. After only three years in Cambridge he resigned his Platt Fellowship on his marriage to Anne, the daughter of Admiral Beecher, and was inducted to the parish of Pilton in Rutland. It was a small living which had a population of a mere forty-five souls, and still only an annual income of £80 as late 1905. Here Ellicott embarked on what was to become a life-long habit of disciplined study and writing.

He began by producing a series of commentaries on the Pauline epistles. He was wary of the newly emerging science of biblical criticism and his writings reflected a reverence for the traditional catholic interpretation of Scripture. His commentaries were both readable and scholarly, and were widely read until Bishop Lightfoot's writings began to appear. Galatians, Ellicott's first commentary, appeared in 1854. Those on Ephesians, the Pastoral Epistles, Philippians, Colossians and Philemon and Thessalonians appeared between 1855 and 1859. 1 Corinthians, the last to be published, came out in 1887 (Romans and 2 Corinthians never materialised).

In view of the scale of Ellicott's output, it was small surprise that he was chosen to succeed Richard Chevenix French as Professor of New Testament at King's College, London in 1858. In the same year he was Select Preacher before the University of Cambridge and published his sermons under the title of *The Destiny of the Creature, and other Sermons.* He aimed particularly to appeal to the younger generation, and stated that his object had been 'to put before the young, the generous and the impressionable, some high and ennobling scriptural truth'. Ellicott was aware that this was a high objective to realise but he wrote: 'if I have pointed out ever so generally to one lone wanderer in this world's dreary wilderness the narrow way of Christ, then I shall solemnly rejoice, and my joy no man shall take it from me'.[30] The following year Ellicott was Hulsean Lecturer to the University of Cambridge and took as his theme *Historical Lectures on the Life of our Lord.* They were published in one volume in 1860 and proved to be one of his most popular books, reaching a sixth edition in 1874.

Partly as a result of his lectures, together with his distinguished scholarship, Ellicott was elected to the Hulsean Chair, which he held along with his chair at King's College. His tenure of these academic positions proved to be short-lived since the stage was now set for his promotion to high ecclesiastical office. In 1861 Ellicott was made Dean of Exeter, whose diocese had been for thirty years under the heavy hand of Henry Phillpotts. 1863 then brought what proved to be the final move, when Lord Palmerston appointed him to the united Sees of Gloucester and Bristol.

Harold Browne went up to Emmanuel College, Cambridge, in 1827 at the age of seventeen. It was described as 'a very idle though very gentleman-like College'.[31] Not surprisingly young Harold developed a taste for rowing and was stroke for the college boat.[32] Perhaps because of his activities on the river Cam he graduated in 1832 with only a third class in the Classical Tripos. He was not, however, one who was easily discouraged and in the following year he carried off the Crosse Theological Scholarship. Then in 1834 he gained the Tyrwhitt Hebrew Scholarship, adding to it the Norissian prize in 1835. For two years he held several minor college offices before being elected to a fellowship at his college in 1838.

In 1846, however, he married Elizabeth Carlyon and therefore exchanged his fellowship, according to custom, for a succession of short charges, in Stroud in Gloucestershire and then in the city of Exeter. This was followed by a spell of six years as Vice-Principal of St. David's College, Lampeter, before he returned to the Exeter Diocese as incumbent of

Kenwyn-cum-Kea in Cornwall and the vicarage of Heavitree on the out-skirts of Exeter.

Browne was chosen as Norrisean Professor of Divinity in 1855 and proceeded to the degree BD in the same year. He settled with his wife and family into Newnham Cottage a comfortable house at the back of the Colleges. Although an academic, his heart was always in pastoral work, and he endeavoured to retain his parochial charges, relying on curates for help, and returning for spells during the university vacations. Eventually Browne's attempts at these dual roles, including troubles with his curates,[33] proved too much, and he left Heavitree in January 1858 but continued as a Canon of Exeter for another seven years.

In 1853 Browne published *An Exposition of the Thirty Nine Articles* which was the substance of his earlier lectures at St. David's College. As a result he was hailed 'as the upholder of a moderate and conservative high church position'. Once he had confined his energies to the University alone, Browne's theological output increased. He contributed an article on 'Inspiration' to *Aids to Faith*, William Thomson's counter blast to *Essays and Reviews*, and he replied to Colenso's radical liberal writings in a piece entitled *The Pentateuch and the Elohistic Psalms* which was published in 1863. In a letter from Cambridge to a friend he wrote: 'What a sad business in Colenso's apostasy! It is difficult to call it by a milder name!'[34] Browne's opinions gained wide acceptance in many quarters and public opinion marked him out for promotion, which came in January 1864, with offer of the See of Ely.

William Jacobson was elected to a scholarship at Lincoln College, Oxford, on 5 May 1826. He suffered a period of severe sickness before his finals and took only a second class degree in Classics. After a brief spell in Ireland he returned to Oxford and was elected a fellow at Exeter on 30 June.[35] Jacobson was ordained deacon in June 1830 and took on a curacy under Archdeacon Clerke at St. Mary Magdalene, in Oxford. In 1832 he was appointed Vice-Principal of Magdalen Hall later Hertford College and with encouragement from the Principal he set about improving the quality and standard of its undergraduate education. J.W. Burgon observed that throughout this time Jacobson was 'a thoughtful and laborious student of divinity'.[36]

Jacobson married Eleanor Jane Turner on 23rd June 1836. She came from his home area and was the accomplished daughter of Dawson Turner, Esq., a banker of Great Yarmouth. William remained Vice-Principal of Magdalen until 1848, during which time he also served as perpetual curate of Iffley, a small village on the outskirts of Oxford. In 1848 he was appointed Regius Professor of Divinity, which carried with it a canonry of Christ Church, Oxford, and at that time also the Rectory of Ewelme, Oxfordshire. His lectures in the university were highly regarded. Canon Farrar of Durham once said: 'My conviction is that Jacobson's lectures were of the greatest importance, and would have ranked in the highest class of excellence had they been delivered as a course on *Theologische Encyclopaedie* in a German University'. Jacobson had remained in the university continuously since his undergraduate days and was honoured by it when chosen as Public Orator in 1842 and as Select Preacher in 1838 and 1842. Dean Burgon wrote that 'his was essentially an upright, earnest God-fearing life' whose integrity won him the respect of his contemporaries.[37] In politics Jacobson was a Liberal, and he chaired William Gladstone's election committee at Oxford in 1865. It was in fact this which resulted in Palmerston putting his name forward for the bishopric of Chester, when it fell vacant on the death of John Graham later the same year. Gladstone wrote to Palmerston to the effect that it would greatly strengthen his chances of success if his campaign manager were to be elevated in this way.[38]

Parochial Experience

As has been noted, Lord Palmerston, prompted by Shaftesbury, was concerned to have bishops who would relate well to ordinary people. For this reason, in his first ministry he made a particular point of appointing men who had a solid base of parochial experience. It is significant that thirteen out of his fourteen English appointees had worked in parish life either as curates or incumbents. Of the six men promoted by Palmerston during his first period of office, each had served as a curate, followed by six or more years as an incumbent or priest in charge.

Montagu Villiers, the first Palmerston bishop, had begun clerical life as an assistant curate to the evangelical Edward Girdlestone (1805-1884) in the parish of St. Mary's Deane, Bolton-le-Moors. The day after being ordained priest, Villiers became Vicar of St. Nicholas Church, Kenilworth, where Robert Sumner, the father of Bishop John Bird and Charles Richard Sumner, had been incumbent from 1773 to 1802. Apart from one or two minor skirmishes with the local Presbyterian minister, William Field, Villiers' stay in Warwickshire was uneventful. In 1841 Lord Lyndhurst, the Lord Chancellor, appointed him to the wealthy Rectory of St. George's Bloomsbury. It was in this setting for the next ten years that Villiers was to gain a rich and varied pastoral experience. Most of the seventeen thousand parishioners were poor, and Villiers and his five curates worked constantly. Villiers himself was a conscientious visitor who achieved a reputation for 'befriending poor cobblers, trying to comfort sick cabmen and luring ragged children to school'.[39] *The Times* newspaper spoke of him as a 'hardworking, much-trudging pastor'. 'People are not unmoved', said its columnist, 'when they see a man who might be enjoying the pleasures of fashionable life giving himself up with the most perfect devotion to the religious and when they see the brother of an earl ... toiling resolutely in the back streets of a London parish.'[40] Villiers was an able preacher who had the unusual gift of being able to communicate the Christian message to the working classes. He spoke to the Y.M.C.A. and was a firm advocate of lay ministry, which he supported by raising funds for the City Mission and the Church Pastoral Aid Society.

While at St. George's, Villiers wrote a paper entitled *On the Necessity and Value of Lay Agency in the Church*. In it he emphasised the many calls on the parochial minister's time and urged that if they 'cannot do it themselves, they should at least get others to do it for them'.[41] *The Gentleman's Magazine* commended his 'hardworking' endeavour and his 'admirable' management of parochial schools.[42]

Charles Baring's parochial experience was in much the same pattern as Villiers'. Soon after his marriage he settled into the country living of Kingsworthy in Hampshire. Then in 1847 he was appointed to the important benefice of All Saints, Marylebone, where he was a renowned preacher. Like Villiers he became a staunch advocate of lay agencies and a promoter of schools. However in 1850 he was preferred to a valuable living in Limpsfield in Surrey, but after a year he succeeded Dr. Monk as Bishop of Gloucester and Bristol. Charles Longley, like many of his contemporary clerical tutors, engaged in pastoral work. He took on the curacy of the then quiet village of Cowley, which was just a mile or two from the city centre. Initially he served under the incumbent, Thomas Vowler Short, who was later Bishop of St. Asaph. In 1823 he succeeded him as incumbent. In this rural location Longley encountered at first hand the hardships of working-class living. Despite being an able teacher, Longley found the life at Christ Church somewhat irksome and longed to be involved with people.

In 1827 he accepted from one of his pupil patrons the country living of West Tytherley, near Stockbridge in Hampshire. The population was only about five hundred souls, and Longley had time to take in pupils from the aristocracy and gentry. In due course, Charles Sumner, the Bishop of Winchester, made him a rural dean, but he did not hold the office for long, for in 1829 Vowler Short put his name forward as headmaster of Harrow, a position which in itself brought a large pastoral responsibility.

On passing his degree in 1835 Tait was immediately appointed a tutor in his college. He was ordained the following year and soon felt the need to be engaged in pastoral work beyond the walls of Balliol. To the amazement of his friends but with encouragement from Bishop Bagot he was licensed as curate to the united parish of Toot and Baldon and March Baldon. The two churches were in a bad state of repair, there was no salary and no vicarage house. To complete the gloomy picture, the vicar, the Reverend Hugh Willoughby, was resident abroad and in ill health. Notwithstanding, Tait rose to the task of tending to the needs of the agricultural labourers who occupied the rows of straggling cottages. Later, when his Balliol responsibilities extended, Tait enlisted the help of two friends,

Mr. Johnson, tutor at Queen's and Charles Golighty of Oriel. For five years Tait retained the sole responsibility for the Baldons, riding or walking from Oxford several times in a week. It was his custom to stay Saturday nights in the parish and return for the college service on Sunday afternoon. According to his son-in-law and biographer: 'To the very close of his life he used to recount with a certain humorous pathos the quiet obstruction offered by the farmers to his Sunday School, and the difficulties of a rustic congregation on a hot summer's day, and the petty quarrels and flirtations and ambitions of his village choir'.[43] Although the pastoral responsibilities of Baldon were modest to say the least, they provided a lasting basis for what was to follow. When Tait gave his Primary Charge to the clergy of the Diocese of London some sixteen years later he said: 'I cannot remember how, when a curate in a small village in Oxfordshire. . . . '[44]

Both Pelham and Bickersteth, the other two appointed by Palmerston during his first ministry, were also men who had wide parochial experience prior to their episcopates. Pelham had a variety of differing charges. He was ordained in 1834 by Bishop Blomfield of London and placed in sole charge of the parish of Eastergate in the Diocese of Chichester. Then in May 1837 he was instituted to the vicarage of Bergh Apton, a large village about eight miles south east of Norwich. Here he remained for fifteen years, spending much of his time promoting the cause of the foreign missions in the county and diocese. His services were recognised by his appointment to the office of rural dean. He later became a canon of Norwich Cathedral and Chaplain to the Queen in 1847. Then in 1852 he became perpetual curate of Christ Church Hampstead, where he remained only three years before being instituted to the Crown living of St. Marylebone on the recommendation of Lord Palmerston. Pelham was resident for only two further years in this position before being consecrated by the Bishop of Norwich in succession to Bishop Hinds. It was in these settings that Pelham learned the values of visiting and the importance of trying to make worship relevant to the needs of ordinary people. In this connection he edited a small collection of *Hymns for Public Worship* which was published in 1855.

Robert Bickersteth was made deacon in Peterborough Cathedral in 1842 and served as curate of Sapcote until the following year, when he moved to work under the Reverend T.C. Granger at St. Giles Reading. In 1845 he moved on to join Archdeacon Dealtry in the parish of Clapham. Dealtry was one of the leading figures in the evangelical world, and it was while working with him that Bickersteth emerged as a preacher of note and influence. As a result, at the end of 1845 Dr. Dealtry offered Bickersteth the incumbency of St. John's, Clapham Rise. Here his evening sermons attracted a wide spectrum of all classes. The Reverend Clement Cobb, who was Bickersteth's curate at Clapham, commented: 'The plain and unecclesiastical church had its best ornament in the eighteen hundred people who filled every seat that was constructed'. Bickersteth usually preached for fifty minutes, and there were no complaints about long sermons![45]

In 1851 Lord Truro offered Bickersteth the living of St. Giles-in-the-Fields, which he accepted. It was not difficult for a preacher of his ability to fill the building on Sundays, but he set himself the greater task of providing pastoral care at the grass roots level. Bickersteth mapped out the whole parish into districts, and eleven Scripture Readers and City Missionaries were paid exclusively for spiritual work among the destitute and poor. Each worker was personally responsible to Bickersteth and was required to meet with him fortnightly in the vestry. Bickersteth opened the Sunday School and put energy into supporting local National Day Schools. He also sponsored meetings of the 'Labourers' Friendly Society' which had the objective of improving the dwellings of the poor. Since Palmerston was specifically looking for men of proven pastoral experience, it was inevitable that Bickersteth should come to his notice. Thus it was in November 1857 he received a letter from the Prime Minister offering him the See of Ripon. He was consecrated on 18 January 1857.

As Shaftesbury himself made clear, Lord Palmerston did not in his second term of office appoint bishops solely on the basis of proven pastoral experience. Shaftesbury had not expected his step-father-in-law to be Prime Minister for any length of time, and he had therefore urged in the early days that men who could relate to ordinary people were wanted. However, the situation in the early 1860s demanded the appointment of men who were able to defend the orthodox faith against the challenges posed by the publication of *Essays and Reviews* and Coleno's *The Pentateuch and Book of Joshua Critically Examined*. However, it is striking that seven of the eight men appointed in Palmerston's second term nevertheless had some experience of parish life.

Joseph Cotton Wigram had begun his ministry in 1822 as curate of St. Mary, Leytonstone, 'a chapelry within the parish of Layton [sic]'. Described as 'a straggling village about six miles from London upon the Epping road' Leytonstone contained the country residences of many of the commercial inhabitants of London.[46] After five years in this prosperous rural setting, Wigram went to take charge of the district Church of St. Luke's, Berwick Street within the parish of St. James, Westminster. Here he mingled and rubbed shoulders with people from all walks of life. Among the parents of the five hundred children Wigram baptised in 1828 there were coachmen, bricklayers, shopkeepers, servant labourers, tailors and shoemakers.[47] During his twelve years of ministry Wigram started a systematic scheme of visiting, with a team of between eight and eighteen visitors who were to find out the sick and communicate conditions of need to the clergyman.[48] By the end of Wigram's time the Berwick Street conventional district had been divided into more than sixty smaller units, with special charities being distributed in seasons of distress and extreme cold.[49] The number of schools was increased, from three with two hundred and twenty scholars, to twelve with more than one thousand two hundred scholars. A lending library was established with two thousand six hundred loans being registered in 1837.[50] Wigram also saw St. Luke's rebuilt on a new site at a cost of £12,210, with increased facilities.[51]

In 1839 Wigram moved to what was a total contrast in ministerial terms, the tiny parish of East Tisted, some four and a half miles South west of Alton. This isolated rural community had an acreage of two thousand six hundred and two, and a population in 1851 of two hundred and twenty-nine.[52] In most years there were half a dozen baptisms and one or two weddings.[53] In 1850 Wigram, who had been appointed Archdeacon of Winchester in 1847, moved to the parish of St. Mary's in the heart of Southampton's dockland. Here for a further ten years he experienced the problems associated with a rapidly growing population in a cosmopolitan sea-faring community.

Samuel Waldegrave's experience of parish life was confined to Oxford and a college country living. He was ordained deacon in 1842 and served his title at St. Ebbe's, Oxford having Charles Baring as his fellow curate. While at St. Ebbe's he took a leading part in building the district church of Holy Trinity which was within the parish bounds. He married in 1845 and relinquished his tutorial fellowship, accepting in its place the college living of Barford St. Martin near Salisbury.[54]

Francis Jeune was made deacon in 1832 but does not appear to have had experience as a curate. The years immediately following his ordination were spent in Canada as tutor to the sons of Sir John Colbourne (Lord Seaton), a fellow Channel Islander who served with distinction at Waterloo. Soon after his return to England, Jeune took up as Headmaster of King Edward's School, Birmingham. Among the boys he earned a reputation as a hard disciplinarian. Francis Galton, one of the school's distinguished pupils wrote: 'I do not like the Doctor (Jeune) taking our class, he expects the grammar said more perfectly than we can and he thrashes the lower part of the body for every mistake they make . . . this morning he thrashed eleven fellows in eight minutes'.[55] On the positive side, Jeune was very farsighted and recognised that, as well as being a centre of classical excellence, the school must provide a balanced education which gave adequate time to modern languages and mathematical and scientific pursuits.[56] The school, he said, 'must cater for the wants of the great commercial community'.[57] Jeune's remarkable success, according to *The Times*, 'recommended him to the favourable notice of the Liberal ministry, whose politics he strongly espoused when most of the clergy disdained all connexion with "whigs" or "whiggery" '.[58] It was not altogether surprising, therefore, when Lord John Russell offered him the post in the place of his upbringing, that of Rector of St. Helier and Dean of Jersey, a position with quasi-episcopal powers. It was a demanding assignment in which Jeune worked immensely hard and, among other projects, took an active role in the establishment of Victoria College in St. Helier.[59] Jeune remained on the Channel Islands until 1843 when he returned to Oxford as Master of Pembroke College, which had a canonry at Gloucester Cathedral attached to it. He continued in the university for more than twenty years, when he was raised to the episcopate.

Of all the Palmerston bishops William Thomson had the most chequered parochial experience. One of his biographers wrote that until he finally arrived at York as Archbishop 'his life is one long catalogue of tasks half-done or even hardly attempted'.[60] He was curate of St. Nicholas, Guildford for two years from 1842-1844. He followed this with a one-year curacy at Cuddesdon before returning to Queen's College as tutor, and rapidly rose to become Chaplain, Dean and Bursar. He was then Rector of All Souls, Langham Place for less than a year, before returning to Queen's as Provost from 1855-1860. He was then ten months Bishop of Gloucester and Bristol before being translated to the archiepiscopal See of York. This latter elevation came so quickly that, when Thomson announced it to his young twenty-five year old wife, Zoe, she replied with great alarm 'Oh do go to bed'.[61] It had been said in a light-hearted moment to Samuel Wilberforce, that every time Zoe Thomson gave birth to another child he got another promotion. To this the bishops replied that he hoped she wouldn't have any more. On being asked why, he replied wryly that there were only two steps left: Canterbury and glory! Yet for all Thomson's university association, his brief pastoral assignments brought him into contact with ordinary men and women. This common touch remained with him to the end of his days. He would invite members of the York Factory Girls Club into the gardens at Bishopsthorpe and mix and chat with them with ease and freedom. He would stop and talk to mothers and children in the streets, and give his money to help the needy and distressed. He truly merited his title 'the people's archbishop'.

For all his academic achievements, Harold Browne was rich in pastoral experience. He was one of those rare individuals who seems to have been able to study at a high level, be there for people and enjoy the pleasures of a relaxed home and family environment. At Kenwyn-cum-Kea Browne purchased a horse and used it for visiting all parts of his charge.[62] His parish was carefully organised and each curate had his division as a kind of sole charge. Browne also established district visitors, whose responsibility it was to furnish him with details of sickness and specific needs, for smaller areas. He enjoyed the good will of all the Non-conformists in his locality and won the confidence of the Methodist Minister at Tregavethan.[63] The wide extent of the Cornish living led Browne increasingly to see the value of obtaining unordained assistance. In 1854 he read a paper entitled *Thoughts on the Extension of the Diaconate and on Lay Agency* to the ruridecanal chapter of Powder. It was later printed at their request.[64]

Ellicott and Jacobson both enjoyed periods of rural ministry before they gave themselves to academic pursuits, Ellicott as Hulsean Professor of Divinity at Cambridge, and Jacobson as Regius Professor of Divinity at Oxford. Ellicott took up the small living of Pilton in Rutland in 1848, remaining there for ten years. The experience must have proved a valuable basis for his later ministry as bishop, as the content of some of his addresses such as *The Church and the Rural Poor* and *The Spiritual Needs of Country Parishes* make plain.[65] Jacobson was made deacon in 1830 and accepted a curacy under Archdeacon Clerke at St. Mary Magdalene's, Oxford prior to his appointment as Vice-Principal of Magdalen Hall in 1832. Despite these responsibilities, which lasted until 1848, he became perpetual curate at Iffley in 1839 and later published a volume of his addresses under the title *Sermons preached in the Parish Church at Iffley*.[66]

Of all Palmerston's bishops, Henry Philpott seems to have had the least experience in terms of church-based pastoral ministry. He was made deacon in 1831 and ordained priest in 1833 in the Chichester Diocese.[67] In 1845 he was, however, elected to the Mastership at St. Catharine's College, Cambridge, which had a residentiary canonry in Norwich Cathedral attached to it. During all his university activities Philpott always arranged that his three months residence in Norwich should fall in the summer. This meant that he was able to fulfil all his duties as Vice-Chancellor and as Master of his college. Despite having lived a secluded ivory tower existence within the university precincts, Philpott emerged as a bishop with a wonderfully caring and sensitive disposition. *The Times* reported of him: 'When the agricultural depression fell heavily upon his large country diocese, his clergy learned the practical character of his sympathy, there was no bounds to his unostentatious generosity, up to the point which left him sufficient for the singularly simple wants of his wife and himself and his small household'.[68]

Churchmanship

There has been a tendency in some quarters to support the view that Palmerston's English bishops were evangelicals to a man. This supposition probably stemmed from Samuel Wilberforce's comment that they were 'wicked appointments'. In point of fact eight of the fourteen were evangelicals, namely Baring, Bickersteth, Pelham, Wigram, Waldegrave, Thomson and Jeune. As such they were all firm supporters of the *Lord's Day Observance* and other major evangelical societies. In addition they were all strongly wedded to the teachings of the English Reformation, an aspect which is considered in detail in a later chapter. Two of the others, Tait and Browne, had strong evangelical convictions, but neither were happy to be regarded as evangelicals full-stop, although Tait was at times very close to being so. Longley, Ellicott, Philpott and Jacobson are probably best considered as moderate high churchmen.

Of the evangelicals Villiers, Baring, Bickersteth, Wigram and Waldegrave were 'Recordite' in their sympathies. That is, their convictions were those propagated by the more extreme evangelical periodical *The Record*. They were firm believers in the verbal inspiration of Scripture, who were interested in prophecy and the end times, and proclaimed the Second Coming of the Lord with an insistent urgency. They saw God's hand of judgement in the events of the times such as Cattle plagues,[69] outbreaks of cholera, the Indian Mutiny and the crisis in Crimea. Apart from their avowed hostility to ritualism, Thomson and Jeune were from the more 'moderate' school of evangelicalism, which was less insistent on the second coming and, generally speaking, more actively engaged in social reforming activities.

Montagu Villiers was generally regarded as being an extreme low church evangelical. Among other things he 'told young men to avoid theatres as an 'unmixed evil', and to look well to their steps in the ballroom'.[70] Villiers seems to have experienced an evangelical conversion during his time as Vicar of Kenilworth. A neighbouring clergyman who had heard him preach a special sermon, afterwards took him aside and pointed out that his discourse was deficient in its doctrine of salvation. The result of this was that he came 'to regard Christ in a way he had not done before'.[71] One of the first things he did after his change of heart was to stand up in front of his own people and 'to declare to them that hitherto he had been teaching them error'. Henceforth, he declared that he was determined 'to know nothing among them save Jesus Christ, and Him crucified'.[72]

John Pelham was, like Villiers, a man of strong evangelical convictions. *The Christian Observer,* on his promotion to the Bench, commented that 'every Christian's heart, familiar with the character and history of the man – must rejoice in the appointment'.[73] *The Church of England Monthly Review* spoke of Pelham as 'a man of sound Evangelical views, and much practical experience' whose elevation augured 'much good . . . to this important see'.[74] Pelham's Recordite convictions were perhaps most clearly evidenced shortly after his arrival in Norwich, when he called together the city's clergy and Non-conformist ministers to consider the possibility of holding a special service in all the churches 'as an opportunity for united prayer and humiliation before God in connection with the present disastrous events in India'.[75]

Charles Baring was commended by *Evangelical Christendom* on account of 'his reputation for sound evangelical doctrine and decided personal piety'.[76] The same journal went on to inform its readers that his views were substantially those 'devoutly cherished by the great body of Scottish Presbyterians and English Wesleyans and Non-conformists'.[77] These convictions stand out in his charges and published sermons. The concluding words of his 1857 visitation address are typical:

And in proportion as you determine to know nothing among your flock but Jesus Christ and him crucified, in such proportion will you find the preaching of the cross a weapon, mighty through God to the pulling down of strongholds, casting down imaginations, and every high thing that exalted itself against the knowledge of God and bringing into captivity every thought to the obedience of Christ.[78]

Robert Bickersteth was equally well-known throughout the country as a man of deep evangelical commitment. He came from a prominent evangelical family. His uncle, Edward Bickersteth, was an influential figure and acknowledged evangelical leader in the years immediately following Simeon's death. His father John 'gloried in the title evangelical', although he always repudiated the charge of being 'a Low Churchman'.[79] Robert's son and biographer later wrote that 'the name of the Bishop of Ripon was a household word throughout the evangelical world'.[80] His cousin, Edward Henry Bickersteth who later became Bishop of Exeter, spoke of him as 'the standard bearer in the front rank of evangelical churchmen'. He continued that, whether he was in the family circle of his own home, or on the public platform or in the House of Lords, 'one motive animated him, the constraining love of Christ'.[81] Indeed, Robert Bickersteth's evangelicalism was apparent in every aspect of his ministerial life: in his preaching, in his support of evangelical societies and lay agencies, his strong adherence to the inspiration and authority of Scripture, and his hostility to things Roman and the Papal Aggression in particular.

Joseph Cotton Wigram, who was consecrated as bishop of Rochester in May 1860, came from a family in which there was a strong Christian influence. His younger brothers George Vicesimus (1805-1879) and William Pitt (1806-1870) were both active in Christian ministry. The former experienced an evangelical conversion one evening in June 1824 after having seen the battlefield at Waterloo,[82] and subsequently joined the Brethren movement after a meeting with John Nelson Darby at Oxford in 1829. William Pitt was appointed by Joseph Cotton as his chaplain in 1860 and subsequently became Vicar of Latton in Essex in 1864. The likelihood is that this religious influence came early through their mother, Lady Eleanor Wigram (1767-1841). She is known to have played a dominant role in the Anglican Church in Walthanston and the surrounding locality. In 1824 she founded the Ladies Auxiliary of the Church Missionary Society, which soon became more successful than the male-run branch.[83]

Joseph Cotton was typical of the 'Recordite' school of evangelicals. He was a forthright and dignified preacher who emphasised Reformation doctrines and stressed the second coming of Christ. He was also an enthusiastic supporter of the Church Missionary Society and backed George Gorham in the baptismal regeneration controversy.[84] Wigram's evangelicalism was later widely denounced as excessively narrow when, in his first charge on 5 November 1860, he warned his clergy against playing cricket and sporting beards and moustaches.[85] He also warned against 'cards, the theatre and following the latest fashions in dress too closely'.[86] For this *The Pall Mall Gazette* ungenerously denounced him as 'nothing less than a prude' and as one of 'the narrowest bishops'.[87]

Samuel Waldegrave was an evangelical much in the same mould as Wigram. He served his curacy at the evangelical church of St. Ebbe's, Oxford, having for his fellow curate Charles Baring. His theological convictions were those of the Reformers; he preached for conversion and actively supported missionary societies. As a bishop his strong links with Non-conformists and his participation in the Exeter Hall meetings earned him the odium of *The Saturday Review*, a paper singularly hostile to both evangelical religion and Whig politics.[88] It denounced him as a 'fanatic' whose religion is 'not one whit superior to that of the conventicle and the revivalist'.[89] In reality Waldegrave was a gracious and scholarly individual with an interest in prophecy and an avowed opposition to ritualism.

The two Palmerston appointees whose evangelical convictions might best describe them as 'Moderates' rather than 'Recordites' were William Thomson and Francis Jeune.[90] William Thomson appears to have experienced his first Christian impressions as a youngster in his family home environment. His grandfather, William, seems to have been a Scottish Presbyterian Minister. Later, at the age of forty-one he wrote in his diary: 'I resolve therefore from henceforth to serve God . . . As all my powers, small as they are, proceeded from God, so too they should return in setting forth His glory and centering all affections upon Him'.[91] A prominent evangelical journal described Thomson's views as substantially those of Charles Baring, whom he had succeeded at All Souls Church in London.[92] Frederick Arnold recalled him as 'the image of the evangelical preacher',[93] one who demonstrated that 'the simplest evangelical truth is not inconsistent with the highest mental power and the best mental culture'.[94] Thomson, who, according to Arnold, preached as 'a dying man to dying men',[95] became very popular with the many lawyers and others who made up his congregation in Langham Place. Baring-Gould pointed out that the high church Party viewed Thomson's episcopal preferments with distaste because they regarded him as the man of most ability in the Evangelical party.[96] They saw in his promotions Shaftesbury's desire for a 'strong man' to put down the beginnings of ritualistic practice in the north of England.[97] Bishop Wilberforce in particular never forgave Thomson for his elevation to the archiepiscopal see to which he himself had long held aspirations. It grieved him deeply that his own former curate should have scuppered his greatest dream, especially as he perceived Thomson's capabilities and qualifications to be considerably less than his own.[98]

Neither Archibald Tait or Harold Browne could be construed as members of the evangelical party, but both were profoundly influenced by evangelical experience. At times Tait appears as close as it was possible to be an evangelical, without actually being one. A foolscap sheet was found in Tait's desk shortly after his death. On it he described how, at the age of ten or twelve, he had stayed with his brother Crauford in Miss Rutherford's house at Glendevon. Here he had a deep spiritual experience of 'the reality and nearness of the world unseen'. He had concluded his reflection as follows: 'O Lord, keep me to the end, washing me in Christ's blood, and making me fit for that glorious and holy presence, which at that early age I faintly realised'.[99] A little later, when a student at Glasgow University, he greatly valued the evangelical preaching of Dr. Welsh at Ramshorn Church which he usually attended on Sundays.[100] When he first arrived at Balliol College he was much influenced by the writings of Sumner and his circle.[101] In 1843 Tait married Catherine (1819-1878), the daughter of William Spooner, the evangelical Rector of Elmdon and later Archdeacon of Coventry. After the strongly evangelical upbringing she had come from she was for some years under the influence of the Oxford School.[102] When Tait was appointed to the bishopric of London *The Church of England Quarterly Review* stated that 'Dr Tait is an excellent man of business . . . and is evangelical without being fanatical'.[103] Tait did most of the things which were expected of nineteenth century evangelicals. He supported major societies like C.M.S., he advocated lay ministry and made positive relationships with Non-conformists, he experimented with new and evangelistic services, he preached in the open air, and took part in the celebrated Exeter Hall and theatre services which were designed to reach out to the working men and women of London. In the judgement of Lord Shaftesbury, with whom Tait enjoyed cordial relations, he was the 'mildest of Broad Churchmen'.[104] Perhaps the validity of Shaftesbury's assessment was best seen in Tait's peaceable stance over the Hampden affair in 1847, and his refusal to join any of the more extreme protestant societies such as the Evangelical Alliance.

Harold Browne's feelings for evangelicalism were in many ways a reflection of Tait's although from an ecclesiastical standpoint his sympathies were inclined towards moderate High Church rather than Broad. Harold's first encounter with evangelicalism was as a young man preparing for university. His biographer commented: 'Browne in common with almost every man of religious feeling in these days, came more or less under the influence, intellectual and spiritual of the evangelical school of thought'.[105] Although in later years Browne distanced himself from the more extreme elements within mid-Victorian evangelicalism, according to Kitchin, he 'ever retained that higher sense of duty to God and man, that taste for parish work, and those deep convictions as to the spiritual nature of religion, which came to him from these early surroundings'.[106] Shortly after his enthronement as Bishop of Winchester, Harold Browne gave an address in which he said: 'I have always called myself evangelical, but I am equally ready to call myself a high churchman. I believe very thoroughly in both'.[107] Where Browne's commitment to high church principles was most apparent was in his view that there was an unbroken line of bishops, which ran from the earliest times by the laying on of hands, through to the present. It was seen also in his appreciation of the church's festivals and his understanding that grace was always conveyed in baptism whether the recipient was a child or an adult.[108]

Modern church historians seem uncertain about where to place Ellicott in terms of churchmanship. David Edwards and P.T. Marsh seem happy to refer to him as a 'moderate Evangelical'.[109] Owen Chadwick included him with Evangelical bishops such as John Charles Ryle and Arthur Hervey,[110] while M.A. Crowther relied on Ellicott's self-description as an 'Evangelical' when he opened a debate on Diocesan Synods in 1867.[111] Lord Shaftesbury on the other hand, in a letter to Palmerston dated 18 November 1862, wrote that 'Ellicott, whom you think of for the Bishopric of Gloucester, is a very moderate and judicious man, formerly Hulsean Professor of Divinity, and now Dean of Exeter by your appointment – He would be linked with the moderate High Churchmen'.[112] It was probably in part for this reason that G.R. Balleine refuted the myth that Palmerston, on Shaftesbury's advice, invariably recommended evangelicals as bishops, and he commented that Ellicott and Jacobson were distinctly high churchmen of an older school.[113] Ellicott himself, in giving his charge to the clergy at his triennial visitation in 1878, stated: 'The views generally mentioned in these Addresses, so far as they represent the views of any party in the Church, are those of what may perhaps be conveniently termed the Constitutional Party'.[114] This 'Party of the Centre', according to Ellicott, united 'the best spirits both of the Old High Church and of the great Evangelical party'.[115] If evidence were wanting that Ellicott was not a convinced evangelical, it could be found in his sermon entitled *Communion with the Departed* in which he said we are now 'realising more clearly the nearness between the seen and the unseen company of the faithful'.[116] It was seen also in his lack of emphasis on preaching the cross and conversion when he gave pastoral advice to his clergy.

Of the three remaining Palmerston bishops, Longley, Philpott and Jacobson, Longley and Philpott were moderate high churchmen and Jacobson belonged to the Broad Church party. Whilst at Ripon, Longley became the focus of high churchmen in the north of England. On his arrival in the diocese he stirred the anxieties of evangelicals by choosing Charles Dodgson, a moderate Tractarian and father of Lewis Carroll, as his examining chaplain. Evangelicals found his views on baptism, which were substantially those of Bishop Phillpotts of Exeter, particularly objectionable.

Longley was much respected by Samuel Wilberforce, who periodically sought out his company and was much impressed by his unambitious temperament.[117] Longley as it proved was vehement in his opposition to all expressions of ritualism, including incense, vestments and above all, the use of the confessional. He was also staunchly attached to the reformed stance of the *Book of Common Prayer*. His high church convictions did, nevertheless, reveal themselves in a number of aspects of his ministerial life. He had a high view of the office of a bishop and structured his new diocese of Ripon in a hierarchical and paternalistic manner.[118] He did not promote lay agency in the way that his evangelical colleagues on the Bench did, preferring instead groups of travelling missionary clergy who would be planted in the heart of the mining communities. Here they would work with the consent of the incumbents concerned, but under the direction of the bishop.[119] He also had a high view of the rite of Confirmation and of the grace it conveyed to the recipients.[120] An incident which particularly distressed Longley was Queen Victoria's insistence, despite his protestations, that the Prince of Wales' marriage to Princess Alexandra of Denmark was arranged in 1863 for a day in Lent.[121]

Philpott was described as high church 'but of the moderate school'.[122] Jacobson, on the other hand, was seen as 'a good man' who 'at present belongs to no extreme school of Theology'.[123] Shaftesbury had two concerns about him: that 'he can of course, have but little parochial experience', and 'I am not aware that he has any power of preaching'.[124] Nevertheless, he was still happy to endorse Jacobson's candidature. 'You could', he wrote to Palmerston, 'safely and conscientiously appoint him. He is absolutely fit'. Others have regarded Jacobson as 'a high churchman of the Scholarly sort'[125] and Dean Burgon saw him as a man of 'severe and exact orthodoxy'.[126] Such a view is certainly endorsed in statements made by Jacobson in his visitation addresses. For example, in 1868 he urged his clergy to make use of the creeds, particularly the creed of St. Athanasius.[127] He also insisted on his clergy sticking 'consistently and closely' to the rubrics of the Prayer Book.[128]

In sum, and taken as a whole, it is clear that Palmerston's English bishops were born of aristocratic and influential homes. In addition to Shaftesbury's hand in their appointments, almost all of them had sufficient personal or family connections to recommend them to those in high places. Academically speaking, their attainments and scholarly output was high. Several of them were university select preachers, two of them gave Bampton lectures, and Browne and Thomson produced standard works on doctrine and logic which went through several editions.

Almost all the Shaftesbury English bishops had some parochial experience, although that of Philpott and Jacobson was small and Thomson's was erratic and piecemeal. Against this, however, can be set the wide-ranging and varying endeavours of the first ministry bishops, Villiers, Baring, Longley, Tait, Pelham and Bickersteth. These men between them did in fact achieve what Shaftesbury had hoped when he appointed them. They won 'the affections of the people', they secured the establishment and they promoted true and sound religion.[129]

IV

Pastors of the People

By the time Palmerston's bishops began their episcopates the Industrial Revolution was reaching its full heights. Associated with it was a very rapid growth in population. Many large towns had seemingly mushroomed in size almost overnight. Birmingham, for example, had 73,000 inhabitants in 1801 but by 1901 this had reached 890,000. Similarly, Manchester was recorded as having reached 84,000 living within its boundaries in 1801, but a hundred years later this had swollen to 645,000. Most other large industrial towns and cities experienced similar growth in the Victorian era, although there were distinctive local variations. It was noted that the average increase in population in Great Britain in the years 1841-1851 was 12.5 per cent whilst in Northumberland it was 14 per cent and in Durham it was 27 per cent.[1] In 1863 the population of London was found to be nearly three millions and increasing annually by about 44,000.[2] These two inter-related aspects, the rising population and the burgeoning of mines and factories, brought with them a host of attendant problems.

One of the most obvious of these was the state of some parishes. Many were far too large and totally unmanageable, at least by a solitary incumbent, even if he had the help of a curate and perhaps a lay mission worker. Lord Shaftesbury himself was acutely aware of this problem and in the year that Palmerston took office he wrote: 'The parochial system is, no doubt, a beautiful thing in theory and is of great value in small rural districts; but in large towns it is a mere shadow of a name'.[3] Archibald Tait wrote in 1863 of some parishes in his London diocese as being 'totally unmanageable from their vast extent' and of 'the necessity of their immediate subdivision into separate districts, each with its new church'.[4] Elsewhere there were problems of a different kind. According to the visitation returns of 1865 the Vicar of Hull, W.P. Bulmer, had been absent from his parish for half a century and had entrusted all the responsibilities of his office to a curate. Three large churches, St. John, St. James and Christ Church, were all situated in densely populated areas but they had no geographical parishes of their own. In Middlesborough there were problems of a similar nature. The incumbent of St. Hilda's had never been resident and left matters to his curate to attend to. At York there were twenty-four independent churches within the city boundaries. G. Eese, the incumbent of All Saints Church, wrote: 'I am convinced that nothing can raise the Church in York but the revival of the parochial system and fixed pastoral relations with the people'.[5]

With the only structure for social, moral and spiritual care being a parochial system which needed radical overhaul, it was inevitable that the poor and criminal elements of society were going to be the losers. Archibald Tait, in his Charge of 1866 to the clergy of London, gave the following graphic account of conditions in a conventional district of an east end parish consisting of 10,000 people, some 4,000 of whom were Jews.

> Not one family in six possesses a blanket or a change of clothing. Not one person in a hundred habitually attends a place of worship. Of 228 shops in the district, 212 are open on Sunday. About seventy, however, are closed on the Saturday the Jewish Sabbath. Not half the Gentile adults can read. Half the women cannot handle a needle. Our Mothers' meeting has seventy members, half of whom, though living with men and having families are unmarried, and this is the proportion throughout the gentile district. Nine families out of ten have but one small room in which to live, eat and sleep. Not one family in six possesses a change of clothing. Not one in four has any bedding beyond sacking containing a little flock or chopped straw (a miserable substitute for a mattress) . . . Not one in twenty has a clock, and not one in ten a book. Many of the houses are in the most wretched condition of dirt and filth, walls, ceilings and staircases broken and rotting. Drunkenness, brawling, blasphemy, and other sins are fearfully prevalent.[6]

Almost all the English dioceses contained at the very least some areas with similar pockets of indigent poverty and squalor. Even the diocese of Carlisle, often perceived as a rural enclave with its hills and lakes, had its industrial blackspots. Observers noted 'the lofty chimneys and many windows of the factories in our cathedral city' together with 'the coal black sheds and the burning furnaces of the neighbouring counties'.[7] Archbishop William Thomson reported on the low state of morals and religious knowledge in parts of his diocese. He quoted from a report to 'The Children's Employment Commission' which revealed that Sheffield youth on the threshold of adulthood had 'a degree of ignorance of religion . . . such as could not be surpassed on the banks of the Zambesi'. 'Lads of seventeen', it continued, 'do not know the name of Christ, of the Bible, of the Queen'.[8]

If conditions in the industrial towns and cities were bleak, the environment in which rural labourers found themselves was often little better. In East Anglia and the Midlands, where John Pelham and Harold Browne and a little later, Francis Jeune, served the dioceses of Norwich, Ely and Peterborough, not only were many of the cottages in a very bad state of repair, wages were low and in the seventies there was to be a widespread rural agitation generated by Joseph Arch's 'National Agricultural Labourers' Union'. *The Royal Agricultural Commission on the Employment of Children, young persons and women in Agriculture* illustrates something of the appalling conditions of many farm workers' dwellings.

The Reverend James Fraser, who investigated a great many cottages in Norfolk and parts of Suffolk, stated in his report:

> The majority of cottages that exist in rural parishes are deficient in almost every requisite that should constitute a home for a civilised community. They are deficient in bedroom accommodation . . . imperfectly supplied with water . . . full enough of draughts . . . many . . . are lamentably dilapidated and out of repair.[9]

It was also the case that many rural labourers experienced both physical hazards and moral temptations that were little different in their intensity from those faced by their counterparts in the towns. The *Stamford Mercury* described one such tragic accident on a farm at Yaddlethorpe near Brigg.

> A girl named Eliza Stocks aged 16 . . . had been cutting bands upon the stage, and some loose straw was thrown over the drum hole and the steam partly shut off. The girl had forgotten her knife, and returning for it. . .put her foot upon the straw, which immediately gave way, and her foot was caught in the drum, which dragged in her leg smashing it to atoms, and the machine was not stopped till it reached her thigh, then it brought the works to a stand. . . .
> The poor sufferer died at 3 o'clock the following morning.[10]

An observer of agricultural labourers in Yorkshire in the 1860s noted 'the utter want of moral and religious training that pervades this class'.[11] The want of cottages, as Archbishop Thomson saw it, was 'a great ill' causing the young to live with 'a knot of loose companions in the farmer's house instead of in a separate dwelling with his wife and children'.[12] Bishop Harold Browne, in his charge to the Ely clergy in 1865, spoke of one great evil in the diocese, 'the system of young and old, male and female, working together in gangs under a leading gang master'.[13] The poor, he stated, were aware that such work is 'injurious to their bodily health and still more injurious to their spiritual health' but they find it hard to live without the few extra shillings their children are able to contribute to family purse.[14] Browne urged his clergy to allow children to plait straw in at least one school period a day. If they were not permitted to make a little money in this way they would stay away from school altogether. Unemployment and its attendant ills was also a perennial feature of life, both in the towns and the countryside. Samuel Waldegrave, for example, noted that in Carlisle the number of cotton operatives out of work together with their wives and families, amounted to very nearly six thousand.[15]

Pastors of the People

In the light of these kinds of problems Palmerston sought to move away from appointing bishops who were high church and scholarly, in the mould of Howley, Hinds and Blomfield. He selected, rather, men who had themselves worked in parishes and knew the conditions of the working classes

from first-hand personal acquaintance. These Palmerstonian prelates recognised the need for bold initiatives which would engage with the poor
and lift them up out of their situation and, if possible, give them education
and a spiritual framework for their lives. Inevitably, because they came
from similar backgrounds and shared common theological and political
convictions, many of their episcopal strategies had a common emphasis.

Church Builders

One major tactic which was shared by almost all the Palmerston bishops
was that of church building. In this they were quite probably influenced
by the Sumner brothers, John Bird who was Archbishop of Canterbury
from 1848-1862, and his younger brother, Charles, who held the See of
Winchester from 1828-1869. John Bird Sumner had seen a marked rise in
Church attendance in his diocese of Chester in the 1830s and 1840s. His
strategy for church planting on a wide scale had a proven influence in
drawing into the Christian community previously unchurched people
groups. As he himself observed in his charge of 1841: 'Numerous are the
places, where, a few years ago hundreds, if not thousands, of families
were congregated without any regular provision for their spiritual culture'. He continued: 'The visitor of these districts now, will not only find
a house set apart for the worship of God but . . . the general aspect of a
Christian community, where recently all was barren'.[16] The success of
Sumner's church extension was widely known, and indeed Sir Robert Peel
had paid tribute to it in the House of Commons.[17] In addition, Montagu
Villiers, who Palmerston appointed to Carlisle in 1856, had served his
curacy under Sumner in Chester Diocese and Joseph Cotton Wigram had
spent the greater part of his ministry in Hampshire under Charles Sumner.
In view of this, it is not surprising that the majority of Palmerston bishops,
particularly those of evangelical convictions, began to press on their diocesan clergy the urgent need for what, in present day terms, would be described as church planting. Charles Baring, in his first charge to the clergy
of Gloucester and Bristol, spoke of the lack of church accommodation in
the diocese. 'There are', he declared, '114,535 immortal souls within the
limits of this diocese who could not, however much they might desire it,
join the public worship of God according to the rites of the Church of
England'.[18] Samuel Waldegrave noted that in his diocese of Carlisle there
were fifty hamlets and villages where a place of worship was needed because the parish church was more than two miles distant.[19] He also stressed
the urgent need for more church buildings in the city of Carlisle. 'There
we have, by the recent census' he stated, 'a population of 30,443 souls,
and church accommodation for, at the utmost 4,600 souls . . .'[20] William
Thomson was conscious of 'the rapid increase of the population in some
of the manufacturing portions of the diocese'. He urged 'the greatest exer-

tions on the part of all church people to keep pace with it by building churches . . . and supplying pastors'.[21]

In order to facilitate an increase in the amount of church building, many of Palmerston's bishops either started diocesan church building societies, or devoted a good deal of time and energy to expanding and developing existing ones. Incumbents were urged both to receive contributions and to preach annual sermons on behalf of church extension, which would then be followed by special collections. Charles Baring suggested that each incumbent preach one sermon a year before Easter for diocesan education and church building.[22] Charles Longley worked particularly hard in the matter of church extension and established 'Bishop Longley's Fund' for that purpose.[23] Some years later in 1861 Robert Bickersteth, his successor in the See, found it necessary to beef up support for the project. Out of two hundred and twenty charity sermons preached in 1860 'the cause of our Church Building Society', he bemoaned, 'was practically ignored'.[24] On a subsequent occasion Bickersteth spoke in more forthright terms: 'I make a personal request to each incumbent in the diocese not to let this year pass without having a sermon and collection in church in aid of the funds of our Church Building Society'.[25] Twelve years later Bickersteth was, however, able to 'thank God and take courage' that in the period 1873-1876, the amount of £98,773..16s..9d had been raised in the diocese for the increase of Church accommodation.[26]

Early in his episcopate Joseph Cotton Wigram issued an appeal to his clergy of the diocese of Rochester informing them of 'the need of continued aid in the work of church building'. 'Only ninety churches in the two archdeaconries (Herts and Essex) have as yet received assistance from our diocesan society, and its income remains miserably small'.[27] A church extension society had been established for the Archdeaconry of Worcester at the time Henry Philpott arrived to take charge of the diocese in 1860. In an address which he gave in June 1865 he expressed his pleasure 'that the Archdeaconry of Coventry have established a similar Church Extension Society'.[28] Nine years later, at his 1874 visitation, Philpott commended the three diocesan extension societies for the archdeaconries of Worcester, Coventry and Birmingham 'to the more liberal support of all the people of the diocese'.[29]

In the light of these endeavours, together with other more locally based efforts and private donations to specific projects, some of Palmerston's appointees achieved remarkable results in terms of new church buildings and the restoration of existing ones. Whilst Charles Baring was Bishop of Durham one hundred and nineteen new churches were erected at a cost of £363,830, affording accommodation for 40,530 worshippers. Charles Baring expressed his strong disapproval of the restoration of Durham Cathedral on the ground that the expenditure 'might have been more beneficially employed' in the building of new churches in needy and populous areas.

For this reason he declined to attend the service to mark the re-opening. He stated that 'I cannot consistently take part in a service to inaugurate the completion of the recent alterations in the noble mother church of the diocese when I have frequently expressed my regret that these alterations have been undertaken'. Many of the clergy shared Baring's views in the matter and over two hundred of their number, including the overwhelming majority of incumbents of the large and more important parishes of the diocese, declined the invitation.[30] Archibald Tait, who established 'The Bishop of London's Fund', was able to report in 1865 that he had consecrated fifty-three churches in the previous three years. All except seven of them were new.[31] During the episcopate of Robert Bickersteth a total of one hundred and fifty-eight churches were consecrated, of which ninety-two were new parish churches, forty-seven were churches rebuilt or enlarged and nineteen were chapels of ease.[32] Bickersteth spoke of his delight at having consecrated twenty-one new churches in the previous five years.[33] Later, in 1876 he once more rejoiced that he had been permitted to consecrate sixteen new churches since his previous visitation.[34] Philpott expressed his satisfaction to the clergy of Worcester 'at the number of new churches being opened as well as the restoration work in progress on the Cathedral'.[35] William Thomson proved to be a most effective facilitator in the matter of church extension. The strategy developed by the archbishop was to promote the formation of local church extension societies in the main towns and centres of the diocese. Their work was fostered by the central diocesan society which had been established in 1861. Between 1861 and 1889 they had promoted the building of ninety-one new churches and thirty-one mission chapels, as well as the enlargement of one hundred and five churches.[36]

William Jacobson, Palmerston's last appointment, consecrated forty-five churches between 1865 and 1871.[37] In addition, in the previous three years he had given licenses for worship in forty-five places and to twenty-eight of them without any limitation.[38] Remarkably, Francis Jeune reported that in the four years prior to 1867 'not less than one hundred and sixteen churches, that is about one sixth of all the churches in the diocese [Peterborough], have been rebuilt, enlarged, or else wholly or partially restored'.[39]

Promoters of Education

Palmerstonian bishops were not blinkered ecclesiastics who believed that the erection of church buildings were the be-all and end-all of mission, particularly in regard to the working classes. They recognised that planting new congregations had to go hand in hand with a holistic approach which addressed moral, social and educational needs. For this reason many of them gave as much, or more time, to the promotion of education within their dioceses. A great deal of their energy was devoted to the building of new church schools, sponsoring teacher training institutions and encouraging Sunday schools and evening classes.

Montagu Villiers soon showed himself anxious to improve education in the diocese of Carlisle. Throughout Cumbria he found that the educational provision was poor. The old school buildings were 'totally unfit for the purposes of education', and 'teachers betray the want of proper training'.[40] In 1856 it was reported that 'in the whole of Westmorland . . . there are but two certified teachers'.[41] During Villiers' tenure of the diocese considerable progress was made through the efforts of George Moore. Villiers commended his unflagging efforts in establishing competitive examinations for the children of the church schools. In 1858 some eight hundred children were examined in the All Hallows district in the presence of Villiers, local clergy, and other dignitaries including the Government Schools' inspector. The annual examination proved to be so positive in its effects that it was gradually expanded throughout Cumberland and later into Westmorland.[42]

Archibald Tait showed himself to be a very forward thinker in regard to the value of a school. He publicly urged the principle of establishing a school and setting a teacher to work before a church is built.[43] Like Archbishop Sumner before him he recognised that a school room could also be used as a place of worship on Sundays. Charles Longley, when he had been elevated to the primacy, urged clergy to establish evening schools. Such institutions, when they are fostered by the parish minister and lay assistants will prove 'instruments of great good in a parish'.[44] Robert Bickersteth saw the urgent need to establish facilities for the education of the poor. 'I would strongly advise an effort to be made', he said, 'in every parish where at present no church school exists, to establish one'.[45] Bickersteth was himself a strong supporter of the Church of England's National Society.[46]

Samuel Waldegrave, who succeeded Villiers at Carlisle, found only one hundred and forty-one endowed schools in Cumberland and Westmorland and that part of Lancashire which was included in his diocese. He urged the necessity of raising adequate funding to make substantial improvements in the situation.[47] At a later point Waldegrave impressed on his clergy the need 'to rally round the Carlisle Diocesan Society'.[48] Francis Jeune, who had in his earlier years been a headmaster in Birmingham, was grateful to discover on his arrival at Peterborough that 'only in forty-six parishes, that is one parish in twelve, is there no school'.[49] Most of these parishes he found on investigation were small and within reach of schools.[50] He did, however, express his grave concern that there were a number of schools in the diocese which ' are in a lamentable state as to discipline and attainment'.[51] Joseph Wigram, who had himself been general secretary of the church's National Society for some years, was glad to ascertain that 'nearly one seventh of our people are directly under the pastoral influence of our public church schools'.[52] A cause for still higher gratification, in his view, was that the number of evening schools had both increased in number and improved in quality.[53] Longley also rejoiced to find in his Canterbury diocese that 'there are 128 parishes where there is an adult school, in which the clergyman takes an active part'.[54]

Most bishops, Palmerston's included, saw the establishment of some form of inspection as the starting point for improving the quality and standards in their church schools. It was the case that schools which received state funding through the National Society were required to submit to government inspectors. Other church schools could be inspected under schemes organised by the diocese concerned. Charles Longley was one who valued the work of his 'Canterbury Diocesan Inspector of Schools' and was heartened at his reports, particularly in regards to religious education, though he had apparently observed 'an almost total lack of Geography, Grammar and History'.[55] John Pelham appointed diocesan inspectors in every rural deanery of the Norwich diocese. Most of these were clergymen and Pelham gave them high praise because they gave their time and service free of charge. In the mid 1860s there were two hundred of his schools under Her Majesty's inspectors and upwards of five hundred under diocesan inspection arrangements.[56] Waldegrave, who was very anxious to improve the standard of education in his largely rural diocese, requested each of his rural deans to make arrangements with managers to inspect all of the schools within their bounds. If they were unable to accomplish this in person they could, with episcopal approval, appoint a deputy.[57] Wigram operated a system of voluntary inspection in Rochester based on the National Society's paper of 1851. He found it brought evidence of improvement as well as offering the prospect of future advance in standards.[58] Both Francis Jeune and Henry Philpott praised the work of their respective diocesan inspectorates. Jeune extolled 'a large number of excellent clergymen' who had undertaken the duty of school inspection.[59]

One particular value of the diocesan inspectors' work was that they ensured a good standard 'in the religious and moral teaching of the lambs of the flock'.[60] Philpott, in his visitation address in June 1874, praised his two diocesan schools' inspectors who in the previous year had visited 547 schools belonging to 308 parishes.[61]

Like most other Palmerston bishops, Philpott welcomed the 1870 Forster Education Act's requirement that voluntary schools should submit to government inspection. Whilst it was the case that Her Majesty's inspectors did not include religious education within their brief, their work was nevertheless regarded by Philpott as improving the efficiency of teaching and increasing the intellectual capacity of the children.[62] Robert Bickersteth came to value the system of government inspection which, he observed, produced a proper examination system for the pupils. The problem he faced in his Ripon diocese was that there were insufficient sums to pay for inspectors' salaries. In order to go some way to meeting this difficulty, he made use of rural deans or incumbents.[63] Both William Thomson and William Jacobson were also among those who were positive about the 1870 Act. Thomson spoke of it as 'an honest measure and likely to be 'worthy' of the church's support'. It had been 'framed with great care and certainly in no hostile spirit towards religious education'.[64] Jacobson pointed out to some of his concerned clergy that the Act 'does not subvert existing educational arrangements. It avails itself of these, and proposes to supply all ascertained deficiencies'.[65]

In addition to their giving active support to the practice of inspection, the bishops proposed other ways of improving the level of children's education. Longley, for example, suggested a system of prizes which increased in value the longer children remained in school.[66] He also, on another occasion, told his clergy that children should not be excluded from school simply because their parents did not wish them to learn the church catechism. It was better for them to come to school rather than spend their time in idleness and bad company. Longley felt the situation was acutely bad in the countryside, where children were withdrawn from school at a very young age to work in the fields in order to supplement their parents' wages, which were lower than those of the town workers.

Others among the Palmerston bishops were active promoters and supporters of teacher training institutions, which they regarded as another key to bettering the level of children's performance. John Pelham was proud to relate that 'our Diocesan Training Institution has continued to maintain its high character' and that its examination results were 'amongst the best in the country'.[67] Robert Bickersteth was instrumental in founding and raising money for the building of the Ripon Diocesan Training College and laid the foundation stone on 1 February 1860.[68] He later expressed his thankfulness for the 'Female Training School' which was opened in August 1862.[69] Bickersteth was a frequent visitor to the college and often sat and talked with the students. His son later wrote that 'to the end of his life his interest in the college never flagged. He made a point of being present at the meetings of the Committee of Management'.[70] Joseph Cotton Wigram extolled the 'excellence of our training institution at Hockerill'. 'The qualifications of its teachers', he declared, 'have been acknowledged throughout the country'.[71] He regarded the college as 'a third guarantee' along with new school buildings and voluntary inspection, for the improved quality of education in the diocese.[72] William Jacobson reported in 1871 that both the training colleges at Warrington and Chester were in a 'very satisfactory condition'. The former had one hundred school mistresses in training and the latter fifty school masters.[73]

Palmerston's bishops were as much, if not more, school builders as they were church builders. Charles Baring, for instance, saw no fewer than one hundred and eighty-three elementary schools erected or enlarged in Gloucester diocese during his episcopate. Robert Bickersteth was heartened to discover in 1870 that there were only thirty-five benefices in his diocese in which there was no church school. Following the Forster Act he pressed the clergy of those parishes to make prompt efforts to provide a school where distinctive religious teaching and the catechism can be an established part of the curriculum.[74] Francis Jeune was pleased to report that only in one out of twelve parishes in his Peterborough diocese was there no school, and in most of those there was a school within easy walking distance.[75]

Religious Education

Almost to a man the Palmerston bishops saw religious education as the foundational discipline. It was this which provided children and adolescents with a moral framework for life. Their view was that RE teaching should be done confessionally to bring the children to a Christian commitment, and for this reason they advocated both instruction from the Bible and lessons from the church's catechism. Montagu Villiers was grieved to report in 1858 that most schools in his Carlisle diocese displayed a painful deficiency in religious knowledge. He was adamant that 'Moral and religious training, the exercise of the reflecting powers of the mind, and the habit of applying knowledge, must form very important items in our educational systems'.[76] Charles Longley deprecated 'the establishment of any system in which religious teaching shall not be integral and . . . an all pervading element in the instruction of children'.[77] John Pelham was insistent that school managers, and clergy in particular, should ensure that the teaching of scripture, the liturgy and the catechism had 'a distinct and prominent position' in children's education.[78] Robert Bickersteth, in his address to his clergy in 1870, underlined that ' at all cost' the religious instruction and religious tone of our elementary schools must be maintained.[79] Samuel Waldegrave spoke of 'the constant vigilance and effort required to keep Religious and Moral education on the curriculum'. He continued: 'Let clear, let full, let fearless scriptural teaching, be given in our schools'.[80]

Henry Philpott spoke with delight of the high profile of religious education in all parts of his diocese, with the exception of the city of Birmingham where the position was lamentable.[81] William Thomson was dismayed at the very high degree of ignorance among children in the city of Sheffield which could not, he said, 'be surpassed on the banks of the Zambesi'.[82]

Following the 1870 Education Act only four hours a day of secular education was required. William Jacobson therefore urged that in the Chester diocese, wherever circumstances permitted, the hour preceding morning school should be secured for religious instruction.[83] He went on to point out that because many schools would no longer offer religious education it was 'more important than ever' to save Sunday school teaching from being 'wearisome'.[84] Palmerston's prelates of all shades of theological opinion were strong advocates of the value of Sunday schools. Villiers told his clergy that their school machinery was 'utterly incomplete' unless it included a well-worked Sunday school.[85] Robert Bickersteth told his clergy that they should spare no effort to make their Sunday school attractive.[86] Sunday schools, in his view, should be short and bright. He did not recommend children being brought into adult church services which to little children are 'unintelligible, and therefore painfully boring'.[87] Archibald Tait, when Archbishop of Canterbury, urged clergy to give careful attention to Sunday school instruction[88] and William Jacobson commended 'well conducted' Sunday school teaching which had, he said, 'great abiding influence on after life'.[89]

Concern for the Poor

The earlier nineteenth century appointments to the episcopal bench were in the main men who were high churchmen and scholars. They were well-respected, particularly in courtly circles, but they tended to stand aloof from the man and woman in the street. Archbishop Howley was a revered personality, Bishop Kaye of Lincoln was a learned scholarly divine, and Hampden of Hereford was a theologian who lived among his books and wrote on Christological topics. Lord Shaftesbury, however, had long had a heart for the poor and feared that the Established Church was far too distant from them. He therefore chose to commend to Palmerston, particularly in the early years of his first ministry, men who had demonstrated a practical concern for the poor in their parochial work, men who had a proven capacity to relate to them and communicate the Christian faith to them. So, if some of the bishops of the earlier part of the century were 'Princely Prelates' the new appointees of Lord Palmerston were in contrast, for the most part, 'pastors of the people'. They were men who did their utmost to minister to the needs of the working-classes and the poor among them in particular. They exhorted their clergy to make the church building more welcoming and to experiment with shorter forms of services, and develop the art of preaching which was anecdotal and related to life. A number of Palmerston bishops were able preachers themselves, and spent their weekends assisting their clergy in parochial missions, and putting in an occasional appearance at the Exeter Hall informal evening services for the working men and women of London.

Like many before them, the Palmerston bishops had a strong dislike for the practice of selling and letting church pews. Not only did this custom give the best seats to the wealthy, it also led to the creation of class divisions within the house of God. Charles Longley condemned the sale and letting of pews in parish churches. He called it a 'grievous abuse' and pointed out that it had been pronounced illegal in the Church courts.[90] Some years later when at Canterbury, he made the same point urging the importance of having all churches 'open to the parishioners without any payment for their seats'.[91] William Thomson was also vehement that letting and hiring seats 'creates inequality in the house of God'.[92]

Of all the Palmerston bishops, Thomson was possibly the one who most captured the hearts of ordinary people. His popularity with the working classes was underlined when he visited Sheffield in February 1869 and addressed nearly a thousand working men. He held them in rapt attention for an hour and a half. A labourer who proposed the vote of thanks said that if they had had such archbishops in the past there would have been very little 'secularism' among working men. Thomson, who had a tall and manly frame, earned himself the title of 'The People's Archbishop'. Robert Bickersteth was another who enjoyed the respect and affection of the working classes of his diocese. He moved freely among them and preached to them in their mills and factories. On one occasion he endeared himself to the mining community when he went to the scene of a colliery explosion to help comfort the families of the bereaved.

Probably no bishop in Victorian times equalled Charles Ellicott's celebrated gaffe in regards to the working classes. He was making the after dinner speech to the annual Gloucestershire Farmers' Union gathering in 1873, at a time when the agricultural labourers' union agitation was reaching a crescendo in the surrounding countryside. Attempting to inject a moment or two of laughter into the proceedings he said that when union delegates were addressing the meeting, if the village horse pond stood invitingly near they would know what to do! For ever afterwards the unfortunate Ellicott was denounced from union platforms and in delegates' addresses as 'the horse pond bishop'.[93] Ellicott, who was actually quite a sensitive man, did his best to make atonement for his error and even on one occasion invited some of the union leaders to his palace in an attempt to help them settle their differences with the farmers.[94] A little later, in October that same year, in his Triennial Visitation Address he urged his clergy to adopt a conciliatory attitude to the agricultural union question.

> Let us not shrink from making it plain that as ministers of the
> gospel, and as servants of Him whose kingdom is not of this world,
> that we deem it no duty of ours either to advocate or to censure
> these combinations and unions which the difficulties of our own
> times may have made some sort of transitoreal necessity. . . .[95]

In this Charge, *The Church and the Rural Poor,* Ellicott went on to urge his clergy to maintain a 'gentle impartiality' and, where possible, to provide allotment land and to establish friendly societies and working-men's clubs. He also counselled patience, kindness and helpfulness. As a result of such behaviour 'it will be seen in the end that England's country clergy have ever been true friends of England's country poor'.[96]

Harold Browne, who was first an incumbent in rural Cornwall and then in Devon, had developed a particular concern for farm workers and their families. In an address to his Ely Diocesan Conference in 1871 he condemned the 'wretched and crowded dwellings' and the 'unwholesome sanitary state' and 'general discomfort' surrounding them. 'We must endeavour', he said, 'to improve the dwellings of the poor'.[97] Shortly before leaving Ely for Winchester, Browne sponsored a very practical discussion on 'The Duty of the Church, clergy and laity in relation to the disputes between Labour and Capital'. In his own pastoral contribution he said that he believed that 'communism and socialism are really the earnest strugglings of the human heart for a state of society which the Christian church ought to supply'.[98] He went on to commend the efforts of clergy in general for having tried to raise the social conditions of the agricultural labourers, for having defended them against oppression, ministered to them in poverty and sickness and provided almost the only education available to them at all.

William Jacobson demonstrated his compassion for the poor when he visited the cholera-ridden suburbs of Liverpool in 1866. Perhaps even more praiseworthy were the efforts made in the same year by Archibald Tait and his wife, Catherine, as they gave themselves to the communities of East London which had been devastated by Asiatic Cholera. Although unwell himself Tait summoned a meeting of the clergy of Bethnal Green, Stepney and Spitalfields which endeavoured to make arrangements which might aid the sanitary authorities. Tait wrote to *The Times* of the desperate needs of the sick and the orphaned children. His letter brought a response of £3,000 within twenty-four hours and a total of £70,000 was subsequently collected.[99] Catherine Tait visited the dying at Wapping and Middlesex hospitals. Later, for about five years, she hired a house in Fulham for orphan girls. In 1871 it was moved to the Isle of Thanet where large premises which could take eighty children were established as a result of Mrs Tait's personal endeavours.[100]

Joseph Cotton Wigram had himself seen at first hand the conditions of poverty experienced by both the rural and the industrial poor. He had worked in central London, then in rural Hampshire, followed by a number of years in Southampton's dockland area. In the year following his consecration as Bishop of Rochester he called together a conference of clergy and laity at Chelmsford. The subject of their discussion was 'The present state of the Labouring Classes, their circumstances, peculiar temptations, domestic and social occupations, ordinary recreations, & c., & c, with the best methods of improving their material, social and religious condition'.[101] Wigram revealed the same concern in his second visitation address in 1864 when he highlighted the needs of several particular occupational groups: the Thames boatmen, the brickfield workers, the large number of bargemen at Grays, and the chalkmen, cement workers and pottery men of Kent and Essex. He urged the need for lay assistants to help the clergymen extend practical and spiritual care to the needy groups of labourers. In January 1867 Wigram sent a circular to all his clergy urging them to encourage members of their congregations to visit and make contact with working class men and women in their neighbourhood. He felt this was particularly urgent in those parts of the diocese where there are 'factories for silk, paper, & co., our straw-plaiting districts; our brick-makers, chalk, cement and pottery workers. . . .'[102]

There is no doubt that the Palmerston bishops made much greater efforts to encourage their clergy to reach out to the poor in a way that some of their predecessors had not. Certainly on a personal level they mixed much more readily, and involved themselves in the concerns of working men and women more than the earlier generations of bishops had done. Having said that, they still, on occasion, breathed an air of paternalism and superiority. Harold Browne declared 'we', meaning 'we' the clergy, must endeavour to 'improve the dwellings of the poor'.[103] There is no hint of 'empowerment', of giving the labourers the wherewithal to accomplish the task themselves. Browne was also inclined to moments of condescension. Advising clergy on the procedure for visiting an agricultural labourer in his cottage he said: 'When you enter a peasant's hut do not keep on your hat, do not use the airs of a superior; speak always kindly . . .'.[104] Joseph Cotton Wigram unconsciously uttered a similar remark when he wrote in a circular that 'from year to year, scarcely a labourer or an artisan has a friendly visit from a neighbour of higher station than himself'.[105]

Support for Home Missions and Lay Agencies

The Palmerston bishops were firm believers in the value of the parochial system of pastoral care and from time to time they said so in their charges and addresses. But like Lord Shaftesbury himself they recognised that in areas of dense population the parish unit was inadequate. The rural parson who ministered to a few hundred souls could indeed pastor his flock, but in the towns the incumbent needed other lips and hands to reach out in mission to the ranks of the disadvantaged and indigent poor.

In his charge of 1864 Joseph Cotton Wigram spoke of the 'great things' which had been accomplished by the ancient parochial organisation.[106] Yet in the same address he admitted that it needed to be 'supplemented every here and there by helps'.[107] Harold Browne was also of the opinion that 'the old parochial system is not flexible enough to cope with the difficulties which meet the church in large cities'.[108] In his view 'it must be supplemented by new machinery and more distinct co-operation'.[109] In his charge of 1865 he declared that what seems most desirable is 'not to supplant or even materially to modify the parochial system anywhere, but to support and strengthen it, and supply its deficiencies'.[110] Among several others Longley was acutely aware of the problems of the parishes 'of our crowded towns of upwards of 20,000 souls'. [111] As a high churchman his solution was to propose a body of missionary clergy who would labour in certain needy parishes under the bishop, with the incumbent's approval.[112] All the rest of Palmerston's appointees, however, were firm advocates of appointing lay agents to assist the clergymen.

When he was Rector of St. George's, Bloomsbury, Montagu Villiers had read a paper entitled 'On the Necessity and Value of Lay Agency in the Church'.[113] He referred to the clergyman' s many tasks which included 'systematic house to house visiting, caring for the sick, preparing three Sunday services, Sunday school work, ministering to his own soul and caring for his family'.[114] He then declared, 'clergymen are not dogs in the manger. If they cannot do it themselves, they should at least let others do it for them'.[115] He went to lay it down as 'a positive duty' that lay agency should be employed.[116] On being promoted to the see of Carlisle, Montagu Villiers had adequate scope to put into effect what he had earlier advocated on the basis of his own parochial experience. Amongst other schemes he supported the initiative to provide a scripture reader in every market town in the diocese. Together with Francis Close, the Cathedral Dean, he helped to establish the 'County Towns Mission'.[117]

Tait saw some of the great benefits of lay agents[118] in the early 1860s in his London diocese where they were employed in conventional districts of overgrown parishes. Tait also valued the success of Scripture Readers[119] part of whose salaries were derived from the funds of 'the Diocesan Home Mission'.[120] Robert Bickersteth prized the services of 'a goodly number' of lay readers in his diocese. These were 'spiritual' men whom he formally licensed to assist incumbents in such tasks as visiting the sick, assisting with Bible classes, Sunday schools and cottage and mission room services.[121] Bickersteth also established a 'Scripture-Readers Society' which in 1864 supported twelve scripture readers in various parts of the diocese.[122] In his charge to the clergy at his Triennial Visitation of 1864 Bickersteth declared: 'I commend this society to the support of both the clergy and the laity of the diocese'.[123] Harold Browne greatly desired to establish a similar system of lay readers to that of Bickersteth's in his Winchester diocese. It concerned him that men who might have been enthusiastic lay evangelists in the Church of England were finding ready opportunities in the Free Churches.[124] Browne was a strong defender of parochial boundaries and would not countenance successful clergymen 'encroaching on the privileges of his neighbour'. In his view, the 'deficiencies' of the parochial system needed to be strengthened from other quarters, and in particular by home missionary agencies.[125]

William Jacobson regarded the growth of lay ministry in his diocese as one of 'the most healthful and cheering signs of the times'.[126] He encouraged his clergy to welcome and foster it wherever possible. In 1874 he announced that a course of lectures had been established for those wanting to minister as lay readers.[127] According to *The Chelmsford Chronicle*, Joseph Wigram, in his primary visitation address in the town's parish church, urged 'the aid and co-operation of the laity in tilling the vineyard of the Lord, and bringing souls into the folds of Christ'.[128]

In the 1860s and 1870s several Palmerston bishops emerged as strong advocates of the use of lay women for specific roles within the parish. Significantly, this was the time when the Salvation Army was beginning to use women as leaders and speakers to great effect. Archibald Tait was inspired by the example of women who had served the wounded during the Crimean War. In the light of this, he was of the opinion that the time had come when bishops and clergy must consider in detail how Christian women living in the community could minister to the sick and poor.[129] He laid down a series of guidelines for such female institutions. Although he personally held all vows whether 'actually taken or mentally implied' to be 'wrong',[130] he nevertheless spoke in terms of high praise of those sisters who had ministered to the dying during the east London cholera epidemics.[131] A further difficulty which Tait had with regard to many of the London sisterhoods was their ritualistic practices, and in particular their reservation of the communion elements and 'a devotion to the Blessed Virgin Mary, going far beyond what the Church of England approves'.[132]

Harold Browne, who also greatly valued the role women were able to play, saw matters in much the same light as Tait. At Ely he allowed the establishment of an order of deaconesses in Bedford as an experiment.[133] On 5 February 1869 in his palace he admitted Miss Fanny Elizabeth Eagles as a deaconess to serve in the parish of St. Peter's, Bedford, with the proviso that she should continue steadfast in the work 'for two years at least'.[134] There was no suggestion of her being under any binding vow. She was given a mandate 'to seek out the sick, poor and impotent folk' and 'to instruct the young in schools or otherwise, minister to those in hospitals, prisons or asylums'.[135] Unlike the female officers of the newly emerging Salvation Army who were given total equality in status and opportunity, Fanny Eagles' role was one of subservience. Her charge included 'setting aside all unwomanly usurpation of authority in the church'.[136]

In December 1870 Browne called a meeting at Ely which resulted in a document that defined the office of deaconess and indicated its duties.[137] In May 1872 Browne convened a further gathering and seventeen bishops signed a paper entitled *The Principles and Rules of Deaconesses*.[138] Thus began a very important chapter in the ministry of women, which a century and a quarter later would lead to their full ordination. Following his translation to Winchester in 1873, Browne gave more general encouragement to the work of deaconesses, though he still steered clear of admitting to the office any women who were bound by solemn vows. In due course he was able to establish a training college for the order at Portsmouth, which was perhaps the most needy town within his diocese.[139]

The evangelical Joseph Wigram was another who pioneered the development of women's ministry within the parish setting. At his second Triennial visitation he gave vent to his convictions:

> I cannot withhold an expression of my deep conviction that in very many parts of the diocese we need the introduction of a considerable female agency – mission women, and such-like female helpers as have been brought to bear in other parts for relieving the sorrows and checking the grosser habits of their own sex.[140]

Such, Wigram declared, 'are invaluable aids to a clergyman'.[141] William Jacobson at Chester also advocated women's work within the parishes[142] though he also was adamant that there should be no vows. 'All the good that sisters can do, and it is not a little', he said, 'may be done without any scandal arising out of eccentricities . . . There must be no vows of celibacy . . .'. Jacobson felt some characteristic dress might be expedient but not of a colour 'that would depress further, the sinking spirits of invalids'.[143]

Relationships with Dissenters

The 1851 Census of Religion had revealed the growing strength of English Non-conformity. In particular it had demonstrated that a slightly greater percentage of the population worshipped in the Free Churches than did in the Church of England. Whig politicians such as Lord Palmerston were anxious neither to alienate dissenters from their party nor to see them as antagonistic towards the Established Church. Some of the earlier high church bishops had regarded dissenters with considerable disfavour, and Palmerston was anxious that such a state of affairs should not continue. Encouraged by his step-son-in-law he therefore sought to appoint to the Bench men who would endear themselves to the many Methodist, Baptist and other Non-conformist members of the working classes.

Montagu Villiers, Palmerston's first appointee, had an immaculate pedigree in so far as good relationships with dissenters were concerned. He worked 'vigorously' with them and commended them for their church-building in Carlisle: 'I do not ignore, nor do I undervalue the labours of my Non-conformist brethren, nor am I insensible to the kindness and courtesy I have met with at their hands'.[144] When he lay dying *Evangelical Christendom* noted that 'his illness had evoked sympathy from all quarters, dissenters as well as churchmen'.[145]

Charles Baring urged on his Gloucester and Bristol clergy 'the duty of toleration, of charity towards our dissenting brethren'.[146] Whilst presiding over the London diocese, Tait consistently upheld the rights of Non-conformists and perhaps nowhere more so than in regards to the Burials Bill. His biographer later wrote of his archiepiscopate that 'he repeatedly urged upon the clergy the advantage, and even the duty of such co-operation as is practicable' with ministers of other denominations.[147] John Pelham promoted good relationships with Non-conformists and on one occasion in 1857 invited representatives of their ministers to come to his palace to consider the possibility of holding a special service of prayer and humiliation in connection with events in India.[148] Robert Bickersteth attracted the friendship and support of great numbers of dissenters, who flocked to hear his preaching and to support his occasional evangelistic efforts. His son wrote: 'My father greatly valued the friendship and esteem of members of the non-conformist body'.[149] In his Charge of 1876 he thanked God 'that there are pious, devoted and Non-conformist ministers of the New Testament supplementing the work of the Church in their efforts to evangelise the people'.[150] Archbishop William Thomson had a warm admiration for the dissenters, with whom he maintained good relations. In Convocation on one occasion he spoke of the debt his own diocese owed to them in the previous century, when the Anglican Church was 'idle and remiss'.[151] He continued, 'And whenever you hear the name of Wesley, and contemplate the doings of the Wesleyan body, let it be with a certain thrill of shame that the Church of England then parted with what it might have kept'.[152] According to bishop Ellicott's obituarist Non-conformists 'confessed themselves to be indebted to him for his co-operation in all good work for the furtherance of religion and the good of the community'.[153]

More and Better Clergy

Basic to this whole desire on the part of Palmerston's appointees to be pastorally concerned for the people of their dioceses was a constant and growing supply of better trained and equipped clergy. Almost all of them made constant and strident efforts to recruit Oxford and Cambridge graduates and to improve the stringency of their ordination examinations and post-ordination training.

Montagu Villiers saw the number of graduate clergy increased during his Carlisle episcopate.[154] At his visitation address in 1861 Robert Bickersteth stated that he held nine ordinations in the previous three years, there being eighty-three deacons and eighty-six priests. He reported his wish 'to raise the standard both of intellectual and spiritual qualification for the work of ministry'.[155] At a later point he reported ten ordinations in the previous three years but with only seventy-seven deacons and seventy-two priests. Fifty-two of these were from Cambridge, twenty-two from Oxford and twenty-one from Dublin; the rest receiving their education in a theological community.[156] During William Thomson's archiepiscopate eight hundred and ten deacons were ordained in the Diocese of York.[157] Seventy-one per cent of them were graduates, the majority of them being from Cambridge. Thomson saw to it that the standard ordination examinations were improved. Like Bickersteth he was of the opinion that theological colleges sometimes gave poor quality education.[158] He also opposed the practice of allowing men who had been ordained for the mission field returning after only a short period and taking charge of a parish.[159] Ellicott, on the other hand, seems to have taken particular interest in the affairs of the Gloucester Theological College having given curacies to a number of its students.[160] In 1865 Browne reported that he had ordained fifty-one priests and twenty-eight deacons since his previous visitation. He went on to relate that no one had been admitted to deacon's orders who had no university degree. He trusted that he would never have to break this rule 'as I am convinced of the extreme value of an university education'.[161] Francis Jeune expressed his disappointment that the number of men coming forward for ordination in Peterborough diocese in 1864 had dropped from the previous ten years' average of twenty-two to only sixteen. He expressed his hope that numbers would start increasing on account of Cambridge offering divinity as a degree subject.[162] Pelham reported in 1865 that he had ordained one hundred and nine men to priests and deacons orders since his last visitation. Eighty-six per cent of these were university graduates. He required of his ordination candidates 'a sound knowledge of Holy Scripture and of the Articles and Liturgy of the Church of England' together with a good working knowledge of Latin and New Testament Greek.[163] Henry Philpott was similarly gratified to have ordained one hundred and twenty-two candidates in the three years previous, ninety-six of whom were graduates.[164]

Probably the first bishop whose style of leadership was in observable contrast to that of the earlier Victorian episcopate was John Bird Sumner. He was noted for his frugal lifestyle and his care for his clergy, and his involvement in their personal and ministerial affairs. He was the first archbishop to give up the practice of driving to the House of Lords in a coach and four, preferring instead to walk, umbrella in hand. Sumner was concerned that the Church should reach out to the masses in the industrial towns and cities. In the effort to achieve this, he built churches and schools and emphasised the importance of lay agency.[165] The Palmerstonian prelates as a group adopted many of these Sumnerian strategies in their dioceses. Since they represented nearly half the bench of bishops in the early-1860s they brought about a significant change in the pattern of English episcopacy. They did not live in the fashion or style of princely prelates who were distant from the affairs of their dioceses, rather they were pastors of the people. They were men who came alongside their clergy, visited them in their rectories, and when the opportunity arose assisted them in their services.

V

Essays and Reviews Bishops

Outwardly speaking, the middle years of Victorian England were regarded by many contemporaries as a period of confidence, when church attendance was at a relatively high level[1] and the great missionary societies continued to expand their spheres of work as the British Empire extended across the face of the globe. Indeed, such was the mood of optimism that some churchmen began to speak and write in almost millennial terms, believing that the great missionary movement was suddenly going to usher in that thousand-year period of bliss 'when the earth would be filled with the glory of God as the waters cover the sea'.

The Background to the Essays

Below this veneer of apparent confident assurance, however, cracks of doubt were beginning to appear even by the 1820s and 1830s. These stemmed from two main sources. On the one hand the discoveries in science were beginning to challenge the traditional view of world origins and the status of man, whilst on the other the newly emerging techniques of higher criticism emanating from Germany were posing serious questions about the nature of the biblical material and, in particular, about the historicity of the New Testament gospels.

The first scientists to pose serious questions were a group of eminent geologists styled the 'catastrophists' on account of their assertion that the earth's crust had evolved over a very long period of time in a series of 'catastrophes' each of which included creatures at a higher level of organisation. Problems were therefore raised about the Genesis narrative, which not only required the creation of a solar system, the earth, plants, animals and man in a six-day period, but also required a particular order of events, with land vegetation preceding marine life. The result of this was that thinking Christians began to part with the traditional view, that the Genesis account of the creation was to be understood historically or scientifically.

Charles Darwin (1809-1842) was very much a part of this group of scientists, and his work built on the findings of several of them, notably Charles Lyell (1795-1875) and Adam Sedgewick (1785-1873). Darwin is generally acclaimed as the first person to have devised a complete and scientific theory of evolution, his views posing a direct challenge to the idea of special acts of creation. They also threatened the status of the human race, which Darwin suggested in his later volume *The Descent of Man* had evolved from a species akin to the ape and monkey genera. Darwin's evolutionary theory was based on the notion that 'the fittest survive', and many sensitive individuals began to question whether a loving God could really have devised a creation which was based on suffering and bloodshed.

Running in parallel with these questionings, English biblical scholars were also beginning to grapple with new emphases in biblical studies which were emanating from Germany. The substance of their theorizings was that the biblical documents were overlaid with layers of mythical material and that this, coupled with successive re-writings and editings, had totally obscured their historical value. The problem, as they perceived it, was an impossible one of separating fact from fiction. All of this led scholars to a more critical approach to the biblical literature and its interpretation. The various books had to be assessed in terms of their genre which might be saga, law, wisdom, prophecy or poetry.

The Publication of Essays and Reviews

English theological scholars began to be influenced by these developments in varying degrees. One such group were seven Anglican churchmen, who in the spring of 1860, published a collection of articles under the title *Essays and Reviews*.[2] The authors were Frederick Temple (1821-1902), headmaster of Rugby and later Archbishop of Canterbury, and Rowland Williams (1817-1870), Professor of Hebrew and Vice-Principal of St. David's Lampeter, who also held the small Wiltshire living of Broadchalke. Williams was a brilliant classical scholar, orientalist and theologian but somewhat hot-headed and contentious. Baden Powell (1796-1860) was Professor of Geometry at the University of Oxford, while Henry Bristow Wilson (1803-1888), who was one of the tutors who condemned Tract 90 in 1841, was Vicar of Great Staughton in Huntingdonshire. Charles Goodwin (1817-78) was the only man not ordained. He was a Cambridge scholar and Egyptologist. Mark Pattison (1813-1884) was a tutor at Lincoln College and Benjamin Jowett (1817-1893), later to be Master of Balliol College, was Professor of Greek in the University.

In a lengthy chapter entitled 'A Time of Preparation 1845-1858' in his study *of Essays and Reviews,* Ian Ellis pinpointed 1845 as a crucially important time. It was in that year that John Henry Newman declared that he had been driven out from the university by the liberals. 13 February 1845 was, according to Ellis, 'the birthday of modern Liberalism in Oxford'. Ellis shows that the scholars whose contributions appeared in *Essays and Reviews* had been working and interacting with one another for a period of fifteen years.[3] The idea of producing such a volume came from Wilson, who put the matter to Jowett who was rapidly coming to be regarded as the leader of the liberal Christian circle at Oxford.[4] He welcomed the idea and explained the project to Arthur Stanley, who was later to be Dean of Westminster, in the following terms:

> The object is to say what we think freely within the limits of the Church of England. A notice will be prefixed that no one is responsible for any notions but his own. It is however, an essential part of the plan that names shall be given. . . . We do not wish to do anything rash or irritating to the public or the University, but we are determined not to submit to the abominable system of terrorism which prevents the statement of the plainest facts and makes true theology or theological education impossible.[5]

The contributions which were made were varied, some of them being more offensive to traditional Christian views than others. Frederick Temple wrote on 'The Education of the World'. He pleaded for the fearless open-minded study of the Bible regardless of the consequence to orthodox belief, as the following passage from near the end of his essay makes plain:

> If geology proves to us that we must not interpret the first chapters of Genesis literally; if historical investigations shall show us that inspiration . . . was not empowered to protect the narrative of the inspired writers from occasional interpolations and forgeries in that Book, as in many others; the results should still be welcome.[6]

Rowland Williams contributed 'A Review of Bunsen's Biblical Researches'. Williams wrote approvingly of many of the *avant garde* views of the German scholar-diplomat, Baron Chevalier Bunsen. He sided with Bunsen's assertions that the Pentateuch was a compilation of 'gradual growth', that Isaiah 40-56 was not written by Isaiah of Jerusalem but much later, that the Book of Daniel was not authentic history and belonged to the second not to the sixth century B.C., that the servant in Isaiah chapter 53 did not refer to Christ but was in all probability Jeremiah or possibly Baruch, and that the epistle to the Hebrews was not written by Paul. These conclusions led Williams to state at one point: 'the Bible is, before all things, the written voice of the congregation' and again: 'The sacred writers acknowledge themselves men of like passions with ourselves. . . .'[7]

Baden Powell wrote 'On the Study of the Evidences of Christianity'. He ruled out what he called 'miraculous intervention as described in the Bible, on the ground that such intervention militated against the orderliness of nature'.[8] Henry Wilson wrote on 'The National Church' in which he gave his own views as to the purpose of the National Church. He contended for a Church with a far less dogmatic basis, capable of embracing much wider sections of the nation. Wilson's views on inspiration were particularly offensive to orthodox Christians. He indicated that the biblical books were not 'miraculously inspired'.[9] 'Nor', he stated, 'did any of the scriptural authors even apply the term "Word of God" to any books of the Old and New Testaments'.[10]

Charles Goodwin wrote on 'The Mosaic Cosmogony'. In his essay he argued that a literal interpretation of the Genesis account of the Creation was at variance with the truths discovered by geologists. He asserted that the creation stories of Genesis were 'nothing but myths created by the Hebrews'. In the final paragraph of his essay Goodwin concluded of Genesis: 'No-one contends that it can be used as a basis of astronomical or geological teaching. . . .'[11]

Mark Pattison wrote on 'Tendencies of Religious Thought in England 1688-1750'. His essay was unpolemical and his role was as an historian of ideas. One of the themes of his discourse was the way in which the eighteenth century had begun to make use of common reason. Theologians of the nineteenth century must, he asserted, go on to use this reason as the judge of revelation.[12]

Benjamin Jowett wrote on the interpretation of Scripture. He was familiar with contemporary German biblical criticism and saw how much it had to teach the English students, hitherto insulated from such influences 'by the blind veneration in which . . . the very letter of Scripture was usually held'. But in the matter of understanding Scripture, Jowett asserted that it must be treated 'like any other book'. 'The first step', he claimed, 'is to know the meaning', and again, 'No other science of hermeneutics is possible but an inductive one'. Jowett spelt the matter out in further detail:

> Scripture has one meaning – the meaning which it had to the mind
> of the prophet or evangelist who first uttered or wrote it, to the
> hearers or readers who first received it. . . . We have no reason to
> attribute to the prophet or evangelist any second or hidden sense
> different from that which appears on the surface.

Because Scripture is 'like any other book', attention must be paid to personal, local, historical and linguistic points of character. This can only be done 'in the same careful and impartial way that we ascertain the meaning of Sophocles and of Plato'.[13]

Reaction to the Essays

Reaction to the Essays was widespread and for the most part unequivocally critical and condemnatory. By and large the Protestant Nonconformists remained somewhat aloof and the main Congregationalist and Methodist scholarly journals made little or no comment. In contrast, however, both the Baptists of the Baptist Union and the Strict and Particular Baptists were forthright in their opposition. *The Freeman*, the Baptist Union's denominational newspaper, began an article on the Essays by stating that 'justice, love and truth compel us to condemn this book'.[14] At the same time, however, the writer was impressed that 'as a controversial book the volume is nowhere disfigured by bitterness or scorn' and each writer seems to be 'imbued with a gentle spirit'. After noting Doctor William's unreserved praise for Bunsen's biblical researches, the volume's contention that the Red Sea 'may be interpreted with the latitude of poetry' and that the fifty-third chapter of Isaiah contains 'no reference to Christ at all', *The Freeman's* reviewer commented on the essayists as follows:

The ultimate issue to which they would lead us is very clear, viz., a rejection of all that the Word of God contains, which we may happen to deem irreconcilable with the dictates of our reason. From henceforth, Scripture would contain no mysteries . . . all God's thoughts absolutely come within the compass of our own.[15]

From within the Established Church itself opposition was not slow in coming. *The Christian Observer*, one of the two main Evangelical periodicals, printed an article on the Essays in June 1860, entitled 'Broad Church Theology'. The reviewer, whose language was emotive and hostile, regarded Rowland Williams as the most dangerous of the essayists: 'He takes up the whole circle of Bunsen's wild profanities, and thus brings into the compass of forty-three pages a mass of reckless infidelity, compared with which the writings of Voltaire and Paine were comparatively harmless'.[16]

The same writer expressed his anger that the essayists considered that the present human race is at 'least twenty thousand years old' whereas Scripture teaches us that 'at a certain time, about 5,860 years ago, the human race was placed on this earth by God'. *The Christian Observer* concluded cynically by stating: 'The present volume is meant to establish the principle that a man may retain the orders and benefices of the Church without believing the Bible'. In short, the volume is the Tract No. XC of the Broad Church'. The other evangelical paper, *The Record*, sounded the same note of alarm and denounced the seven essayists as 'septem contra Christum'.[17]

Aids to Faith

In addition to the rebuttals made by the various Church of England periodicals, two full-length books were also produced. *Replies to Essays and Reviews* (1862) was edited by Samuel Wilberforce, Bishop of Oxford and *Aids to Faith* (1861) by William Thomson, Bishop of Gloucester. Neither volume was acclaimed for its depth of scholarship, and critics regarded the latter as a 'poorish effort'. *The Christian Observer* was a little kinder in its pronouncements and stated that taken together 'they present an aggregate of solid and valuable thought, the like of which the Church has scarcely had offered to her in any former year of modern times'.[18]

Thomson's volume was clearly stronger than that put out by Wilberforce. Significantly, in addition to himself two other contributors, Charles Ellicott and Harold Browne, both owed their promotion not only to Lord Shaftesbury, but also to the fact that they had taken their stand against those who sought to make shipwreck of the orthodox creedal faith. In his preface to the volume Thomson stated their clear objective.

The Essays in this volume are intended to offer aid to those whose faith may have been shaken by recent assaults. The writers do not pretend to have exhausted subjects so vast and so important, within the compass of a few pages but they desire to set forth their reasons for believing the Bible, out of which they teach, to be the inspired Word of God, and for exhorting others still to cherish it as the only message of salvation from God to man.[19]

Harold Browne wrote on inspiration. He began his essay with a lengthy historical survey of the ways in which Christians in successive eras of church history understood the authority of the scriptures. He stated his own position with clarity, that all the canonical books of the Old and New Testaments are 'the oracles of God, the Scriptures of God, the record and depository of God's supernatural revelations in early times to man'.[20] He was unequivocal that the Holy Spirit was the inspirer of the scriptures which are 'an infallible depository of religious truth'. The problem in articulating a specific doctrine of inspiration, Browne saw clearly, was in deciding the relative weights of divine and human influence in the Biblical text. 'We may suppose', he wrote, that 'the human mind was perfectly passive, acting under the influence of the Holy Spirit' or 'we may suppose the mind of the writer or speaker and altogether freely, speaking entirely its own thoughts and words, but . . . derived from Divine Communion'.[21] Browne was reluctant to venture a specific opinion on this issue but his convictions seem to lie mid-way between these two positions. Browne went on to highlight the weakness of the liberal view of inspiration which emanated from Coleridge that scripture 'finds' one in ways and at a depth not equalled by other books. If we go on this principle, Browne asked, 'where are we to stop?' The difficulty is that there may not be very much in the second book of Chronicles which 'finds' us, whereas we may find if we were to read Baxter's *Saints Everlasting Rest* that it finds us on almost every page. 'To carry out Coleridge's principle', he wrote, 'we ought to uncanonise, or reject the inspiration of the book of Chronicles, and set up as canonical the Book of Baxter'.[22] Browne therefore argued that the doctrine of inspiration must rest on something much more objective. He underlined the fact that both Jesus and the apostles cited the books of the Old Testament as 'Scriptures', as the 'oracles of God' and as 'God-breathed'. 'Surely', he added, 'we have no right to say that one part "finds me" and another does not and settle our own Canon accordingly'.[23] Browne supported his plea for a more objective view of inspiration from the fulfillment of Old Testament prophecies and Christ's attestation of them. Referring to the former he asserted 'if the prophets really did centuries before foresee an event, most unlikely, but which we have witnessed as true, they must have had something more than the inspiration of genius or than the exalting of their intuitional consciousness'.[24]

Browne warned against being perplexed 'because some recently discovered geological phenomena seem hard to reconcile with a few verses in one chapter of Genesis'.[25] He concluded by urging his readers to reflect that the first book of the Bible teaches two incontrovertible facts that creation took place at an 'infinitely distant' time from the present, and that man was the last of all animated beings to come into existence.

Charles Ellicott, then Dean of Exeter, also considered the question of inspiration in his essay entitled 'Scripture, and its Interpretation'. His contribution, which extended to a hundred pages, is substantial in both content and argument. He dealt first with the doctrine of inspiration and then went on to consider the principles which should be taken into consideration when interpreting specific biblical texts. Ellicott introduced the subject by examining the liberal challenge that because Scripture is capable of so many differing interpretations, it cannot therefore be held to be 'inspired'. His view is that 'the extent and variety of interpretations of Scripture is exaggerated'.[26] If a careful study is made of the writing of successive expositors it will be found that there is a 'concordia discors' and that 'in many passages' we can find interpretations which may 'stand even the test of Vincent of Lerins, and may justly be termed the traditional interpretations of the Church of Christ'.[27]

Using Jowett's own words, Ellicott declared that we cannot interpret Scripture like any other book, 'when, in the merest rough and outside view, the Scripture presents such striking differences from any book that the world has ever seen'.[28] Clearly the books of the Old and New Testaments must therefore be regarded as 'inspired'. In an effort to explain the meaning of the term Ellicott ventured the following definition:

> Scripture is the revelation through human media of the infinite mind of God to the finite mind of man, and recognising as we do both a human and a Divine element in the written Word, we verily believe that the Holy Ghost was so breathed in the mind of the writer, so illumined his spirit and pervaded his thoughts, that, while nothing that individualised him as a man was taken away, everything that was necessary to enable him to declare Divine Truth in all its fullness was bestowed and superadded.[29]

Charles Ellicott did however agree with the liberal authors of *Essays and Reviews* in rejecting all theories of 'inspiration' whether 'mechanical' and 'dynamic'.[30] He was content to assert that Scripture was 'inspired' but how that 'inspiration' came about he, like his opponents, was not prepared to speculate. He wrote:

> But it may be asked, how do we conceive that this inspiration took place? What is our theory of the process? What do we conceive to be the modus agendi of the Holy Spirit in the heart of man? This we plainly refuse to answer. We know not, and do not presume to inquire into the manner; we recognise and believe in the fact. Individual writers may have speculated; imagery, suitable or unsuitable, may have been introduced as illustrative by few thinkers in early ages; but the Catholic Church has never put forward a theory.[31]

Ellicott nevertheless devoted a substantial portion of the essay to set-ting out arguments in support of the doctrine of inspiration, as well as tracing its development through successive epochs of Church history. He began by underlining Jesus' endorsements of Old Testament in texts such as John Chapter 10 verse 35 'the scripture cannot be broken' and Jesus' promise to his apostles that the Holy Spirit should teach them all things, and bring all things which he said to them to their remembrance.[32] He also stressed St. Paul's claim that his written words were of divine origin.

Ellicott then moves on and shows that the doctrine of inspiration was taught by both the Sub Apostolic Fathers and the Ante Nicene Fathers such as Justin, Irenaeus, Cyprian and Tertullian. He then cites St. August-ine who 'asserts the infallibility of Scripture in language which the strongest asserter of So-called bibliolatry of the day could not desire to see made more definite'.[33]

Ellicott also stressed what he termed 'the subjective argument' for the inspiration of Scripture. By this he meant that 'the Bible has spoken to millions upon millions of hearts, as it were with the very voice of God himself'.[34] He suggested the case of the unschooled simple believer who reads the Bible daily in a devotional manner. Such a person finds in its pages consolation in sorrow, strength in times of weakness and calm in moments of excitement. The sum of these arguments, Ellicott asserted, was a sufficient ground to assert that the Canonical Scriptures are 'inspired'.

Ellicott proceeded to consider the matter of the infallibility of Scripture. 'Was the inspiration such as to wholly preclude errors and inaccuracies?' 'This', he wrote, 'is the real anxious question of our times'.[35] Ellicott consid-ered the accusations of errors of mind, errors of judgement, and errors in matters of fact. In essence, he viewed these alleged failings on the part of Scripture as 'far more doubtful than they are assumed to be'.[36] Many of them disappear when handled by men who have sufficient scholarship to extract the core meaning from Scripture. Nevertheless, Ellicott was not prepared to assert that there were no inaccuracies in scripture. Discrepancies over dates, names and other unimportant matters of fact are plainly evident. In drawing his thoughts on 'inspiration' to a close Ellicott suggested that in so far as Scripture has a human element we may admit to 'incomplete-ness' and 'limitations' but these have no bearing on divine truth.[37]

The second part of Ellicott's essay dealt with the interpretation of Scripture. He set out in a lucid and clear manner five principles which should govern Biblical hermeneutics. First we should interpret grammatically, and care must be taken to ascertain what is the lexical meaning of the individual words. 'We may smile', he wrote, at such a 'thread-bare rule' and yet this rule is the least adhered to by New Testa-ment scholars.[38] Second, we must interpret historically.[39] By reference to historical background and topography the full meaning of a particular text or word written within a text may be drawn out. Third, interpretation must be done contextually. If a text such as Matthew Chapter 5 verse 34 is dislocated from its context, its meaning can readily be distorted. In matters of acute dispute as to the meaning of a particular text, reference should also be made to other texts which are 'more frequently appealed to as final and absolute'.[40] Fourth, Ellicott counselled that interpretation must be done 'minutely'. If all Scripture is believed to be inspired, then the interpreter must not be satisfied until the significance of every aspect of a passage has been tapped. Indeed, he underlined the fact that the interpretation of a text may sometimes be determined by a single word.[41] Ellicott's fifth guide post was interpretation according to the analogy of faith, by which he meant the Nicene and Athanasian Creeds. To those who contended that the creeds were subsequent to the Canon of Scripture, Ellicott countered that they were formulated in substance from the earliest time. In his view the Creeds were 'authoritative summaries of Scripture, and so authoritative guides in interpreting Scripture'.[42]

Ellicott ended his essay on an evangelical note, praying that 'the great Father of love and mercy draw all who love His ever blessed Son, and who, see in Him the propitiation for the sins of a whole guilty world, still nearer together'.[43] He expressed the hope that at the last the household of faith presently fragmented into hostile camps, may be rekindled and re-united in love, and be united in praising and blessing our common Lord.

William Thomson who edited *Aids to Faith*, himself contributed an essay entitled 'The Death of Christ' which was not specifically directed against any of the contributions *in Essays and Reviews*. It was nevertheless a strong defence of the traditional doctrine of the substitutionary Atonement which liberal scholars professed to find so objectionable. Thomson began his argument of elucidating the New Testament teaching on the death of Christ. Whilst Jesus didn't specifically speak of his crucifixion as a 'sacrifice' for sin, Thomson made it clear that the whole concept was implicit in his teaching. It was seen for example, when he spoke of 'My blood of the new covenant' and in his discourse on the bronze serpent lifted up in the wilderness as a pre-cursor to his death.[44] It was also clearly implied in John the Baptist's designation of Jesus as 'the Lamb of God which taketh away the sin of the world' and in the early apostolic preaching. Here he instanced Philip's explanation to the Ethiopian official that the suffering and death of the servant in Isaiah Chapter 53 referred to the sacrificial death of Jesus. He also referred to Paul's proclamation of forgiveness of sins through Christ in his sermon at Antioch[45] and his designation of Jesus as 'the reconciler and as the mediator between God and man'.[46] Thomson also drew out the Petrine doctrine of Christ which 'is connected strictly with that of His work as Saviour and Messiah'.[47] After considering the Johanine epistles and the letter to the Hebrews, Thomson summed up what he understood to be the substance of the New Testament teaching on the death of Christ:

1. God sent His son into the world to redeem lost and ruined men from sin and death, and the Son willingly took upon Him the form of a servant for this purpose; and thus the Father and the Son manifested their love for us.

2. God the Father laid upon His son the weight of the sins of the whole world, so that He bear in His own body the wrath which men must elsewhere have borne, because there was no other way of escape for them; and thus the Atonement was a manifestation of Divine justice.

3. The effect of the Atonement thus wrought is, that man is placed in a new position, freed from the dominion of sin, and able to follow holiness; and thus the doctrine of the Atonement ought to work in all the hearers a sense of love, obedience, and of self sacrifice.[48]

In the subsequent pages of his essay Thomson first demonstrated that this was the doctrine held by both the early Catholic Fathers and some of the later medieval schoolmen. He then went on to examine and counter some of the moral objections against this notion of sacrificial atonement. He cited Irenaeus, Origen and Athanasius. 'Origen', he wrote, 'who is often said to know nothing of the substitutive sufferings of the Lord, asserts them in several passages'.[49] He also drew on Cyril of Alexandria, who wrote that 'He who was free from sin, and had trod the paths of all righteousness, underwent the punishment of sinners, destroying by His Cross the sentence of the old curse . . . "being made a curse for us".'[50] After a series of references from Augustine, Hilary, Ambrose and Gregory of Nazianzus, Thomson stressed the point that it is absurd to claim that the doctrine of the substitutionary atonement was the invention of Anselm.[51] It had in fact a long tradition which was strongly rooted in Athanasius in particular, and in the earlier anti-Nicene Fathers.

Thomson scrutinised the objections which were most commonly raised against the substitutionary atonement in some depth. These included the notion of the vengeful father meting out his anger on his own son, the innocent being punished in place of the guilty, and the whole idea of transference of guilt from one person to another. Thomson began by making the point that these objections arose out of crude one-sided representations. 'It is not true', he wrote, 'that God looked forth on His works to find some innocent man able and willing to bear the weight of His wrath, and found Jesus and punished Him'.[52] Such a view of the matter, he contended, was wide of the truth because God 'took our nature upon Him, and therewith sins of it, at least in their consequences'.[53] Finally, to those who would argue that the substitutionary atonement was cruel because punishment fell on the innocent, Thomson had a counter-argument. Such a sacrifice was not cruel 'if it thereby marks for ever the enormity of sin which needed such a sacrifice',[54] nor was it useless 'if it changed the relation of man to

God . . . drawing all men to Jesus', and nor was it unjust 'because the Father's will to punish never outstripped the Son's to suffer'.[55] Thomson concluded as follows:

> The power of the doctrine of the Atonement has been felt wherever the Gospel has come. It has carried comfort to sinners where nothing else could do so. Wherever the conviction of sin has been deepest, the power of the Cross has been most conspicuous. . . . Let it still be reached; and our lessons from these controversies be that we preach the whole of it, so far as Scripture informs and our mind comprehends.[56]

Essays and Reviews *Bishops*

Archibald Tait suggested that the publication of *Essays and Reviews* had a curious result. It filled the 'Shaftesbury clique' which influenced Palmerston with the idea of championing opponents of the book, rather than merely campaigning for the appointment of more evangelical pastors.[57] Tait himself ruefully reflected that 'Latterly all appointments seemed to be made by Palmerston with no idea than that the person appointed was safe as regards to the *Essays and Reviews* '.[58] Certainly Shaftesbury set on the deliberate course of rewarding, wherever possible, men who had taken up the cause of orthodoxy in the fight against the liberal views of the essayists.

The promotions to the Bench of Bishops of William Thomson, Charles Ellicott and Harold Browne were certainly attributable in large part to their contribution to *Aids to Faith*. Thomson began the project while he was Provost of Queen's College, before his appointment to the bishopric of Gloucester and Bristol.[59] It was not however published until after his consecration had taken place.[60] *Evangelical Christendom* wrote of Thomson having distinguished himself as 'an author in defence of the truth . . . against the bolder speculation of the Seven Essayists'. The article continued: 'To this circumstance . . . it is understood that Dr Thomson owes his appointment'.[61] Charles Ellicott had only been in post as Dean of Exeter for two years when he was offered the bishopric of Bristol and Gloucester, in succession to Thomson who had been translated to York. Although he was not, like Thomson, an evangelical, Shaftesbury was easily reconciled to his appointment. He gave three reasons why he felt Ellicott to be the right man for office, the third of which was 'my own feeling . . . that honour should be done for everyone, whenever occasion offered, connected with answers to *Essays and Reviews* '.[62] Harold Browne was also widely acclaimed for his 'well-reasoned and temperate statement of the orthodox views' in *Aids to Faith*.[63] In consequence he had become well-known as a prominent conservative in the developing controversies over biblical criticism. There seems little doubt that this led to his being offered the See of

Ely in 1864.[64] Significantly, both Palmerston's other two episcopal appointments subsequent to the publication of *Essays and Reviews*, Francis Jeune and William Jacobson, were staunchly conservative in their theological pronouncements.

The Palmerston Bishops stand against Essays and Reviews

The episcopal assault on *Essays and Reviews* began with Samuel Wilberforce's Charge at High Wycombe in November 1860. His forthright homily was a rallying call to conservatives to settle their differences 'to crush the liberal viper which had reared its ugly head'.[65] Wilberforce lambasted those who treated the Bible as legend and deprived prophecy of its supernatural character. Unless divisions were set aside, he declared, we shall be 'robbed unawares of the very foundations of the faith'.[66] Wilberforce, it should be noted, went on to produce a further vigorous and critical attack in *The Quarterly Review* of January 1861.[67] He confronted the authors as a group. In his view, even though the degree of divergence from the Christian faith had of course varied from contributor to contributor, joint authorship implied joint responsibility. The essayists' attempt to combine the advocacy of unorthodox doctrines with the status of clergymen of the Church of England was 'moral dishonesty'. As Wilberforce saw it, the writers had subjected the whole range of supernatural phenomena, whether miraculous or sacramental, to the 'universal solvent of criticism'.

Wilberforce's strident attack on the essays proved to be the clarion call which drew the rest of the bishops as a whole into the fray. Most of Palmerston's appointees took the opportunity to publicly declare their distaste for the views of Wilson and his circle. Samuel Waldegrave, who had only been in post as Bishop of Carlisle for a year, declared that the book was 'not so much the inroad of a new foreign element of mischief, as the outbreak of an infection which has long been stealthily at work amongst us'.[68] The essayists had undermined 'the plenary inspiration and supreme authority of the Bible, the total corruption and certain condemnation of man, the miraculous incarnation and vicarious suffering of the Word for men's redemption' and 'the sovereign election and effectual operation of the Spirit in man's regeneration'.[69] 'How are we to counteract the doubt and the rationalism of the authors of *Essays and Reviews*?', he asked in a rhetorical question during his Charge to the clergy of the diocese. His answer was preach the Bible, 'preach it, in all simplicity, in all fullness, in all boldness'.[70] In order to do this, he continued, we have to have that 'constant fellowship with God in prayer and in study of His word to which we stand pledged by our Ordination vows'.[71]

In his 1861 visitation sermon Robert Bickersteth interpreted *Essays and Reviews* as 'a sign that we have surely fallen on perilous times'. He professed himself incensed that ministers who have willingly subscribed to the 'Thirty-Nine Articles' were propagating opinions held by 'avowed infidels'.[72] In the same address he denounced the contributors who 'scoff at the idea of a direct inspiration from God' and 'exalt the human intellect to the position of sitting in judgement on revealed truth'.[73] In a letter to one of his incumbents, Bickersteth wrote that he did not believe there was a single clergyman in the diocese who had any doubt as to his views on *Essays and Reviews*. It is, he said, 'a pernicious book'.

In his second visitation address Joseph Cotton Wigram made reference to the Essays. He spoke of them as 'the fresh outbreak of the old spirit of scepticism, and more than that opposition to the authority of the word of God'.[74] Henry Philpott, in his 1865 Charge to the Worcester Diocese, fulminated against 'the irrelevant language with which efforts have been made to shake the faith of believers'. He also went on to denounce the 'self-confident, arrogant assaults which the essayists had made on the historical truth of Holy Writ'.[75] Philpott reminded his clergy and churchwardens that the Articles of Religion and *The Book of Common Prayer* make it abundantly clear that the Church of England regards the canonical books of the Old and New Testaments as 'the word of God'.[76] In support of this contention Philpott cited the Ordination Service where, on delivering the Bible to a candidate for ordination to the priesthood, the Bishop is directed to say, 'Take thou authority to preach the word of God'.[77]

Archbishop Sumner's letter on behalf of the bishops

Samuel Wilberforce pressed the ageing evangelical primate, John Bird Sumner (1780-1862), to issue a pastoral directive in response to *Essays and Reviews*. The archbishop responded on 1 February and convened the Bench to debate the matter. There is little record of this meeting apart from a passing reference in Wilberforce's biography, which indicates that the bishops were divided over whether or not there should be a prosecution. Wilberforce spent the night of 2 February at Fulham 'very much tired' after the meeting with three Palmerston appointees London, Rochester and Carlisle.[78] As a result of their discussions Wilberforce produced a memorandum which they all agreed on and sent out. Meanwhile Sumner continued to receive petitions and protests from various deaneries around the country. The result was that on 12 February, following a further meeting of the Bishops at Lambeth, he issued a public reply in response to one of them. The protest, which came from a Dorsetshire rural deanery, typified the shock felt by many conscientious parochial clergy.

> We wish to make known to your Grace and to all the Bishops the alarm we feel at . . . the denial of the atoning efficacy of the Death and Passion of our Blessed Saviour Jesus Christ, both God and Man . . . and the denial also of a Divine Inspiration of the canonical scriptures of the Old and New Testament.[79]

Sumner replied from Lambeth with a letter addressed to the Reverend H.B. Williams, the clergyman whose name was at the top of the list. His statement was a forthright one in which he asserted that his colleagues on the Bench 'unanimously agree with me in expressing the pain it has given them that any clergyman of our Church should have published such opinions as those concerning which you have addressed us'.[80] He continued that 'We cannot understand how the opinions can be held consistently with an honest subscription to the formularies of our Church, with many of the fundamental doctrines of which they appear to us essentially at variance'.[81] Almost all the bishops appended their names to the document. There were one or two absentees, including the Palmerstonian, Henry Philpott of Worcester, but it may simply have been the case that he was unable to be present at the Lambeth debates.

Tait's Prevarications

Of all the Palmerston bishops, Archibald Tait was the most reluctant to bring essayists to book. His close friendship with two of the essayists, Frederick Temple and Benjamin Jowett, made his position awkward. He did, however, draw a distinction between the different essays and the overall harmful effect of the volume as a whole. Although he had proposed taking no action at all, he had nevertheless set his signature on Sumner's memorandum because he could happily agree that collectively the essays had indeed had a destructive impact on the faith of ordinary Christian men and women. Tait made this point when Canon A.P. Stanley wrote a complaining letter to him from Oxford dated 16 February 1861. Stanley was aggrieved that Tait had explicitly stated that he 'saw nothing seriously to condemn in Jowett's Essay and hardly anything in Temple's.'[82] 'Now', he continued, 'he has set his name to a rebuttal of them published in *The Times'*.[83] In reply Tait repeated his earlier assertion that Temple's essay had 'nothing in it, taken by itself, to which such a condemnation as that of the Archbishop's letter can apply'.[84] Jowett's piece has, he also stated, 'a deeply earnest tone about it'.[85] But Tait went on to underline that 'the book of the *Essays and Reviews* as a whole is what has excited so much feeling'.[86] In a letter to Temple the following day he made the same point: 'For my own part I draw a marked distinction between the tone and substance of the several contributions to the book called *Essays and Reviews*'.[87] Tait's position was undoubtedly a difficult one, because in his earlier days as an Oxford tutor he had urged his university undergraduates to undertake a critical study of the Bible. Furthermore, he had stated that if they took his advice, he for one would never join in treating them unjustly.[88] Frederick Temple felt Tait's change of tone keenly. 'If you do not wish to alienate your friends, do not treat them as you have treated me'.[89] Tait wrote in his diary of 24 February 1861, 'Anxiety as to the judgement of the Bishops on Essays and Reviews. Fear of misunderstandings with old friends'.[90] A further entry for 7 March 1861 highlights the conflicting issues with which Tait was having to grapple.

> How difficult is my position . . . we have had a great duty – to express our disapproval; a great duty also, I think, to guard the accused from ill-usage: a great duty to the Church to guard its doctrine: and to watch for its children likely to be led astray by any appearance of persecution.[91]

The extract suggests that Tait's position as a bishop had caused him to move to a more conservative standpoint. His role was no longer challenging undergraduates to think, but earnestly to convey a simple gospel message to the poor of his burgeoning London diocese. The Palmerstonian years had moved the Church on from its earlier liberalism to a more orthodox position, and Tait undoubtedly felt the impact as he contemplated the outcry and alarm of the British public.

Convocation and Prosecutions

Wilberforce and many of the bishops still felt that *Essays and Reviews* needed a stronger and more corporate disapproval on the part of the Church. In the recently revived convocations they had an instrument ready to hand. The necessary arrangements had been made by Parliament enabling the southern province to meet in Convocation in 1854 and the northern in 1861. On 26 February 1861 a debate was initiated in the lower house of Canterbury, in which most of the speakers criticised the volume and expressed their shock that clergymen should have written it. On 13 March Sumner called his Episcopal colleagues together to consider the opinions of the York convocation.

On 12 March, a petition was presented at Lambeth asking for action against the volume. It was signed by more than 8,000 clergy. When Convocation met again on 14 March the bishops agreed to Wilberforce's motion that the Lower House be requested to appoint a committee to report on the volume. Archdeacon Denison was voted chairman and a report was presented to the House for their consideration. The session was poorly attended and the Lower House voted by 31 votes to 8 that 'there are sufficient grounds for a synodical judgement on *Essays and Reviews*. The Upper House of Bishops eventually pronounced against the book as containing 'false and dangerous statements, and reasonings at variance with the Church of England'.[92]

At this point two of the essayists were prosecuted. Bishop Walter Kerr Hamilton (1808-1869), the Tractarian diocesan of Salisbury, instigated proceedings against Rowland Williams, who had recently been instituted to a living in his diocese. The case came before the court of Arches in June 1861. Later in the year similar action was taken against Henry Wilson in the same court. Wilson was censured on several counts, including denying that the Bible was written under divine inspiration, which contradicted articles six and twenty. Williams was similarly condemned for his opinion that 'the Holy Scriptures proceed from the same mental power as has produced other works'. The court gave sentence on 15 December 1862 and both men had to pay costs and were suspended from their benefices for a year.

The two defendants appealed against this sentence to the Judicial Committee of the Privy Council. The judges eventually met in February 1864 and decided that it is not penal for a clergyman to maintain that the 'Bible is the expression of devout reason, and therefore to be read with reason in freedom' or that the Bible is 'the written voice of the congregation'. The court's decision, which was given by Lord Westbury, dismissed all the charges brought against Williams and Wilson. On the accusation that Wilson had denied eternal punishment, it maintained that he had not denied a judgement at the end of the world. Westbury thus went down in history as the judge who had 'dismissed hell with costs'.[93] On the issue of the inspiration of the Bible, the Committee did not feel able to state categorically that Wilson or Williams had contradicted either the formularies or Articles of the Church of England.

The Primates' Pastoral Letters on Essays and Reviews

The problem for many people was the fact that the Law Lords had supported the essayists and more than that, with the presence of bishops among their number. Why hadn't the bishops, who had been present at all of the deliberations, protected the interests and doctrines of the church? Tait and the lay judges were unanimous in their acquittal of both Williams and Wilson but both Palmerston primates, Longley of Canterbury and Thomson of York, dissented. In order to make their position clear each of them published a pastoral letter setting out their views.

Longley's *Pastoral Letter* addressed to the clergy and laity of his province was dated 14 March 1864. He took Rowland Williams to task for his opinion that 'the Bible is before all things the written word of the Congregation'.[94] On this view, Longley contended, Holy Scripture 'must be the word of man; and can have no more authority for the establishing of doctrine, than such expressions of devout reason as we have in the works of Hooker, Taylor and Barrow'.[95] Longley's view was that the scriptures are 'the word of God' and 'our only infallible authority concerning matters of faith and practice'.[96] On the matter of the everlasting punishment of the wicked, Longley declared that he considered the doctrine 'to be clearly indicated in the Commination Service, the Burial Service, the Apostles' Creed and the Athanasian Creed'.[97]

William Thomson issued his *Pastoral Letter to the Clergy and Laity of the Province of York* to coincide with Longley's address to the southern province. He had received many representations and letters from clergy and laity urging him to make plain his views on the Privy Council's reversal of the Court of Arches' condemnation of both Williams and Wilson. As a member of the Council he was inhibited from a full disclosure of the proceedings, but he nevertheless was unequivocal in stating his personal position. He noted that the pleas of Williams and Wilson had both been upheld by the Council's judicial committee, despite the fact that they had maintained that 'the Bible is not the word of God' and that 'it is the word of devout men'.[98] In contradistinction Thomson pointed out that 'the Bible is spoken of as the word of God in the 19th, 20th, 22nd and 24th Articles'.[99] He asserted that if it is maintained that 'the Bible is not the word of God but only contains the word of God' then there is no touchstone which shall tell us whether a given passage is part of the word of God or the word of man therewith entangled'.[100]

Thomson also sided with Longley in strongly defending the traditional understanding of the doctrine of everlasting punishment. 'Everlasting', he wrote, 'must mean lasting for ever, never coming to an end.'[101] 'The Church of England', he continued, 'believes in a life that lasts for ever for the good, and in an everlasting punishment for the wicked.'[102] He concluded his sixteen page missive by urging all clergy to be 'zealous in teaching the pure word of God'.[103]

The archbishops' pastoral letters certainly went some way towards overcoming the uncertainty and the confusion which existed in many quarters of the Church and nation. Both Longley and Thomson had strenuously denied that the Church was party to the final decision. In fact Longley had been unequivocal in a speech to Convocation. 'I do not acquiesce in the terms of the judgement', he declared, 'and therefore I am not responsible for the words [of acquittal]'.[104] For his part Thomson maintained that the 'so-called Judgement' was only a statement for the guidance of the public of the grounds upon which the advice to the Crown would be based'.[105] In this way both primates to a large extent succeeded in standing apart from the Privy Council's verdict, without seeming to present too much of a divided front from Bishop Tait who had sided with the lay members.

Condemnation in Convocation

The judgement of the Privy Council showed clearly enough that the State would not lend its weight to endorse doctrinaire religious beliefs or penalise clergymen for views which were unorthodox. The stage was thus set for the Church to take matters into its own hand. The bishops in Convocation had so far avoided episcopal condemnation of *Essays and Reviews* but the situation now seemed to demand it. Convocational condemnation was not slow in coming, indeed the rapidity of it certainly displayed an air of indignity.

Denison's high-church supporters convened a meeting in the Music School at Oxford, and a declaration which unequivocally endorsed biblical inspiration and eternal punishment was passed. The pronouncement asserted:

> We, the undersigned presbyters and deacons in Holy orders of the Church of England and Ireland, in common with the whole Catholic Church, maintain without reserve or qualification the inspiration and Divine authority of the whole canonical Scriptures, as not only containing, but being the Word of God, and further teaches, in the words of our blessed Lord, that the 'punishment' of the 'cursed', equally with the life of the 'righteous', is 'everlasting'.[106]

Within three weeks every incumbent and curate in England and Ireland received a copy of the declaration urging them for the love of God to sign it. Nearly 11,000 out of a total 24,800 clergy did so. At the same time 137,000 signatures were collected from the laity and presented by a deputation to the two Archbishops at Lambeth Palace.[107] Numbers of them also wrote to Tait in 'sadness of heart' urging him 'even now' to express his repudiation of what Dr Pusey called the 'soul-destroying judgement' of the Privy Council.[108] Tait was not happy with the declaration, maintaining that it meant that Scripture was an infallible guide, in every single syllable, not only as to faith and doctrine but physical science in addition.[109]

Notwithstanding Tait's opposition, a motion of condemnation was passed in the Lower House of Convocation, carried by 39 votes to 19. In the Upper House it was carried by 8 votes to 2, the minority consisting of the Bishops of London and Lincoln.[110] Tait subsequently reflected in a private memorandum:

> The folly of the publication of *Essays and Reviews*, and still more, of Stanley's ill-judged defence of them in the *Edinburgh Review* . . . have so effectually frightened the clergy that I think there is scarcely a Bishop on the Bench, unless it be the Bishop of St. David's, that is not useless for the purpose of preventing the widespread alienation of intelligent men. . . . Meanwhile I feel my own vocation clear, greatly as I sympathise with the Evangelicals, not to allow them to tyrannise over the Broad Churchmen. . . . What is wanted is a deeply religious liberal party, and almost all who might have formed it have in alarm, deserted. . . . The great evil is that the liberals are deficient in religion, and the religious are deficient in liberality. Let us pray for an outpouring of the very Spirit of Truth.[111]

In these reflections can be seen the rightness of Shaftesbury's assessment of Tait as 'the mildest and gentlest of Broad Churchmen'. Clearly he agreed with his colleagues on the Bench that the spirit which emanated from the essays was damaging, but at the same time he wanted to keep open the doors of honest and thoughtful inquiry.

Following the condemnation in both Houses of the Convocation the issue died down and only re-surfaced in 1869 when the Crown appointed one of the essayists, Dr. Temple, Headmaster of Rugby School, to the See of Exeter. Harold Browne, whom Palmerston had appointed to Ely in 1864, was invited to be one of the consecrators. He had serious misgivings about the matter and his clergy wrote to him that they had 'witnessed deathbeds of hopeless infidelity entirely brought on by this volume'.[112] Browne wrote to Temple asking him if he would write back 'affirming his belief in the Catholic creeds . . . the Atoning Sacrifice on the Cross, and that you do not doubt the special supernatural inspiration of the Prophets and Apostles'.[113] Temple, however, felt himself unable to accede to Browne's wishes in the matter.[114]

In summary, it is clear that Palmerston's bishops played a major role in the heated controversies which surrounded the publication of *Essays and Reviews*. Several of their number owed their promotions to their active opposition to the volume. Collectively the Palmerston appointees created a climate which generated hostility to the views expressed by the essayists and, as individuals, almost all of them publicly pronounced and wrote in condemnation of the essays in their pastoral letters and charges.

VI

Leaders of the Clergy

At the beginning of the nineteenth century bishops tended to stand aloof from their clergy. Part of the reason for this was that they had very little legal authority over their clergy. It wasn't until the passing of the Stipendiary Curates' Act of 1813 and the Consolidation Act of 1817, together with the Pluralities Act of 1838 that they achieved sufficient powers to reform clerical abuse and malpractice. Thus Frances Knight observed that in these early years 'a bishop's disciplinary powers over his clergy were more or less confined to issuing ultimations with non-residence and curates' licenses, and to dangling the prospect of the augmentations from Queen Anne's Bounty as a carrot to prevent clergy from misbehaving'.[1]

By the fifth and sixth decades when Lord Palmerston held office, episcopal influence had increased considerably, and politicians of all persuasions looked to the bishops to continue to reform the structures of the Church as well as bringing the behaviour of their diocesan incumbents into line. The Palmerstonian prelates were therefore both, aware of the needs of their clergy because of their own parochial experience, and in a better position to lead them forward as they grappled with a whole range of personal, social and economic issues.

Clerical Income

In 1867 Anthony Trollope published *The Last Chronicle of Barset,* the final volume in 'The Chronicles of Barsetshire' series. The central focus of this novel revolved around Mr. Crawley, the scholarly but poverty stricken perpetual curate of Hogglestock. On account of his very low stipend of £120 per annum he was forced to depend on the patronage of others, and in particular the wealthy Dean Arabin of Barchester Cathedral. Crawley and Arabin had been very close friends at university but life had treated them both very differently, the one reaching high ecclesiastical office and the other finding himself on the bottom rung. On account of his being constantly distracted by his impecunity, Crawley became somewhat absent-minded, to the point where he couldn't always remember where some of the money which was given to him had come from. The result of this was that Crawley came under suspicion of having stolen a cheque for twenty pounds, and was committed by the magistrates to stand trial in the County Court. Eventually it transpired that this money had in fact been given to him by Mrs. Arabin and he was freed. The book has several other sub-plots including the struggles between the high church Grantley faction and the low church Proudie following, but the focus on poverty was an apt commentary on clerical life in the 1850s and 1860s. Indeed, at the close the book Trollope wrote that 'my object has been to paint the social and not the professional lives of the clergymen'.[2]

The Carlisle diocese of the 1850s and 1860s was perfectly reflected by Trollope's portrayal of Mr. Crawley of Hogglestock. The diocese was the poorest in England and Wales. Over half the 260 incumbents received less than £100 per year, with some of the poor mountain clergy receiving stipends of only £50 per annum. When Bishop Villiers unexpectedly arrived in Troutbeck he had a strange encounter with its parish priest. He asked a shepherd if he knew where he could find the incumbent. The shepherd retorted: 'He is before you, my Lord: I am he'. The bemused bishop replied that Sewell would be better employed among his parishioners. William Sewell's response summed up the plight of the poorer clergy: 'My Lord, when you find me better remuneration, I can probably afford to lay aside assisting my neighbours; and I shall be very glad to give up salving sheep'.[3]

In his first charge to the clergy in 1858 Montagu Villiers expressed his 'very great regret' that the value of the benefices in his diocese were 'so miserably small'. 'There are', he continued, 'scarcely any livings yielding such an income as can support a clergyman without calling upon him for expenditure of his private fortune'.[4] In the same address Villiers did also tender thanks to Mr. Howard of Greystock Castle who, together with land-owners and occupiers, had spent much time in addressing the ecclesiastical commissioners on the subject of poor livings in Cumberland and Westmoreland.[5] Despite these endeavours the struggle to raise clergy incomes proved an uphill task, and by 1864 two-thirds of those whom Villiers had ordained had left the dioceses to seek for more favourable circumstances.[6]

Villiers' successor at Carlisle, Samuel Waldegrave, found the situation only marginally improved. Speaking in 1864 he bemoaned the fact that fifty-one pastors still had no home to call their own. He also drew attention to the fact that 'ninety-six benefices still fall short of £100 per annum: sixty-four exceed that sum but do not attain £150'.[7] In an effort to rectify this situation Waldegrave stated that, since 1861, £109,000 had been devoted to the work of church and parsonage building and benefice aug-mentation.[8] He said it was the aim of the diocese that 'poor benefices in public patronage will be augmented to the minimum stipend of £300 per annum'.[9] Three years later, in his visitation address of 1867, Waldegrave noted that the number of poor livings in the diocese was still little improved. 'Eighty of our ministerial charges,' he bemoaned, 'are still endowed with less than one hundred pounds per annum, and seventy-five more with less than one hundred and fifty.'[10] On his arrival in the Gloucester diocese in 1856, Charles Baring was disconcerted to find that ninety-four benefices in the diocese had no parsonage house. He also expressed his concern that 'there are 183 incumbencies in this diocese with an income not exceeding £200 per annum'.[11]

When William Thomson was translated to the archiepiscopal See of York he gave himself unstintingly in an effort to tackle the problem of clerical poverty. Shortly after his arrival in 1863, 420 livings in the diocese were found to be below £300 per annum in value and 160 yielded less than £100.[12] Thomson was deeply concerned over the matter because it prevented the clergyman from encouraging and engaging in the work which he considered should form the basis of his ministerial life.

> A clergyman cannot efficiently promote schools, or libraries, or aid the sick and suffering without setting his flock an example in the duty of giving; and therefore in such cases he has the dire alternative, either of diminishing further by activity his small income, or of allowing his poverty to overrule him into action.[13]

Thomson vowed that the campaign to augment diocesan stipends would continue until every benefice which had a population of 500 was raised to £300 per annum.[14] The main source which Thomson used in his endeavours was grants from the Ecclesiastical Commissioners. During his tenure at York they gave the diocese grants with a capital value of close on a million pounds.[15] The York Diocesan Church Building and Endowment Society also contributed £16,800 towards the endowment of livings, and by July 1889 it had raised the incumbent's income in eighty-six parishes.[16] In 1886 Thomson firmly opposed the proposal to pool benefice incomes into a common fund with a view to equalising all diocesan stipends. To do so, he felt, was to abandon one of the great strengths of the Established Church. Each incumbent was a corporation with an endowment and to forfeit it was, in his view, to abandon one of the unique strengths of the national Church.

One of the great problems which Thomson and his episcopal colleagues encountered in their endeavours to raise clerical income was the fluctuating value of the price of corn, and therefore of the income from tithes. This meant that when the country was later hit by the agricultural depression in the 1870s and 1880s many clergy suffered a fall in their income along with the farmers. The incumbent of Barnby-on-Don, for example, lost £100 in three years to one farmer. At Fishlake, also in the York diocese, the value of the living fell in 1883 from £354 to £302, but the clergyman was only able to collect £213.[17] No scheme of benefice augmentation, it seemed, was able to counteract the vicissitudes of the agricultural market in the last quarter of the nineteenth century, and the Archbishop was reduced to writing to *The Times* in 1887 and again in 1890 asking the public for subscriptions to alleviate clerical poverty.[18]

Like Thomson, Joseph Cotton Wigram found himself having to grapple with the problem of poor livings in his Rochester diocese. He found 181 benefices had an income of less than £200 per year, and 38 of those 181 had an average value of only £75 per year.[19] The basic pay of curates he found to be 'just below £100 per year with a house rarely being found'.[20] Wigram proposed to raise the level of all the poorer livings to £200 per annum.[21] He took the opportunity in his second visitation address to urge on his clergy 'the importance of proper management of church property'. In particular he was insistent that proper income should be secured from land rents. He felt that if this matter was not taken in hand it might be very difficult to rectify matters in the future.[22]

Both Harold Browne and William Jacobson also expressed their concern at the low level of clerical incomes in their respective dioceses. Browne rued the fact that many of his curates were on incomes of less than £100 a year, and Jacobson spoke of the need to augment the value of small benefices.[23] 'It is painful,' he reported 'to find that we have fifty-five so-called beneficed clergymen whose incomes are under £200 a year . . . and that the incomes of twenty-nine are below £100 a year, of whom nine have no houses provided for them.'[24] Under Jacobson's influence a *Diocesan Fund for the Augmentation of Inadequately Endowed Benefices* was started in 1870. During his episcopate £93,250 was contributed in an effort to raise the income of small livings. Jacobson himself made a yearly contribution of £100.[25]

Clerical poverty, as Trollope so well highlighted, was clearly a major issue for many mid-Victorian clergy. The diminishing value of tithe payments at the behest of the fluctuating agricultural markets was a factor in many cases, which was beyond the capacity of the church authorities to cope with. It was nevertheless apparent that the Palmerston appointees made energetic and valiant attempts to grapple with the problem. In so doing they achieved overall a measure of success.

Pastors to the clergy

The majority of the Palmerstonian bishops, as has been noted, had themselves enjoyed parochial ministerial responsibility. Most of them therefore well understood from their own experience the problems of grappling with both rural and urban inner city parishes. They made it their aim to stand alongside as well as to lead their clergy in the tasks of ministry.

Charles Longley, who saw himself very much in the role of a pastor to his pastors, devoted part of his first charge to the Diocese of Durham to a consideration of the role of the bishop as he understood it. He was adamant that, if people generally were ever going to value the episcopate, then the bishops of the church must 'endeavour to identify ourselves with our clergy'. This identification will mean that,

> we must throw hearts and minds into our dioceses, and be known
> among our flocks, as St. Paul was among his; we must strive to be

the friends, the fathers, the counsellors of the clergy . . . supporting the brethren in their parochial trials and perplexities, encouraging the timid, and arousing the lukewarm, letting as many congregations as possible in our diocese hear from time to time from
our lips the words of eternal truth, and giving the poor parent in
each parish the opportunity of seeing that besides their appointed
minister, there is the chief pastor of the diocese, who cares for the
souls of their children, and is furthering plans for their spiritual
benefit. Such, my reverend and dear brethren, is the estimate I
have of the duties and responsibilities of a Bishop.[26]

Although Longley was a moderate high churchman, his views on the
role of a bishop were shared and endorsed by most, if not all, of the
Palmerstonian appointees. Significantly Robert Bickersteth, who was sometimes referred to as 'the evangelical of the evangelicals', lived out Longley's
ideal in all the aspects of his long episcopate at Ripon. Palmerston's bishops both made themselves available to their clergy and, in addition, devoted considerable amounts of time to travelling around their dioceses
visiting and encouraging their clergy, either in their homes or through deanery meetings and retreats. Samuel Waldegrave, for example, informed his
clergy that he wished to make himself 'as accessible as possible' to them[27]
He urged them to write to him as fully and as freely as they were able and
stated that his house would always be open to them. For those clergy who
found his residence too far distant he made it his rule to be present every
Wednesday at noon, unless previous notice was given, at the home of his
secretary, Mr. Mounsey, in Castle Street, Carlisle.[28]

Among those bishops who were noted for visiting their clergy, John
Pelham of Norwich was an outstanding example. It was his custom in the
early days of his episcopate to arrive at a country parsonage on a Saturday
afternoon and spend the evening quietly with the incumbent and his family. He became a great favourite of the clergy children and displayed a
remarkable ability for remembering all about them. On Sunday morning,
if there was an early Holy Communion service he took part in it, and then
preached at the morning, afternoon and evening services. It was also his
custom to visit the Sunday school and speak to and encourage the teachers. Before leaving on Monday Pelham would inspect the day school and
have interviews with the church wardens and other officials.[29] In his charge
of 1865 Pelham spoke of his delight at 'becoming better acquainted, not
only with clergy, but with the scenes and features of their work in the
Lord'.[30] He further commented that 'It would be the desire of my heart, if
it were possible, personally to visit every parish, and to take part with
every pastor in his ministrations, both in the church and in the parish'.
Unfortunately the size of his diocese, as he went on to point out, meant
that it would take more than twenty years to make a complete tour of his
entire charge. Pelham was convinced that his involvement in parish affairs

beyond the confines of the church was an effective way of extending the Church's influence among the local population. In the six years preceding 1865, Pelham visited 354 parishes and preached and took part in the worship of 154 of them. In addition he inspected 204 schools and held 39 meetings of local clergy.[31] Charles Baring's obituarist in the *Durham County Advertiser* extolled his open-door policy to his clergy:

> He has fulfilled that important function of a bishop – the exercise of hospitality; kind and considerate to all with whom he came into contact, he was a father to the clergy, and ready to promote their plans of labour. His house was ever open to them and his hospitable table, and the memory of many a pleasant word spoken at such times has sunk into loving hearts, which will be gratefully remembered for years to come. [32]

Like Pelham, Robert Bickersteth was noted for his constant travelling about his diocese visiting, and encouraging his clergy in their ministry. It was his practice on these occasions to preach three times on a Sunday, often extemporaneously without notes. *The Christian Observer* lauded his 'clear, plain, powerful and energetic delivery of the most prominent doctrines of the gospel' which 'has fixed the attention of all classes, and attracted immense congregations, including every denomination of Dissenters, in all principal towns, and many villages which lie within his diocese'.[33] Montagu Bickersteth later wrote that his father was strongly possessed with 'the parochial instinct' and that he was never happier than when he was spending a weekend assisting an earnest clergyman in the work of his parish. Bickersteth also showed himself a ready support in times of crisis. Typical was the occasion when he went out to assist the Reverend Clement Cobb in Barnsley, following an explosion at the Oaks Colliery on 12 December 1866. He spent the entire Sunday visiting, comforting and praying with the sick and injured.[34] Robert Bickersteth became a familiar figure in every quarter of his diocese and there was apparently very little which escaped his observation.[35]

It was not only Palmerston's evangelical appointees who were diligent visitors of their clergy: both Charles Ellicott and William Jacobson, for example, were diligent in this matter. Frederick Arnold noted that, despite his constant output of scholarly writing, Ellicott was a consistent visitor of his clergy.[36] In order to keep a closer touch with clergy at the local level, Ellicott often gave several different visitation addresses at selected centres within the diocese. Jacobson was also noted for 'his concern and consideration for clergy'.[37] He took particular care over other Christian workers who laboured alongside the incumbents in the parishes.[38] During the outbreaks of cholera in Liverpool in 1866 Jacobson visited the affected areas supporting and encouraging local clergy.[39] Henry Philpott, who had less pastoral experience than any other bishop appointed by Palmerston, nevertheless demonstrated a remarkable capacity to make pastoral contact with his clergy and be aware of their individual needs.[40]

Rural Deans

At a time when suffragan bishops were few, the Palmerston bishops valued the support and advice of their archdeacons. Wigram for example 'gratefully acknowledged' the counsels of his three archdeacons in his charge of 1865.[41] Charles Longley spoke of his archdeacons as 'the eye of the Bishop in overlooking that part of the diocese committed to his care'.[42] In his visitation address in 1865 Bishop Pelham acknowledged how much 'I have been indebted, throughout the eight years of my episcopate, to the valued counsel of the three Archdeacons'. Charles Ellicott enjoyed cordial relationships with his archdeacons and met with them on a regular basis.[43] One of their number, J.W. Sheringham, who was Archdeacon of Gloucester, was a lifelong friend.[44] During his ten-year episcopate at Ely, Harold Browne sought to recast and strengthen the organisation of his diocese. He saw his own role as that of 'head and father' of his diocese, and then beneath him, as his chief lieutenants, his four archdeacons of Ely, Bedford, Huntingdon and Sudbury. Through his archdeacons he aimed to have contact with every individual parish in the diocese.

Archdeacons, however, were few in number and in large dioceses their capacity for making contact with local clergy was necessarily limited. Additionally, some archdeacons were regarded as over-bearing and as too much in league with the bishop. In an attempt to ease the burden on archdeacons and to overcome other difficulties of communication, diocesan bishops turned increasingly to the help of rural deans.

The office of rural dean had a long history stretching back to the Reformation. At the beginning of the nineteenth century, however, Exeter appeared to be the only diocese where rural deans were engaged in their customary activities of being pastorally responsible for the incumbents, churches and parsonage houses within their deaneries.[45] Rural deans had largely fallen into disuse in the late seventeenth century[46] but they re-emerged as important personnel in the Victorian Church. This revival, which became noticeable in the 1820s, was possibly encouraged by growing Parliamentary concern for the industrial heartlands in the post-Napoleonic war years. It was also stimulated by the publication in 1835 of William Dansey's *Horae Decanicae Rurales*.[47] This was a lengthy study of more than 900 pages in which Dansey supported his ideas on the functions of rural deans from works in other European countries. By the late 1830s some bishops were beginning to widen the responsibilities of rural deans. No longer were they simply required to keep a watch on their non-resident neighbours they were also charged with superintending and later inspecting National Schools. Additionally, the Church Discipline Act of 1840 assigned them a special role in the investigation and prosecution of clergy within their deaneries, a development also well-portrayed by Anthony Trollope. In his Last Chronicle of Barset Dr. Mortimer Tempest of Silverbridge Rectory was required by Bishop Proudie, as Josiah Crawley's rural dean, to set up a five man commission to examine the charges brought against him of stealing, albeit unwittingly, a cheque valued at £20.[48] As Frances Knight has shown rural deans were often much better placed, having first hand knowledge, to arbitrate in more local disputes. Being also fellow incumbents they were trusted as being more sympathetic in such matters.

By the time Lord Palmerston took office, rural deans had become the recognised instruments of pastoral care for the clergy at grass-roots level. Most of those chosen for office were incumbents who were known to be trustworthy and conscientious. Inevitably, Palmerston's bishops, some of whom had themselves been rural deans, not only valued the office, but extended and developed it as a key part of their strategy of caring for and leading their clergy.

Although the ancient office of rural dean had begun to enjoy something of a revival in a number of dioceses in the 1830s and 1840s, none were appointed in the Carlisle Diocese until January 1858, when Montagu Villiers established eighteen new rural deaneries within the two archdeaconries of Cumberland and Westmorland. As he saw it, rural deans would bring him into a closer contact and relationship with his clergy. Significantly perhaps, Villiers didn't confine his selection merely to those who shared his own churchmanship. Only three of his appointees can be positively identified as evangelicals. They were Thomas Dundas Harford Battersby, Samuel Peach Bonflower and John Dayman. Two others were high churchmen and at least four of the remaining promotions were made on the basis of long ministries within the diocese.[49] In his first charge to the clergy Villiers stated that, in arranging the work of the diocese, he had had recourse 'to that which has been found of the greatest services in other places, I mean the appointment of rural deans'.[50]

Robert Bickersteth, although known for his staunchly evangelical opinions, was, like Villiers, not governed by party politics in the choice of his rural deans. The Reverend H.D. Cust recalled a meeting of rural deans in the library of Bickersteth's palace and reflected that there were 'representatives of all parties'. Some of their number were 'the most independent spirits of the diocese, and these the selection of the bishop'.[51]

At the beginning of his episcopate in the Bristol and Gloucester Diocese, Charles Baring spoke of 'the valuable aid' received from the rural deans. Their observations eased his task of correcting 'that which is faulty and setting in order the things that are wanting'.[52] At his second Triennial Visitation Baring urged all clergy to take the trouble to regularly attend the half yearly ruri-decanal meetings. In addition to the value of the topics considered on these occasions, Baring believed the opportunities for interchange of thought and discussion amongst his clergy were of great benefit. He also went on to point out that grants to needy parishes were often made on the basis of information gathered at the rural deanery chapters.[53]

Charles Longley arrived in Durham, having found the organisation of rural deans 'a manifest advantage to the Church in my late diocese'.[54] It was no surprise, therefore, that he believed that the administration of his Durham diocese could not be satisfactorily accomplished without the establishment of rural deans in due subordination to their respective archdeacons. He regarded the rural dean as the archdeacon's 'eye' and coadjutor but also 'as a general referee to whom the Bishop may apply for local information in matters of importance within his deanery'.[55] On his translation to the archiepiscopal see of Canterbury, Longley continued to endorse the value of rural deans whom he thanked for the aid they had given him in 'helping to ascertain the state of the diocese in respect of the churches and of parsonage houses'.[56] Like Charles Baring, Longley also underlined the importance of the local rural decanal meeting. 'I sincerely hope,' he said, 'that chapters will be regularly held from time to time in each Deanery, for the discussion of subjects bearing upon the welfare of the Church.'[57]

There had been no rural deans in the Norwich Diocese for a century and a half until Bishop Stanley recreated them in 1842. In his early days in the diocese John Pelham made these officials the immediate channel for communicating with his clergy.[58] Later he extended the scope of his forty-three rural deaneries and urged his clergy to be diligent in their attendance at the half yearly meetings whose importance he considered as 'great'.[59] Pelham saw the deanery meetings as 'occasions for mutual counsel and interchange of opinion among the clergy . . . strengthening mutual co-operation in the work of the Church'.[60] Pelham held an annual meeting of all his rural deans at which they discussed diocesan strategy and the way in which he could best keep episcopal oversight of the diocese.

Archibald Tait introduced rural deans for the first time in the metropolis of his London diocese in 1861[61] and William Thomson created five new rural deaneries in the diocese of York.[62] Charles Ellicott declared that 'every diocese in the Kingdom can bear witness to the efficacy' of the ruri-decanal synod, although he feared that in the Gloucester diocese deanery resolutions 'generally do not come sufficiently to the surface'.[63] At Chester William Jacobson revived ruri-decanal action throughout his diocese[64] and in 1868 he 'heartily' thanked his rural deans for their 'great goodwill' and for 'the very important services which they have continually rendered'.[65] He regarded rural deaneries as the best places for clergy and laity to come together and consider the work of the Church.[66] Three years later, in his second visitation address, Jacobson expressed himself very gratified that nine of the Chester rural deaneries had organised conferences at which laymen and clergy met together to discuss the work of the Church.[67] In 1861 Joseph Cotton Wigram set himself the task of visiting all his fifty rural deaneries before his next triennial visitation of the diocese.[68]

Harold Browne gave a good deal of thought to the matter of rural deaneries. He found it impossible to contemplate a diocesan synod bringing his 700 clergy together with one lay representative from each parish. He therefore recognised that rural deaneries were 'much more practicable and useful'.[69] Browne felt that in this context laymen and clergy could meet twice a year and discuss practical but not doctrinal questions. The results of these conferences could then be gathered up and conveyed by one or two representatives to an annual assembly. 'The system of rural deans', he declared, 'ought to answer all the purposes of the more unwieldy Diocesan Synods.'[70] In 1864 Bishop Browne sought the opinion of all his clergy on the matter of rural deans. When he had received all the replies he convened a conference on 13th and 14th December of all rural deans together with his archdeacons. The meeting determined that ruri-decanal conferences should include all incumbents and licensed curates. Further, it resolved that rural deans should summon regular meetings consisting of the clergy, the church wardens of each parish and selected laymen up to one third of the number of parishes in the deanery.[71] One particular problem which Browne encountered was that some clergy refused to answer returns sent out by rural deans and would only communicate with the bishop directly.[72] Notwithstanding this particular difficulty, Browne, along with his Palmerstonian colleagues, remained totally committed to the value and usefulness of rural deans.

Diocesan Conferences

The mid-Victorian years witnessed a widespread growth in diocesan consciousness. Not only was this generated by a revival of the role of archdeacons and archdiaconal visitations, together with the re-establishment of rural deaneries, but it began to be focused in diocesan conferences. In 1871 George Moberly, Bishop of Salisbury, convened the first diocesan conference with a proper constitutional basis and a minimum ex officio membership.[73] Harold Browne of Ely, however, was one of the first to experiment with such gatherings. In 1864 and 1865 he held what were termed 'informal diocesan conferences'. Initially they consisted largely of clergy but in 1868 they were thrown open to the laity. Browne's conferences considered church education, the inspection of schools, parochial organisation and home and foreign missions.[74] William Thomson also worked along similar lines and first held unstructured regional conferences at Sheffield, Middlesborough and Hull in 1869, and a further one at Doncaster in October the following year. Later these conferences were held biannually. The archbishop felt that the diocesan conference was a much more effective means of promoting fellowship among the clergy and laity than their listening to a visitation charge from their chief pastor. It was also more representative of the church than the revived Convocations, as there was room for the laity to take a full part. Thomson was firmly of the opinion that attendance on their part enabled them to develop a wider interest in the Church's mission.[75]

Robert Bickersteth, who was an astute observer of the times, called together an informal diocesan conference early in 1870. There were no constitutional elections and membership was by personal invitation from himself. The gathering discussed certain important topics such as foreign missions and national education. In the years which followed, Bickersteth, together with his archdeacons and rural deans, produced a provisional constitution. Certain people were ex-officio members, a few were nominated by the bishop and the rest were elected. Although this new Ripon diocesan conference had no legislative powers it formulated decisions and framed resolutions.[76] William Jacobson also established a diocesan conference in the Chester diocese in 1870, Dean Burgon commenting that it was 'one of the earliest assemblies of the kind'.[77] At the bishop's suggestion the diocesan conference established a fund for the augmentation of impoverished benefices.[78]

The Conduct of Worship

The Palmerston bishops devoted a good deal of their visitation addresses to encouraging their clergy in the conduct of worship. Montagu Villiers, for example, was a firm advocate of two Sunday services. He was well aware of the difficulty of trying to sustain a second service in country areas where the population was small, but he insisted that 'the best mode of airing a church is keeping it well used'.[79] In 1856 he expressed his delight that there were less than sixty churches in the diocese with only one Sunday service. John Pelham also rejoiced in the diminishing number of churches in which only one Sunday service was held. He urged that the promise of 'the Lord's presence even to two or three, require and encourage the pastor to gather his flock however small their number.[80] Speaking in 1865, William Thomson rued the fact that there were still a hundred and eighteen churches in which two legally required Sunday services were not held. He trusted that these exceptions would disappear before the time of his next visitation. Charles Ellicott sought to encourage his clergy where possible to hold three services each Sunday. In 1874 he expressed his great satisfaction at the growing number of churches in the Bristol area which were now complying with his wishes.[81]

Ellicott's concern for three Sunday services reflected a growing trend among bishops in general that their clergy should place a greater value on the sacrament of Holy Communion. It is significant that, despite the ritual abuses which were surrounding the conduct of the Eucharist in some quarters in the 1860s, the Palmerston bishops, evangelicals included, continued to urge more frequent celebrations. Montagu Villiers, for example, felt the practice of holding only three or four communion services a year 'a most injurious tendency'.[82] He expressed the hope that it would be kept as a monthly ordinance.[83] Charles Baring reflected that there had been some improvement in the number of churches in the Gloucester diocese holding more frequent Holy Communion services. There was however still much room for improvement.[84] When at Durham, Charles Longley expressed his sorrow that in one third of the churches in the diocese Holy Communion was administered less than six times a year. He commended 'a minimum of once a month'.[85] Some years later, when he had moved on to Canterbury, he found himself having yet again to complain that in sixty-five churches Holy Communion services were held less than six times a year. He reminded his clergy of the benefits of the Sacrament which are 'the strengthening and refreshing of their souls'. It should not, he declared, 'be the faithful pastor's wish to stint his flock of this rich pasture'.[86]

At his visitation of 1865, John Pelham rejoiced 'to find throughout the diocese a more frequent ministration of the Lord's Supper'. In 302 churches services were held monthly and on principal festivals. In 109 churches Holy Communion was held from eight to twelve times a year and in 304 churches six to eight times. Nevertheless in 287 churches the rite was celebrated on only three occasions. Pelham's opinion was that the clergyman should 'aim at leading his flock, however gradually, to attend this blessed ordinance at least once every month and on the great festivals'.[87]

In his first charge, Robert Bickersteth complained that there were still a considerable number of churches where Holy Communion was celebrated less frequently than once a month. In each succeeding charge he both noticed a growing improvement and continued to stress the importance of frequent and regular attendance. High churchmen in the diocese of Ripon had little cause to complain that he did not give the Sacrament a prominent place in his public teaching. In his visitation address in 1861 he noted that in 306 churches Holy Communion was still held less than once a month which he described as 'a deplorable neglect of the sacred ordinance'.[88] On a later occasion he urged clergy who did not hold Holy Communion services for their people at least once a month to reconsider their practice. In his opinion such infrequency was 'to deny them a privilege which it is our duty to afford'.[89]

Bickersteth's fellow evangelical, Joseph Cotton Wigram, was also an advocate of more regular attendance at Holy Communion. Shortly after his consecration as bishop he made plain his disapproval that there were some 270 churches in the diocese in which the Sacrament was observed on less than twelve occasions. In 64 of those 270 churches the number of Holy Communion services were only four or less during the course of the year. William Thomson made it clear in an address to the York diocese that 'too many clergy are neglecting to give sufficient opportunity to their people to attend Holy Communion'.[90] Thomson spoke of the Lord's Supper as 'the holy rite which brings us close to Jesus' and regretted that there were 276 parishes where services were held less than twelve times a year.[91]

Charles Ellicott was remembered by his college obituarist as a bishop who encouraged more frequent services of Holy Communion.[92] Under his leadership there was a steady increase in the frequency with which Holy Communion services were held within the parishes under his jurisdiction. When he first took up residence in Gloucester there were only fourteen churches in the whole diocese in which Communion was administered weekly. By 1873 there were thirty-two churches in the archdeaconry of Gloucester alone in which there was a weekly celebration.[93] The evangelical, Francis Jeune, shared Ellicott's feelings in the matter. On coming to take charge of the Peterborough diocese he felt 'some anxiety' that there were 338 parishes in which the Lord's Supper was celebrated less than once a month. In 129 of these there were only four occasions in the year.[94] Although Jeune had a strong dislike of the ritualism with which second generation Tractarians surrounded the Eucharist he was adamant 'that the Holy Sacrament ought to be administered at least once a month, and at the great festivals in every church'.[95] Jeune regarded attendance at Holy Communion as sign of spiritual life. He stressed that 'he who has found peace with God by faith in the Atonement on the cross will not be slow to show forth the Lord's death, and to claim at his table the full benefits of his Passion'.[96]

Philpott and Jacobson, who were broad church and high church respectively, both shared the views of their other Palmerston colleagues. Philpott believed that every clergyman should give his parishioners an opportunity of receiving Holy Communion at least twelve times a year.[97] He was an advocate of evening Communion services and stressed that it was no law of the Church of England that attendance should be preceded by fasting.[98] William Jacobson also advocated monthly Communion as a minimum[99] and expressed his regret that some churches in his Chester diocese 'have only seven or eight administrations in the course of the year'.[100]

The Occasional Offices

It was not only on the matter of Holy Communion that Palmerston's bishops had strong views, as several of their number gave their clergy guidance as to the conduct of the occasional offices. Baptism, the rite of entry into the Christian Church, had come into prominence early in the previous decade. George Cornelius Gorham had refused to entertain the view that baptised infants were always automatically ipso facto regenerate. His diocesan Bishop, Henry Phillpotts of Exeter, had in consequence refused to institute him to the living of Brampford Speke near Exeter, and a lengthy legal battle had ensued. In Gorham's time and before, many clergy had followed the custom of baptising children privately instead of during the statutory services of Morning or Evening Prayer. The Gorham controversy had helped to focus the Church's attention on what had, like Holy Communion, become a somewhat neglected ordinance.

The Palmerstonian bishops, having themselves for most part been conscientious pastors of the people, were desirous to set matters to rights. One of their major concerns on this score was that baptism should be administered at public worship as the *Book of Common Prayer* enjoined. It seemed to them logical that if the Sacrament of Baptism was a kind of passport to Church membership it made sense to have it at times when the whole church membership was gathered for worship. Thus Charles Longley, soon after his arrival at Canterbury, expressed his displeasure that there were a hundred and twenty-six churches in the diocese in which baptism was not administered 'at the stated times when the congregation are present at the service'.[101] Longley felt strongly that to hold baptisms at times other than at Morning and Evening services was to deprive infants of the prayers of the congregation, and deny church members the opportunity of being reminded of their own Christian faith.[102]

Pelham, Bickersteth and Wigram were all also warm advocates for holding baptisms during times of public worship. Pelham was gratified to find that public baptism, 'once in such general disuse in the diocese, is more frequently adopted'.[103] He was of the opinion that if clergy took time to properly instruct their people it would not be a problem for them to accept a Baptism service once a month in the context of Morning or Evening Prayer.[104] Bickersteth observed with thankfulness that 267 out of 422 benefices held baptismal services when the whole congregation was present.[105] He reminded clergy that baptisms should be held on Sundays 'when the most number of people come together'.[106] His words did not appear to fall on good ground since in 1876 the number of benefices had increased by fifty to 472 but the number holding public Baptism services had fallen to 243.[107] Wigram indicated that public Baptisms took place in 423 churches in his Rochester diocese but not in 221.[108] 'Would that public Baptism were celebrated in all!', he declared in his charge of 1864. A public baptism was in his view 'a memento to every man . . . of the profession he is bound to carry out'.[109]

Both Ellicott and Jacobson, who were 'mild' high churchmen, favoured public Baptisms. Ellicott, speaking in 1876, was glad that 'the cases in which Holy Baptism is not administered in the face of the general congregation . . . are now comparatively few'.[110] William Jacobson recommended to his clergy that baptisms be held at the time fixed by the rubric and went on to state, probably for the benefit of his more evangelical clergy, that this was 'a wholesome regulation in the judgement of Bucer'.[111]

As the nineteenth century progressed, more and more people were living outside the pale of the Church. It increasingly happened that those who were brought for burial came as total strangers to anything Christian. The result of this was that many clergy felt profoundly unhappy about the wording of the Prayer Book Funeral service. Several of the Palmerston bishops not only shared their clergy's disquiet over the matter, but advocated changes in the wording. Charles Longley saw clearly the problem of pronouncing a heavenly certainty over the corpse of an unbelieving, unbaptised person. Nevertheless his view was that, unless the minister was sure the party died a hardened sinner, he should not grudge to a departed brother 'the expression of hope, however faint it may be, that he will be accepted through the mercy of his heavenly Father, and the merits of his Saviour'.[112] Longley expressed himself happy to go along with those who wanted to make 'reasonable change' to the liturgy, but he warned against those who sought to 'obliterate all traces of dogmatic Christianity from our formularies'.[113]

Charles Baring received requests every year from Gloucester clergy to alter or omit passages from the Burial service.[114] He regretted that he had no power to sanction change to even one or two expressions. Baring felt that what was wanted was an additional rubric 'enabling the officiating minister under exceptional circumstances, with the written sanction in each case of the bishop, to omit the expressions to which objection is taken'.[115] Such a move, he contended, would offend no real friend of the church and would go a long way towards assuaging those who were urging for revision.[116] Archibald Tait took an altogether different view of the legality of minor changes to the liturgy. He declared 'that a clergyman may, even now, omit any part of the services including the much discussed clauses in the order for burial or baptism for example, with the sanction of the bishop'.[117] *The Christian Observer,* commenting on his opinion believed that it would be found to be correct.[118]

Although several of the bishops appointed by Lord Palmerston were prepared to make minor concessions to the form of words, particularly in the Burial service, they were united in opposing any kind of full revision of the liturgy.[119] To most of them such a move was to open a can of worms which would raise fundamental doctrinal issues which might well pull the Church apart. Longley praised the Reformers for their 'enlightened and comprehensive spirit' which resulted in 'the surpassing excellence of our present liturgy'.[120] He considered the Prayer Book not only to be a precious aid for personal devotion but 'a bulwark against the in-roads of error'.[121]

Robert Bickersteth shared Longley's judgements on the matter and deprecated any attempts to revise or alter the *Book of Common Prayer.*[122] He was more than ready to concede that it contained words which needed altering, but he was adamant that any major scheme for change would bring 'great danger to the peace and unity of the Church'.[123] Bickersteth gave his full support to the 10,000 clergymen who had signed a petition against Prayer Book revision in 1860.[124] Charles Ellicott delivered an address in 1874 at Cirencester Parish Church under the title of 'Revision of the Rubrics'. His view was that the proposed revision in 1875 would open up too much controversy. He felt it would be wise to alter as little as possible, and spoke of the Prayer Book as 'the bond of wisdom as well as of peace, – that keeps us all together'.[125]

Confirmation

At the beginning of the nineteenth century there was a bad tradition surrounding many Confirmation services. Candidates were for the most part ill-prepared and the services, which were often irrelevant, were frequently followed by riotous festivities. When Vernon Harcourt,who was Archbishop of York for forty years from 1801 to 1847, appeared in the Minster to confirm, the vergers would shout above the noise and talking, 'Silence for the Archbishop', whereupon his Grace would ascend the pulpit. When the time came for the actual Confirmation prayer, he would lift up his hands over the entire congregation and invoke the Holy Spirit upon them. Such a procedure did not engender reverence and it also left people confused as to who had been Confirmed and who had not![126]

For much of the nineteenth century dioceses were still large and travel difficult, particularly in the winter months. Bishops were also often away from their people for long periods when there were debates in the House of Lords or other business to be attended to in London. All this meant that the number of occasions when bishops were available to hold Confirmations were limited. The custom which many of them continued to follow therefore, was to hold area services in the larger market towns with local clergy from a wide area bringing their candidates in. Thus in 1829, for example, Bishop Kaye of Lincoln confirmed 1,090 candidates at one service in Bedford.[127] Dr. Corrie, Master of Jesus College, Cambridge from 1849-1885, remembered having been Confirmed in Grantham church with 7,000 to 8,000 other candidates. He recalled 'a scene of indescribable confusion with oranges being sold in the church and public houses being ready for them before they came out'.[128]

There were other problems associated with the rite of Confirmation. In rural areas in particular, people had superstitious views about it and believed it to be an insurance against demonic ills and a cure for certain diseases.[129] For many, Confirmation was a means by which they marked their passing from childhood into the beginning of adulthood. Large numbers who were Confirmed never made their first Communion on the Sunday following, and thereafter attended church only for the great festivals. A further problem was that Confirmations were often attended by treats, special teas and other festivities. After a Confirmation service at the Alford village of Lincolnshire in 1837 it was reported that many of the people went straight from the church to the public houses, where the attractions included 'lewd women' and dancing, as well as drink.[130] In an effort to restore law and order the clergy were instructed to call for the assistance of constables.[131] There were similar episodes at Lincoln and Louth three years later, where many of the newly Confirmed of both sexes, streamed into the public houses and the day ended with displays of drunk and disorderly behaviour.[132] In rural areas in particular, young labourers moved a good deal, looking for new situations or seeking employment at the annual hiring fairs. Numbers of them who were attracted by the prospect of another feast were Confirmed on more than one occasion, notwithstanding the strictures of their local clergy. Confirmation, it seems, remained popular in the first half of the nineteenth century, and many young people were prepared to walk long distances to receive the laying on of the bishop's hands.[133]

Lord Palmerston's episcopal appointees, along with others on the Bench, wanted to reform the rite in such a way that the candidates not only had a faith to confirm but continued in it. Charles Baring was concerned that some Confirmation services in Gloucester diocese had been 'productive of much levity, if not serious mischief'.[134] He regretted that 'the frivolous' regarded confirmation as a 'holiday' and a 'season of dissipation'. He also urged clergy to provide food in some private house before the service 'so that the young should have no necessity or excuse for entering a public house'. Baring's strategy for grappling with these ills was to hold services where possible on Sundays, so that parents and sponsors could attend and doubtless exercise a restraining hand where necessary. His policy was to hold more frequent local Confirmations, which prevented larger numbers of candidates who might cause a public nuisance by coming together in some central market town.[135] At Durham Baring held 671 confirmation services in which he confirmed 45,397 females and 30,307 males.[136]

Most of the Palmerstonian bishops impressed on their clergy the need for adequate preparation of those who they presented for Confirmation. Villiers believed it was better for clergy to refuse candidates than to present them unprepared to the bishop.[137] Charles Longley spoke of confirmation as 'the most deeply interesting office in which I your bishop can be engaged'.[138] He urged clergy to take particular care in their preparation of candidates because Confirmation is often the time of 'their true conversion to God'.[139] Like Baring, Longley announced his intention to hold more frequent confirmations; 'biennially in the larger towns of the diocese, and triennially in all other places.'[140] John Pelham also increased the number of Confirmations, which he held at one hundred selected points within the diocese. This strategy meant that no parish church was more than three miles walk from one of the chosen parishes.[141]

Robert Bickersteth took a great deal of time and trouble with his Confirmations. It was his practice to visit the remoter parts of his diocese on alternate years and when he did so he usually combined it with a holiday. His son, Montagu Bickersteth, recalled that he would often leave home in his own carriage, accompanied by his wife and one or two children, and travel up through the Dales enjoying the hospitality of many friends along the way.[142] Bickersteth was a stickler for punctuality, and on one occasion when he missed his train he reached the service on time by travelling on the engine of a goods train. Bickersteth stressed to clergy 'the precious opportunity which the preparation of candidates affords for exercising a wholesome influence upon the youthful members of your flock'.[143]

William Thomson soon began to improve matters in the York Diocese. The custom of serving sherry and cakes in the vestry after Confirmation services disappeared,[144] and the Archbishop forbade the girls to wear anything that might distract attention, particularly that of the young men.[145] Referring to the instruction of candidates Thomson urged his clergy, 'Oh be very zealous in the blessed work of preparing them!'[146] Thomson held Confirmations every year in the large centres of Sheffield, Hull, York, Scarborough and Middlesborough. In the smaller towns such as Doncaster and Whitby, Confirmations took place every second year, and in rural areas every third year.[147]

Harold Browne made Confirmation a priority during both of his episcopates, at Ely and at Winchester. He urged his clergy that Confirmation presented 'the most blessed opportunity' of appealing to the hearts and consciences of the young. It was his view that there should always be something akin to a Confirmation class in every parish. He also urged all incumbents, at some point before the service to speak in private to each candidate about their faith, and to ensure that they took Holy Communion on the first Sunday following the Confirmation.[148] Browne's neighbouring bishop, Francis Jeune of Peterborough, informed his clergy that he was making greater use of the railways in order to increase the number of Confirmations being held in the diocese.[149] William Jacobson similarly expressed a willingness 'to be ready to minister Confirmation in every year in all the more populous places, and wherever else it may, with good reason be desired'.[150] Jacobson also advocated that clergy always have some ongoing course of systematic instruction available for those who wished to be Confirmed.

Most of the bishops Lord Palmerston appointed were insistent that fifteen was the minimum age at which young people should be Confirmed. Longley wanted clergy to stick rigidly to this rule[151] as did Bickersteth, Pelham and Jacobson, the latter drawing support from Archbishop Grindal's sixteenth-century injunctions.[152]

In the early decades of the nineteenth century, as has been observed, Confirmations were often infrequent occasions, and the level of preparation of the candidates either inadequate or totally lacking.[153] The Palmerston appointees made sterling endeavours to increase the number of occasions on which they administered Confirmation, and for the most part they were successful in raising the number of candidates in their dioceses. John

Pelham Confirmed 33,700 men and women between 1858 and 1867, although he did not mark any great rise in the number being Confirmed.[154] Robert Bickersteth reported that he had Confirmed 3,753 candidates during the first year of his episcopate.[155] In the three following years the average number of candidates was 3,900, although Bickersteth reported that 'the number of persons who have been Confirmed during the last three years in this diocese is very much below what it ought to be'.[156] By 1883 Bickersteth had greatly improved the situation. In that year 10,781 individuals were Confirmed in 63 centres. This represented an increase of nearly 200 per cent, against a population rise of only 50 per cent.[157] William Thomson, who had done much to ensure his clergy improved their preparation, saw a steady increase in the number of those coming forward for Confirmation. During his episcopate nearly 200,000 people were confirmed which was proportionately twice the average that had been reached before 1863. The total for the three years ending in 1865 was 4,651, whereas the three year period ending in 1889 saw an increase to 8,958.[158]

Harold Browne was able to report that he had held twice as many Confirmations in his first year at Winchester than his predecessor Samuel Wilberforce had achieved in his first year in the See.[159] Frances Jeune stated that he had Confirmed some 18,304 people of both sexes and all ages in the three year period from July 1864 to July 1867. William Jacobson saw a dramatic upturn in the number of Confirmations in his Chester diocese in 1871, when he extended the number of locations from 29 in the previous year to 94.[160] Henry Philpott on the other hand did experience a decline in the number of his candidates. He reported 17,510 confirmees in the three years preceding his visitation of 1874, as compared with 20,180 in the three prior to his 1871 visitation.

Advice on Preaching

The weakness of nineteenth-century Anglicanism, Mark Pattison maintained, was in the pulpit. Benjamin Jowett, one of the contributors to *Essays and Reviews,* also deplored the poor quality of Church of England sermons. Preaching, as he understood it, was an art that required careful study and instruction. At a time when theological colleges were in their early stages there was little or no opportunity for clergy to improve their preaching. Jowett once sardonically recounted a University sermon on the clergy's lack of education which was best illustrated by the sermon itself! It was a 'wretched performance; no reason or meaning in it; very trivial and childish in parts'.[161] Against this background, the Palmerstonian bishops issued an abundance of advice and guidance to their clergy on the preparation and delivery of their sermons. Several of their number were themselves preachers of considerable ability, who had drawn large crowds during their earlier parochial ministries. Villiers, for example, had demonstrated a real ability to make the Christian message resonate for the working classes during his time at St. George's, Bloomsbury. He apparently 'always preached extempore'. George Moore, a Cumbrian-based evangelical philanthropist, observed that 'his powers of preaching are great'. Not surprisingly, Villiers was soon in demand outside his diocese. In May 1857 he preached at one of the special services at Exeter Hall, and in 1859 addressed a special congregation of the working classes on his favourite theme 'The Coming of the Lord'.[162] Bickersteth had packed his church in Clapham Rise to the doors, and William Thomson had drawn a large following of the more fashionable Londoners during his short spell at All Souls, Langham Place. Bishop Ellicott was also renowned as 'an excellent preacher'[163] and Archibald Tait, who took part in the Exeter Hall services for the working classes, proved also to be a capable open-air speaker.

The bishops appointed by Lord Palmerston had a variety of practical advice to give to their clergy about preaching. Villiers urged that they would 'preach more usefully' if they visited their people and kept in touch with what was happening in their lives.[164] Charles Baring was particularly concerned that many of his clergy were not able to gain the attention of 'the less educated portion of their flock'. He counselled them not to shrink from the use of common every day expressions or homely illustrations. Too many incumbents, in his view, feared criticisms of simplicity from the families in the great pew. He advocated careful study and preparation to be followed by writing out the words in longhand. Then, if possible, the sermon should be committed to memory.[165] Samuel Waldegrave counselled the clergy of Carlisle to preach simply and scripturally and to give time to their preparation.[166] William Thomson was adamant that a sermon 'should abound with life, love, instruction and practical advice'.[167]

Harold Browne reminded his clergy on one occasion that five million people in the country were living in neglect of the Church and its Sacraments. This, in his opinion, meant that there was insufficient active proclamation of the Gospel.[168] His general advice to preachers was to take a passage, expound it, and then deduce practical lessons from it.[169] He was also adamant that clergy have committed to them 'the ministry of reconciliation; and its message that "God was in Christ reconciling the world unto Himself, and not imputing their trespasses unto them"'.[170] A number of other Palmerston bishops shared Browne's insistence on an unequivocal declaration of the Gospel message. Montagu Villiers urged that the foundation of all preaching must be 'Christ and Him crucified'. He was insistent that only that which exalts Christ will produce conversions.[171]

Robert Bickersteth achieved a reputation for being a 'preaching prelate'. He was chosen as University Preacher in 1857 and his sermon made a profound impression on his audience, who listened with rapt attention.[172] Evangelism was always on his heart and he assisted on two occasions in 1875 and 1883 in town wide missions to Leeds. In 1875 he delivered addresses in factories and warehouses every day, over a week and a half period.[173] He was adamant that no sermon was worthy of the name 'which did not contain the message of the Gospel urging the sinner to be reconciled with God'.[174]

Archbishop William Thomson took part in three Sheffield missions which were held in 1872, 1876 and 1883. One of his biographers suggested that, in his capacity to mingle with all classes of people and preach so effectively to them, he was probably unique among the members of the Bench of Bishops.[175] In the mission of 1876 it was estimated that he delivered over twenty-five addresses to 25,000 people.[176] Although Charles Ellicott did not share all of Thomson's evangelical convictions, he nevertheless urged Gloucestershire clergy to 'preach the blessed and salutary doctrine that Christ Jesus came into the world to save sinners'.[177]

Palmerston's bishops were well aware that for preaching to be effective it was necessary that it should be reinforced by godly Christian living. Several among them were ready to make this point quite strongly. Pelham, for example, emphasised that clergy must be 'men of holiness'. 'Our lives', he declared in his charge of 1865 'must savour of that Christ whom in our pulpits we preach'.[178] He pleaded the importance of prayer asserting its 'inseparable connection' with ministerial usefulness.[179] Robert Bickersteth, who is reckoned to be the first bishop to have held a retreat for his clergy, stressed the need for that 'sacred character which befits sacred office'.[180] Twelve years later he again emphasised 'the absolute necessity' of personal holiness on the part of his clergy. Noting the business and the restlessness of the age, he was adamant 'as to the necessity of time for prayer and meditation in God's word'.[181]

Henry Philpott concluded his charge of 1874 by reminding his reverend brethren to give diligence to prayers and the reading of Scripture.[182] William Thomson ended his charge of 1865 by praying that his clergy would lead consecrated holy lives. Harold Browne urged that in the many commitments of a pastor's life, prayer must be kept as a necessity.[183] Joseph Cotton Wigram enjoined the need for people from all walks of life to make family prayer a top priority among domestic duties.[184] In 1863 he produced a slender volume entitled *The Cottager's Family Prayers*.[185] It contained simple short prayers for each day of the month related to a theme such as 'Peace in Believing', 'The Family of Christ' and 'Self denial'.[186]

Support for Missions

The 1850s and 1860s were a period in which societies for promoting missionary activity both at home and abroad were reaching a high point. As Peter Williams has pointed out, the second half of the nineteenth century was to see 'a phenomenal growth in missionary commitment', with the numbers of missionaries increasing dramatically.[187] The growing concern for the lost, both within the nation and beyond, was reflected in the bishops' concern that the incumbents of their dioceses should be active promoters of missionary societies.

Of all the evangelistic agencies the Church Missionary Society was the most popular with the bishops appointed by Palmerston. Among others, they endorsed the work of The Society for the Propagation of the Gospel and Church Pastoral Aid Society. Montagu Villiers commended to each incumbent the idea of doing something annually for the cause of the Gospel at home and abroad. Overseas he commended The Society for the Propagation of the Gospel, The Church's Mission to the Jews and The Irish Church Mission. At home he advocated The Church Pastoral Aid Society and The Diocesan Scripture Readers Association.[188] In 1857 Charles Longley urged the clergy of Durham to preach at least two sermons a year in support of both home and overseas missions.[189] In his later years at Canterbury he continued to urge incumbents to devote at least one sermon a year to the cause of Church of England Missions.[190]

Archibald Tait first became interested in missions in 1841 while he was still a tutor at Balliol College. Together with three other colleagues he founded a small society, the members of which read fortnightly papers on missionary topics. Tait spoke at the C.M.S. Annual General Meeting in 1857 and in the same year founded a Diocesan Home Mission.[191] John Pelham hailed the increased giving to mission societies in his Norwich Diocese, from £13,000 in 1857 to £16,000 in 1865, as a token of growing spiritual life.[192] He nevertheless bemoaned the fact that 'there are still so many churches and parishes in which no regular collection is made either for home or foreign purposes'.[193] Both Bickersteth and Waldegrave were warm supporters of C.M.S. and C.P.A.S.. Bickersteth reported the total missionary giving from the Ripon diocese in the three years prior to 1867: C.M.S. received £12,305 and S.P.G.received £8,849, while C.P.A.S. with £5,240 was the first among the home societies.[194] Samuel Waldegrave, in his first visitation to the Carlisle Diocese, expressed his warm confidence in the C.P.A.S. and in both C.M.S. and S.P.G. Whilst he was delighted that 116 churches had devoted sermons to the support of C.M.S., and a further 57 to S.P.G., he was concerned that 94 parishes had shown no public commitment to mission.[195] Joseph Cotton Wigram issued an annual appeal to the churches of his Rochester Diocese for support for home and foreign missions. He customarily selected one or two societies and requested that sermons be preached in parishes on their behalf, and collections made between Easter and Trinity Sunday.[196]

In the early part of the nineteenth century there had been strong calls to the Episcopal Bench on the part of politicians to reform the Established Church. Such demands seemed only reasonable, since bishops were after all peers of the realm. Vigorous steps were taken to facilitate improvements, particularly with the establishment of the Ecclesiastical Commission in 1836. For many clergy, however, the steadily increasing power of the bishops which followed in its wake was not something they welcomed. Indeed the majority both resented it and were suspicious of it. By the 1850s, with the revival of rural deans and the greater use of archdeacons, some of the earlier distrust had been dissipated, although there were still many doubters who perceived archdeacons and rural deans as agents of the bishops.

As a group of fifteen English prelates appointed by Lord Palmerston they were strongly influenced by evangelical convictions or Whig political opinions. Inevitably therefore, as has been observed, they were set to reform the work and structures of their dioceses. In so doing they set a new tone. They gave themselves to visiting, meeting, teaching and encouraging their clergy. Bishops such as Villiers, Pelham, Bickersteth and Thomson in particular, spent much of their time helping clergy in their mission and evangelistic work. Men of the calibre of Archibald Tait didn't merely commend the usefulness of open air meetings, they preached in factories and street corners themselves. Palmerston's appointees were also able administrators, who emerged as figureheads who were widely known and respected in their dioceses. Collectively the Palmerston bishops represent a significant step forward in the character of English episcopacy. Here were bishops who pastored their clergy, who worked with them and who sought to raise their incomes along with their educational and spiritual attainments. In their leadership of the clergy there can be little doubt but that Palmerston's bishops established new emphasis in pastoral care and initiated new ways of organising, supporting and facilitating their ministry.

VII

Conservative and Reformed Theologians

In the early years of the nineteenth century most Church of England members happily accepted the orthodox creedal faith. Clergy subscribed in good conscience to the Thirty Nine Articles of Religion and were glad to accept the doctrines enshrined in the liturgies of the *Book of Common Prayer.* In particular they were more than happy to endorse Article 6 which asserted the 'sufficiency' of Holy Scripture and that the canonical books of the Old and New Testaments 'contained all things necessary for salvation'. Few questioned the assertion of the articles that 'the Bible is God's Word'.

Early nineteenth-century Christians held a view of the scriptures that had been taken over from the Greek thought of the early catholic church and had been further reinforced by the Reformation. They thought of God literally breathing the Scripture into the writers of the biblical documents. The result of this was that the Bible was held to speak authoritatively on all matters, whether they related to man's relationship to God or the scientific origins of the universe. The ordinary Christian man and woman at the beginning of Queen Victoria's reign regarded the Christian religion as an historical religion. It concerned the story of God's historical acts in relation to his people. It was therefore understandable that the story of the Creation and the Fall should have been accepted as describing an historical event. Indeed Archbishop James Ussher's calculation that the world was created in 4004 BC was printed in the margin of the Authorised Version Bibles which came off the university presses right up to the beginning of the nineteenth century.

Throughout the Victorian era a number of influences and movements combined to send a series of shock waves through traditional Anglican theology. In 1833 John Keble's celebrated 'Assize Sermon' condemned the 'National Apostasy'. Parliament and the nation had turned their backs on the National Church. What was needed was a stronger ecclesiology which would call people to a new respect for the Established Church. Keble, and the other early leaders of what became known as the Oxford Movement, began to teach that the Church of England was a 'divine Society' because it could trace its origins all the way back to St. Peter and apostolic roots. This apostolicity, according to John Henry Newman, was passed down from the apostles who appointed the first bishops, who in turn laid their hands on their episcopal successors and so on down to the

1830s. The Church, instead of being seen as 'the faithful company of Christ's people', came to be regarded in much more ethereal and institutional terms. It was 'the mystical body of Christ' which conveyed saving grace through its episcopally validated sacramental system. Tractarians claimed that men were joined to 'Christ by being joined to His Church'.[1]

This idea that the Church of England was a branch of the catholic church brought in its wake doctrines which, as they developed, began to run counter to the Reformation theology enshrined in the Articles of Religion and the *Book of Common Prayer*. The most notable of these were that the Church of England priest had a mediatorial and sacerdotal function, and that the episcopate was essential for the *esse* of the Church. Indeed, Newman declared that every bishop of the Church whom we behold is 'a lineal descendant of St. Peter and St. Paul after the order of a spiritual birth'.[2]

A concomitant of Tractarian teaching about the nature of the church and ministry was a growing conviction that righteousness was not merely imparted to the believer on account of his or her faith in Christ, but also given and infused through the sacraments and the life of obedience. From the 1840s onwards numbers of the Oxford men began to return to the medieval notion that Justification was a lifelong process maintained and nurtured by good works. Inevitably such teaching provoked hostility on the part of the majority of the bishops and guardians of the Church.

Running in parallel with these developments in ecclesiological doctrine a number of other factors combined to undermine people's faith in the reliability and inspiration of the Bible. Essentially this challenge emanated from two sources: scientific discoveries and the new discipline of Biblical criticism. The work of Charles Darwin and other scientists such as the geologist, Charles Lyell, posed a number of serious questions to biblical literalism. It seemed clear for example, that the earth's crust had evolved over a very long period of time and certainly many aeons before 4004 BC. Findings also demonstrated that marine life was likely to have preceded land vegetation, and Darwin's theory of 'natural selection' showed there was a close relationship between species, and that modification occurred and could be transmitted to succeeding generations. Part of Darwin's theory of evolution involved the extinction of some species and the survival of others. If species were designed in such a way that they had either become extinct or had been considerably modified from their prototype, this did not appear to demonstrate strong evidence for a faultless original design on the part of a perfect all-knowing, all-wise designer.

At the same time as scientific discovery was presenting these challenges to the Christian faith, assaults on traditional beliefs were also coming, not from unbelievers but from the theologians themselves, in the form of the newly emerging science biblical criticism. The heartland of this new discipline was among the German universities, which had many more chairs of divinity than their English counterparts. The chief threat of the critics was their contention that the biblical books of both the Old and New Testaments were overlain with mythical embellishments. This meant, in their view, that it was virtually impossible to separate fact from fiction. Thus, when attempts were made to study the gospels, it was virtually impossible to construct an accurate historical picture of Jesus. Albert Eichorn, for example, maintained that 'only a slender thread' of that primitive Gospel believed by the apostles ran through the first gospels. In 1846 George Elliot translated David Frederick Strauss's *Life of Jesus* into English. Strauss claimed that the task of producing an accurate historical biography of Jesus was beyond the bounds of possibility. The miracles of the Virgin Birth, Resurrection and the Ascension of Christ were, in his view, of little historical significance.

Many of these assaults on Christian orthodoxy found their focus during Lord Palmerston's premiership. In 1859 Charles Darwin published his celebrated volume *Origin of Species,* in which he set out the first full scientifically researched theory of evolution. Darwin's writing brought a challenge to the status of man. Although he was reluctant to speculate on the matter in this first work, he gave explicit argument to support the evolution of the human race in his later volume, *The Descent of Man,* which was published in 1871. His works raised serious questions about the uniqueness of man and tended to minimise the extent of the Fall. Clearly, if humanity merely evolved from a community of descent which included the monkey in particular, the traditional doctrine of the Fall was undermined. On this understanding men and women never were in a state of perfection from which a first human pair could have turned away.

Darwin's *Origin of Species* was followed in the very next year by *Essays and Reviews*, an all Anglican collection of scholarly articles, which embraced the findings of both geologists and biblical critics. As has been noted,[3] the individual contributions of the seven essayists varied in their degree of offensiveness. Matters then reached a much greater pitch in 1861 when John William Colenso, the colonial Bishop of Natal, questioned the historicity of much of the early books of the Old and New Testaments, and went on to deny some of the fundamental Christian doctrines which were endorsed by the *Book of Common Prayer.*[4]

The bishops whom Lord Palmerston appointed during his two ministries came from a variety of churchmanships and theological backgrounds, yet they proved themselves to a man to be bulwarks of orthodoxy. Not only did they take their stand on the inspiration and sufficiency of Scripture, they championed the doctrine of the Protestant Reformers in their teaching of Justification, the Atonement and the Church, Ministry and Sacraments.

Biblical and Creedal Orthodoxy

The bishops Palmerston appointed were deeply concerned lest the faith of their clergy was being undermined by the liberal biblical critics of mid-Victorian England. Most of them devoted a considerable amount of pen and ink to rebutting what they saw as dangerous and threatening views. In their diocesan charges in particular, they set out arguments in support of the inspiration and infallibility of Scripture. In his visitation address in 1861, Robert Bickersteth urged his clergy to uphold the doctrine of inspiration. 'Show,' he urged, 'in what sense you regard the Bible to be an inspired record; not because you take it to be the production of men of brilliant genius, but because you believe it to have been written by men who spoke as they were moved by the Holy Spirit.'[5] The bishop went on to draw a distinction between a mere human production on the one hand, and a divine on the other. Only in the case of the latter 'can you hear the voice of the ever-living Jehovah.'[6] Having once established the point that the Bible is divinely inspired, Bickersteth vehemently defended the accuracy of biblical history. His opinion was that once this authority and reliablity of Scripture is denied, basic faith and doctrine are undermined.[7] The writer who penned the narrative was also the person whom the Spirit employed to unfold key doctrines. If the biblical writer ignorantly or wilfully recorded, as true, occurrences which never took place, he is not entitled to belief when he speaks of doctrine.[8] Bickersteth went on to argue for the Divine Inspiration of Scripture on the grounds that its many books, form a coherent whole with one idea pervading the entire volume from Genesis to Revelation.[9] He was deeply concerned at the liberal outpourings of the early 1860s and 'implored' his clergy to teach their people 'that the whole Bible is the infallible record of the mind and will of God, conveyed by direct inspiration to holy men of old who spake by the Holy Spirit'.[10] Bickersteth warned against setting up human reason as a divinity against the Divine mind expressed in Scripture. He was adamant and unequivocal.

> The Bible, like its author, is pure and unchangeable truth – truth without admixture or error – truth, which is now what it ever was, and ever shall be – truth which is fitted to enlighten the understanding, correct the judgement, sanctify the heart, and save the soul.[11]

Samuel Waldegrave of Carlisle was, like Bickersteth, very impressed with the coherence of Scripture as an argument for its inspiration.[12] He referred to the Bible's sixty-six separate documents, at one period in Chaldee, at another in Hebrew and at a third in Greek. He then reminded his hearers of the differing genres of biblical literature: notably psalm, proverb, prophecy and gospel, written by a variety of men at separate points in time and from diverse cultural backgrounds, yet 'all revealing the mind and purpose of the Triune Jehovah'.[13] Waldegrave was also adamant as to

Scripture's 'infallible pages'. In a sermon on the nature of the Christian ministry, he urged his hearers not to look for authority to the early Church fathers of the undivided early catholic Church, or even to the fathers of the Reformation. He was emphatic, that there could be only one sure basis, namely 'what saith the Lord'.[14]

Henry Philpott, who came to the See of Worcester as a recognised member of the broad church school, nevertheless adopted a thoroughly conservative stance in response to the controversy which followed the publication of *Essays and Reviews*. He was very ready to underline the fact that 'our authorised formularies express a clear judgement that the whole Bible is the word of God'.[15] Although, in contrast to Bickersteth and Waldegrave, Philpott displayed a certain reticence to express his own views, he did remind his clergy of Hooker's doctrine that Scripture is sufficient provided it is used for its appointed purpose.[16]

Both William Thomson and Charles Ellicott, who had written in defence of biblical inspiration in *Aids to Faith*, did much to encourage the study of the Bible. When Thomson was Provost of Queen's College, Oxford, he persuaded the university authorities that a certain level of biblical knowledge should be taken into consideration in the final honours examination.[17] While Ellicott was incumbent of the country living of Pilton in Rutland he began a series of commentaries which were both scholarly and devotional. His commentary on Galatians came out in 1854 and those on Ephesians, the pastoral epistles, Philippians, Colossians and Philemon, and Thessalonians, followed successively in 1855, 1856, 1857 and 1858. All reached four editions. Until Bishop Lightfoot's commentaries began to appear in the later years of the century, Ellicott's commentaries were recognised as the best in the English language, and they were widely read. Ellicott wrote in 1873 of the vital need for 'plain dogmatic truth, as resting on Scripture' to be proclaimed from the Church's pulpits. In another address given at the re-opening of Holy Trinity Church, Clifton on 8 January 1874, he again referred to the dangerous current tendency 'to set aside the scriptures as an ultimate authority'.[18] His view was that ultimately this would lead to the denial of the personality of God.[19]

In November 1891 Ellicott published a volume entitled *Christus Comprobatur or The Testimony of Christ to the Old Testament* in which he maintained the trustworthiness of the historical events recounted in its pages. He was not impressed by the work of liberal biblical critics, who assumed that most of the Old Testament history books had been remodelled and generally tampered with by a mysterious priestly source designated 'P'.[20] His contention was that Jesus' endorsement of biblical authorship and events was a sufficient guarantee of their veracity.[21]

Ellicott devoted the greater part of his life to the study of the Bible, and chaired the committee which Convocation appointed to produce a Revised Version of the Bible. He regarded this as the great work of his life and termed the work of revision as 'the greatest spiritual movement that has taken place since the Reformation'.[22] In total, 407 meetings of the Revision Committee were held in Jerusalem Chamber of which Ellicott attended 405. As chairman it fell to him to present to Convocation the New Testament in 1881, the Apocrypha in 1896 and the references in 1899.[23]

Significantly, another of Palmerston's appointees, Harold Browne, chaired the panel which revised the Old Testament. Although he was concerned that the work took him away from his diocese rather too much, his mastery of Hebrew made his presence a necessity.[24] His group worked together for fourteen years and held eighty-five sessions, most of which lasted for nine days.[25]

In his visitation address of 1867, Francis Jeune spoke of his concern regarding those who 'don't believe in the inspiration of Scripture any more than Luther, Bacon or Shakespeare were inspired and they don't believe the Resurrection or Ascension to be historical facts'.[26] Such individuals, he maintained treated the Bible in the way that they treated any other book.[27] Jeune was equally scathing towards those who argued for the interpretation of Scripture by the Church, or by the conciliar infallibility of the Pope. Nothing in the Bible, he maintained, suggested the infallibility of any assemblage of men or the infallibility of the successor of Peter.[28] In his earlier years as Master of Pembroke College, Jeune had reminded members that the Established Church with which the university was so intimately linked 'rests on Scripture'.[29] He advocated the teaching of every science as vitally important for the development of students. Significantly he went on to make the following declaration:

> Our object is primarily to form Christians and to train ministers of religion. The word of truth and the learning which more particularly qualifies men rightly to divide it, must be the greater staple of our teaching.[30]

With Newman's departure to the Church of Rome still fresh in everyone's minds, Jeune underlined the crucial importance in matters of controversy of 'appeal to the word of God as interpreted by reason and sound criticism'.[31]

Significantly, both the high church Charles Longley and Henry Philpott shared the stance of the evangelical Palmerston bishops in the matter of scriptural authority. Longley reminded the clergy and laity of his Canterbury diocese that St. Paul had endorsed the Old Testament as 'given by inspiration of God' and that the church declared that 'God has caused all Holy Scripture to be written for our learning'.[32] Longley was a firm advocate of the Bible as a basis of spirituality. It was for him a solace in times of sickness, a source of strength in moments of temptation, a guide and comfort in daily living and a means of support in the hour of death. He urged all clergymen to hand on the scriptures 'as the word of God'[33] and to regard it as 'our only infallible authority concerning matters of faith and practice'.[34]

Speaking against the background of doubt engendered by liberal theologians, Philpott was clear that the Church of England formularies judged 'the whole Bible to be the word of God'.[35] He reminded his readers of Hooker's doctrine of the 'sufficiency of Scripture' but stressed that no infallible information was given in things for which the scripture was not intended.[36] Philpott expressed himself grateful for the work of biblical scholars who scrutinised the text and meaning of scripture. He urged all clergy to make themselves acquainted as much as possible with the results of their inquiries, in order to be able to 'minister the real meaning of what our blessed Lord has caused to be written for our learning'.[37]

Arising out of their understanding and interpretation of Scripture, several of Palmerston's evangelical bishops had a strong notion of God intervening both in the events of their diocese and in the affairs of the nation. Samuel Waldegrave, for example, preached a sermon entitled *The Cattle Plague a Warning Voice to Britain from the King of Nations*.[38] In it he observed that the counties which made up his diocese were more seriously affected than many parts of England. He urged every clergyman to give a day to pray and fast in view of the crisis. Waldegrave based his homily on two texts from the book of Jonah, and made the point that when the people of Nineveh repented of their godless ways, God's fierce anger abated and he spared the six-score thousand inhabitants and also much cattle.[39]

Waldegrave reminded the people of his Carlisle diocese that some four years previously the rod of the Lord's anger 'fell upon our manufacturing regions'.[40] The present distress, he declared, made self-examination a matter of extreme urgency. The bishop identified two major sources of the present divine displeasure: 'the sins of the priests' and 'the increasing desecration of the Lord's Day'.[41] He went on to condemn the widespread use of Sunday labour in the environs of the city of Carlisle, where thousands were 'weekly robbed of the moral and physical repose which God designed for them'.[42] Perhaps not altogether unsurprisingly Waldegrave was emphatic that the Lord was 'deeply angered' at the way liberal scholars, 'men of foremost rank', had practically rejected the Bible and denied its basic teachings on the Fall of man, the Blood of Christ and the work of the Holy Spirit.[43] He concluded by expressing his conviction that the British nation had been directly blessed in proportion to her commitment to the Biblical Protestant faith.[44] He urged his clergy to humiliation and repentance.

In a similar vein, Joseph Cotton Wigram believed that the heavy early autumn rains which had threatened to bring disaster to the harvest in September 1860 were a divine appointment. However, when disaster seemed imminent and the rains were averted, Wigram was adamant that 'the Providence of Almighty God has been shown'.[45] He wrote a circular letter to all his clergy and urged them to use public prayers of thanksgiving in their churches for a few Sundays.

Grappling with Bishop Colenso

John William Colenso (1814-1883) was a celebrated missionary and Bishop of Natal. In his earlier years he had been a Fellow of St. John's College, Cambridge, and had followed this with a spell in a Norfolk country living. Whilst at Cambridge he was much influenced by Frederick Denison Maurice's universalism. As a result, when he went out to Africa in 1853 he felt it unnecessary to convert the indigenous peoples he encountered there, but instead he merely taught them. On his arrival, Colenso quickly set about the task of translating the Old and New Testaments into Zulu. He was much perturbed when his Zulu assistant expressed his revulsion at the brutal command of ancient Hebrew law in Exodus 21, verses 20 and 21. The experience challenged Colenso to re-think a whole range of issues including the Creation, Deluge and Flood stories. In 1861 the bishop created a stir by his questioning of the doctrine of eternal punishment in his *Commentary on the Epistle to the Romans.* This, however, was nothing compared to the positive uproar which resulted when he began to publish his *The Pentateuch and Book of Joshua Critically Examined* between 1862 and 1879. In this volume Colenso occupied himself with the minutiae of Old Testament detail, such as the great ages of the heroes of the patriarchal era, and the logistical and mathematical problems associated with the temple ritual and the wilderness wanderings. In one chapter based on Joshua chapter 8, verses 34 and 35, he considered how Moses could have read all the book of the Law before all the congregation of Israel, a company he calculated on the basis of Exodus chapter 12 to be 'not less than two millions'.[46] 'Surely', he commented, 'no human voice, unless strengthened by a miracle of which the scripture tells us nothing, could have reached the ears of a crowded mass of people, as large as the population of London.[47] In another section, Colenso considered the size of the Court of the Tabernacle in relation to the number of the 'whole congregation of Israel' who were, according to Numbers chapter 10, verses 3 and 4, ordered to gather at the door of the tabernacle. Colenso assumed that they must have stood in consecutive lines not just in front of the door but the width of the courtyard, in which case they would have stretched away 'a distance of more than 100,000 feet, in fact, nearly twenty miles![48] Colenso commented: 'It is inconceivable how under such circumstances "all the assembly", "the whole congregation" could have been summoned to attend "at the door of the Tabernacle" by express command of Almighty God.[49] In another discussion related to the Tabernacle, Colenso considered the sacrificial duties of the priests, of whom there were only three, Aaron till his death and his two sons, Eleazar and Ithamar. Just attending to the childbirth offerings of approximately 250 births a day each priest would daily have had to eat '88 pigeons for his own portion, "in the most holy place".'[50] Colenso concluded with a scornful dismissal of the Pentateuch by stating that the 'narrative, whatever may be its value and meaning, cannot be regarded as historically true'.[51]

For his painstaking researches Colenso's metropolitan, Bishop Gray of Capetown, a Tractarian conservative, deposed him in 1863.[52] Colenso, however, appealed to the Judicial Committee of the Privy Seal who reversed sentence in his favour in 1865. The controversy dragged on even after his death and the schism in the South African church was not healed until 1910.

Colenso's views were deeply offensive to the mid-Victorian public and there were a number of public rebuttals in the Christian press and published sermons. The Palmerstonian bishops who, as has been observed, were conservative to a man in matters of biblical authority, pronounced against Colenso in the strongest of terms. Charles Longley showed no hesitation in declaring his conviction as to the unsoundness of Dr. Colenso's teaching, and affirmed that he was justly deposed from the episcopate.[53] He also expressed his satisfaction in 1864 that so many published replies, already amounting to about fifty, had been made to Colenso's attacks on the Pentateuch and the Book of Joshua.[54]

The Bench of bishops met together on several occasions in January and February 1863 to discuss Colenso's writings. On 9 February Archibald Tait drafted an address on behalf of the Episcopal Bench to Bishop Colenso, who was then in England, which urged him to 'earnest prayer and deeper study of God's Word', that he might 'under the guidance of the Holy Spirit, be restored to a state of belief in which you may be able with a clear conscience again to discharge the duties of our sacred office'.[55] Bishop Tait in a later speech in Convocation had not the slightest doubt that Bishop Colenso had 'published most dangerous books – books of the tendency of which I doubt whether he was fully aware when he published them'.[56] 'Colenso', he continued, 'has already done sufficient to convince us [the bench of bishops] that he is quite unfit to exercise the office of a Bishop in the Church of England'.[57]

Bishop Gray of Capetown was a man of staunch conservative theological opinion, who found it hard to accept Lord Westbury's judgement of 1865 that he had no coercive or legal power over Colenso. In fact the Privy Council's decision went even further, in that it declared no appeal could be made to the Archbishop of Canterbury since it was the Crown's prerogative to receive colonial appeals. Tait and the majority of English bishops sympathised with Gray's displeasure at Colenso's views, but they did not agree with his decision to excommunicate him. In their opinion Gray was acting outside the bounds of what was legal, and was at the same time acting against the prerogative of the English Crown. William Thomson shared Tait's views in the matter. He was strongly hostile to liberal theology and higher criticism in general, but he felt it was crucial not to allow Gray to exceed the limits of office. For this reason Thomson declined to attend the first Lambeth Conference of Bishops, on the grounds that the American and Colonial bishops might undermine the policy of the English bishops in the matter of Colenso. In spite of Longley's assurance that the matter would not be discussed, Thomson still refused to attend. Events proved his decision to be correct when Archbishop Longley succumbed to pressure by Gray and allowed the matter to be debated. The end result was that a rival Bishop of Natal was consecrated in 1868, which led to further unhappy and divisive consequences.

Thomson's personal opinions on the critical biblical scholarship of Colenso's school were never more vehemently displayed than in his comments on Ernest Renan's *Life of Jesus*. 'It must be ranked,' he wrote, 'as one of the greatest outrages that has ever been offered to that Name which stands upon the title-page'. He continued: ' "The Away with Him!" is a sentimental rhapsody of 460 pages, endurable but for the insolence of its praise, in which the supposed decadence of a moral nature is described.'[58] Thomson was also called upon to reiterate his views in 1865 in response to the preaching and writing of one of his own incumbents, the Reverend Charles Voysey. Voysey was first appointed curate of Healaugh near Tadcaster in 1863 and then became Vicar in 1865. From 1865 to 1868 Voysey issued a series of sermons entitled *The Sling and the Stone*. In them he maintained that the whole system of Pauline theology rested on the supposed fall from perfection of Adam and Eve, and that once this myth had been exploded, the system fell to the ground. Apart from the miracles he doubted the doctrine of the Atonement, and even the Incarnation and the Trinity. Following a hue and cry on the part of evangelicals and ritualists, Voysey was brought to book by Thomson. After having failed to persuade him to recant, the archbishop was reluctantly forced to begin proceedings against him. His views were condemned by the Chancery Court of York and later by the Judicial Committee of the Privy Council to whom he subsequently appealed. The latter body concluded that 'he advisedly rejected the doctrines on the profession of which he was ordained a minister of the Church'.[59] He was given a week to retract from the errors on which he had been served judgement but he refused to comply. He wrote to the registrar reasserting those same views with the result that he was summarily deprived from office under the great *Heresy Act*, 13 Elizabeth C12, 'for ministers to be of sound religion'.[60]

John Pelham found it 'startling' that the courts of law did not find in Colenso's writings 'any sufficient cause for a judicial condemnation' of his opinions. He found it hard to accept that Colenso's conscience had not led him to resign his position as a Bishop.[61] He was, like others, thankful 'for the many able publications which have been called forth for the maintenance of the faith and the refutation of the false teaching by which it is assailed'.[62] He felt it was important for clergy to inform themselves about the advance of scientific research so that they could deal competently with objections and difficulties which arose from biblical criticism.[63] Samuel Waldegrave of Carlisle accused Bishop Colenso of betraying with a kiss the Scriptures. 'By one traitorous blow,' he declared, he has deprived us both of Moses and the prophets, and also Him of whom Moses in the law and the prophets did write.[64]

Waldegrave was forthright in his condemnation of Colenso's writings, which he regarded as 'no novelty'. Colenso's mathematical musings were, in his view, first aired and refuted centuries previously. The Bishop of Natal's 'fearful aggravation' had betrayed Christ's Church and perpetrated 'treason against the Lord of Lords and King of Kings'.[65] Waldegrave's main line of defence against Colenso was the coherence of Scripture. He also contented himself with demonstrating the Church of England's belief in the inspiration and authority of Holy Scripture, by means of copious quotations from the *Articles of Religion* and the liturgy of the Prayer Book.

In 1863 Harold Browne delivered and published five lectures entitled *The Pentateuch and the Elohistic Psalms.* This was a direct reply to Colenso in which Browne made an erudite defence of the integrity of the early books of the Old Testament. Amongst other things he answered Colenso's charge that the law of Moses was inhuman by elaborately contrasting the Mosaic code with the laws of other nations in the ancient world.[66] Browne spoke of Colenso's 'apostasy' and 'deeply regretted' the course which his writings adopted.[67]

Joseph Cotton Wigram wrote to Bishop Colenso in December 1862 and forbade him to preach in any churches of the Rochester diocese. His letter, according to *The Christian World*, was 'a model of politeness and firmness'. The same paper praised Wigram's 'zeal for Christ's truth' and 'the spirit' in which he wrote.[68] A fortnight later *The Chelmsford Chronicle* printed Wigram's reply to seven rural deaneries who had written corporately expressing, 'cordial sympathy with, and gratitude for' his recent letters both to them and to the Bishop of Natal. In his closing paragraph Wigram expressed his strong concern for the Bishop of Natal and urged his clergy to pray for him.

> I feel deeply for the position into which the bishop of Natal has been betrayed through his precipitancy and reliance on his own great mental powers. May God forgive and turn him into the right way. . . . I entreat you dear brethren to offer up prayer fervently to God on his behalf, that the Holy Spirit would indeed bring him to the acknowledgement of God's truth, and do his own great work as the comforter in settling, grounding and establishing him for ever in the faith from which he has so greatly and grievously erred since he solemnly pledged himself, at his ordination and consecration.[69]

Supporters of the Protestant Reformation

At a point in time when the Tractarians were expressing doubts about the Reformation settlement and teaching doctrines which ran counter to the Thirty Nine Articles of Religion, the bishops whom Palmerston had appointed emerged as forthright exponents of Protestant teaching and practice. Robert Bickersteth's son wrote of his father's 'unwavering adherence to the scriptural principles of our Reformed Church'.[70] He preached a sermon in 1854 entitled *Romanism in its Relation to the Second Coming of Christ* in which he identified the Church of Rome with the man of lawlessness, of 1 Thessalonians chapter 4, whose activities would precede the return of Christ. Near the conclusion of his address he thanked God that the Protestant heart of the English nation was still sound. He was glad that the spirit of Protestantism was not dead, and rejoiced that 'the blood of the martyrs yet flow in our veins' and 'the flame-shroud of Latimer has not yet been extinguished'.[71] A year or two later after his consecration as bishop of Ripon he appeared to have mellowed a little in his attitude to Romanism. In April 1858, while acknowledging that there were strong political and social grounds for denouncing Rome, he felt that it would be 'unbecoming' to do so when preaching on behalf of the Reformation Society.[72] According to his obituarist, Charles Baring's 'antipathy to ritualism' was founded on 'his reverence for the Reformed Church of England and his dread lest the introduction of practices which he considered akin to those of Rome should utlimately cause the church to recede from Protestant principles and return to Romanism'.[73]

Samuel Waldegrave was of the opinion that 'exactly in proportion as Britain has maintained her Protestant character, at home and abroad, has God solidly blessed her among the nations'.[74] In a sermon which he preached to the Church Missionary Society on 4 May 1868, he reminded the congregation that the Church of England stood pledged to the doctrine of Justification by Faith without works of the law. It was this doctrine which Luther, Calvin, Ridley, Latimer and other Reformers had proclaimed, and which the fathers and founders of the Church Missionary Society had found to be faithful.[75] Henry Philpott similarly 'heartily' accepted the settlement of the 'polity which was made at the time of the Reformation of the Church of England'.[76]

William Thomson had strong reformed convictions and like Waldegrave was conscious of the debt owed to Martin Luther. In a sermon entitled 'Martin Luther, His Mission and Work', he spoke of Luther having done 'a great work in the secret souls of men . . . and sensibly influenced the march of freedom and civilisation'.[77] Although he happily accepted the Anglican position of the threefold ministry, he had no belief in the apostolic succession of bishops or the mediatorial role of the priesthood. He was vehement that neither a priest or the Blessed Virgin could ever intercede for the human race. It was, as he saw it, the glory of the Reformation that it removed the priest from between God and man.[78]

Despite his desire not to be labelled either 'evangelical' or 'high church', Charles Ellicott was deeply attached to Reformation and the doctrines taught by the sixteenth century reformers. In an address on the 'Revision of the Rubrics' he declared that to the Reformation 'we owe the return to the true aspects of that great doctrine . . . on which all vital and personal religion and all true morality absolutely rests – Justification by Faith in Christ Jesus'.[79] Ellicott went on to relate that he had been taught to reverence the English Reformation 'from my earliest childhood' and that he intended to remain true to that teaching to the end of his days.[80] Four years later in another sermon, 'Some Present Dangers of the Church of England' Ellicott again spoke of himself as 'deeply attached to the Reformation'.[81]

Harold Browne was, according to his biographer, strongly attached to the principles of the Reformation. He referred again and again to their clear protest against medieval religion and constantly reiterated that his faith was in Christ the Redeemer as displayed in the teachings of the English Reformers.[82] Francis Jeune of Peterborough was similarly firm in the Reformation principle of 'the sole and unapproachable authority of Divine Scripture'.[83] He forcibly reminded a gathering of his clergy that the Reformers did not appeal to the undivided Church when they sought to purify English Christianity, but rather to Scripture alone.[84] He noted that Rome was prepared to assert that we are justified by faith, but unwilling for the Reformation insistence on faith only.[85]

Conversionism and Crucicentrism

David Bebbington outlined four key characteristics of evangelicalism: Conversionism, activism, Biblicism and Crucicentrism.[86] Both Conversionism and Crucicentrism, or the insistence on the Cross and the Atonement, were prominent features in the ministry of most of the bishops whom Lord Palmerston appointed. They were particularly marked in the teaching and addresses of those who were evangelical in their churchmanship, although both Ellicott and Browne shared their convictions in the matter.

Montagu Villiers was insistent on the need to make conversion the central aspect of the ministry. He urged all preachers to speak as 'a dying man to dying men',[87] and to ensure that they exalted Christ in such a manner that conversions would follow.[88] Charles Baring urged incumbents in his diocese 'to know Jesus Christ and Him crucified' and to preach the Cross, a weapon 'mighty through God to the pulling down of strongholds'.[89] John Pelham exhorted his clergy 'to understand the Cross for themselves' in order that they might preach Christ and Him crucified.[90]

Robert Bickersteth impressed upon his 'Reverend Brethren' the need 'to dwell much upon the central truth of the whole scheme of the Gospel, the Atonement effected by our Saviour Jesus Christ, when He died upon the cross'.[91] Samuel Waldegrave emphasised that the aim of the Christian ministry is 'the salvation of souls'.[92]

William Thomson took as the theme of his Bampton Lectures of 1853 'the atoning work of Christ',[93] and emphasised the expiatory character of the Atonement. He typified evangelicals of his day in his insistence that the Atonement should be the burden of the Church's preaching.[94] Bishop Thorold of Rochester observed in later years that 'the sacrifice of Christ was the constant theme of Thomson's sermons' and that 'his secret hope and trust and joy were in the cross'.[95]

Tait, Ellicott and Browne, although not in the evangelical school of Villiers, Baring, Pelham, Bickersteth or Thomson, nevertheless shared their insistence on the Atonement and conversion. Tait for example charged his hearers at his 1866 Visitation 'to spread the Gospel of your Master' and to 'preach the Lord Jesus Christ faithfully in your sermons and in your lives'.[96] Ellicott urged that 'we of the clergy preach the blessed and salutary doctrine that Christ Jesus came into the world to save sinners'[97] while Browne stressed that 'the peculiar office of Christ's ministers is to preach ... that "God was in Christ reconciling the world unto Himself" '.[98] On one occasion Browne wrote to one of his former curates, Mr. Knott, who was on the point of being received into the Church of Rome. He impressed on him 'the need of implicit reliance on Christ alone for salvation'.[99]

Eschatology

Christian eschatology is concerned with the last things, and in particular with the return of Christ, millennial bliss, death, judgement, heaven and hell. In the nineteenth century these matters were keenly debated and hotly contested with considerable intensity. They were the subject of many denominational controversies and issued in a spate of books and pamphlets. There were, of course, a variety of reasons which underlay these arguments and debates. They included recurrent revivalism with its notion of the imminent return of Christ, and the expectancy that God would pour out his spirit in the last days. These were periods of great political and social uncertainty which caused many, but particularly the poor, to contemplate the end of their time in the present vale of tears and the hope of the millennial kingdom of justice and plenty. The Victorian era was one of great missionary endeavour and many concerned themselves with the destiny of the Christless heathen, both overseas and in the large and burgeoning towns and cities of the Industrial Revolution. All of this was compounded by the emergence of biblical criticism and the debates about myth, anthropomorphic language, and the moral question of whether a just God would condemn to hell those who had never had any opportunity to respond to the Christian message. It was inevitable therefore that the bishops whom Lord Palmerston appointed would be taken in varying degrees with these eschatological issues.

The 1820s were a decade of turmoil, with unemployment following the end of the war with France. Bread prices were high and rioting and rick burning featured in many southern counties, where the situation was particularly acute. Against this background, Edward Irving proclaimed the imminent return of Christ from his London pulpit in Regent Chapel. His preaching attracted many of the fashionable, the well-to-do middle classes, and even some members of Parliament. At the same time John Nelson Darby and a small group of influential aristocrats, including Lady Powerscourt, established the Brethren Movement. Darby was also insistent on an imminent parousia, and a number of prophetic conferences were organised which began to impact, the intelligentsia of the evangelical world. This in turn influenced some of the evangelical bishops whom Palmerston appointed. Robert Bickersteth's uncle, Edward Bickersteth, was a student of end time prophecy, and Joseph Cotton Wigram's brother, George Wigram, became a prominent leader of the Exclusive Brethren and edited their journal, *Present Testimony*.

Montagu Villiers became preoccupied with Pre-millennialism and each year from 1842 he invited prominent evangelicals to give Lent addresses on the Second Coming of Christ.[100] Robert Bickersteth was also a firm advocate of the pre-millennial return of Christ. In a sermon preached in 1854 he explained that the second advent would not take place until there had been widespread apostasy. This 'falling away' he linked with the man of lawlessness described in Paul's letter to the Thessalonians.[101] H. Kirk-Smith, William Thomson's biographer, stressed how much he lived his life in the light of the Lord's return. Thomson himself declared at the Norwich Church Congress that 'the vision of that future glory of our Lord is needed to keep up our hearts'. 'Christ', he went on to declare, 'shall one day be universal king.'[102]

Arising out of his Old Testament interests, Harold Browne published a thin volume entitled *A Course of Sermons on the Prophecies of the Messiah*. Later he expressed his deep concern at the way in which Liberal scholars denied 'the existence of prediction at all in the Old Testament, and especially predictions of the Messiah'.[103] Joseph Cotton Wigram gave a lecture in 1850 entitled 'The Advent of the Lord the present Glory of the Church', which was later published in a volume edited by William Wilson. In it he stressed that the day of Christ's coming will be one of 'peculiar resurrection blessedness for the saints'.[104] The blessedness, he asserted, lay in the thousand year reign in which believers will participate on Christ's return.[105] Wigram had a very literal view of this end time period. In another address he spoke of the Jews returning to their land, Jerusalem being exalted over the earth, and David's son occupying 'as he has never done, the promised throne'.[106]

Despite a growing enthusiasm on the part of some evangelicals for pre-millennialism, post-millennialism (which resonated with the creeds, the Thirty Nine Articles of Religion and with radical millenarian groups such as the Chartists), remained the dominant view of the century. Significantly, Samuel Waldegrave devoted his 1866 *Bampton Lectures* to an extended argument in support of Post-millennialism. In contrast to the views of Wigram, Waldegrave did not view Jerusalem as having dominant role in the end time.[107] He saw the future Kingdom as 'essentially spiritual in character'.[108] Waldegrave argued that when Christ the perfect comes, the imperfect must be done away. Since during the millennium therefore, Satan is not yet destroyed, Christ must return after the thousand year period has come to an end. Waldegrave stressed that when Christ returns he will 'confer a blessing far greater than that of millennial sabbatism'.[109] Indeed at his advent the Lord will bestow on believers 'perfect consummation and bliss both in body and soul.[110] As Waldegrave perceived it, the appeal of pre-millenarianism 'was in direct opposition to creed and Scripture alike'.[111]

No aspect of eschatology was more keenly debated in Victorian times than that of hell. Mrs. J.W. Lea, who contributed an essay to a volume entitled *The Church and the World* (1866) asserted that 'no one interested in theology could have lived through the last few years, without having the awful question of future punishment forced upon his thoughts'.[112] Few would have disagreed with her. The problem, as many high churchmen saw it, was that to take away hell was to take away the ground for holiness. Pusey, for example, urged one of his congregations to 'remember the parching flame, the never-dying worm, the everlasting fire, the gnashing of teeth, "the smoke of torment" which "goeth up for ever" '.[113] Newman also regarded eternal punishment as 'the critical doctrine' indeed 'the very characteristic of Christianity'.[114] Evangelicals regarded eternal punishment free from any symbolic interpretation as an essential doctrine of the Christian faith. 'Why?', many asked, 'would Christ have lived and died a sacrificial death if there was no punishment from which the human race needed to be saved.' For the great missionary societies the removal of hell was the removal of the raison d'être of evangelism.

The doctrine of hell and eternal punishment came under threat from several quarters in the mid-Victorian years. Biblical critics such as the writers of *Essays and Reviews* cast doubt on reliability of Scripture. Some thought the language must be interpreted figuratively. Others felt that eternal punishment was overly vindictive and could not be justified on moral grounds. All this combined to produce some hotly debated controversies and many sharply worded tracts and pamphlets.

In the disputes over hell the bishops appointed by Palmerston emerged as champions for what they saw as creedal orthodoxy. Samuel Waldegrave, for example, urged his clergy to faithfully declare that 'there is a great assize near at hand' and that 'the dead shall be judged out of the things written in the books'.[115] 'Everyone unwashed in His Blood', he declared, 'shall without doubt thus perish everlastingly.'[116] However, it was Archbishops Longley and Thomson who, in the wake of *Essays and Reviews,* stoutly defended both hell and everlasting punishment against the liberal onslaught. Both issued pastoral letters on the subject to their respective provinces. Longley was vehement that no distinction could be drawn between the word 'everlasting' as applied to the blessings of the righteous, and as applied to the future punishment of the wicked. He wrote to his clergy and laity:

> I am sure you will beware of giving any other interpretation to the word 'everlasting' in the passages of our formularies which relate to the punishment of the lost, than that of 'eternal' in the sense of 'never ending'. For whatever be the meaning of the word in these passages in the case of the lost, the same must be its meaning in the case of the saved.[117]

William Thomson, in his 'Pastoral Letter to the Province of York' expressed himself in a similar vein to Longley. 'Everlasting', he wrote, 'must mean for ever, never coming to an end. The Church of England believes in a life that lasts for ever for the good, and in an everlasting punishment for the wicked.'[118]

Clearly, the bishops whom Palmerston appointed stand out as orthodox and Protestant in their convictions. Regardless of their churchmanship or theological position, they all defended the inspiration and authority of Scripture. To a man they stood out for the Reformation settlement of the Church of England and subscribed with personal conviction to the doctrine of the Substitutionary Atonement and Justification by Faith alone. In an epoch which was beset with doubt and scepticism they stood firm for the tenets of traditional creedal and historic Christianity. As theologians they proved themselves able to set out a reasoned defence of the faith against liberals and agnostics alike. Most undoubtedly won the acclaim and respect of their clergy.

VIII

Anti-Ritual Bishops

The English Church in medieval times had, of course, been part of the western Catholic Church. English worship in that era before the Reformation was characterised by a good deal of ritual centred on the Mass and the sacramental system. In addition there were many monastic houses with their daily rounds of processional services and sung offices which contributed to the development of ceremonial. Much of this heritage was eradicated by the sixteenth century Protestant reformers in their desire to recover a simpler way of religious life and worship that was more in keeping with the New Testament and early church practices. For the most part English Church worship remained plain and unadorned until the middle years of the nineteenth century, when a series of events combined to create a renewed desire to recover medieval ritual in the Church of England.

The impetus towards ritualism in the nineteenthth century came from the second generation of the Oxford Movement. The first phase of Tractarianism 1833-41 had been purely concerned with doctrinal issues. In particular, Tractarians had been concerned to argue that the Church of England was part of the one undivided Catholic Church and that through an unbroken line of episcopal hands the spirit of the apostles had been passed down to the present bishops. Despite this strong doctrine of the Church as the Divine Society there had been no ritual accompaniments in the worship of the first phase of the Oxford Movement. In fact right up until the time he left the Church of England in 1845, Newman celebrated Holy Communion in a cassock, surplice and scarf standing at the north end of the communion table. Pusey likewise was, in this early phase, against what he termed 'provocative trappings' and 'popish toys'.

Emphasis on the undivided Catholic Church

Several factors led the second generation of the Oxford Movement to adopt ritualistic practices. First and most basic was their emphasis on the undivided Catholic Church of the first five centuries. The first generation leaders of the Oxford Movement, and Newman in particular, had looked back to what they termed the 'Via Media' or middle position which characterised the undivided Catholic Church of the first five Christian centuries. Newman contended in tracts 38 and 41 that in this era the church was neither Roman on the one hand nor Protestant on the other. As the Tractarians studied the life and worship of this period of church history, they found many doctrines and practices which Protestantism had obscured. These included, for example, regular fasting, prayers for the dead, prayers to the Saints, the veneration of Mary, an emphasis on virginity (celibacy), monastic communities, a belief in the real presence of Christ in the Eucharist and the idea that the bread and wine change in substance when the priest called the Holy Spirit down on them.

Ritualism arose out of a desire to reach the poor

Second, there was a missionary motive behind the desire for increased ritual. Robert Linklater, a ritualist who worked for eleven years in London's east end in the parish of St. Peter's-in-the-East, wrote of the murky atmosphere of fog and dust which pervaded the narrow alleys and courtyards of his pastoral charge. The children were in his words, half-maimed 'many of them stunted . . . deformed and sickly-looking'.[1] In such an atmosphere it was felt that the unemotional, arid services of low-church Protestantism would never touch the poor. Indeed, Blomfield described the average church service of the 1850s as being 'blank, dismal, oppressive and dreary'. 'Matins and litany', he continued, 'with a sermon lasting the best part of an hour, in a cold gloomy Church, was not the kind of worship to appeal to a man or woman with no education or little imagination'.[2] The Tractarians therefore determined to reach the people for whom dull grey buildings had little appeal with 'mystery, movement colour and ceremonial'.

The Romantic Movement

This desire for colour and movement was further re-inforced by the Romantic movement. Victorian England was captivated by what is generally referred to as the Romantic movement, which looked back with warmth and esteem to 'Merrie England' of the medieval period. It manifested itself in the arts, literature and architecture. The Romantic ideal was a reaction to the growing emphasis on nationalism, scientific discovery and cold logic. In literature it was seen in the novels of Sir Walter Scott, in painting it was most visible in the Pre-Raphaelite School, who sought to recover the insights of the medieval artists before Raphael. In architecture it was everywhere apparent in the growing taste for the medieval Gothic style buildings.

The Camden Society

Partly influenced by this Romantic movement was the Cambridge Camden Society, named after the antiquarian William Camden (1551-1623). It began as The Ecclesiological Society in 1837, started by John

Mason Neale (1818-1866) and a small circle of associates, most of whom were undergraduates who enjoyed visiting and studying old churches. It was formally founded in 1839 with the following aim: 'to promote the study of Gothic Architecture and Ritual Arts and the restoration of mutilated architectural remains'. The Camden Society sought to ensure that all new churches were erected in the Gothic style and that all restorations were carried out after the pattern of Medieval buildings. The Society kept lists of specially approved architects. Among them were Sir Gilbert Scott (1811-1878), William Butterfield (1814-1900) and Augustus Pugin (1812-1852). The latter had such an enthusiasm for Gothic that on one occasion his friends presented him with a Gothic pudding![3]

The Middle and Upper-Middle Class Taste for Ritualism

In the fashionable suburbs which were springing up on the outskirts of many towns and cities there was a growing taste for more elaborate housing. Door steps and hall ways were frequently laid with brightly coloured tiles. The upper class Victorian drawing room was often ornate and rich in rugs, hangings and furniture. In some areas such as Kensington, Chelsea or Brighton ritualism represented a transference of the Victorian house into the context of the church building. As Owen Chadwick put it: '. . . It was natural that the religious sentiment should desire to ornament churches in conformity with the better tastes of the generation.'[4]

Religious Orders

In the later years of the nineteenth century the second generation of the Oxford Movement encouraged the re-founding of religious orders, and the need arose for devotional offices which were beyond the scope of the Prayer Book services. Monks, nuns and other members of religious communities felt the need for stillness, quiet and contemplation. It was in the context of the newly formed religious houses that the doctrine of the real Presence and the practice of Reservation and Benediction began to develop.

The Ornaments Rubric

The ritualists were further encouraged by the 'Ornaments Rubric'. This was printed with the preface to the 1552 Prayer Book and was retained in the front of the 1662 *Book of Common Prayer*. The rubric stated explicitly that 'such ornaments of the Church, and the ministers thereof, at all times of their ministration shall be retained and be in use, as were in this Church of England, by authority of Parliament in the second year of the reign of King Edward VI'. Thus the ritualists were able to maintain that they were simply adhering to the original regulation and that it was perfectly legal to wear 'a white albe plain with vestment or cope and to celebrate', not at the north side of the table but 'afore the midst of the altar' as specified in the *Book of Common Prayer* immediately before the Prayer of Consecration. At this level it was quite hard to take action against the ritualists. They argued, for example, that the vestments, far from being illegal, were the only legal form of dress at Communion. However, it should be noted that in the trial of John Purchas for ritualistic innovations in 1870 the use of this rubric to justify ritualistic practice was brought to an end. This was done on the basis of the Act of Uniformity which, whilst it sanctioned the rubric of 1549, also added the words 'until the order shall be therein taken by authority of the Queen's majesty'. 'Such order', it was argued, had been taken because in 1566 Archbishop Parker had issued Advertisements which condemned all vestments but the surplice. Although Elizabeth I didn't actually sign the bill, she clearly assented to its provisions because the use of vestments in the Mass entirely disappeared. It is perhaps worth noting at this point that the number of ritualistic churches in England was not large. The main concentration was in the south and in London in particular. In 1882, out of 903 churches in London, thirty-seven had vestments, ten used incense, forty-five had candles on the altar and 270 used the eastward position for the celebrant at Communion.[5]

Opposition to Ritualism

Inevitably, those bishops whom Lord Palmerston had appointed who were evangelicals were outspoken in their opposition to ritualism. What is more significant is that those who were mild high churchmen and from the broad church party were equally vehement against the innovations of the second generation of the Oxford Movement.

Montagu Villiers was described by his obituarist as 'one who shrank from the shadow of Roman Catholic practices'.[6] From the outset of his episcopate he made his position perfectly clear. He had 'no sympathy with those who are wholly Romanists, and he had none for those who are semi-Romanists'.[7] On his arrival at Carlisle he found only a small minority of clergy who had Tractarian sympathies. He expressed his thankfulness that no encouragement had been given in the diocese to the dissemination of views diametrically opposed in spirit to the writings of the Reformers and to the Scriptures of truth'. He congratulated his clergy on

the all but complete absence . . . of those doctrines which, if by subtle reasoning, they can be distinguished from, are yet so near akin to the errors of Romanism as to have perverted many who were once members of our Reformed Protestant Church.[8]

Charles Baring denounced 'the disgraceful and dishonest proceedings of several of our body' who had in recent years sought 'to deny the Protestant principles of the Church of England and to palliate the most flagrant errors of the Church of Rome'. These 'weak-minded persons' had forced upon unwilling congregations 'frivolous changes in dress and authorised novelties in ornament and ceremonies'. What worried Baring was that the British public in general would come to regard the clergy as a whole as 'traitors in heart' whose real allegiance was to the Papal See.[9] Whilst at Durham, Baring's uncompromising aversion to ritualistic practice sometimes brought him into conflict with his clergy. In particular he was engaged in a protracted dispute with the Reverend Doctor Dykes, the vicar of St Oswald's church, within his cathedral city. Baring refused to license the Reverend George Peake as his curate, unless he received pledges that he would not be allowed to take part in certain specified practices which had been judicially declared illegal. He further demanded a promise from Peake to that effect in writing. Dr. Dykes then appealed to the courts in January 1874, with the result that Baring was shown to have 'established his right to receive pledges if he chose to exact them'. During the course of the dispute 3,300 of the laity signed an address in support of Baring and pledged between £7,000-£8,000 should the judgement have gone against him. Significantly, although Dykes differed strongly with Baring in matters relating to ritual, he had a high personal regard for his Diocesan and wrote in one of his letters: 'I will yield to none in sincere appreciation of your personal character, your honest goodness, your warm sympathy, your generous kindness, your open-handed liberality, your single-hearted transparent sincerity of purpose, your genuine Christian simplicity and your untiring zeal in your Master's service'.[10]

John Pelham was also worried at ritualistic developments in his Norwich diocese. He warned clergy not to introduce practices or ceremonies not prescribed by the Church into their services.[11] He made it plain to them that if they did so they were in breach of their ordination pledges. Robert Bickersteth, who shared Pelham's evangelical convictions, had spoken out in strong terms against Tractarian innovations some time before his elevation to the episcopate. In a sermon entitled *Papal Aggression* preached in 1850, he denounced 'the dishonest pretence of Churchmanship' under which Tractarians had laboured to indoctrinate the minds of the people with Romish error.[12] He spoke of 'the figment of apostolic succession' and expressed contempt for the 'sixty or seventy perverts from the ranks of the clergy of the Church of England' who had forsaken the Reformed Faith during the past nine years.[13] On his arrival at Ripon he expressed his happiness that the diocese was, with comparatively few exceptions, free from the 'trouble' of ritualism. The danger, as he saw it, was that ritual symbolised doctrine, and what is witnessed in the spectacle of worship, will in the end come to be taught in the pulpit.[14]

Samuel Waldegrave warned of the dangers of ritualism which, he said, had 'betrayed many of our brethren into the embraces of Rome'.[15] He also regretted that lay people were being alienated from the Established Church by the introduction 'ritualistic novelties'.[16] He denounced 'sensuous ceremony' as a system which is 'addressed to the fancy and the senses'. He had no time for those clergy who 'let form, and colour, and music, and incense, all combine to lend their delights to the office in which, clad in garments unused for three hundred years, you elevate the host before the prostrate, the adoring throng'. Waldegrave's major contention against ritualism was simply that 'Christ is not there', despite all the 'histrionic representations' of him which were common in Puseyite churches.[17]

William Thomson saw ritualism as diverting the energies of the Church from her vital mission to overthrow atheism and counteract infidelity. He entered a protracted dispute over the advanced ritual at St. Matthew's Church in Sheffield, where Gladstone had appointed G.C. Ommanney, a member of the Confraternity of the Blessed Sacrament, as incumbent in 1882.[18] The clergy of the area were united to a man in their opposition to his ceremonial innovations, and during the following year, the vicar of St. Luke's Solly Street, who was a militant Irish Protestant, broke with customary ecclesiastical etiquette and preached in St. Matthew's Parish Schools on the evils of ritualism. Notwithstanding, advanced ritualistic practices continued and opposition from within the parish soon began to surface. Walter Wynn, one of the churchwardens, wrote to the archbishop complaining of twelve abuses. These included the mixed chalice, the use of wafer bread, prostrating during the Prayer of Consecration, the elevation of the paten and the chalice and a 'white-tablecloth with five small crosses worked thereon'.[19] A lengthy and acrimonious exchange of letters between Thomson and Ommanney then ensued. Matters took a turn for the worse when Ommanney disclosed the entire correspondence to the editor of *The Sheffield Telegraph* complaining that he had been misrepresented.[20]

The situation further deteriorated when Wynn grew impatient at Thomson's inability to restrain Ommanney's ritualistic practices. He wrote to Thomson accusing him of inaction and likening him to the King of France who marched his 30,000 men up the hill and down again in a fine demonstration which achieved nothing. The archbishop reprimanded Wynn, who in consequence divulged their intemperate correspondence to *The Sheffield Telegraph*, who published it in their columns. The outcome was far from satisfactory from Thomson's point of view. Not only had his injunctions proved ineffectual but, on Easter Day 1884 there were 260 communicants in St. Matthew's Church with a Sunday School attendance of 250.[21]

Apart from the debacle of St. Matthew's, Thomson's diocese was relatively free from ritual controversy. This, however, was in part due to the fact that he generally refused to ordain men of extreme ritualistic sympathies, and several times revoked the licenses of rebellious assistant clergymen. Amongst a number of confrontations Thomson refused to li-

cense a curate at St. Martin's, Scarborough, on account of the use of coloured stoles, the mixed chalice, wafer bread and the practice of placing
bread fragments in the chalice. The archbishop was also accused of intrigue
in a dispute involving the parish of Bridlington. The parish was in the
patronage of the Simeon trustees and was staunchly low church. The incumbent of the adjoining parish sought to provide a more colourful service for those in the locality by erecting a temporary iron building, right on
his side of the boundary. A curate was appointed and the chapel soon
became well-attended. Thomson then succeeded in promoting the building of a church a short distance away on the Bridlington side of the boundary and securing the appointment of a pronounced evangelical incumbent
to it. Not only did this diminish the congregations in the iron chapel, but
further hostility was caused when in 1871 Thomson refused to license the
iron building because the new incumbent no longer supported it.

One of Thomson's biographers wrote that he 'never became reconciled
to the spread of ritualism'.[22] Nevertheless it could be countered that his
strong stance against ritualist clergy helped to stem the flow of what might
have become a rising tide in his diocese and other parts of the north. In a
letter penned in later years to his friend, James Fraser, the Bishop of
Manchester, Thomson wrote:

> The position of those who want to keep the Church of England in
> her old position has got very trying for a time. You and I must both
> expect to feel it. Will there ever come a time when it will be thought
> a crime to have striven to keep the Church of England as repres-
> enting the common sense of the Nation? I suppose it may; but I
> shall not see it. I have gone through a good deal; but I do not re-
> pent of having done my best.[23]

Francis Jeune, who was consecrated Bishop of Peterborough in June
1864, was well-known for his Protestant convictions in earlier years. When
Master of Pembroke College in 1845 he preached a sermon before the
University entitled *The Studies of Oxford Vindicated*. In it he declared that
the object of the University was 'primarily to form Christians and to train
ministers of religion'.[24] In view of this fact, he continued, the Bible and
'the learning which qualifies men rightly to divide it, must be the great
staple of our teaching'.[25] Against the background of Newman's recent departure into the Church of Rome, Jeune was unable to resist raising the
spectre of the Oxford Movement, and the very damaging effect it had had
on the reputation of the university. He spoke of the 'humiliating attempts'
on the part of ritualists 'to introduce a fantastic symbolism into the sanct-
uaries which were cleansed, three centuries ago, for the service of the
spirit of truth'.[26] Such innovations had alienated the laity from the Establishment and hindered the spread of episcopal government in the British
colonies. In the following year, in another sermon, Jeune deeply regretted
that some of the worst practices of Rome have been introduced into more

than one of the places of education connected with the Church of England.[27] In his only diocesan charge Jeune expressed his strong disapproval of 'the ritualistic excesses which have startled us of late years'. He singled out for particular mention, altars, incense, gestures, embroidery, worship of the Virgin, auricular confession and 'I know not what others'.[28]

Among those Palmerstonian bishops who were not members of the evangelical party, Longley, Tait, Ellicott and Browne were all forthright in the opposition to ritualism. While he was still at Ripon, Longley had a remarkable encounter with the ritualist faction of St. Saviour's Church, Leeds in the spring of 1851. He had earlier consecrated the building in 1845 but only after a lengthy correspondence lasting nearly a year with Edward Pusey, who was one of the project's leading sponsors. Pusey had tried to insist on a number of points which Longley found objectionable. Two of the most contentious items were a stained glass representation of the Virgin Mary crowned, and another design which portrayed her seated in the centre surrounded by the apostles as the Holy Spirit descended on each. Other matters of dispute included communion plate inscribed with prayers for the dead, prayers being said within or just in front of a chancel screen, and the officiating clergyman's back being turned to the congregation during the liturgy.

Eventually these matters were acceded to and the church was consecrated. It did not, however, bring an end to the troubles. On All Saints Day 1846, the Reverend G. Mullen of Oxford preached a sermon in St. Saviour on the intercession of the Saints which contained a number of passages which had to be censured. In April 1848 the Reverend Thomas Minster was appointed to the vicarage and soon began the practice of holding private confession. On this matter he was strongly rebuked by Longley in January 1849. A year later Longley received complaints from parishioners that the officiating clergyman was standing in a position which was not legal at the time of the consecration, and that a large cross had been erected over the rood screen. This was followed by a protest in the Spring of 1850 at the mode of infant baptism, which included lighted tapers and other medieval traditions. One of the assistant clergy preached a sermon in which he taught that Confirmation, Absolution, Unction, Holy Orders, Marriage, Baptism and the Lord's Supper were all sacraments. Inevitably matters came to a head, and in 1851 Longley revoked the license of one of Minster's curates, the Reverend H. F. Beckett. Shortly after this he received a letter signed by 660 persons, 220 of whom were communicants, praying that they might not be separated from their pastors. Longley responded by expressing his gratitude to the clergy of St. Saviour's for their dedicated commitment and pastoral care during the cholera outbreak. 'At the same time,' he continued, 'this exemplary conduct cannot blind me to the peril of the course they have been pursuing.'[29] He underlined the fact that five out of six of their recent assistant priests had defected to Rome. He for one was not prepared to tolerate these clergy 'encumbering the ritual of our Reformed Church with pompous ceremonies'.[30] He drew his piece to a conclusion by stating that 'From the recurrence of the dangers to which you were exposed under the ministry of your late deluded teachers, it will be my duty to protect you as far as in me lies'.[31]

When Longley moved on to Durham in 1857 he was glad to find that the peace of the diocese had not been disturbed by ritual extravagances or the revival of obsolete ceremonies and vestments.[32] Later, when Archbishop of Canterbury, Longley found himself having to face the issue of ritualism in the Church as a whole. Referring to the ritualists on one occasion in 1868, he stressed that they 'are a noisy, but not numerous section of our Church'.[33] It was their forwardness in expressing their views that gave 'an erroneous expression that they were a more important body than they really are'.[34] Returning to an earlier theme he stressed to his Canterbury diocese that the 'self-denying and devoted' living of the ritualists cannot be used to justify 'the great mischief ' which had been caused by their activities and general conduct.[35] He also rebuked those ritualists who were strict in their observance of church order in many aspects, but then omitted certain parts of the church service when it suited them.[36]

Archibald Tait came from a Scottish Presbyterian background, and his early Protestant upbringing was to remain influential on the convictions of his later years. While still a tutor at Balliol College, he had signed the protest against Tract 90 in which Newman had tried to argue that 'The Thirty Nine Articles' could be interpreted in a way that was favourable to Roman Catholicism. Twenty years later Tait found himself at the head of the largest and busiest diocese in England. Already, even before his arrival, London had been the stage of several controversial outbreaks of ritualism. The Reverend W.J.E. Bennett, Vicar of St. Paul's, Knightsbridge, had appealed for funds to build a district church of St. Barnabas, Pimlico, which was consecrated by Bishop Blomfield on 11 June 1850. Both churches adopted 'advanced ritual' which included the wearing of vestments. As a result of the tussles which followed, Bennett resigned the living and was replaced by the Hon. Rev. Robert Liddell, who continued in the same vein. In December 1855 the Consistory Court of the London diocese directed that a number of changes were to be made in the ritual of both places of worship. Liddell appealed to the Privy Council and Tait, who had only just been consecrated Bishop, was required to act as one of the assessors who handed down the first of many ritual judgements. Among other things, Liddell was required to remove the stone altar from St. Barnabas' Church and replace it with a wooden table. The cross attached to the Communion Table was illegal and had to be taken away, and the use of certain embroidered altar linen discontinued.[37]

The disputes which Tait had with Liddell marked the beginning of a number of similar cases in his diocese. On 5 March the bishop found it necessary to rebuke the Reverend Edward Stuart, an 'advanced ritualist', and one of the original founders of 'The English Church Union'. He informed Stuart that he had 'no authority in St. Mary Magdalene, Munster Square to light candles on the Communion Table in broad daylight, except when they may reasonably be considered necessary or convenient for the purpose of light'.[38] Tait showed a certain degree of magnanimity in his dealings with Stuart, whilst at the same time stressing the need for adherence to the Reformed Faith. He wrote to him in a letter:

> I am anxious to allow you as great liberty as possible in so apply
> ing the services of our Church as you deem most likely to affect
> your people's hearts, but you will grant that a heavy responsibility
> devolves on me not to sanction the introduction of innovations or
> returns to old usages of the unreformed Church which I believe
> likely to break down the barriers which mark in the minds of sim
> ple people the distinction between our worship and that of Rome.[39]

Tait went on to state that, although he had no intention to bring the matter to the courts, he hoped that Stuart would drop the practices objected to.[40] However, Stuart refused to comply with the bishop's requests on the grounds that the Prayer Book rubric sanctioned the use of lights on the Communion Table.[41] This brought a further rebuke from Tait who greatly regretted 'that you should think it right to disobey my command on your private interpretation of what you deem to be the law'.[42]

Tait's encounters with Stuart were followed by a number of more vehement struggles, including a further dispute with the parish of St. Paul's, Knightsbridge, this time over the matter of Confession. The most prolonged and public struggle, however, concerned the parish of St. George's-in-the-East and its mission church, St. Peter's, London Docks. The Rector of the benefice, the Rev. Bryan King, and the priest in charge of St. Peter's, Charles Lowder, were unflinching in their commitment to the revival of ritual. King was not one who could introduce change in a conciliatory manner and his congregation steadily dwindled. In 1856 the situation worsened when King announced his intention to begin the use of the, then almost unheard of, Eucharist vestments. The dissatisfied of his congregation voiced their discontent by absenting themselves from services and general grumblings, but matters came to a head in 1858 when Tait's attention was called to a 'Romish' Catechism and a number of ritualistic books and tracts which were being circulated in the parish. Among other things, these clearly taught Confession, Transubstantiation and the supremacy of the Bishop of Rome as 'the Patriarch of the West'.[43] Tait at once confronted King on the matter in person and then wrote to him at length the next day. He advised that both King and Lowder should express their disapproval of the Catechism which he acknowledged may have been circulated by 'those two of your curates who lately joined the church of Rome'.[44] He also warned King once more against the use of 'foolish vestments'.[45]

This already tense conflict was considerably heightened in May of the following year when the vestry of St. George's appointed the Rev. Hugh Allen as a lecturer. Allen was already well-known for his vehement 'no Popery' crusading, but Tait was powerless to block the appointment, since an Act of Parliament passed in George II's reign gave the vestry the right to nominate a lecturer who should 'be admitted by the Rector to have the use of the pulpit from time to time'.[46]

On the first Sunday after his licensing, Allen entered the pulpit to tumultuous applause and supported by a noisy band of followers. Elated by their success they invaded the normal service on the Sunday following, where their presence created such clamour and violence that the clergy and choir had to be taken from the building with a police escort.[47] The presence of a large number of constables kept matters in check until the end of the year. However, when their presence was withdrawn on 1 January 1860, the Church service disrupted into a state of anarchic disorder. Bryan King himself later wrote:

> The whole service was interrupted by hissing, whistling, and shouting. Songs were roared out by many united voices during the reading of the lessons and the preaching of the sermon; hassocks were thrown down from the galleries, and after the service, cushions, hassocks, and books were hurled at the altar and its furniture. I myself, and the other officiating clergy, had been spat upon, hustled, and kicked within the Church, and had only been protected from greater outrages, for several Sundays past, by the zealous devotion of some sixty or eighty gentlemen who attended from different parts of London.[48]

The conflict went on almost without a break for six months and the matter was raised in Parliament on several occasions. Tait made it plain that while both sides continued to stand firm on their legal rights there was little hope of breaking the impasse. The weekly scenes of noisy irreverence, shouting the psalms to drown out the choir, coughing and banging of pew doors continued unabated. Eventually Bryan King was persuaded to go abroad for a year, and on his return accepted a country living in the Diocese of Salisbury. Matters then began to return to something like normality, and the pastoral work of the parish resumed in the hands of Charles Lowder and Alexander Mackonochie.

Tait had a number of other skirmishes with ritualists in his London diocese. These included a dispute over the use of altar lights at the Chapel of All Saints in Margaret Street. This new church had been erected at the expense of private donors to replace the earlier unecclesiastical building. Local Protestant stalwarts urged the bishop to use the occasion of his Consecration sermon on 28 May 1858 to protest against the 'Popish mummeries' of its ornaments and services. Tait adopted a more temperate stance. He took as his text, 1 Corinthians chapter 8 verse 9, 'Take heed lest by any means this liberty of yours become a stumbling-block to them that are weak'. He urged the congregation in all their worship to surround themselves, through the Lord Jesus Christ's help, 'with a beauty far above that of outward adornment – the beauty of pure Gospel faith, and of a simple, earnest, self-denying Christian life'.[49]

Further struggles took place following the Consecration of the new church of St. Alban's Holborn in February 1863. Initially there were disagreements between Tait and Mackonochie over the use of altar lights and the nature of Christ's presence in the Eucharist. Then in December 1867 a case was brought to the Court of Arches by Mr. John Martin of the Church Association. The Dean of Arches, Sir Robert Phillimore, decided in favour of altar lights, but pronounced against the mixing of water and wine in the chalice and the use of incense. The judgement regarding altar lights was, however, reversed on appeal in December 1868. There was a further exchange of letters between Tait and Mackonochie over the intercession of the Blessed Virgin Mary.[50]

In all his dealings with the ritualists, Tait showed himself to be open to discussion, but he stood firm against any practice or custom which militated against the Reformed doctrines of the Church of England. In the latter years of his London episcopate he enjoyed cordial and warm relationships with Lowder and Mackonochie, both of whom were respectful of his authority. Robert Brett, who was a ritualist churchwarden at St. Matthias, Stoke Newington under five incumbents, wrote of Tait: 'I feel great respect for him, not only for his office, but personally for the many great efforts which he displays in advancing the cause of the Church, and also for acts of personal kindness to myself, and especially for tender sympathy in times of bitter trial'.[51] This is not to say that Tait could not also be firm. When Consecrating St. Michael's Church, Shoreditch, he found a large group of ritualist clergy, several of whom were wearing coloured stoles. He ordered them in a firm voice 'Take off these ribbons, gentlemen', whereupon they took them off and laid them in the vestry.[52]

In his charge of 1866 Tait made his views on ritualism abundantly clear. He condemned those who had taken it upon themselves 'so to alter the whole external appearance of the celebration of the Lord's Supper as to make it scarcely distinguishable from the Roman Mass', and who had introduced into other services 'change of vestment or ornament quite alien to the established English usage of 300 years'.[53] If these clergymen could not be persuaded to desist from such practices then recourse to the law would have to be made as a last resort. The fact that ritualism attracted large congregations was in Tait's opinion no argument in its favour. 'Amongst the multitudes in our large towns,' he said, 'everything which is eccentric or even unusual, either in teaching or practice, will have many admirers'.[54]

In January 1874 Queen Victoria wrote to Tait, who was now Archbishop of Canterbury, that 'the defiance shown by the clergy of the high church and ritualistic party, is so great that something must be done to check it, and prevent its continuation'.[55] She urged, among other things, an attention to the Prayer Book rubric with a presumption to outlaw ritualistic practice. One of her chief worries was that 'as things stand at present the archbishops' and bishops' authority is brought absolutely into contempt'.[56] Tait replied on the day following that he had discussed the matter with senior bishops, who had 'by an almost unanimous vote' authorised the Archbishops of Canterbury and York to draw up a bill to be brought into Parliament. This would empower diocesans, assisted by certain of the clergy, to control the services of the Church. Tait expressed himself reluctant to make any alteration to the rubric.[57]

Throughout his episcopate Tait proved himself to be a consistent opponent of ritualism. In an obituary *The Record* praised 'his masculine mind' which had caused him to fight against the inroads of Tractarianism and ritualism.[58] It was the general opinion of his contemporaries that Tait handled the ritualists with statesmanlike firmness. In the end, even clergy such as Lowder and MacKonochie who dealt in advanced ceremonial came to respect and admire him.

Charles Ellicott's view was that ritualism first arose out of an aesthetic desire to do outward honour and reverence to God in the services of public worship.[59] He also spoke of it on another occasion in 1873 as a reaction to the growing uncertainty over key Christian doctrines. He took the view that in a climate in which all things were 'shifting and opinionable', many were finding it necessary for the sake of their congregations to 'make the truth more objective, and revert to practices and ritual that may seem to form the best standing protest to the doubts and scepticism of the times'.[60] Later Ellicott expressed himself more strongly against the ritualists maintaining that their ceremonial was an expression of Romanism which would carry the Church back into the twilight and shadows of pre-Reformation England. He rebuked ritualist clergy for having 'a conscious and unconscious desire for power over the souls and spirits of men'.[61]

Like Tait, Ellicott had a number of struggles with ritualist clergy in his diocese. There appear to have been two major pockets of activity, one in Bristol and, later in the century, a group of churches centred on St. Mark's Church, Swindon. According to a contemporary chronicle at St. Paul's Church, one of the parishes in the group:

> the services are highly Ritualistic. On special occasions the altar is ablaze with candles, there are processions with banners and the chanting of processional hymns; members of the congregation bow their heads and cross themselves and those in office bow the knee as they pass the altar.[62]

Ellicott's approach to the ritualists in his diocese was somewhat peremptory compared to that of Tait. It was epitomised in a comment to one of his diocesan clergy: 'I always deal with every case wherever any number of parishioners complain. Where there is no complaint, I don't interpose'.[63]

In Bristol, Ellicott's first confrontation was with the congregation of All Saints, Clifton, a church which had been specifically built to facilitate Tractarian ceremonial. In the year of its opening, 1868, there were 279 Easter communicants, a figure which steadily increased until it reached a pinnacle of 742 in 1892. Two years after the passing of the Public Worship Regulation Act three laymen made charges to the bishop alleging ceremonial irregularities. These included eucharistic garments, lighted candles on the altar during Communion, and the holding of monastic offices of Terce, Sext and Nones. Ellicott's treatment of the incumbent, Randall, was beset with contradictory decisions regarding the licensing of curates. He further refused to conduct Confirmations at the church 'so long as lights and vestments were in use'.[64] At St. Raphael's church, also in Bristol, many of the features of advanced ritualism were in evidence. These included vestments, lights, mixed chalice, incense, Stations of the Cross, Crucifixion and Elevation at the Consecration. In 1877, 'without a word of warning' Ellicott demanded that H.A.Ward, the parish priest, desist from these practices. He agreed to comply save in respect of vestments, lights and the mixed chalice, which he maintained were sanctioned by the Ornaments Rubric. Ellicott thereupon withdrew Ward's license and the church was closed for 15 years. A similar situation occurred at the new church of The Holy Nativity, Knowle in 1883 where the incumbent, Robert Ives, provoked the bishop's displeasure by erecting 'baldachino' over the altar. The bishop refused to consecrate the church unless Ives resigned and removed the offending item. Ives did resign but it is doubtful whether the Catholic ethos of the parish worship changed significantly, since he was succeeded by a former curate of All Saints, Clifton.

The most celebrated ritual case which confronted Ellicott during his Gloucester episcopate was at Prestbury, where the incumbent was the Reverend John Edwards. Edwards, who adopted the family name of Bagot de la Bere in 1879, was a modern Tractarian parish priest. On his arrival in Prestbury in 1860 there were 39 communicants on Easter Sunday. At Easter 1880 there were four services with a total of 253 communicants. In 1873 Charles Combe, a parishioner and tailor by trade, made complaints about ritualistic practices in St. Mary's to Ellicott, who soon began proceedings against the vicar. It proved impossible for Edwards to object that Combe was a Dissenter, since Combe declared that he was 'as good a churchman as ever I was', but had been driven from his parish church by illegal practices there.[65] These included eastward position of the celebrant at the Eucharist, mixed chalice and altar lights. Edwards was found guilty and after a series of further court cases was sentenced by the Dean of Arches to be deprived of his living. By his refusal to acknowledge the authority of the Courts Edwards had placed himself in an untenable position. He had also, so Ellicott claimed, put himself outside the bishop's jurisdiction. There was a certain note of unpredictability in Ellicott's dealings with ritualists, later culminating in an astonishing volte-face with Randall. In 1889 he reconciled himself with the Vicar of All Saints, lifted the prohibition, offered him a canonry at Bristol Cathedral, and in 1892 commended him for the vacant Deanery of Chichester. Significantly also, he appointed Henry Bromby, a noted ritualist, as Randall's successor at the church. The following year, he made the decision to reconsecrate St. Raphael's, which had been closed for fifteen years, and reinstated the former priest-in-charge.[66]

In summation it is clear that Ellicott shared with the other Palmerston appointees their deep concern over the emergence of ritualism. He did not, however, possess quite the same sensitive approach as Tait when it came to dealing with individual ritualists. The reason for this was in all probability that he had persuaded himself that it was 'the collective force of these elements which constitute our present danger'.[67]

Harold Browne, who had 'great sympathy' with the evangelicals, was deeply distressed to see young men in their youthful enthusiasm endeavouring to copy the ways of Rome.[68] He shared Ellicott's view that the reviving of medieval customs and ritual would inevitably lead to a return to doctrines which had been deliberately rejected by the Church of England at the time of the Reformation. Among other things Browne was particularly concerned at the introduction of hymns to the Virgin Mary, and the weakening effect that an exaggerated view of her would have on the preaching of the Atonement.[69] In an address preached in 1865 Browne warned that 'ritualism will lead to demands for Liturgical Revision'.[70] Great care must be taken, he urged, 'before we lay one finger on a treasure so sacred'.[71] At a much later point, in 1889, Harold Browne sat as one of the assessors at the prosecution which ruled against the saintly Bishop of Lincoln, Edward King, for using unauthorised ceremonial during a celebration of Holy Communion on 18 December 1877 at the Church of St. Peter-at-Gowts in Lincoln.

William Jacobson, a scholarly high churchman, nevertheless had no liking for new or extreme ritual. According to Dean Burgon, 'he dreaded the dangerous tendency of the later Tractarian teaching'[72] and refused to be identified with it any way. At the same time Jacobson was unique among Lord Palmerston's appointees in that he steadfastly refused to write a single pamphlet or speak out against ritualism in any of its forms. To have done so, he believed, would only have proved counter-productive. He had scarcely been in office for twelve months when the clergy of Chester and its neighbourhood addressed him on the subject of ritualism. His reply was that no good could result from any pronouncement against ritualism unless it could be sustained by law. He also made the point that if he were to invoke the Prayer Book rubrics against ritual he would have to insist on the same uniform strict adherence on all other aspects of the liturgy.

Holy Communion and the Real Presence

In their opposition to ritualism the Palmerstonian bishops focused their attention on three key aspects: the doctrine of the Presence of Christ in the Eucharist, the use of vestments and the introduction of confessionals. On each of these matters they were unanimous.

Like most evangelical bishops, Montagu Villiers advocated a monthly Holy Communion service rather than the customary practice of having the sacrament only three or four times a year. He was nevertheless convinced 'as strongly as you can be, of the Protestant doctrine that the elements remain unaltered in substance; that is, the bread and wine are neither changed into nor joined with the real body and blood of Christ'.[73] Charles Longley was also unswerving in this same opinion. In 1857, when in Durham, he asserted that the Church of England's teaching on the matter could be summed up in the words of Richard Hooker that 'The real presence of Christ's most blessed body and blood is not to be sought for in the sacrament, but in the worthy receiving of the sacrament'.[74] Years later, during his Canterbury archiepiscopate, he re-iterated the same point stating that Jesus' words of institution 'cannot be construed to signify that the natural body of Christ is present in the sacrament'.[75] For this reason Longley refused to allow adoration of the bread and wine, and further rejected any notion that the Body and Blood could again be offered up as a satisfaction for sin. To entertain such a view was a failure to recognise that the offering Jesus made was 'a perfect redemption, propitiation, and satisfaction for the sins of the whole world, original and actual'.[76]

Robert Bickersteth was of the opinion that all ritualistic innovations were connected with Holy Communion, and in particular to the teaching of a localised presence of Christ in the bread and wine. In his outright rejection of this doctrine Bickersteth declared:

> If we are to understand by the Doctrine of the Real Presence that Christ is in any sense bodily present, by virtue of the act of consecration, in or with the sacramental elements, this is a doctrine which is not maintained in the Articles or the formularies of the Church of England, nor can be held consistently with those standards of belief.[77]

Henry Philpott took the view that the bread and wine remain unchanged, for the simple fact that the Prayer Book of 1559 still referred to them as bread and wine, even after the prayer of Consecration.[78] For this reason, as he saw it, the practice of adoration was nothing less than idolatry and 'to be abhorred by all faithful Christians'.[79] For William Thomson, the Eucharist was the central and most holy act of worship. There was, however, no real presence of the Lord in the consecrated elements, rather it was 'a memorial' of the Lord's passion.[80] Thomson was a 'receptionist'. As he understood it, the sacraments did not contain God's grace, they simply bestowed it into the hearts of those with faith. Thomson spoke of believers drawing near to Christ to 'taste more strongly the sweetness of His love and the efficacy of His atoning death'.[81] In his Bampton Lectures he gave further clear expression to this conviction that it was in right receiving that Christ's presence is appropriated:

> The effect is not magical, but moral; the sacraments confer the grace of God, they do not contain it; they are channels, not fountains. Nor are they the sole or the peculiar means of conveying to believers the effects of our Lord's Incarnation.[82]

Harold Browne similarly rejected any notion of a localised presence of Christ in the Communion elements. In a published correspondence which he had with the Rev. John Molyneux, an incumbent in the Ely diocese, Browne denied his assertion that Christ was especially present on the altar between the candlesticks.[83] He went on to stress that there is 'a special, though spiritual, presence of Christ in the Holy Communion and that the faithful receive spiritually His Body and Blood'.[84] Browne concluded his exchange with Molyneux by expressing his great anxiety about ritualism which he felt would only lead to schism.[85]

William Jacobson, who shared Browne's high-church sympathies, was equally adamant against any notion of a material presence of the Body and Blood of Christ in the sacrament. He pointed out any such teaching was explicitly denied in a Council debate held just four days before the publication of the second Edwardian Prayer Book.

Vestments

The use of mass vestments including the alb, chasuble and stole were, as has been noted earlier, a prominent aspect of ritualism. Many ritualist clergy adopted the custom of standing at the east side of the Communion Table or altar with their back to the people. In such a position the priest was held to be adopting a mediatorial role between the altar and the congregation. This was taken to imply that the priest was making a sacrifice on behalf of his people, as had been the custom in pre-Reformation England, when the Mass was offered up for the sins of the living and the dead. Ritualists attempted to justify this position on the basis of the rubric immediately before the Prayer of Consecration in the 1662 service, which speaks of 'the Priest standing before the Table'. However, this understanding was in contradiction to the fourth rubric at the beginning of the service enjoining the priest to stand 'at the north side of the Table'.

The Palmerstonian bishops were adamant to a man against Romish innovations in clerical dress. Charles Longley for example, was apprehensive about the introduction of vestments which had not been used in parish churches for three hundred years. As he saw it, they would inevitably be used 'to countenance and advance certain doctrines of the Church of Rome, repudiated by our Church in her liturgy and articles'.[86] In an address to his clergy, he observed that the use of such vestments identified the Holy Communion in the minds of the participants with 'the offering to God a sacrifice of the Body and Blood'. In short it changed the role of the minister who wore such vestments to that of a sacrificing priest.[87] As Longley understood it, the Ornaments Rubric sanctioned only the use of surplice and hood in parochial church services. He pointed out that, during the past three hundred years, seven hundred bishops had sanctioned no other form of clerical dress.[88]

Bishop Charles Baring, when at Durham, suspended the Reverend Francis Grey, Rector of Morpeth, from the office of rural dean because he had worn a black stole with three crosses embroidered on it.[89] Archibald Tait roundly condemned the use of vestments.[90] The fact that large congregations were attracted to some ritualist churches was no argument in favour of their proceedings.[91] In his view the actual numbers committed to ritualism was 'very small'.[92] In December 1858 Tait wrote to Rev. Bryan King, the incumbent of St. George's-in-the-East in his diocese, 'deeply regretting' that you should think it right to assume the unusual garments you describe to me'.[93] In the autumn of the following year Tait remonstrated with the churchwarden of St. George's and announced his determination to put a stop 'to such follies'.[94] Robert Bickersteth, when Bishop of Ripon, wrote to a clergyman who had adopted vestments that 'they are almost insepara-bly associated with the tendencies to Romish error and superstition'. He continued by stating that he did 'not believe it possible for you or any other clergyman who makes such innovations to acquit himself in the judge-ment of the Church at large'.[95]

Charles Ellicott, who had a number of struggles with the clergy in his diocese regarding the introduction of vestments, proved to be a staunch opponent of their use. Along with several of his fellow bishops he argued that the Ornaments Rubric did not make vestments legal. In a sermon en-titled 'Vestments and the Position of the Celebrant' which he preached in Malmesbury Abbey, he stressed that it had been the custom for three hun-dred years that only the surplice be worn for services in parish churches.[96] Regarding the position of the celebrant at Communion, Ellicott did not wish to see any change in the Prayer Book Rubric. He concluded his ad-dress voicing 'his deepest anxiety' on the question of the Eucharistic vest-ment, be it the cope or the chasuble'.[97]

Ellicott did once very reluctantly put on a cope (which was legal in cathedrals) and mitre, in a procession from the Chapter House on Christ-mas Day 1891, but he removed the mitre on entering the Cathedral and refused to wear it inside the building.[98] Ellicott's son wrote of his father 'I believe he once and once only wore the vestments presented to Bristol Cathedral. He had no love, I think I may say, for vestments'.[99]

In 1867 Ellicott became a member of the Royal Commission on Ritual and the Rubrics. Four reports were issued, the first two of which dealt with vestments. The Commissioners deemed it expedient 'to restrain in the public services all variations in respect of vesture'.[100] During a Commission meeting in 1867, Samuel Wilberforce recorded in his diary: 'Bishop of Gloucester, as always now, hot and intemperate in trying to force on condemnation of the chasuble'.[101]

In summary, Ellicott's dealings with ritualism were somewhat ambivalent. On the one hand there was the public figure who condemned the extremists in his own diocese. On the other, the pastor who was able to sympathise with those who shared his high view of the sacraments and wanted to lift the public church services above a level of dull formality.

The Confessional and Priestly Absolution

The second generation of the Oxford Movement introduced the practice of Confession during the 1840s. Numbers of them were influenced in this by Edward Pusey, who himself started the practice with Keble as his ear in 1846. In the same year Pusey preached a sermon entitled 'Entire Absolution of the Penitent', in which he pressed for the use of sacramental Confession. He appealed for support for the practice to the Prayer Book order for the Visiting of the Sick, which provided for a moment of personalised Confession and Absolution.

Along with other colleagues on the Episcopal Bench, the Palmerstonian bishops were unanimous in their outright condemnation of the practice of Confessional. Montagu Villiers expressed himself thankful that his diocese appeared to be clear of 'the filthiness of the confessional'.[102] Robert Bickersteth warned his diocese against 'all the dark abominations which are connected with the confessional'.[103] Samuel Waldegrave, Bishop of Carlisle, preached a sermon in January 1867 which was subsequently published entitled 'The Apostolic Commission on Auricular Confession and Priestly Absolution'. He began by defining what he understood as confession, which was not 'that general and open confession' nor 'that exceptional confession of the sick or dying penitent'. What he meant was 'that minute, that prolonged, that exhaustive confession of every thought, every word, every deed of ill, which needs to be drawn forth by questioning, detailed and often necessarily polluting, from the inmost recesses of memory and conscience'. Waldegrave continued: 'The whole scheme is a fond thing, vainly invented and hath no warranty of Holy Scripture'. His advice to those who felt drawn to make a confession was 'resist the very beginning of this evil'.[104]

Waldegrave took up the matter again later in the same year in his charge to the diocese. He warned against the practice of auricular confession which 'invests you with power over the maidens and matrons of your flock'. He continued: 'Its noxious influence places human society itself at your feet'.[105]

William Thomson was unequivocal in his condemnation of the use of the Confessional. In a speech to Convocation in 1878 he objected that 'it would sap the family life of this country, sow discord between husband and wife, diminish the legitimate authority of the parent over the child, and put the priest, who has a much slighter responsibility, in the place of those in whom God has placed full responsibility'.[106] Thomson put a further argument against private Confession. It was not good, he declared, that when sins have been committed, that the priest should have to bear the weight of them alone in his mind.[107] Francis Jeune, the evangelical Bishop of Peterborough, joined the hue and cry against the confessors. He reminded clergy that it was only after the Lateran decree of the year 1215 had rendered Auricular Confession obligatory upon all members of the Western Church that it was used. 'By what means is forgiveness to be obtained by believers?,' Jeune asked. 'By confession of sins to him who forgives.' 'Other absolution', he declared, 'we need not.'[108] He concluded: 'If our Church regarded Absolution and Confession as the provision made by God for the pardon of sin, she could not refrain from enforcing them'.[109] Charles Ellicott spoke of confession as 'often repulsive in its practice and details'. He was particularly concerned at the way in which it placed individuals under the influence and direction of the parish priest.[110] Henry Philpott spoke of private Confession and Absolution as 'calculated to move, more perhaps than any other practice which was deliberately laid aside by our Reformers, the aversion and indignation of the people of this country'.[111] In his view, Confession encouraged 'exaggerated and false notions of the power committed to a priest by ordination'. He was concerned at the emotional damage caused to both the confessors and the priests who listen to them.[112]

Among the Palmerston bishops, Longley and Tait both had to deal with particularly difficult instances relating to private Confession. The Reverend Thomas Minster, who was Vicar of St. Saviour's, Leeds in Longley's Ripon diocese, began the practice of Auricular Confession within a year of his appointment to the benefice. Longley admonished Minster and all his coadjutors at St. Saviour's to confine themselves to practices which the Church of England distinctly authorises.[113] Matters reached a crisis point when a young lady was urged to make her confession to one of the assistant clergy, the Reverend H.F. Beckett. She recounted to Longley that he asked her 'if I had any indecent connection with any young men, and if I have anything to do with any person but my husband'.[114] After her confession the woman was told to kneel down in order to receive Absolution. In the process Beckett 'touched me, which alarmed me, and I jumped up'. Although it is clear that no major impropriety had taken place, Longley described Beckett's dealings with the woman as moral compulsion and revoked his license.

Archibald Tait had a not dissimilar situation in his London diocese when

Alfred Poole, the curate of St. Barnabas Church, Pimlico requested Susan Buckingham to make her confession. Buckingham, who lived by prostitution, had fallen on hard times and sought relief from the Parish Visitors. Poole refused any money until she had made sacramental Confession. This took place in the vestry when it was all but dark. The door was locked, or 'secured' as Poole later put it, and he proceeded to ask Buckingham questions 'of a very personal and intimate nature'.[115] On these grounds Tait decided that Poole was causing scandal and injury to the Church. He therefore withdrew his license and urged him to 'reflect on the dangers to which such a course of action as you have adopted may expose both yourself and those over whom you exercise influence'.[116] Poole subsequently appealed to the Archbishop of Canterbury who confirmed the Bishop of London's action in July 1858. Poole then went to the secular court who required Sumner to hear the appeal. His verdict was that the proved allegations 'constituted good and reasonable cause for the revocation of his license'.[117] The matter of private Confession and Absolution reached a high point in 1873 when upwards of 60,000 lay members of the Church of England petitioned the Archbishops of Canterbury and York against the practice. Tait and Thomson replied to their Memorial jointly in a published item which included the following lines:

> THE ARCHBISHOPS OF CANTERBURY AND YORK –
> We believe that through the system of the Confessional, great evil has been wrought in the Church of Rome, and that our Reformers acted wisely in allowing it no place in our Reformed Church, and we take this opportunity of expressing our entire disapproval of any such innovation, and our firm determination to do all in our power to discourage it.[118]

Opposition to other Aspects of Ritualism

Although the major focus the Palmerston bishops was centred on the Real Presence, vestments and the Confessional, there were other aspects of ritualism to which, on occasion, they took strong objection. Charles Longley, for example, denounced the practice of the priest standing in the eastward position when consecrating the bread and wine.[119] Harold Browne also retained a lifelong dislike of the eastward position because it fostered a tendency to confuse Holy Communion with sacrifice.[120] He later emphasised to his clergy that the Laudian prelates stood, and encouraged others to stand, at the north end of the table.[121] Browne felt strongly that churches should have Communion 'Tables' rather than altars since a table indicated the commemorative nature of the sacrament.[122]

Archibald Tait also strongly advocated the use of tables for Holy Communion and during his disputes with Robert Liddell he ordered him to remove the altar from St. Barnabas Church, Pimlico, and to substitute 'a wooden table'.[123] William Jacobson of Chester, despite his strong high church convictions, stood always at the north end of the table when celebrating Communion.[124] He was also adamant that the Holy Communion must not be spoken of as 'the mass' since in the English mind the word was so strongly associated with 'distinctly Romish tenets'.[125] Longley shared Jacobson's convictions in the matter. He urged his clergy in Ripon not to think or speak of Holy Communion as being an occasion when a sacrifice is offered for sin.[126] Much later, when 'Primate of All England', he devoted a large section of his last diocesan charge to an attack on ritualism. Among many other things he declared that 'the only sacrifice which we are spoken of as making is the offering of ourselves, our souls and bodies'.[127]

The year 1850 had witnessed the restoration of the Roman Catholic hierarchy for the first time since the Reformation. In 1852 Newman had preached his celebrated sermon entitled 'The Second Spring' at Oscott Chapel near Birmingham, and thus had begun what many referred to as the 'Papal Aggression'. People in England in the eighteen fifties and sixties began to fear the possibility that the nation might return once more to Roman Catholicism. Against a background of rising Irish immigration, a residual folk Protestantism began to surface in many quarters of the country. In some areas of Liverpool and London it issued in mob violence against ritualist clergy. It therefore becomes all the more understandable that the bishops Lord Palmerston appointed, whose convictions were already firmly Protestant, should have denounced ritualism with such fervour.

IX

Palmerston's Bishops in Parliament

Lord Palmerston did not appoint bishops who would stand behind his party's policies solely from a political motive. Although his personal commitment to the Christian faith was nominal, he valued and supported the Church of England as an institution. He therefore worried that the wrong episcopal voices, or the lack of competent opinion, would result in the lay members of the Upper House who did not always understand the issues at stake, being led astray.[1] For this reason political considerations were always of secondary concern to Palmerston in his church appointments. Evelyn Ashley who was for a time Palmerston's private secretary, wrote:

> I can certainly of my own knowledge assert, that the one way in which a clergyman would not get preferment, was to commence his letter of application by a statement of his political principles, thus making them a ground of claim.[2]

In the event, almost all the bishops Palmerston appointed were strongly aligned to the Whig cause. Only Joseph Cotton Wigram and Henry Philpott were not of 'Pam's' Politics. It was probably for this reason that Owen Chadwick remarked that 'Palmerston was not as unmoved by political advantage as he professed to be'.[3] Indeed, Chadwick asserted, 'he was as eager as any prime minister not to have bishops who would speak against the government in the House of Lords'.[4]

Wigram's father, Sir Robert Wigram, was elected M.P. for the borough of Fowey in Cornwall in 1797, but after the Union sat for his native town of Wexford. He gave unswerving support to the Tory policies of William Pitt and was President of the Pitt Club.[5] Joseph Cotton's elder brother, Sir James Wigram (1793-1866), was Tory M.P. for Leominster.[6] Neither Wigram nor Philpott, it should be noted, caused Palmerston any embarrassment in Parliament. Wigram is only recorded as having spoken once in a debate, and that on the subject of education[7] and Philpott achieved a reputation for seldom attending the House of Lords.[8]

The remaining twelve Palmerstonians shared nineteen appointments between them. They were all either drawn from Whig families or developed strong Liberal convictions. Montagu Villiers' brother, George, was a Whig and in Palmerston's diplomatic service. Charles Baring's younger brother, Thomas, was Lord Melbourne's Chancellor of the Exchequer, while Archibald Tait became a Whig by conviction during his Oxford undergraduate days.[9] Charles Longley's father-in-law, Sir Henry Brooke Parnell

(1776-1842), to whom he owed his preferment, was recognised as an active and useful member of the most liberal section of the Whig party.[10] John Pelham's father, Thomas Pelham (1756-1826), joined the Whigs in 1794.[11] Samuel Waldegrave belonged to a great Whig family, his obituarist noting that 'though his political sympathies were with that party, he strongly dissented from their policies about the Irish Church'.[12]

Robert Bickersteth's son and biographer recalled that 'on questions of general politics my father was in the main a Liberal'.[13] William Thomson and Francis Jeune were both men of strongly held Liberal views, while William Jacobson actually owed his preferment to the fact that he had been chairman of Gladstone's election committee at Oxford.

Although Palmerston's bishops proved capable enough as pastors and administrators in their dioceses,[14] most of them failed to live up to his hopes that they would prove to be those who made solid contributions to the debates of the Upper Chamber. Longley, Frederick Arnold recalled, 'did not often speak in the House of Lords, but, when he did, his observations were always received with marked attention'.[15] Having been Head-master of Harrow and a prominent member of the Oxford University Commission, he spoke with noted authority on education issues. In point of fact, Longley's endeavours were perhaps not as infrequent as Arnold suggests, and they were certainly well above the level of most of his fellow Palmerstonian colleagues. Although Hansard cannot be guaranteed to record every speech made in the House, its records do nevertheless provide a fairly accurate indication of a peer's commitment and contribution in the House of Lords. From the time of his appointment by 'Pam' to the See of Durham, until his death in 1868, he spoke on some sixty-one occasions.[16] Aside from Archbishops Tait and Thomson, Ellicott and Browne proved to be the next best contributors, the former speaking on some twenty-eight occasions and the latter seventeen. Next in order of the number of recorded speeches given, came Samuel Waldegrave with eight and Robert Bickersteth with six. Waldegrave's obituarist noted that he did 'distinguish himself as a speaker in Shaftesbury's Anti-Ritualistic Bills in 1867 and 1868'.[17] Robert Bickersteth was observed by his son to have taken part in the debates only 'occasionally'.[18] His biographer recorded his great reluctance to leave the diocese and speak in Parliament. On those days when he did, he displayed 'capable eloquence.[19] He spoke with forcefulness in the debates on marriage with a deceased wife's sister and the disestablishment of the Irish church.[20] Of the remainder, Montagu Villiers made four speeches, Baring three and Wigram and Jeune one a piece. Pelham, Philpott and Jacobson were the most reluctant and there is no record of their ever having opened their mouths in the Upper Chamber. Despite Jacobson's learning and academic stature as a former Regius Professor of Divinity at Oxford, 'it is believed', said Arnold, 'that he never once opened his lips in the House of Lords'.[21] *The Times* reported of Henry

Philpott that 'he very rarely appeared in the House of Lords, though in the days when peers' proxies were allowed he sometimes caused his vote to be recorded'.[22] Significantly, John Pelham's obituarists make no mention of his ever having been present or taken an active part in any debate.

Among the Palmerstonian appointees, William Thomson and Archibald Tait were the most active in Parliamentary affairs. *Hansard* indicates that Thomson spoke on some seventy-three separate occasions, and made significant contributions to The Dilapidations Bill which he introduced in 1871[23] and to The Public Worship Regulation Bill of 1874, in which he actively supported Tait. Thomson also brought forward the Clergy Discipline Bill in 1888.[24] But of all Palmerston's bishops it was Archibald Tait who proved to be far and away the most significant figure in the Upper Chamber. Indeed for a generation he was the most prominent episcopal influence on the floor of the House. From the time of his Consecration as Bishop of London in November 1856, to his death in December 1882, he gave one hundred and ninety-three speeches. In addition there are a hundred and ten reported contributions by him during the committee stages of various bills. The great majority of Tait's speeches related to ecclesiastical affairs, but by no means all. For example, he spoke in a number of education debates[25] and in The Supreme Court of Judicature Bill in 1873.[26] Tait also concerned himself with environmental issues including railway building, atmospheric pollution and sulphurous acid.[27]

Tait's joint biographers, Randall Davidson and William Benham, noted that in the earlier years of his episcopate he believed it was vital that bishops should keep abreast of political affairs.[28] For that reason, when he was first at London he went far more frequently than any other Bishop to the Peers' Gallery of the House of Commons.[29] The same writers went on to remark of Tait that 'From the House of Lords he was scarcely ever absent when anything was going on'.[30] It was doubtless this which accounted for his extraordinary influence in both Church and national affairs. 'A man can't sit here every night', Tait said on one occasion, 'without people wanting to know what he comes for and listening to what he's got to say.' The Archbishop's Westminster robing room apparently became a place of consultation and debate. A clerical colleague recalled 'almost as many interviews of first rate importance in that room as either at Lambeth or Addington'.[32] Many of those who contacted Tait in this way were malcontents and Parliamentary opponents who would not have made their way to his palace at Lambeth. Of Tait's Parliamentary speeches, Lord Granville, who could hardly be a better judge in the matter, wrote the following:

> Having probably heard every speech he made in the House of Lords,
> I should like to say a few words as to his position in that Assem-
> bly, and the hold he obtained over its members. Of all our great
> speakers none had more the gift of persuasiveness, after all the
> chief merit of public oratory. Whatever might be the disposition of

the hearer on the particular question in discussion, it was difficult not to want to agree with the speaker. This feeling was produced by a sense of his strength, earnestness, gentleness and charity. . . . I may be wrong as to the causes which I have given for it, but I have no doubt of the power he exercised over the minds of his peers.[33]

Tait's chaplain during the last six years of his life invariably accompanied him to the House of Lords and heard every speech the Primate made. Only one he recalled as being ineffective, and that was his last, a response to the Duke of Argyll's proposal for an alteration in the parliamentary oath. His voice was unprojected and his manner diffident. Tait's comment as he returned to his room was: 'They didn't listen to me. It is the first time for twenty years. My work is done'.[34]

According to his son-in-law, it was a constant source of regret to Tait that his fellow bishops made so little of their Parliamentary opportunities.[35] The majority of his Palmerstonian colleagues, including Samuel Waldegrave with whom he was particularly close, must therefore have been a disappointment to him. This said, it can be countered that together they did make a vigorous contribution to a number of issues which in their views were crucial.

Palmerstonian Episcopal Contributions in the Lords

Clerical Income

As might be expected, Lord Palmerston's bishops gave themselves most readily to specifically religious issues, and in particular those which related to evangelism, worship, the clerical office, church property and privilege. Among their most urgent concerns was the falling income of the clergy, which was notably acute in rural dioceses where the tithe became increasingly hit by the widening agricultural depression. Montagu Villiers informed the House in April 1860 that matters in his diocese were 'even worse' than those in the diocese of Durham to which the previous speaker had made reference. In Durham there were 28 livings under £100 per year, but their Lordships, he said, would be surprised to learn that in the Diocese of Carlisle there were 120 livings under £100 per year.[36] In another debate on clergy income, Tait pointed out that a recent Burial Act had resulted in considerable loss of fees which had 'fallen very heavily on many of the clergy'.[37] The matter of clerical and parochial income continued to weigh heavily with Tait. In 1860 he moved the second reading of the Union of Benefices Bill stating that it was the intention that a wealthy parish should resource the needs of a poorer adjoining parish. The bill provided that any diocesan bishop should have the power to set up a Commission to consider uniting two adjacent benefices where such advantage could be achieved.[38] A little later in the same year Tait spoke in favour of a similar principle during the course of the Ecclesiastical Commission Bill. He urged that the Church Commissioners should not be permitted to divert income derived from large properties in inner city parishes when the people living within them were in 'great spiritual destitution'.[39]

Experimental Services

The need to reach out to the unchurched, and particularly to the working classes was a major priority with all of the Palmerstonian bishops. In the Spring of 1857 Lord Shaftesbury, and a group of associates who also shared this concern, arranged a series of Sunday evening services at the Exeter Hall in London. Some of the foremost evangelical clergy, including Bishops Montagu Villiers and Robert Bickersteth, agreed to take part, and Tait, whose diocese it was, gave his sanction to the proceedings. The hall was packed to the doors every Sunday evening with large crowds of working class people, and the national press carried headlines such as 'Extraordinary movement in the Church of England' and 'Spurgeonism in the Church of England'.[40] During one of the sittings of the Upper Chamber, Viscount Dungannon put a question to Tait, as Bishop of London, regarding the legality of 'certain evening discourses being held at the Exeter Hall in London'.[41] Were such services in unconsecrated buildings legal, and did Tait approve of them? Tait replied that he believed such occasions to be perfectly legal under the terms of the Act for the Better Securing of the Liberty of Religious Worship which had been brought in by Lord Shaftesbury. Tait went on to give his full support to what was taking place:

> not only do I consider these meetings to be strictly legal, but they are in the highest degree expedient. I believe from my heart, that there are thousands of people in this metropolis and other large towns . . . who have not entered a place of worship for many years. . . . I believe that those who are conducting these meetings have most earnestly at heart the welfare of the labouring classes of this country.[42]

After a time however, a hue and cry was raised against this innovative worship in the Church press. The incumbent of the parish in which the Exeter Hall stood, the Rev. A.G. Edouart, was persuaded to assert his legal rights and to veto the proceedings as being contrary to Canon Law. 'I am setting my face,' he said, 'against a proceeding altogether irregular, which, if permitted would prove thoroughly subversive of all discipline and . . . destroy that form of sound words so essential to the purity and power of our branch of Christ's Church.'[43]

As a result of Edouart's protest, Tait was compelled to advise that the services should be discontinued. Lord Shaftesbury's response was to immediately introduce a Bill into the House of Lords to deprive an incumbent of the right of veto. Samuel Wilberforce successfully protested against the Earl's 'indecent haste', with the result that he was forced to withdraw his measure in favour of a milder proposal put forward by the Archbishop of Canterbury. Sumner's Religious Worship Amendment Bill was warmly supported by Tait 'because he believed it would accomplish everything which the bill of the noble Earl proposed'.[44] He continued that 'the bill of the most Rev. Primate exactly made law that which did take place in the case of the Exeter Hall services'. Tait felt that it was 'a remarkable sign of the times that all the Prelates of the Church of England should agree that such services were necessary'.[45] In the Bill's second reading, Robert Bickersteth stated that he had preached at one of the Exeter Hall special services. He was of the opinion that the congregation contained 'a greater proportion of the working classes, than he had ever 'seen assembled in any church whatever'.[46] He 'deeply deplored' the fact that a movement which promised to advance true religion within the Church of England, more than any other which had been initiated for many years, should have been stopped by a single incumbent. Although Tait acknowledged the rightness of Edouart's protest, he believed he had acted 'very indiscreetly'. The issue caused Tait serious reflection on the whole issue of an incumbent's right to control all forms of Church of England worship within his parish boundary. He spoke on the matter at some length during the course of the debate.

> The parochial system must of course be maintained; but the law did not maintain that system in all cases. Where it was proved that the parochial system was used to give clergy a monopoly rather than secure the rights of the laity, the law of the land had over-ridden the parochial system. . . . It was never the intention of the law to give the incumbents a monopoly which should stand in the way of the teaching of the Gospel.[47]

With Tait's support the bill passed through the Lords, but it was withdrawn in the Commons. In the intervening period, however, Lord Shaftesbury and his associates restarted the Exeter Hall services, having been counselled that they could deprive Mr. Edouart of his legal power of veto if they avoided using any liturgical forms. Although Edouart disputed the validity of this advice he decided to leave the matter with Tait, who assured him that he would keep a careful check that services didn't get out of hand.[48]

For Tait the Exeter affair had a positive outcome, since it strengthened his hands in his determination to open Westminster Abbey and St. Paul's Cathedral for Sunday evening services for ordinary people. Despite a variety of objections, including financial, which Tait overcame by personally raising funds, the first such service was held under the dome on Advent Sunday. A crowd variously estimated in the newspapers as being between 10,000 and 100,000 had to be turned away, and Ludgate Hill was completely blocked for some time. Other similar occasions followed in Westminster Abbey and a series of 'Special Services for the People' at Bethnal

Green also took place, with Tait as one of the preachers.[49]

The question of holding Divine Service in theatres was not one to die away quickly. In February 1860 Viscount Dungannon once again drew the attention of the Upper House to the Performance of Divine Service at Sadlers Wells and other theatres by clergymen of the Church of England on Sunday evenings. He expressed his intention to move a resolution that they were 'highly irregular' and 'calculated to injure rather than advance the progress of sound religious principles in the Metropolis'.[50] Tait refused to be drawn at this point but was forced to make a statement on the following Friday when the Viscount formally tabled the matter before the House. Tait's defence was that the use of theatres was essentially a private initiative on the part of certain Christian men who felt a deep responsibility to reach out to the poor sections of the community. In his view 'they had acted wisely in not consulting the heads of the Church in entering on an experiment which might, after all, have not been successful'.[51]

Revision of the Liturgy

Many Victorian clergy were of the opinion that certain aspects of the Prayer Book services were inappropriate to the unchurched or too difficult for ordinary working class people to understand. For this reason there were periodic heartfelt demands for changes in the wording or for shortened adaptations of Morning and Evening Prayer. Some of the Palmerston bishops were very sympathetic to these pleas, but when it came down to the business of making specific alterations they began to fear that it would open the door to doctrinal changes of which they would disapprove. The Palmerstonian bishops were all strongly wedded to the Reformation doctrine enshrined in the Prayer Book services, and were particularly wary of suggested alterations which might result in ritualistic innovation. In July 1859 Lord Ebury presented a petition to the Lords from a group of Church of England clergy for a revision of the liturgy. He informed the House that 'he merely wanted to shorten the services'.[52] Tait, in making a reply, said that there was a danger of mixing up two very different questions: 'whether the services should be shortened was one question – whether the doctrines embodied in the services should be altered was another'.[53] He noted that the petitioners said they didn't want to introduce any new doctrine but they did not say how many doctrines they wished to be left out.

Lord Ebury was persistent in this matter and less than a year later, in May 1860, he put down a resolution for a 'Royal Commission to Revise the Book of Common Prayer and the Canons of the Church of England'.[54] Tait once again responded, and repeated his earlier warning that 'they could not have any excision without leaving some fear'.[55] He went on to acknowledge that alterations might bring back some who had seceded but it might by the same token 'alienate those who remain'.[56] The resolution was declined but Lord Ebury later attempted to force the issue. On a further occasion, a year later, he presented 'A Petition of Members of the Church of England and Ireland, praying for an Address to Her Majesty to Appoint a Commission to Inquire into the subject of the Book of Common Prayer'.[57] Tait was once again on hand to champion the cause of those who wanted to ensure there would be no doctrinal alteration to Church of England. Tait did, however, express his preparedness within certain limits to consider some shortening of services.[58]

It is significant that in another debate in the House in May 1863 on the Uniformity Amendment Bill, Archbishop Longley took his stand on the same principle of not changing the Church's doctrinal position. He pointed out that the Act required that a clergyman should declare in the church in which he officiated his unfeigned assent and consent to the use of everything in the Prayer Book. To change this declaration so that the clergyman 'would merely conform to the Liturgy' was not a change he could countenance.[59]

A further aspect of mission which was raised on a number of occasions was that of increasing the number of bishops. The population in many dioceses, particularly those in the industrial north, had increased considerably, to a point where they were pastorally unmanageable. For this reason there were a number of proposals to subdivide existing Sees and to promote schemes for the introduction of suffragans to assist in the administration of Confirmation. From time to time these matters were raised in the House. The view of most of the bishops whom Palmerston appointed was that some limited expansion was to be welcomed, but that if this was on too wide a scale not only would the status of the episcopate be devalued, but clergy might feel themselves under too much scrutiny. Speaking in The Subdivision of Dioceses Bill in March 1861, Tait put suggested that Cathedral Deans should also act as Suffragan Bishops. He had been a dean for seven years, and two of those years had been lost in vain attempts to find out what were the distinct duties of his office. He believed that nothing would be more satisfactory than that 'their duties should be rendered more distinct and useful'.[60] Montagu Villiers also contributed to the debate. Villiers favoured only a limited extension of the episcopate and warned against 'those who wanted to multiply the episcopate indefinitely'. In his view too many bishops would 'devalue the status' of the office and result in bishops who 'pried too much into the lives of their clergy'. Villiers quoted Bishop Ellicott, who had recently written that too many bishops could result in 'injudicious and mischievous meddling.[61]

In a later Bill of the Increase of the Episcopate, Charles Longley expressed his 'opinion most emphatically' that in places where the population had greatly increased 'enlarged Episcopal supervision should be supplied'. Longley went on to describe the present plan for only three new dioceses, Bodmin or Truro, Southwark and St. Albans as 'a plan of most moderate dimensions'.[62] During the second reading of the Bishoprics

Bill in March 1878, Charles Baring echoed Palmerstonian episcopal opinion. He pointed out that the population of Durham had increased more rapidly since the last census than anywhere else in Britain. At the same time the number of benefices and the number of his clergy had more than doubled. All this put greater demands on the bishop and made it increasingly difficult for him to pastor his clergy. With regard to the extension of the episcopate in general, Baring felt that there was also a danger of 'over officering' just as much as 'under officering'. Clergy, in his view, 'did not seem inclined to submit to that larger degree of interference which an increase in the number of bishops would imply'.[63]

Church Rates and Burials Acts

At the beginning of the nineteenth century Non-conformists suffered a number of disabilities which made them more or less second-class citizens. Two of their major grievances were the payment of Church Rates and the burial laws, which meant that in most instances they were not able to have their own pastor to officiate at the graveside of one of their own members.

According to the law every parish was bound to maintain the fabric of the parish church. The churchwardens were able to call together a meeting of all 'occupiers of property' and levy a rate which everyone, including those who were not members of the Established Church, was bound to pay. The rate was not only for the material upkeep of the church building, but also for the maintenance of church services and the salaries of certain officials, including the parish clerk.

As early as 1793 the parish vestry meeting at St. Peter's, Thetford, refused to agree a rate at all. The Church made an application to the courts but the judge's ruling was that the wardens could not compel people to pay a rate if the majority were against it. In 1825 a further attempt was made to prevent vestries exercising this prerogative of refusing a rate. However, on this occasion the court ruled that all the churchwardens could be compelled to do was to call another vestry to reconsider the matter. As the nineteenth century progressed there was growing hostility to the payment of Church Rates and a number of large cities, such as Sheffield where Nonconformity was strong, refused the rate.

From time to time various bills to abolish Church Rates were brought before Parliament, the first being in 1834. In a speech in July 1859, Archibald Tait pointed out to the House that the Established Church did have some right to expect subscriptions from the people. He highlighted the fact, for example, that 83 per cent of the existing schools for the poor were in connection with the Church of England, and in the matter of marriages some 84 per cent of the total were solemnised by her ministers.[64] In Tait's view it was most extraordinary that because 500 parishes had refused to grant a rate, the government should pass a bill which would make it law to abolish the rate in all the remaining 11,000 parishes. Tait urged that this matter be tested out in a Committee of the House.[65] In a further debate later the same month, Tait reminded those who were seeking to abolish Church Rates that these payments had produced £100,000 a year more than the Ecclesiastical Commissioners had been able to accumulate for annual distribution.[66] Finally, in 1868 Gladstone's Liberals carried into law the Compulsory Church Rates Abolition Bill. Longley, Tait and Thomson all spoke in the House during the second reading.

Longley stated that since the government had made it clear that it was not their intention to oppose the second reading of the Bill, 'it would be vain for anyone to suppose that the motion could be defeated'. He nevertheless rose 'for the purpose of satisfying his own conscience, by stating the reasons why he could not accept the principle of the Bill'. Although many of the town parishes had rejected the rate, Longley pointed out that it was still levied in the vast majority of country parishes. He did not see 'why those parishes should be deprived of the right which they had enjoyed for centuries – of making rates for maintaining the fabric of their churches'. It would give the poor the privilege which they had for centuries enjoyed, 'of having repairs and services of the church defrayed by the landowners'.[67] Significantly perhaps, Longley failed to mention that many of the rural poor were either dissenters or resented the Established Church's allegiance with squirearchy and farmers. Longley also feared that the burden of maintaining the fabric of the church once the rate had been abolished would inevitably fall on the clergy, who were overburdened already. Longley went on to state that 'the principle of religious equality lay at the bottom of the bill'. Such principles, he warned, 'would lead to the disestablishment of the Church and State'. For these reasons he entertained strong objections to the bill.[68]

Archibald Tait took a different view of the Bill, stating that he had no intention of opposing the second reading, since he was a member of the Select Committee of the House which had examined a considerable number of witnesses and considered the matter with a great deal of care.[69] He was, however, concerned that the present Bill proposed a blanket repeal of all the Church Rates, which would result in the ending of many local agreements, of which nobody really knew the consequences. He instanced the case of St Botolph's, Bishopsgate, whose late rector procured a private act by which the rates were totally ended and the maintenance of the church paid for out of the parish tithes. In contrast to Longley, Tait felt that in country parishes where the rate was still levied 'disaffection was even there creeping in'.[70]

William Thomson said he did not feel enthusiastic about the measure but that 'he believed the time had come when it was necessary that the irritation and ill-feeling attending this controversy should be done away with'. He would, he stated, do nothing to impede the further progress of the measure. He did, however, warn that some of the Bill's clauses contained principles which would gradually turn what had once been the poor man's Church into the Church of the rich.[71]

With the passing of the Compulsory Church Rates Abolition Bill the parish vestry, whose responsibility it had been for generations to keep the parish church in a state of good repair, ceased to have any significance. People had warned that the abolition would lead on to the disestablishment of the National Church, but their fears proved to be unfounded.

The question of burial was a major grievance suffered by Nonconformists. As matters stood, whenever a committal took place in the parish churchyard the law required that only a clergyman of the Established Church could officiate, and that he must use only the Book of Common Prayer service. Free Church members deeply resented the fact that they were unable to have the ministry of their own pastor at such a time of grief and sorrowing. An Act of 1852 enabled corporations in large towns to provide municipal cemeteries. This relieved the situation somewhat in the more densely populated areas but did nothing to resolve the problem in the majority of the nation's parishes.

Church of England clergy felt strongly against allowing Non-conformist ministers the right to officiate in the parish burial grounds for a variety of reasons. Some claimed it would open consecrated soil to heretics. Some, such as Father George Drury, the Rector of Claydon with Akenham in Suffolk, even included Non-conformists among them! For most however, the bill was seen as an invasion of clerical rights and privileges.

During the 1860s and 1870s a number of Burials Bills were brought before Parliament, several of them promoted by the Liberal M.P., Mr. Osborne Morgan. Then in the Spring of 1877 the Tory government brought forward a Burials Acts Consolidation Bill. It was a somewhat lengthy proposal with eighty-eight clauses including sanitary provisions the experts declared to be 'very good'. Tait spoke in its favour during the second reading, which was carried in the Lords by a majority of 39 votes, which included thirteen bishops. Then remarkably the Government withdrew the one clause which dealt with the religious difficulty. Tait was indignant because it was largely on the strength of this provision that he had supported the bill. 'My Lords,' he said, 'the time has undoubtedly come when this matter should be settled . . . and defective as the clause in question was, it promised to give us some sort of solution to the difficulty . . . It is not desirable that the Bill should go forward as a simple measure of sanitary reform.'[72] Unexpectedly Lord Harrowby, a staunch Tory, then proposed an amendment in favour not only of the 'silent funeral' which the government had withdrawn, but even the dreaded Non-conformist service beside the open grave. This amendment was carried, Tait siding with Lord Harrowby's amendment. In view of this defeat the Tories withdrew the bill, blaming the Archbishop for what had happened.

The General Election of 1880 brought Gladstone back to power and this made it certain that the Burials question came to the forefront once more. In May 1880 Lord Chancellor Selborne wrote to Tait:

> The Burials Bill will be introduced into the House of Lords . . . .. It will, in the enactments as to the alternative of silent burial, or burial with religious service, and as to the safeguards against disorder, etc., be in conformity with the amendments to the Bill of 1877 which were carried on Lord Harrowby's motion, in the House of Lords.[73]

The bill was introduced on 27 May by Chancellor Selborne, and on the motion for its second reading Bishop Wordsworth of Lincoln moved for its rejection in an emotional and detailed speech. He pointed out to the House that nearly 16,000 clergy had signed a petition for its rejection and he 'fully shared their wishes and their fears'.[74] He went on to predict that the Burials Bill would be 'an Act for the burial of the Church of England herself' whose provisions 'would be a dishonour to Almighty God'.[75] Tait unexpectedly rose immediately to reply, in what proved to be a masterly speech. He began by speaking with warmth in his respect for Bishop Wordsworth and then continued as follows:

> What is that which is to be dishonouring to Almighty God? Is it to be supposed to be a dishonour to Almighty God that, over the grave of one who is at present buried in silence, someone may offer a Christian prayer, or read a portion of the word of God. . . . I cannot believe that my right rev. brother really thinks that this uttering of a few words of a Christian prayer by any relative or friend, or by an individual appointed by the relatives, or the reading of portions of Scripture, will be dishonouring to God. I believe his mind was so occupied with what he supposes to be the inevitable consequences of the passing of the Bill that he forgot to consider what the measure itself is . . .[76]

Tait continued in a simple and clear way to outline the central principle of the Bill as he understood it. 'It is,' he said, 'to allow the burial, with religious rites, of persons who at present suffer under the grievance of being prevented from being buried with those religious rites.'[77] Tait's conception of the Church of England as a National Church was clearly a strong motivating factor behind his support for the bill. He believed that as a national church it should 'be ready to embrace all in the nation who are anxious to join it'.[78] For this reason he wanted to be magnanimous towards those of other denominations. He pointed out that at that very moment the Established Church was working with Non-conformists in producing a new translation of the scriptures, and that under the auspices of both Houses of Convocation. He also reminded his hearers that 'we use their hymns and they use our prayers'.[79] For these reasons Tait felt it to be his duty to support the second reading of the Bill. After a long and keenly contested debate, the second reading was carried by a majority of 126 votes to 101. It subsequently passed through the Commons and the committee stages with the provision still intact.

The bill's passing into law provoked the animosity of many country clergy. Numbers of them wrote in protest to the archbishop that they intended to resist by force any Non-conformist ministers who took advantage of the Act. As matters turned out there was very little evidence of graveyard hostility, and prophecies of doom and martyrdom proved totally unfounded. In all of this, Tait had proved himself to be a masterly and magnanimous leader in the Church and nation.

Ritualism and the Public Worship Regulation Act

Reference has already been made in the previous chapter to the long wranglings which took place over ritualism in the 1850s and 1860s by Lord Shaftesbury, to whom so many of the Palmerstonian bishops owed their appointments. The Earl had worked tirelessly against the introduction of such rites and ceremonies, which he regarded as contrary to the Reformation settlement. There were protests and counter-protests followed by litigation in the Church courts, but the outcomes were frequently protracted and inconclusive.

Issues of ritualism surfaced in Parliament in 1860 when there was rioting and disorder in London's East End, most notably in the Church of St. George's-in-the-East. Trouble had begun in 1856 when the Rev. Bryan King introduced the, then almost unheard-of, Eucharistic vestments. He then caused further antagonism by circulating 'Romish' tracts which urged that children as young as seven years of age should go to Confession and that 'the bread and wine become the Body and Blood of Christ'.[80] Matters reached a crisis point when the congregation elected the Rev. Hugh Allen, a distinguished 'no Popery' preacher, as Parish Lecturer with the right to use the pulpit from time to time. It was not long before Allen's Protestant following started to attend the usual services. Sunday after Sunday there was rioting, disorder and buffoonery. Books and kneelers were hurled from the galleries and King was shouted down by anti-ritualistic rent-a-mobs as he tried to read the liturgy.

Questions were asked in the Lords of Tait, as Bishop of London, about this lawless behaviour within his diocese. He responded by pointing out that the law was clear, namely that anyone who disturbed any minister in the discharge of his duty should be taken before the nearest Justice of the Peace and stand trial before the next Quarter Sessions. The problem, Tait observed, 'was identifying who the disturbers were'.[81] Some weeks later he was able to tell the House that a Sunday evening service at St. George's had 'passed off quietly', though he added that sixty policemen had been stationed inside the building. Tait blamed 'foolish vestments' as the major root cause of the disorders, and in another speech urged clergy 'not to irritate the feelings of the Protestant Congregations who were placed under their charge'.[82] When further outbreaks of disorder occurred later in the summer Tait was quick to defend the Rev. Hugh Allen to members of the Upper Chamber. He was an able preacher commended both by Archbishop Sumner and the Bishop of Cashel, who spoke of his 'zeal and efficiency'.[83]

The gathering storm over ritualism eventually prompted The Royal Commission on Ritual in 1867, but even this proved ineffectual in so far as stemming the tide of Romish practice was concerned. Protestant churchmen therefore reluctantly reached the conclusion that the only way forward was the introduction of Parliamentary legislation. This would open the way for the secular courts to take matters in hand and, it was hoped, bring clarity to what was rapidly becoming a very confused state of affairs. The majority view in the Upper House was that if such legislation was to be introduced it should come from the episcopal benches rather than from the somewhat rougher designs of the Earl of Shaftesbury. Against this background a meeting of the bishops of both provinces was convened at Lambeth on 13 and 14 January 1874. A Bill was then drafted in the first instance by the two archbishops, who endeavoured to take on board as much as possible the advice which Convocation had given four years before.

Once the provisions of the proposed bill became known there was vigorous opposition from the high church party and a series of somewhat vehement letters from Edward Pusey appeared in *The Times* in the last two weeks of March. An aspect of the bill to which objectors took particular exception was the setting up of diocesan councils to investigate alleged cases of ritualism. The Council, under the presidency of the bishop of the diocese, was to consist of three incumbents and five laymen elected respectively by the clergy and churchwardens. It was the lay membership which was to be elected by churchwardens which high churchmen found hard to accept. On the other hand, low churchmen, such as the redoubtable Dean Francis Close, were of the view that the bill was far too mild in its provisions to have any significant regulatory effects. 'Believe me, my dear and respected Lord,' he wrote to Tait, 'a very much more radical measure will now alone satisfy the aroused and sensitive laity.'[84]

Eventually, on 20 April 1874, Archbishop Tait rose and laid on the table of the Upper House a bill entitled An Act for better administration of the Laws respecting the regulation of Public Worship. In doing so he made it abundantly clear that it was not the intention to change any ecclesiastical laws. 'On the contrary', he said, 'it is our desire that the laws of this Reformed Church of England should be observed, and therefore what we request of your Lordships is to give us greater facilities in the administration of those laws.'[85] After having assured the House that his colleagues on the Bench desired to approach the subject as free from party bias as possible, he went on to state that the proposed bill had been provoked by the extremes of ritualist practice lately witnessed in a number of

parishes. He referred in particular to the recent Privy Council condemnation of the Rev. John Purchas for having a lighted candle and a large
metal crucifix on the Communion Table. In addition he was also charged
with having in the church a modelled figure of the infant Christ with two
lilies on either side and a stuffed dove suspended over the font. These
things, Tait pointed out to their Lordships were 'condemned as dangerous
innovations in the worship of the Church of England'.[86] The archbishop
referred to other things which are 'of a very grave character' such as the
introduction of 'Confession-boxes' and 'invocations to the Virgin Mary
and the Twelve Apostles'.

Tait ended his speech by stressing stressed that the process of obtaining
judgement in the Church's Court of Arches was slow and very expensive.
By way of example he cited the costs of the case brought against W.J.E.
Bennett, Vicar of St. Paul's, Knightsbridge, which had amounted to £11,015.
10s. 6d. Tait emphasised that the proposed bill in no way sought to alter
the laws of the Church but merely aimed to help with their administration.
The requirement which they were proposing was that in the first instance
a complaint regarding ritualism should be heard by the bishop and three
assessors with a right of appeal to the archbishop.[87] William Thomson, as
Archbishop of York, spoke in support of Tait and underlined the fact that
the bill was not advocating anything other than a new legal process whereby
'the law when once clearly ascertained, may be put into force'.[88]

The bill received its second reading on 11 May 1874. In his speech Tait
stated that he fully believed that the authority of bishops, if the bill became law, would be supported by all three major parties in the Church.
Tait had expected a strong reaction, particularly 'from those who were
likely to have their offences visited'[89] and he expressed his surprise that
there was so little opposition. After a debate which lasted for seven hours
the bill was read for a second time.

When the committee stage began the archbishops found themselves
facing a shoal of amendments from various sections of the House. One of
the most significant changes was Lord Shaftesbury's proposal that a single
lay judge, appointed by the archbishops, should replace the two existing
provincial judges, and would hear all representations under the Act without
the intervention of either diocesan courts or the preliminary Commission
of Inquiry. Neither Tait nor Thomson were happy with Shaftesbury's clause,
but realising that it was widely supported in the House they reluctantly
agreed to accept it rather than jeopardise the bill. After five further nights
in committee the bill was read for the third time and sent down to the
Commons, where it was received with enthusiasm. The Prime Minister,
Disraeli, spoke warmly in its favour as a bill 'to put down Ritualism'. The
Act received royal assent early in August. Few realised it at the time, but
it was to turn some of the prosecuted ritualists into martyrs for the cause,
thereby unexpectedly gaining public sympathy for their stance.

Other Concerns

By the end of 1874 the impact in the Lords of Palmerston's appointees to the Bench was dwindling. Villiers, Wigram, Longley, Waldegrave and Jeune had all died. Pelham, Philpott and Jacobson rarely attended the House and if they did, they never spoke in debate. Bickersteth preferred to stay within his diocese, and only journeyed to London if it was imperative for him to do so. Thus the Palmerston voices which continued to be heard were those of Tait, Thomson, Baring, Browne and Ellicott.

A debate took place on the Confessional in June 1877 to which both Tait and Ellicott contributed. In the course of his speech Tait warned against those who endeavoured to pry into the secret thoughts of the human heart in matters of delicate character.[90] He spoke of 'the very evil results' of Confession and 'the harm' it will do to the minds of the clergy concerned. Charles Ellicott drew the House's attention to a clergyman in his diocese who he suspected of being a member of the Society of the Holy Cross, an organisation which advocated the use of the Confessional.[92] As Ellicott was on the point of instituting him to a living in his diocese, he required him to sign the following paper which he then read out.

> I herewith notify to you (the Bishop of the diocese) that I have withdrawn from the Society of the Holy Cross, and that I distinctly repudiate the work entitled, 'The Priest in Absolution'.[93]

Tait spoke against Lord Thurlow's proposal to open museums and art galleries on Sundays.[94] It had been argued that this was a measure which would provide greater leisure opportunities for the working classes, but Tait's view was that there was no proof that this was wanted. More than that, he was adamant that the proposed bill would 'deprive them of that day of rest which they greatly valued, and which had been so conducive to the prosperity of this country'.[95] Tait urged members to look at 'the evils which existed on the continent of Europe in this matter'.[96]

Throughout his time in the Lords, Tait made speeches on a wide variety of topics. Whilst it was the case that the majority of his contributions were on specifically Church related issues, he also addressed the House on a broad range of other matters. For example, in 1860 he spoke during The Endowed Schools Bill.[97] Three years later in the Subscription Bill he argued for a simpler form of words for those receiving the MA degree at Oxford.[98] In May 1863 he presented a petition, praying their Lordships to withhold their sanction from a bill before Parliament which authorised the construction of a railway viaduct across Ludgate Hill. Two years later Tait expressed his hostility over proposals to expand Fulham Gas Works to cover a further 150 acres, with increased pollution of the Thames.[99] In 1868 he offered his views on army chaplains, artisans' dwellings and university tests.[100] In 1873 he contributed on several occasions to the Supreme Court of Judicature Act.[101] In 1876 he spoke on sulphurous acid and Elementary education.[102] In 1879 he turned his attentions to the Canal Boats Act, and in 1881 concerned himself with the Alkali and Company Works Regulation Bill.[103]

No other Palmerstonian bishop was able to come anywhere near to Tait's energetic and wide-ranging contributions to the debates of the Upper House. Ellicott, a keen naturalist, spoke during the Wild Bird Law Amendment Bill and the Cruelty to Animals Law Amendment Bill[104] in 1864 and Harold Browne on insurance against sickness and old age in 1880, on teaching in the Universities of Oxford and Cambridge in 1882, and on the Criminal Law Amendment Act in 1884. But their output, like the other Palmerston bishops except perhaps Thomson, didn't compete with their Primate's.

In Retrospect

Looking back over their Parliamentary contributions, it seems clear that the majority of Palmerston's appointees to the Bench didn't realise his hopes. He had wanted bishops who would make sound and articulate speeches in the Upper House, and thus prevent uninitiated lay peers being misinformed as to the central issues of Church politics. With the exception of Tait, Thomson and Longley, the majority of Palmerstonian bishops played only a small part, even in the major Church bills such as the Public Worship Regulation Act, the Compulsory Church Rates Abolition Bill and the Burials Act. With the exception of Wigram and Philpott they were Whig in their convictions but, on occasion, they showed themselves to be above party politics, particularly in matters in which the Church was concerned. Tait, for example, was perfectly willing to support Disraeli's bill to curb ritualism, until it eventually proved unworkable. Perhaps a more obvious example was seen in The Irish Church Bill. Although it was an avowedly Liberal measure crafted by Gladstone's first ministry, Baring, Ellicott, Tait, Pelham, Bickersteth and Philpott all voted against it.[105] Browne devoted a section of his 1869 Visitation Address to attacking the Bill, and Bickersteth in his lengthy and forthright speech in the Lords suggested that it would 'not have a feather's weight in producing contentment and peace in Ireland'. He believed the legislation would prove 'a blow to Protestantism and a triumph to Romanism'. Indeed, he said, 'it will exasperate Protestants without conciliating Romanists'.

Palmerston had wanted bishops who would be both good pastors known and respected in their dioceses, and at the same time speak competently in the Upper House. It is clear that all of his appointees fulfilled the first requirement, but although they made solid contributions on major church issues, most failed in the second. Perhaps they were weakest in failing to bring a Christian voice to bear on the major social and international issues of the day such as industrialisation, education, poverty and social reform.

X

Palmerstonian Episcopacy

In a letter written in the mid 1880s to the Christian Socialist, Thomas Hughes, Mr. J. Bryce, a fellow of Oriel College, reflected on the changing nature of English episcopacy during the course of the nineteenth century.

Few changes in our modern England have been more remarkable than the character of the bishops of the Anglican Church and the way they are regarded. Forty or fifty years ago they were usually rich, dignified and rather indolent magnates, aristocratic in their tastes and habits, moderate in their theology, sometimes to the verge of indifferentism, quite as much men of the world as pastors of souls. Now and then eminence in learning or literature raised a man to the bench; there were 'Greek Play' bishops, such as Monk of Gloucester, and the Quarterly Review bishops, like Copelston of Llandaff, whose powerful pen as well as wise administration marked him for promotion. But on the whole the prelates of those days were more remarkable for their tact, their adroitness and suppleness, than for intellect or moral eminence among the clergy so far as they were respected. They were respected as part of the solid fabric of English Society, more than for personal merits. But they were often a mask for political invective and literary sneers. The revival within the Church of England which has gone on all through this century began from below, and reached the bishops last. Palmerston's choice generally fell on men of earnestness, though they may have been sometimes narrow and unlearned. When High Churchmen began to find their way to the bench under Lord Derby and Mr. Gladstone, they showed as much religious zeal as the Evangelicals, and more gift for administration. The popular idea of what may be expected from a bishop rose and the bishops rose with it.[1]

It is the purpose of this final chapter to point up in more detail the nature of these changes which Hughes observed during the course of his long lifetime. The Palmerstonian bishops, whom he clearly saw as being at a pivotal point in these developments, are contrasted both with the earlier episcopate as well as with the generation who were raised to the Bench in the fifteen years after 1865.

Their Church Party Allegiance

As a group of prelates Palmerston's bishops were clearly in marked contrast to the appointments which had been made during the first half of the nineteenth century. Of eighty-eight English episcopal appointments made between 1800 and the time Palmerston took office in 1855, only nine, or 10.2% were from the evangelical party.[2] Of the twenty English bishoprics filled during Palmerston's first and second ministries eleven or 55% were filled by evangelicals. Of the fourteen men promoted by 'Pam' to English sees, eight were members of the evangelical party and three others, Tait, Ellicott and Browne had strong evangelical sympathies. Tait had married Catherine, the daughter of William Spooner, the evangelical Archdeacon of Coventry, and retained her evangelical faith throughout her life. Her husband was also described by *The Church of England Quarterly Review* as 'evangelical without being fanatical'.[3] Both Charles Ellicott and Harold Browne also frequently expressed their indebtedness to the evangelical party. The Bench of Bishops during Palmerston's period of office represented the greatest concentration of evangelicals in the nineteenth century. Indeed at one point in 1860, 10 of the 23 English sees were occupied by evangelicals.[4]

Palmerston's appointees reveal a spirituality which typified mid-Victorian evangelicalism. Most obviously they were both prayerful themselves, as well as advocating the importance of a prayer discipline to their parochial clergy. Montagu Villiers emphasised 'personal piety' particularly, 'prayerfulness' and visitation of the congregation.[5] Charles Baring urged the clergy and people of Gloucestershire to be 'patient' and 'prayerful' students of Scripture. Samuel Waldegrave assembled his family every morning for worship. No matter who his guests were they were expected to attend. Joseph Cotton Wigram had published *The Cottager's Family Prayers* in 1863. It contained prayers and readings for each day of the month. In the preface Wigram urged that in each house and cottage there should be a fixed time when parents, children and everyone in the house should say the Lord's Prayer and read a proper prayer. Archibald Tait made frequent recourse to prayer while he was working. Many of his diary entries are brief extracts from his daily round punctuated with short petitions. Typical of many such instances is the entry for 22 December 1850.

> I have been very busy for others, Lord, grant that the growth of holiness in my own soul may keep pace with my activities for others. The difficulty for such a character as mine is inward holiness. Outward activity comes naturally. Lord replenish me with the grace of Thy Holy Spirit. O Lord, give me holy thoughts, may I have no desire but to glorify Thee.[6]

In another entry a quarter of a century later Tait wrote: 'It is a glorious employment, this preaching of the everlasting Gospel, and good for one's own soul at least, whether it reaches others or no. But I want a life of greater, deeper, truer prayer'.[7] Tait emerged as an intensely spiritual man of God who drew deeply on divine resources in the moments of great suffering and sadness which afflicted him. During his time as Headmaster of Rugby School he had been stricken with a fever from which it was anticipated he would die. Tait submitted himself to God, praying that if his life was spared he might be useful in the service of the Church. He never forgot the watching care of his young wife who sat with him through all his choking paroxysms, ever ready to pray with him and repeat biblical texts and hymns.[8]

Just a few years later when Archibald and Catherine were installed in the deanery at Carlisle, brutal tragedy struck hard when five out of their six daughters died within a period of a few short weeks during a particularly virulent outbreak of scarlet fever. For more than two months Tait was so overcome with grief that he was unable to take up his diary. When he finally did so, he wrote that God had dealt 'very mysteriously with us'. They had passed through deep waters yet they resolved to submit, for the 'sweet memories' of their daughters' little lives, comforted in the knowledge that each was 'now in the arms of the Good Shepherd'. Further suffering was to befall them again when their only son, Craufurd, died on Wednesday 29 May 1878, aged only 29 just a few months after his induction to the parish St. John's, Notting Hill. On 12 November Tait's second daughter was married, but yet more tragedy was to follow when only days later Tait's wife, Catherine, unexpectedly took sick and died with congestion of the lungs. As the archbishop passed through these 'vales of misery' he was, like the psalmist of old, able to use them for a well. In each of these trials of sickness and sorrow Tait gave himself to earnest intercession. In the days preceding the death of his beloved son, Craufurd, Tait prayed with him both morning and evening. Tait drew much strength from Holy Communion. Shortly before both his son and his wife died he was able to minister the Sacrament to them, together with other members of the family circle and the household.

When John Pelham died after thirty-six years of devoted service in the Diocese of Norwich, he was reported by *The Times* obituarist as 'a man of deep personal piety' who passed his days 'in contemplation of the unseen world'.[9] Punctuality and regular daily habits were integral to the spirituality of Robert Bickersteth. Life at Ripon was orderly and by the clock. His son recalled that for the greater time of his bishopric his father would rise at six and spend the early morning hours in prayer, meditation and devotional reading. At nine o'clock it was his custom to read prayers in his chapel for the household and the outdoor servants. After breakfast he set himself the task of answering a great pile of letters. He apparently never sought the services of a secretary or chaplain, but succeeded in getting through all his writing in person, on account of his methodical and disciplined habits. On Sundays everyone, including any guests, starting with the youngest members and ending with the bishop himself, were asked to read a hymn. This practice apparently derived from his father's lifelong friend, Mr. Henry Thornton, who was one of the prominent members of the Clapham Sect.[10] Like Wesley before him, Bickersteth felt that punctuality was a vital part of his spirituality. So important did he feel it was to keep his appointments on time that, on one occasion when he missed his train he arrived before the start of the service by travelling in the engine of a goods train.[11]

William Thomson was a strong advocate of family prayers and he urged his clergy in the diocese of York to follow his example. He believed that household prayers should be short, simple and natural. 'When the master of the house kneels with his family to adore the Lord of Lords . . .', he declared, 'a higher meaning is added to their life. . . . God will be there because he is sought.'[12] William Thomson adopted a pattern for the day which was in some ways quite similar to that of Robert Bickersteth. He loved his children and even when he was far away holding Confirmation services he always returned home, often journeying as no other archbishop has done before or since, on the foot plate of a freight train with the engine driver. On his arrival at Bishopthorpe, even if it was three o'clock in the morning, he always wanted to find out how they all were before he went to sleep.[13] Amidst his intensely busy life William Thomson always found time for his children. Like the Bickersteth household, the Thomsons always gathered all the family for Morning Prayers in the Chapel at Bishopthorpe. The Archbishop always put on a surplice for these occasions and hymns were sung. Shortly after the archbishop's death, a visitor sent a letter to his wife recalling the cordial welcome he had received. 'If I may take the liberty of saying so,' he wrote, 'I thought I never saw a more delightful picture of a happy English home than that which I was so privileged to enter, and which has so sadly been broken up.'[14]

One or two of the Palmerstonian bishops were inclined to puritanical extremes in their lifestyle. Perhaps the most celebrated instance was Joseph Cotton Wigram, who in his Primary Charge to the Diocese of Rochester classified card playing, beard growing and cricketing as unacceptable in his clergy. His pronouncement resulted in *The Pall Mall Gazette* describing him as 'the religious prude of the Episcopal bench'.[15] Another paper, *The Saturday Review*, in an article entitled 'A Bishop of Little Things', jibed that 'he omits to warn his clergy that temptation may lurk in the drawing room as well as between the wickets'.[16] Robert Bickersteth, although not a teetotaller, was a zealous advocate of temperance societies,[17] and Montagu Villiers urged men to avoid theatres as an 'unmixed evil' and 'to look well to their steps in the ballroom'.[18] Not all the Palmerstonian evangelicals fell in with such strictures. William Thomson's life was definitely not dull. Balls and parties were held at Bishopthorpe and also when the family went to London. There were also frequent visits to the theatre. The archbishop romped with his children in the nursery, rowed with his sons on the river Ouse, and allowed his wife who was sixteen years his junior to indulge her fancies for pretty clothes.[19]

Palmerston's bishops were, all of them, men who took their relationship to God with great seriousness. Not only did they set aside time themselves for devotional reading and private prayer, they exhorted their clergy and the laity of their dioceses to do the same. It is also clear from their many writings and addresses that they all shared a common and deep concern for the proclamation of the Christian message and its application to the issues of the society of which they were a part.

In his ten years as Prime Minister, Palmerston appointed to nineteen English sees. When he died more than half of the bishops of England were Palmerstonian. In his first ministry the majority of his appointees were evangelicals, men prompted by the influence of his step son-in-law Shaftesbury. In his second period of office, when Gladstone joined the government, Palmerston said to Shaftesbury:

> I should like to be a little cautious in the selection of bishops so as
> to not unnecessarily vex my colleagues, some of whom are very
> high. It is a bore to see angry looks, and have to answer questions
> of affected ignorance. This must not stand in the way of fit men,
> but if we can now and then combine the two, so much the better.[20]

In the event, eight out of the thirteen appointments to English sees in the second ministry went to evangelicals. The principle remained the same, of finding men who were anti-Puseyite, and in some cases scholars who were capable of rebutting the liberal threat epitomised by the writers of *Essays and Reviews*.

In contrast to the predominance of evangelicals among Lord Palmerston's bishops, the generations who preceded them, and those who were their immediate successors, were both very largely high churchmen. In the earlier decades of the nineteenth century this can be illustrated with reference to some of the most influential prelates. For example, Herbert Marsh (1757-1839), who was Bishop of Peterborough from 1819-1839, was a high churchman who maintained cordial relationships with the leaders of the Hackney Phalanx and was at one with them. Bishop Van Mildert of Durham, the last of the 'Prince Bishops', was actually a member of the Phalanx having thrown in his lot with them long before he was raised to the Bench. He maintained close contact with them in the years that followed. Charles Manners-Sutton, who held the Archiepiscopal See of Canterbury from 1805-1828, was a warm friend to the Hackney circle. He selected his chaplains from men who were either among its members or sympathetic to its aims. His successor in office, William Howley, was also a strong high churchman, as was Charles Lloyd, who was briefly Bishop of Oxford and was recalled by J.H. Overton 'as heart and soul with high churchmen'.[21] George Pretyman Tomline, who was first at Lincoln from 1803-1820 and then at Winchester from 1820-1827, was a staunch high churchman who wrote orthodox theological works. Among others who were appointed to the Bench of Bishops in the 1830s and 1840s and who were also high churchmen, were Charles Blomfield who went to Chester in 1824, Henry Phillpotts who was appointed to Exeter in 1830, William Otter (1768-1840) who was at Chichester from 1836, John Lonsdale (1788-1867) who was Bishop of Lichfield from 1843, and Samuel Wilberforce who was promoted to the See of Oxford in 1845.

There were bishops appointed in the first half of the nineteenth century whose sympathies were not with the high church party, but they were the exception rather than the rule. Henry Bathurst (1744-1837) for example, who was Bishop of Norwich from 1805 to 1837, was a broad churchman and a most liberal-minded prelate. On one occasion he was cheered by a crowd when he happened to pass by a political meeting at Lincoln's Inn Fields. Someone who recognised him cried out, 'the Bishop of Norwich, a Reform bishop!'[22] Bathurst's successor, Edward Stanley, shared his Church party allegiance and was widely known for his enlightened views and reforming activities. Richard Bagot (1782-1854) was eased out of Oxford in 1845, and translated to Bath and Wells where his 'timorous ways' were felt to be less damaging to the Church's administration.[23]

The period immediately following Palmerston's death witnessed a marked change in the church party allegiance of the episcopal appointments which were made. In the fifteen years after 1865, fifteen appointments were made, seven by Gladstone, five by Disraeli, two by Lord Derby, and one by Lord Aberdeen. Thirteen of the new bishops held high church views and two, Lord Arthur Hervey (1808-1894) who was consecrated to the See of Bath and Wells in 1869, and William Magee (1821-1891) who was elevated to Peterborough in 1868, did not. Hervey was 'a staunch and thorough Protestant' who 'gloried in the Reformation'[24] and 'inclined to evangelicalism'.[25] Magee came from an evangelical home in Ireland and remained a committed evangelical throughout his days. He was, however, known for his wide sympathies and abhorrence of fanatical views.[26]

Before 1865 the sole episcopal patronage which the Tractarians had received was the appointment of Walter Kerr Hamilton in 1854. His appointment only took place because Queen Victoria was apparently unaware that he was a Tractarian.[27] However, with the coming to office of Lord Derby and Gladstone, some of the episcopal appointees were, as well as being high churchmen, also committed ritualists. George Moberly (1808-1885), who was appointed Bishop of Salisbury by Gladstone in 1869, was on intimate terms with John Keble and made a formal protest against the sentence of degradation which had been passed against William George Ward for the views which he had put forward in his *Ideal of the Christian*

Church Considered. Harvey Goodwin (1818-1891) accepted Gladstone's offer of the See of Carlisle in October, 1869. In 1848, along with John Mason Neale and Benjamin Webb, he established the Ecclesiological Society, which later developed into The Cambridge Camden Society. This organisation had the specific objective of building new churches in the medieval Gothic style in such a way as to promote ritualistic practices. Edward Benson (1829-1896) was chosen as first Bishop of Truro and consecrated at St. Paul's Cathedral on 25 April 1877. His son later wrote of his father's 'own delight in ritualism'.[28] In later years, however, when Benson was elevated to the Primacy in 1882, men like Henry Liddon, who had been enthusiastic at his appointment, were disappointed that he did not give them stronger support.[29] Part of the reason for this may well have been the fact that Benson's father was a 'pronounced evangelical' and that he himself had 'received his first impulse to holy living' under the ministry of the Reverend George Lee, a prominent Birmingham evangelical.[30] Benson genuinely feared that an excess of ritualism in the Establishment might drive out the evangelicals to the detriment of the Church as a whole. For this reason, according to his biographer, 'he thought everything should be done, that could be done, in order to retain them'.[31]

The great majority of the high church bishops who were appointed in the fifteen years after 1865 proved to be very fair-minded and tolerant of the views of other sections of the church, and of the evangelicals in particular. It could be said that, generally speaking, they were more tolerant of the Evangelicals than some of the Palmerstonian evangelicals were of the ritualists in their dioceses. On the other hand it has to be remembered that the *Prayer Book*, ecclesiastical law and court decisions vindicated the Protestant cause. It was perhaps for this reason that Frederick Arnold felt that Samuel Wilberforce 'had perhaps greater toleration for the evangelicals than the evangelicals had for him'.[32] Charles Mackarness wrote of his father John, who succeeded Wilberforce at Oxford in 1870, that 'he belonged to the High Church School; but he was also careful not to give offence to men of other views'.[33] During his episcopate no section of his clergy were ignored or isolated, and the honorary canonries at the cathedral were impartially filled with good men from various parties within the Church. It was said that Mackarness could work 'genially and unaffectedly' with the great sisterhoods of the diocese as well as with C.M.S. and the Church Army.[34] Joseph Lightfoot (1828-1889) was the first man since 1660 to become Bishop of Durham without having held another see. He was consecrated on 25 April 1879 in York Minster. In his diocesan administration and patronage he was, like Mackarness, scrupulously fair. All of those he appointed honorary canons were working in the diocese before he came, with only one exception, a younger man who held a canonry for a time as a lecturer in church history in three northern dioceses.[35]

Their Stance on Ritualism

In the years before Palmerston came to office ritualism had already emerged as a threat to the Church's peace and stability. Newman's reception into the Church of Rome in 1845, followed by several others in the wake of the Gorham case over baptismal regeneration in 1851, led many people to link ritualism with Romanism. 'No Popery' riots had taken place at East Grinstead in 1848 and St. Barnabas, Pimlico in 1850. National suspicions as to the intentions of the ritualists were fuelled by the restoration of the Roman Catholic hierarchy in 1850. Both Charles and John Sumner had pronounced against the Oxford Movement in their Diocesan Charges, John declaring in 1841 that the Tractarians had obscured the crucial doctrine of Justification by Faith.[36] Later, when he was raised to the Archiepiscopal See of Canterbury, John Bird devoted a section of his 1853 Charge to questions raised by the ritualists. He denounced the practice of private Confession and spoke of those who had recently left the Church of England for the Church of Rome as 'victims of delusion'.[37]

However, it was not until the 1860s and 1870s that ritualism began to emerge on a growing scale such that there was widespread public outcry against it. It was therefore inevitable, given Lord Shaftesbury's own hostility to ritualism, that the Palmerstonian bishops who were appointed as a result of his influence would share his views on the matter. Such was the case, and Lord Palmerston's appointees proved to be the most outspoken episcopal critics of ritualism. To a man they denounced practices such as the use of vestments, the mixed chalice, the eastward position of the celebrant and the use of the Confessional. It was Tait, one of their number, who sponsored and carried into law The Public Worship Regulation Act of 1874. It was the Palmerstonian bishops who, generally speaking, were the most ardent in putting down ritualism.

It was inevitable that the bishops who were appointed in the fifteen years after Palmerston would prove less draconian in the measures they adopted with regard to the ritualists. For one thing they were almost all high churchmen, and some of their number actually identified with the ritualists. This meant that, at the very least, their stance was going to be more conciliatory than that of their predecessors. Furthermore, with the passing of time, ritualism came more into the mainstream of church life. In 1876 for instance, Parliament learned that 7,144 parish churches had been restored to Gothic designs since 1840, and that 1,727 new churches had been built in the Gothic style.

George Selwyn (1808-1878) had been consecrated a bishop of New Zealand in 1841. He returned to England for a second visit in 1867 to attend the first Lambeth Conference, at which time Lord Derby offered him the See of Lichfield. Selwyn did not oppose the Public Worship Regulation Act during its passage through Parliament, but in his diocese he made no attempt to enforce it. His biographer noted that 'he declined to abandon faithful priests and their attached congregations to the persecutions of puppet parishioners'.[38] An incumbent wrote to Selwyn in 1869, explaining that he used altar lights in his celebration of the Eucharist, but would give up the practice if ordered to do so. Selwyn replied, pointing out that the law of the land had declared the use of altar lights to be illegal, but he made no request to the incumbent to remove them. Generally speaking Selwyn's diocese was free from ritualistic excesses. After three years in office in which he gained 'an intimate acquaintance with his diocese', Selwyn declared that 'he did not believe there was a single clergyman within its limits who was fairly and justly liable to the imputation of promoting Romish doctrine and teaching'.[39] To another of his clergy, the Reverend C. Boddington, who had raised matters about ritualism, Selwyn replied urging him 'to think most of the mind of Christ and of the peace of His Church'.[40] He also required him 'to offer to those parishioners who desire the ordinances of the Church to be performed in a strictly lawful manner, such convenient opportunities as may satisfy their just and reasonable demands'.[41] Selwyn's biographer summarised his views by stating that 'in matters of ritual he was always tolerant, and increasingly so in later years'.[42]

John Mackarness was generally opposed to ritualism in his Oxford diocese, although paradoxically he defended one of his incumbents, Thomas Carter, the Vicar of Clewer, when a medical doctor named Julius brought charges against him. These included among other things, wearing vestments, mixing wine with water, making the sign of the cross in blessing the congregation, using lighted candles on the altar, allowing 'O Lamb of God' to be sung after the Consecration, and elevating the bread and wine in an unauthorised manner. Mackarness was unwilling to prosecute, but Julius pressed the matter and the court required him to do so. Although Mackarness disapproved of ritualism he was not happy at the prospect of the ageing Carter being committed to prison. He therefore appealed and agreed to be represented by lawyers. In May 1879 and March 1880 the House of Lords upheld the appeal. By his action Mackarness demonstrated that bishops had the legal right to veto ritualistic prosecutions. He had in so doing reduced the effectiveness of the Public Worship Regulation Act.

What had taken place inevitably helped to dissuade members of the Church Association from bringing prosecutions in a diocese where the bishop was in sympathy with the ritualists. On the other hand, where bishops did use the veto against ritual prosecutions, they inevitably ran the risk of being regarded by the public as 'Romanisers'. Some bishops were, however, willing to take that chance, believing that the veto might in some circumstances bring peace to the Church. After the veto case the number of prosecutions for ritualism appeared to decline, although there were still one or two imprisonments. The most notable cases were those of Thomas Pelham Dale in the city of London from 30 October to 24 December 1880,

R.W. Enraght of Bordesley, Birmingham from 27 November 1880 to 17 January 1881; S.F. Green of Miles Platting in Manchester, 19 March 1881 to 4 November 1882.

James Fraser, who was made Bishop of Manchester in 1870, did not believe that the Public Worship Regulation Act should be 'rigorously interpreted or severely applied'. There was little ritualism in his diocese and right at the close of his episcopate in 1884 he stated: 'I have only two churches in the diocese in which illegality in ritual is carried to its highest extent, the clergy of which have utterly despised my admonition'.[43] In 1878 Fraser engaged in an extended struggle with Sidney Fairthorne Green, the Rector of St. John's, Miles Platting, one of the poorer suburbs of South Manchester. Eventually his hand was forced when the Church Association took up the case on behalf of the parishioners. Green refused even to 'submit under protest' to the bishop, with the result that at the end of the statutory period of twenty days the matter passed to the secular court. In due course, in June 1881, Green found himself a prisoner in Lancaster gaol, much to Fraser's great regret. During a lengthy period of imprisonment Fraser conducted an extensive correspondence with Green, offering to bring about his release if he would submit to his episcopal authority. Green's point of principle was that the Prayer Book permitted the ritualistic practice he was accused of and the bishop therefore had no right to condemn them.[44]

Frederick Temple (1821-1902), who was successively Bishop of Exeter from 1869 to 1885 and Bishop of London from 1885 to 1896 before being raised to the Primacy, was generally tolerant of the ritualists although he disapproved of their practices. Soon after his arrival in London he was faced with difficulties at St. Cuthbert's, Philbeach Gardens, where the curate-in-charge was Henry Westall. This was a new church with a district carved out of St. Philip's, Earl's Court. No sooner had Temple consecrated the new church than he was faced with a stream of complaints. These included 'a procession in which the crucifer and numerous acolytes took part, boys wearing red blood cassocks and slippers to match . . . the officiating priest wearing a biretta [and] full eucharistic vestments'. The Mass was rendered 'with full orchestral accompaniment' and 'there were 64! lighted candles on the altar – the lesser lights being ceremonially lighted while the service was proceeding'.[45]

Temple took no decisive action against Westhall, despite being urged to do so by the Church Association and others.[46] The result was a series of unsatisfactory and extended confrontations. Temple adopted a similar stance in April 1888 when complaints were made to him that the new highly coloured reredos which had been erected in St.Paul's Cathedral was 'idolatrous'. Temple rejected the protesters' view that it was 'part of the tide of Romish error and practice which is coming in like a flood upon us'.[47] He also firmly believed in the bishop's right established by Mackarness to veto frivolous prosecution. Temple occasionally heard confessions but not in the way Anglo-Catholics conducted them. He was strongly opposed to the notion of people having the right to demand a priest to listen to their confession.[48]

Bishop Jackson agreed to veto the ritual prosecution of Mackonochie, the incumbent of St. Alban's, Holborn, in 1882. Of the generation who came after the Palmerstonians, the following bishops exercised the right of veto in ritual cases: Temple at both Exeter and London, Harvey Goodwin (1818-1891) while at Carlisle, William Magee at Peterborough and George Moberly of Salisbury.[49] Mackarness was an opponent of Confession but did not believe those clergy who practised it were carrying out 'any conspiracy against the doctrine and discipline of our reformed Church'.[50] Moberly was strongly of the view that there was a rightful use of Confession in the Church of England.[51] James Fraser, on the other hand, denounced the Confessional as 'demoralising equally to priest and penitent'.[52] Although E.W. Benson was happy with a certain amount of ritual, he worried 'lest its elaboration and development should bring about a subordination of the thing symbolised to the symbol'.[53] He was anxious that ritualism was in danger of detracting the Church from the great problems of society.[54] He also felt there was a certain degree of effeminacy associated with ritual. A brief passing entry in his diary stated 'these short surplices, no hoods and coloured stoles don't seem fit for men'.[55]

Like their Palmerstonian predecessors, some of Gladstone's and Disraeli's appointees were strongly committed to the principles of the Reformation. Selwyn, despite being a high churchman, was firmly attached to the doctrines of the Reformers. At his last diocesan conference he was emphatic that the Church of England has 'accepted the principles of the Reformation'. He desired nothing more than 'to carry out those principles to the highest point of spiritual life'.[56] Samuel Wilberforce, who was translated to the See of Winchester on Gladstone's nomination expressed his views on confession and ritualism at a meeting of his archdeacons and rural deans shortly before his death in 1872. He declared that Confession damages the intimacy between husbands and wives and 'poisons' the mind of the priest. Regarding ritual, Wilberforce warned of 'a growing desire to introduce novelties such as incense, a multitude of lights in the chancel and so on'. Such things, he declared, 'are honestly and truly alien to the Church of England'.[57] Lord Arthur Hervey, a low churchman, shared Wilberforce's views. Described by his son as 'a staunch and thorough Protestant', he took a great dislike to the introduction of what he considered 'mere imitations of the ritual of foreign services into our own'.[58]

In summary, it is clear that the generation of bishops who were appointed after Palmerston's period of office were, generally speaking, much less vehement against ritualism as a whole. A few of their number embraced ritualism themselves and the majority of the rest, who were almost all high churchmen, were prepared to be tolerant, believing this policy to be in the best interests of the wider Church.

Their Accessibility

The earlier years of the nineteenth century were not noted as a time in which bishops moved freely about their dioceses or were familiar faces to the people of their parishes. Bishops Kaye of Lincoln, Blomfield of Chester and Monk of Gloucester were prominent members of the Ecclesiastical Commission, but in their dioceses they were somewhat distant figures who gave insufficient attention to their clergy and people. When Monk was at Gloucester, Francis Close, who was incumbent of Cheltenham within his diocese, once remarked on their cordial and gentlemanly relationship: 'He never interfered with me in any one thing that I ever did!'[59] Kaye, Monk and Blomfield represented early nineteenth century bishops who came from scholarly backgrounds. Both Monk and Kaye had been at Cambridge, Kaye as Regius Professor of Divinity and Monk as Professor of Greek. Blomfield had been a college fellow for a time and although he held no distinguished academic position, he sustained a considerable scholarly output in his early years. As a country clergyman he was a pluralist who became heavily involved in county business. He wrote to his friend Monk on one occasion telling him that he had become a Justice of the Peace and a Commissioner of turnpikes and was likely to become a property tax official. He worried that these tasks might interfere with his Greek studies![60] When he became Bishop of London he seems to have engaged in nepotism which did not endear him to the clergy of his diocese. Blomfield, despite his desire for reform, believed an alliance of serious clergy and the gentry provided the most stable social and religious structure. Charles Manners-Sutton and William Van Mildert pursued extravagant living and indulged in lavish entertainments which demanded a high expenditure. Such behaviour hardly created a close bond between them and their impecunious clergy, let alone the undernourished farm workers of East Anglia, or the long-suffering miners of Durham. Henry Phillpotts was another spend-thrift high churchman, although in his case the large sums went on litigation. Always embroiled in lawsuits with his clergy over issues such as appointments, the use of the surplice or baptismal regeneration, he was reputed to have spent more than £20,000 on court cases during his forty-year episcopate.[61]

Clearly there were some reforming bishops in the earlier part of the century who made genuine endeavous to move among the people of their diocese and to pastor their clergy. John Bird Sumner, during his twenty years at Chester from 1828 to 1848 consecrated 232 churches, saw an increase of more than 700 primary schools, held regular diocesan visitations and met the clergy in their homes.[62] He made great efforts to show the poor and the working-classes that there was a place for them in the house of God. On one occasion he even had the locks removed from pew doors during a service in order that those without seat could take up unoccupied private pews.[63] John Bird's younger brother, Charles, when at Winchester had been known to invite the hungry poor into his palace at Farnham and offer them food and warmth. At Winchester he consecrated new churches, opened a training college for teachers, pastored his clergy and held regular diocesan visitations.[64] Samuel Wilberforce, besides being a model reforming bishop, took care over his ordination candidates and was instrumental in founding Cuddesdon Theological College. He created Diocesan Societies for church building, spiritual help, the education of the working classes and the augmentation of poor benefices. He set himself the aim of an hour's devotional exercises at the beginning of every day, and he himself missioned the village parishes of his diocese.[65]

However, when all is said and done, the fact remains that the Sumner brothers and their relative, Samuel Wilberforce, along with Edward Stanley of Norwich, Henry Ryder of Lichfield, and Walter Kerr Hamilton of Salisbury, were exceptional. They stood out as the few who attempted to initiate a new style of episcopacy which made a spiritual impact at the grass roots level in their respective dioceses. In most cases, episcopal visitations in the first half of the nineteenth century were rare. In the Winchester diocese for example, until 1828 no bishop for a hundred years had made more than one visitation.[66]

The majority of the bishops in the early part of the nineteenth century had aristocratic connections. Richard Soloway pointed out that only thirty-eight of a hundred bishops already installed in 1783, or appointed over the next sixty-nine years, lacked any direct familial relationship with the aristocracy.[67] Inevitably therefore, these prelates were identified with the peers of the realm and were, generally speaking, aligned with the landed and commercial interests of the upper echelons of society. Most had little time to grapple with a Church which, in the words of Owen Chadwick, 'had a parochial system adapted to ministry in villages, its clergy gentlemen, its legal framework inflexible and unable to meet new circumstances'. He continued that 'the clergy were learned, well connected, socially acceptable, influential as magistrates are influential'.[68]

In contrast to these earlier generations of bishops, Lord Palmerston had deliberately set out to select bishops who would be accessible to both the clergy and people of their dioceses. For this reason, prompted by his son-in-law, he had often chosen men who had proved themselves in parish work. To a man, the Palmerstonian appointees proved themselves as those who gave themselves to their people and made themselves available to those who most needed their ministrations. They also made particular efforts to be on hand to see and counsel their clergy. The Palmerstonian bishops all held regular Diocesan Visitations, in most cases on a triennial basis. They extended the office of rural dean as being a means whereby they could more effectively communicate with their clergy. They made real efforts to alleviate clerical poverty by building new parsonage houses and raising money to supplement the incomes of impoverished benefices. In the matter of Confirmation services, Palmerston's appointees set themselves to improve on the practice of many of their predecessors. Most held more frequent services and urged their clergy to better preparation and ongoing instruction.

Montagu Villiers, the first Palmerston bishop, journeyed extensively throughout his diocese and set himself the task of preaching in every church. He visited remote hamlets where the local people had never seen a bishop. When he went to All Hallows in August 1857, so many people came to listen to him that for the first time in his ministry he preached to 800-900 people sitting in the churchyard.[69] During his ministry in the Carlisle diocese, Villiers was noted as:

> preaching in the open air, visiting from cottage to cottage, praying with the dying, exhorting the living, elevating to a wonderful degree the tone of morality amongst the working classes in the neighbourhood; besides throwing open his house to the younger clergy, and especially to candidates for holy order.[70]

Charles Longley took his pastoral role with great seriousness. At Ripon his visit to Howarth's parsonage was recalled by Charlotte Bronte whose father, Patrick, was the incumbent. 'He is certainly a most charming bishop,' she wrote 'the most benignant gentleman that ever put on lawn sleeves; yet stately too and competent to check encroachments'.[71]

When later at Durham, Longley urged that 'we, the Bishops of the Church, must be known among our flocks . . . we must strive to be the friends, the fathers and counsellors of the clergy'.[72] Archibald Tait was renowned as a man of the people both at London and later, when Archbishop of Canterbury. When in the nation's capital city he preached in the open air in Covent Garden market, and to the weavers of Bethnal Green. On another day he addressed omnibus drivers and cabmen in a stable yard at Islington. He approved of the Exeter Hall informal services and fought to improve poor livings in the diocese. John Pelham is perhaps the outstanding example of a bishop who was at one with his clergy and people. He made regular visits to each of his rural deaneries in order to maintain close contact with his clergy. During the earlier years of his episcopate it was Pelham's custom to spend a long weekend in a parish, passing time with the clergyman's family, participating in the church services and inspecting the Sunday and day schools. He took his Ordinations with intense seriousness, preparing the candidates with great thoroughness with addresses and charges. It was his practice for many years to invite annually to the palace all those whom he had ordained and who remained in the diocese.[73]

Robert Bickersteth's long episcopate at Ripon contained many reflections of both Tait and Pelham. Like Pelham he enjoyed nothing better than to spend a weekend at the rectory of some conscientious clergyman and to share in the Sunday services, presiding if there was a celebration of Communion and preaching at one of the other services of the day. Along with Tait, Bickersteth was comfortable speaking in the open-air or at factory gates. On one occasion his pulpit was even an enormous Armstrong gun.[74] He took part in the Mission to Leeds in 1875 and preached day after day in the town's churches. Following his predecessor, Longley, Bickersteth took on the semi-parochial charge of North Leys, a small village about half a mile from his parish.[75] Here he constantly visited the sick and the poor. Along with his Palmerstonian colleagues Bickersteth paid particular attention to the Examination of Ordination of his ministerial candidates. So devoted was he to the work of his diocese that he was reluctant to leave it, even when there were important matters to be discussed in the House of Lords.

During his nine years at Carlisle, Samuel Waldegrave proved himself to be a devoted pastor to his clergy and people. He gave himself unstintingly to the work of building parsonage houses and raising the income of the poorer incumbencies. He urged his clergy to carefully scrutinise the candidates they presented to him for Confirmation and he himself took great care with his own addresses on such occasions.[76] During his first Diocesan Visitation he stated the fact that 'I have already striven to make myself as accessible as possible to the clergy'. For those who found it difficult to contact him he made himself available every Wednesday at noon at the private residence of his secretary, Mr. Mounsey, in Castle Street, Carlisle.[77] Joseph Cotton Wigram was recalled by Archdeacon Mildmay as 'emphatically the layman's bishop' and one who was noted for his ready accessibility.[78] He concerned himself with the needs of the poorer clergy, urged the importance of lay helpers in the parish, and took particular care over Confirmation and Ordination services.[79] Charles Baring's Durham obituarist wrote that he 'possessed the love and revered regard of almost the entire clergy and laity of his diocese, to whom his life presented a rare example of piety, Christian zeal, devotion to duty, steadfastness in faith and conviction, and large-hearted benevolence'.[80] When Henry Philpott died after thirty years as Bishop of Worcester, his *Times* obituarist recalled 'the practical character of his sympathy' for his clergy. He gave liberally from his own income to support the needs of the impoverished clergy of his diocese.[81]

William Thomson achieved the distinction of being heralded 'The People's Archbishop' which is inscribed on a memorial stone in Sheffield Cathedral. During the latter part of his life no man equalled him in the affections of the working classes, and it is difficult to overestimate the positive impact which he made in the northern province. In 1869 he addressed nearly a thousand working men in Sheffield, and in June 1883 his artisan admirers presented him with a gift of cutlery.[82] Despite his many responsibilities as archbishop, Thomson ministered in 450 parishes in his diocese in addition to his Confirmation services. Charles Ellicott and Harold Browne, notwithstanding all their biblical scholarly pursuits, were both men of deep pastoral concern who gave themselves to the needs of their clergy. For most of his forty year episcopate Ellicott presided over the combined See of Bristol and Gloucester. During that time he made it his practice to stay in Bristol each month and to preach in the Cathedral on the first Sunday. Because of the size of his diocese he took particular care over his Visitations, often giving different addresses in neighbouring localities. Ellicott lived close to his people and was acutely aware of the problems of interference and the rural poor. He also did his best to mediate in the agricultural labourers' dispute in 1872, when he invited local union leaders to his palace. He took particular care with his candidates for Holy Orders, some of whom in after years recalled the concern and attention he gave during their pre-ordination retreats.[83] Harold Browne fostered good relationships with his clergy. He disliked being called 'Your Lordship' and listened with deference to men far beneath him.[84] He valued his rural deans as his link with the clergy.[85] He took great care over his Confirmation addresses, and when at Ely concerned himself with the problems of agricultural gangs.[86] When William Jacobson died after nearly twenty years of presiding over the See of Chester, his ministry was given fulsome praise in the following paragraph which spoke of his accessibility and care for his clergy:

> He was dignified and yet considerate, a faithful 'overseer' of his clergy without being austere, while he had in a very large measure one New Testament qualification of a bishop, that, namely, of being 'given hospitality'. In fact, his kindness, especially in the cause of charity, was almost incredible, for it was generally understood that during the closing years of his life as a bishop he actually devoted the whole of his large stipend to the benefit of struggling clergymen and deserving cases that stood in special need of pecuniary relief.[87]

When the extent of this evidence is weighed, it is clear that as a group Palmerston's bishops were remarkable for the level of their availability and pastoral oversight of their clergy. Several of their number worked alongside their clergy rather than over them. They were in reality pastors both of their clergy and people in a degree that had not been evidenced in earlier generations. Their high level of involvement with clergy helped to create a mutual bond between them, and by the same token, created a genuine feeling of a diocesan family, with its own head and leader who was known and respected. Clearly the pre-Palmerstonian bishops were not as readily accessible as their successors and nor were they as concerned for the needs of the poor and inner-city areas. The charges of Palmerston's appointees are filled with concern for the working classes in a way that those of their predecessors were not. Bishops like Blomfield and Lonsdale consecrated new churches whereas bishops such as Bickersteth, Tait and Villiers preached in them.

Palmerston and Shaftesbury's concern to appoint men with a wide pastoral experience of parish life had set a new pattern of episcopacy. Significantly it seems to have influenced Gladstone, Disraeli and Lord Derby in the appointments which they made in the period from 1865-1880. Thirteen of the fifteen men who became bishops in that period had substantial parochial experience. The only two who lacked it were Joseph Lightfoot and George Selwyn. Joseph Lightfoot spent his entire career before his consecration in academic life, first as a tutor at Trinity College, Cambridge, then as Hulsean Professor of Divinity. George Selwyn was briefly curate to the Reverend Isaac Gossett, the Vicar of Windsor, before he was consecrated as a bishop for New Zealand at the age of thirty-two. By the time he was offered the See of Lichfield he had had twenty-five years of rich pastoral experience as a bishop in the southern hemisphere.

The most obvious pastors among the Gladstone-Disraeli appointments were Thomas Claughton (1808-1892) of Rochester and later St. Albans, James Fraser of Manchester, Arthur Hervey of Bath and Wells, Richard Durnford of Chichester and John Mackarness of Oxford. Claughton was appointed to the populous parish of Kidderminster in 1841 and remained in post for twenty-six years. Here he established daily services and an efficient system of parochial visiting. He promoted schools and the building of additional churches. He was also an able and effective preacher.[88] James Fraser had two lengthy spells of parish work, first at Cholderton from 1847-1860 where he built a new church, constructed a village school, humoured the local squire and ironed out the little troubles and jealousies among his flock. He then moved to Ufton Nervet in Berkshire where he opened a new day-school and built another church. During his time at Ufton, Fraser was appointed as a Commissioner to report on the elementary and other schools in the United States. This took him out of the country for much of 1865. He was then appointed to serve on the 1867 Royal Commission on the Employment of Children, Young Persons and Women in Agriculture. He had a particular responsibility for the counties of Norfolk, Essex, Sussex and Gloucestershire. His work brought him into close contact with farm labourers and the working and living conditions of the rural poor.[89]

Lord Arthur Hervey, who was appointed Bishop of Bath and Wells in 1869, was instituted to the family living of Ickworth-cum-Chedburgh in Suffolk where he remained for more than thirty years, becoming Archdeacon of Sudbury in 1862.[90] Richard Durnford (1802-1895), who became Bishop of Chichester in 1870, was inducted to the living of Middleton in Lancashire. He remained there for thirty-five years, improving educational institutions, building a new National School and restoring the parish church. He abolished pew rents and erected new churches at Thornham, Rhodes and Parkfield.[91] John Mackarness held a Worcestershire vicarage from 1845-1855 and then had fifteen years as Rector of Honiton in Devon as his preparation for the See of Oxford.

Significantly, whereas four of the fifteen men Palmerston appointed to English sees came of aristocratic families, only one of the fifteen sub-sequent appointments, Arthur Hervey, did so. The middle-class upbringings of the men Gladstone and Disraeli brought to office helped both to bring the episcopate closer to ordinary men and women, and to shed the Church's hierarchy of its seeming alliance with the rich and powerful.

Their Managerial Role as Diocesans

Not only did the Palmerstonian bishops set a new level of accessibility and care, they also established a new emphasis on the bishop as the manager in his diocese. From its second decade onwards the nineteenth century had witnessed the gradual development of what Arthur Burns had termed 'the diocesan revival'. The adoption by the Palmerstonian appointees of this executive episcopal role can rightly be seen as the culmination of this process which Arthur Burns has termed a growth in 'diocesan consciousness'. This development had, he argues, had its roots in the late eighteenth century but also received 'important support from Claphamite evangelicals such as the Sumners'.[92] Burns challenges the traditional view that the reform of the episcopate began with Samuel Wilberforce, and also the influence of Tractarian insistence on the episcopate as the *esse* of the Church.

During the 1850s and 1860s most of the Palmerston bishops devoted a good deal of their energies to supporting and building up existing diocesan societies and organisations. They solicited funds in visitation addresses, by presiding at their annual general meetings and by occasional preaching. They were also in the habit of urging their clergy from time to time to give sermons in support of diocesan causes and to take up collections for them. William Thomson's biographer perceived rightly that his subject 'was amongst the first of a new business-like, administratively-efficient type of Bishop whom the new age was producing'.[93] His fellow Palmerstonians were like him. They were dedicated, hard-working prelates who put their heart and soul into their work. They were not afraid of confronting hard issues, whether it was plurality, non-residence, drunkenness or ritualism. Villiers reorganised his diocesan structure and created eighteen new rural deaneries. He put a great deal of his energy into the Carlisle Diocesan Education Society and travelled throughout his diocese. He was not afraid to discipline, and suspended at least three clergymen for drunken behaviour. Longley and Tait both stood against ritualism, and both established insti-tutions and funds for promoting church extension. John Pelham, too, was a great promoter of education. He completely reconstituted his Diocesan Board of Education and promoted the Diocesan Training College. When Pelham announced his resignation from the See the dean spoke on behalf of the members of the cathedral of his 'most remarkable administration'.[94] At another meeting of rural deans Archdeacon Perowne declared:

We shall miss his authority. . . . In him we always had a leader and a ruler on whom we could rely and to whom we could look up. His grasp of the diocese, though never harsh, was always firm, and while it comprehended the whole, extended so to the several parts, that we often found that our Bishop was better acquainted with our several departments of work than we ourselves were.[95]

Robert Bickersteth was in many ways similar to Pelham in the way that he conducted his diocesan affairs. He too was a conscientious visitor and pastor to his clergy and a great supporter of education; he was the first bishop to conduct an authorised retreat for his clergy in 1866. He was a complete workaholic. His son commented: 'It was the rarest thing during the greater part of his episcopate for my father to take a holiday'.[96] In the autumn of 1880 he said to his daughter with great satisfaction: 'Mr. Oxley has asked me to preach at Harvest Festival at Grevelthorpe (a little village six miles from Ripon), and that fills up my last free day for the next month!'[97]

The bishops appointed by Palmerston in his second ministry followed suit. Samuel Waldegrave was recalled as 'an able administrator' and one who 'will be lastingly remembered in connection with some of the most useful Diocesan institutions'.[98] Ellicott, Browne, Jeune and Jacobson were all likewise skilled administrators, who put their energies to instructing their clergy and ensuring that their diocesan organisations functioned efficiently and well. Jeune was described as probably the ablest man of business in his day at Oxford.[99] In his short episcopate at Peterborough he worked hard to improve education and continued the work of church extension.[100] On his retirement William Jacobson was praised by *The Chester Courant* for his 'great earnestness' in 'the consolidation of his diocese'.[101]

In view of their competence and expertise in the management and administration of their sees, it comes as no small surprise that Palmerstone's appointees were the first bishops to establish diocesan conferences. These assemblies were not only properly constituted democratic bodies, but they were also able to make binding decisions. Chaired by the bishop, they represented both a new level of authority and control for the episcopate and also the completion of 'diocesan consciousness'. Browne introduced a Diocesan Conference as early as 1865 and three years later set up a Diocesan Fund.[102] Robert Bickersteth convoked a conference in 1870 which discussed important subjects including foreign missions and National Education.[103] Subsequent conferences went on to discuss diocesan organisation and finance including Diocesan Societies.[104] William Thomson's first Diocesan Conference was convened in May 1869 and met at Sheffield. Initially they were held annually but later biennially. Thomson valued these conferences because they gave the laity a voice in church affairs. He also felt that the Diocesan Conference was a more effective way of promoting fellowship among the clergy than the preaching of an address at a visitation.[105] John Pelham did not establish a Diocesan Conference until 1879 although he had earlier held a diocesan Church Congress in 1867.[106]

The bishops who were appointed in the years immediately after Palmerston's period of office also proved themselves active and competent diocesan administrators. James Atlay (1817-1894) brought the same thoroughness he had exhibited as incumbent of Leeds parish church to the rural diocese of Hereford. Edward Benson governed the new see of Truro with great competence, establishing a Diocesan Conference and giving great attention to church schools. At Canterbury, despite the pressures of public life, he never lost sight of the pastoral aspect of his office.[107] Richard Durnford was renowned for impartiality and diocesan reorganisation at Chichester, while James Fraser completely re-ordered the structures of his huge industrial diocese of Manchester, and established the first of a number of Diocesan Conferences.[108] Arthur Hervey was regarded by his diocese as a man of tact and firmness. His administration was universally popular with clergy and people.[109] Joseph Lightfoot built on the work of his Palmerstonian predecessor, Charles Baring. He increased the number of rural deaneries and adjusted their boundaries. He divided the single archdeaconry into two and established a Diocesan Conference for the first time in 1880.[110] Frederick Temple not only administered the three sees of Exeter, London and Canterbury judiciously, he sought to address the great social questions of the day, particularly those of poverty, temperance and unemployment.[111]

Their Commitment to a National Church

Contrary to the jibes of Samuel Wilberforce, who denounced Palmerston's bishops as 'narrow' and 'wicked appointments', they were in fact men of broad sympathies who got on well with representatives of other church parties.[112] Robert Bickersteth, for example, shared a cordial relationship with Walter Hook, the Vicar of Leeds, and also chose his rural deans from all church persuasions.[113] Montagu Villiers, although a convinced Protestant evangelical himself, exhorted his clergy to 'care little, then, whether men call you High Church or Low Church, but make sure that by your faithful preaching you are adding to the true Church'.[114]

It was probably for this reason that his successor in office noted that he had 'secured the hearty co-operation, even of the men who differed from him widely in opinion'.[115] Samuel Waldegrave, when a Residentiary Canon at Salisbury, enjoyed cordial and friendly relationships with his Tractarian Bishop, Walter Kerr Hamilton.[116] Perhaps even more remarkable was that John Pelham who 'never swerved from his strict evangelical principles'[117] enjoyed a life long friendship with Henry, later Cardinal, Manning.

Although on first hearing these cross party relationships on the part of Palmerston's bishops might seem a little incongruous, they were perfectly consistent with their vision of the Church of England as the National

Church. Although members of differing church parties and most being evangelicals, they were unanimous in wanting the Established Church to embrace the whole nation and yet without compromising the doctrinal principles of the *Book of Common Prayer* and *The Thirty Nine Articles*. It was for this reason that they all opposed the rising tide of ritualism. They did not want the Church to be hijacked by a narrow faction which would damage its role as a body to whom the whole nation could look to for a lead and for spiritual direction. It was indeed for this reason that Archibald Tait had fought so vigorously to abolish the burial laws which discriminated harshly against the Non-conformists.

Samuel Waldegrave preached a sermon in Carlisle Cathedral in August 1868 entitled *Ministering Kings or Our Established Church a favour from God* in which he began by pointing out that the Church of England 'is a Reformed Church' which was 'reformed by the Ministration of Kings'.[118] He went on to point out that it is 'our National Church' whose organisation is designed to make it 'the channel of blessing to every quarter of our land'.[119] Henry Philpott, when Bishop of Worcester, 'heartily' endorsed 'the settlement of the laws of our ecclesiastical policy which was made at the time of the Reformation'.[120] He was particularly glad that the literal face value interpretation of the 39 Articles and the Book of Common Prayer 'remains the sole test of the soundness of doctrine'.[121] On another occasion Philpott warned of the danger of those who spoke lightly of the National Church and failed to view the prospect of disestablishment with alarm.[122]

William Thomson preached a sermon entitled *The National Church* at the opening of the Cathedral in St. Albans in October 1885. He spoke warmly in favour of the Established Church and particularly the benefits which it had brought to education and to the needs of the sick and the poor.[123] Charles Ellicott found himself worried by those 'who would separate Church from State'.[124] He referred in particular to the danger from the ritualists 'who are now threatening to carry us back into twilight and shadows'.[125] Ellicott proudly identified himself with 'the sons of the Reformation'[126] and lamented the fact that the students at the Diocesan College were showing a 'silently growing distaste for the clear bracing theology of our own Sixteenth century divines'.[127] Ellicott was happy with the supremacy of the Crown over the National Church because he saw it as 'the foundation of our national independence and true Christian liberty'.[128] Harold Browne described himself as one who did not wish to see the Church of England cease to be a part of English constitution.[129] He maintained that disestablishment would destroy the benefits of the parochial system which he believed, in the country at least, were considerable.[130] Indeed it was because of his strong belief in the concept of a National Church that both Browne and Bickersteth strongly opposed Gladstone's bill to disestablish the Irish Church.

The Palmerstonian bishops had, by their recourse to the State and to the secular courts, particularly in the matter of ritualism, but also in the matter of *Essay and Reviews*, demonstrated their belief in the benefits of an Established Church. They valued a national institution for other reasons, including its contribution to education and its parochial system which embraced the whole nation and provided a solid basis for mission. Some of their number, such as Tait and Bickersteth, had even defended the Irish Church against disestablishment.

The years that followed Gladstone's disestablishment bill were a time of uncertainty and Nonconformists in Parliament led by Edward Miall put forward a series of unsuccessful motions for the disestablishment of the Church of England in the early 1870s. However, the situation gradually settled, particularly as the level of ritual prosecutions diminished. Most bishops appointed by Gladstone and Disraeli supported the Palmerstonians as supporters of the status quo. Most probably shared the views of Mackarness of Oxford who recognised 'certain dangers in the Establishment' but did 'not wholly despair of their cure'. For this reason he could not support disestablishment.[131] Others were more forthright in their pro-establishment views. Such was James Fraser of Manchester who 'aimed to make the Church as national as possible'.[132] When Benson succeeded to the Primacy in 1882, he was able to steady the ship, indeed Desmond Bowen observed that 'Archbishop Benson represented a new consciousness among the bishops of the value of the Establishment in terms of catholic mission to the nation'.[133] Gladstone and Disraeli's bishops were also much like their Palmerstonian predecessors in that they were warmly disposed to dissenters and sought to establish good relationships with them. Most supported the Burials Act and the Universities Test Act and the opening of Church of England Grammar Schools to Dissenters. The majority, like Palmerston's appointees, were concerned to raise the standards for Ordination and took care and delight over their Confirmation procedures. Some, such as Mackarness and Fraser, were particularly at ease speaking to the working classes on the shop floor or at the factory gate.

Taken as a whole, Palmerston's prelates were men of sound orthodox beliefs who adhered strongly to the Reformation settlement of the Church of England. They kept high standards in their personal lives, and above all were conscientious pastors of clergy and people. The evangelicals among them certainly cannot be made to bear the malevolent criticisms of Samuel Wilberforce and the Tractarians, who doubtless smarted under the rebukes they received from the Palmerstonians as a whole, high church included. The Palmerston bishops were "Good and Proper Men" who brought a new impetus and style to the episcopal office in the mid-Victorian years. Much of what they stood for was taken up and continued by their successors.

The Episcopal Bench during Palmerston's Premiership

Province of Canterbury

Canterbury	J. B. Sumner (1848-1862)	*C. T. Longley (1862-1868)*	
Bath and Wells	Robert Eden, Lord Auckland (1854-1869)		
Chichester	A. T. Gilbert (1842-1870)		
Ely	T. Turton (1845-1864)	*E. H. Browne (1864-1873)*	
Exeter	H. Phillpotts (1831-1869)		
Gloucester & Bristol	J. H Monk (1836-1856)	*C. Baring (1856-1861)*	*W. Thomson (1861-1862)*	*C. J. Ellicott (1863-1905)*
Hereford	R. D. Hampden (1848-1865)		
Lichfield	J. Lonsdale (1843-1867)		
Lincoln	J. Jackson (1853-1868)		
London	C.J Blomfield (1828-1856)	*A. C. Tait (1856-1869)*	
Norwich	S. Hinds (1849-1857)	*J. T. Pelham (1857-1893)*	
Oxford	S. Wilberforce (1845-1869)		
Peterborough	G. Davys (1839-1864)	*F. Jeune (1864-1868)*	
Rochester	G. Murray (1827-1860)	*J. C. Wigram (1860-1867)*	
Salisbury	W. K. Hamilton (1854-1869)		
Winchester	C. R. Sumner (1827-1869)		
Worcester	H. Pepys (1841-1860)	*H. Philpott (1861-1890)*	

Province of York

York	T. Musgrave (1848-1860)	*C. T. Longley (1860-1862)*	*W. Thomson (1862-1890)*
Carlisle	H. Percy (1827-1856)	*H. M. Villiers (1856-1860)*	*S. Waldegrave (1860-1869)*
Chester	J. Graham (1848-1865)	*W. Jacobson (1865-1884)*	
Durham	E. Maltby (1836-1856)	*C. T. Longley (1856-1860)*	*H. M. Villiers (1860-1861)*	*C. Baring (1861-1879)*
Manchester	J. P. Lee (1848-1869)		
Ripon	C. T. Longley (1836-1856)	*R. Bickersteth (1857-1884)*	

names in italics were appointed by Palmerston.

The Episcopal Bench, 1855-1865

Italic headings refer to appointments by Palmerston.

BARING Charles (1807-1879)
Bishop of Gloucester, 1856-61; Bishop of Durham, 1861-1879

He was the fourth son of Sir Thomas Baring, 2nd baronet, of the eminent banking firm, and Mary, daughter of Charles Sealy, a Calcutta-based barrister. Charles was educated privately and entered Christ Church, Oxford in 1825 where he graduated BA in 1829, MA and DD in 1856. He was ordained deacon in 1830 and priest in 1831. He was Curate of St. Ebbe's, Oxford and then incumbent of Kingsworthy, Hampshire. In 1847 he was appointed Rector of All Saints', Marylebone, where he became a renowned evangelical preacher. In 1850 he was made a Chaplain to the Queen and was also Select Preacher at Oxford. In 1855 he moved to the parish of Limpsfield, Surrey, and in 1856 he was chosen as Bishop of Gloucester. Here he encouraged the clergy in their preaching and pastoral work. In 1861 Baring was translated to the See of Durham where he worked with great energy and effectiveness. During his episcopate 102 new parishes were formed, 119 new churches erected and a further 129 extended and restored. At the same time the clergy were increased by 186, and 183 elementary schools were erected or enlarged in the diocese. Baring was a pronounced evangelical and he refused to license curates to clergy whose ritual he believed to contravene the Prayer Book. Due to failing health he retired from office in February 1879 and died in September the same year.

BICKERSTETH, Robert (1816-1884)
Bishop of Ripon, 1857-1884.

He was born on the 24th of August 1816, at Acton, Suffolk, the fourth son of John and Henrietta Bickersteth. After tuition by his father and a period of medical training, he entered Queen's College, Cambridge, in 1837 and graduated BA in 1841, MA in 1846 and DD in 1856. He was ordained deacon in 1841 and priest in 1842 and was Curate of Sapcote 1841-1843, St. Giles, Reading, 1843-1845 and Holy Trinity, Clapham, 1845 under Dr. William Dealtry (1775-1847). His power as a preacher was soon recognised and at the end of the year Dealtry offered him the incumbency of St. John's, Clapham Rise. He remained there until 1851 when he took up the living of St. Giles-in-the-Fields. In 1854 he was appointed Canon Residentiary and Treasurer of Salisbury Cathedral and on 18 June 1857, was consecrated Bishop of Ripon. He was also Select Preacher at the University of Cambridge in 1857. During his episcopate he concerned himself with church building, education and evangelism and spoke at the Leeds Mission of 1875. He consecrated 155 new churches and began the restoration of the cathedral in 1862. He was an infrequent speaker in the House of the Lords, but his speech against the disestablishment of the Irish church in 1869 was published. Bickersteth took a keen interest in education and was a leading influence in the founding of the Diocesan Training College at Ripon in 1860. Although a zealous evangelical his long episcopate was free from confrontations with ritualists. Bickersteth's health weakened after 1882 and he died at his palace in Ripon on 15 April 1884.

BROWNE, *Edward Harold (1811-1891)*
Bishop of Ely, 1864-73; Bishop of Winchester, 1873-1890

He was born on 6 March 1811, at Aylesbury, the son of Colonel Robert Browne and Sarah, daughter of Gabriel Steward. He was educated at Eton and Emmanuel College, Cambridge, where he graduated BA in 1832, MA in 1836, BD in 1855 and DD in 1864. He was ordained deacon in 1836 and priest in 1837. He became a Fellow of his college in 1837 but resigned when he married in June, 1840 and accepted the sole charge of Holy Trinity, Stroud. He was then successively Curate of St. James's and St.Sidewell's, Exeter. In 1843 he was appointed Vice-Principal of St. David's College, Lampeter, which had a prebendal stall attached in St. David's Cathedral. He was dissatisfied with the running of the college and in 1849 accepted the living of Kenwyn-cum-Kea in Cornwall. In 1854 he was appointed Norrisian Professor of Divinity at Cambridge. For three years he held this position in conjunction with the vicarage of Heavitree, Exeter, with a canonry in the Cathedral. In 1861 he contributed to *Aids to Faith*. On 20 March, 1864, he was consecrated Bishop of Ely. Despite his hostility to *Essays and Reviews*, he officiated at the Consecration of Frederick Temple. As a bishop he advocated lay workers, including deaconesses, opposed ritualism and established a Diocesan Conference in 1864. In 1873 he was translated to Winchester where he carried forward his earlier policies. He chaired two important committees at the 1888 Lambeth Conference. His health began to fail and he resigned in 1890 and died on 18 December 1891. Although he often spoke of his debt to evangelicalism, he was in reality a mild high churchman of the old school. He was a scholar of some distinction and published a large number of sermons and pamphlets.

DAVYS, George (1780-1864)
Bishop of Peterborough 1839-1864

He was the son of John Davys of Rempstone, Nottinghamshire and Sophia, daughter of the Rev. B. Wigley of Sawley, Derbyshire. He entered Christ's College, Cambridge, in 1799 where he graduated BA in 1803, MA in 1806 and DD in 1831. He was ordained deacon in 1806 and priest in 1807, and held curacies at Littlebury in Essex, Chesterford and Swaffham Prior 1817. He held the vicarage of Willoughby-on-the-Wolds, Lincolnshire, 1811-1829 but moved to Kensington Palace in 1827 as tutor to Princess Victoria. In 1829 he was appointed to the rectory of Allhallows-on-the-Wall, London, which he held until 1839 and from 1831-1839 he was dean of Chester. He was consecrated bishop of Peterborough on 16 June, 1839. Here he concerned himself with educational issues. His own convictions lay with the evangelical party but he was liberal and fair minded to all sections of the church and took no active part in either the religious or political controversies of the day. He died at Peterborough 18 April, 1864.

EDEN, Robert John, Lord Auckland (1799-1870)
Bishop of Sodor and Man 1847-1854; Bishop of Bath and Wells 1854-1869

He was the third son of William Eden, first baron Auckland. He was educated at Eton and entered Magdalene College, Cambridge, where he graduated MA in 1819 and BD and DD in 1847. He was ordained deacon in 1822 and priest in 1824. He was Rector of Eyam, Derbyshire, 1823-1825, Rector of Hertingfordbury, Hertfordshire, 1825-1835 and Vicar of Battersea from 1835 to 1847. In addition he was chaplain to William IV 1831-1837 and to Queen Victoria 1837-1847. On 23 May, 1847 he was consecrated Bishop of Sodor and Man. On the death of his brother who was unmarried on 1 January, 1849 he became third Baron Auckland. On 2 June, 1854 he was translated to the see of Bath and Wells. He was a moderate High Churchman. He died at Wells on 25 April, 1870.

ELLICOTT, Charles John (1819-1905)
Bishop of Bristol and Gloucester, 1863-1897 (Gloucester, 1897-1905)

He was the only son of Charles Spencer Ellicott and Ellen, a daughter of a Welshman, John Jones. He was educated at grammar schools in Stamford and Oakham and St. John's College, Cambridge, where he graduated BA in 1841, MA in 1844, BD in 1857 and DD in 1863. He was ordained deacon in 1846 and priest in 1847. He remained in Cambridge as a Fellow of his college until his marriage in 1848 when he became incumbent of Pilton in Rutland. He used the time afforded by his rural parish to write, and during the 1850s produced a string of New Testament commentaries. In 1858 he become Professor of New Testament at King's College, London, and in 1860 became also Hulsean Professor of Divinity at Cambridge. In 1861 he was appointed Dean of Exeter and in the same year contributed to *Aids to Faith*, a counterblast to *Essays and Reviews*. In 1863 he was appointed to the united Sees of Gloucester and Bristol, remaining at Gloucester after the division of the diocese, an episcopate lasting 42 years. Ellicott expressed his indebtedness both to the evangelicals and to high churchmen, but he could not abide ritualism. He denounced Confession and the chasuble in particular, and entered into conflict with some of his incumbents. Ellicott was concerned for his many rural clergy and took great care over his diocesan Charges. He was chairman of the Revision Committee of the New Testament and presented the completed text to Convocation in 1881. He was secretary to the first Lambeth Conference in 1867 and those of 1878 and 1888. He was a moderate high churchman, remembered as 'an excellent preacher' and a warm, outgoing person. He resigned in 1905 and died later the same year at Birchington-on-Sea.

GILBERT, Ashurst Turner (1786-1870)
Bishop of Chichester 1842-1868

He was the son of Thomas Gilbert of Ratcliffe, Buckinghamshire, a captain in the Royal Marines, and Elizabeth, daughter of William Hutton, Rector of Maids Moreton, Buckinghamshire. He was educated at Manchester Grammar School 1800-1805 and entered Brasenose College, Oxford where he graduated BA in 1809, MA in 1811, BD in 1819 and DD in 1822. He was tutor 1816-1820, Vice-Principal 1820-1821, then Principal of Brasenose College 1822-1842 and Vice-Chancellor 1836-1840. He was consecrated Bishop of Chichester on 24 January 1842. His episcopate was marked by dedicated hard work with a particular concern for education. Although he was High Churchman he was a strong opponent of ritualism who attaked the Rev John Purchas's ceremonial innovations at St James' Chapel, Brighton. Gilbert died at the Palace, Chichester on 21 February 1870.

GRAHAM, John (1794-1865)
Bishop of Chester 1848-1865

He was the only son of John Graham, Managing Clerk in the city of Durham. He was educated at Durham Grammar School and proceeded to Christ's College, Cambridge, where he graduated BA 1816, MA 1819, BD 1829 and DD in 1831. He was ordained deacon in 1818 and priest in 1818. He was a fellow and tutor of his college in 1816 and served as Master 1830-1848. He was Rector and Rural Dean of Willingham, Cambridgeshire, from 1843-1848 and chaplain to the Prince Consort 1841. On 14 May 1848 he was consecrated bishop of Chester. Graham was a Liberal in politics but seldom spoke in the House of Lords. His episcopate was marked by his conciliatory and gracious manner, but his warm relationship with Nonconformists caused friction with some High Churchmen. He died at the Palace, Chester on 15 June 1865.

HAMILTON, Walter Kerr (1808-1869)
Bishop of Salisbury 1854-1869

He was the son of Anthony Hamilton, Archdeacon of Taunton and Prebendary of Lichfield and Charity Graeme, third daughter of Sir Walter Farquar. He was educated privately and at Eton and entered Christ Church, Oxford, in 1827 where he graduated BA in 1831, MA in 1833 and DD in 1854. He was ordained deacon and priest in 1833 and was Curate of Wolvercote, near Oxford, 1833-1834 and then Curate 1834-1837 and Vicar of St Peter's-in-the-East, Oxford, 1837-1841. Whilst in the city he came under the influence of the Oxford movement and remained a tractarian to the end of his days. In 1841 he became Canon and Precentor at Salisbury Cathedral where in 1853 he published a pamphlet entitled *Cathedral Reform*. On 14 May, 1854 he was consecrated Bishop of Salisbury on his predecessor's recommendation. He increased the number of confirmations, raised the standard of ordination candidates and established Salisbury Theological College. He rarely left his diocese and enjoyed good relationships with his clergy. His last three diocesan charges aroused considerable dissent on account of his clear teaching of the doctrine of real presence in the Holy Communion, eucharistic sacrifice and priestly absolution. He died in Salisbury on 1 August, 1869.

HAMPDEN, Renn Dickson, (1793-1868)
Bishop of Hereford 1848-1868

He was the eldest son of Renn Hampden, a colonel in the militia of Barbados and his wife, Frances Raven. He was educated privately in England and entered Oriel College on 9 May 1810 where he graduated BA in 1814, MA in 1816. He graduated BD and DD in 1833 from St Mary Hall. He was ordained deacon in 1816 and priest in 1817 and was successively Curate of Blagdon, Faringdon, Hungerford and Hackney. He was Bampton Lecturer and Tutor of Oriel in 1832 , Principal of St Mary Hall in 1833, Professor of Moral Philosophy in 1834 and Regius Professor of Divinity with an attached canonry at Christ Church, 1836-1848. His appointment was opposed by high churchmen, who believed his christological views were unorthodox. As Regius Professor he also held the living of Ewelme 1836-1847 where his pastoral labours were greatly valued. In 1847 amid considerable opposition he was offered the See of Hereford and was eventually consecrated on 26 March 1848. As a bishop he proved an able administrator and his conduct was exemplary. He opposed the re-establishment of the Roman Catholic hierarchy in England. His views were evangelical. He died in London on 23 April 1868.

HINDS, Samuel, (1793-1872)
Bishop of Norwich 1849-1857

He was the son of Abel Hinds of Barbados. After schooling in Bristol he entered Queen's College, Oxford where he graduated BA in 1815, MA in 1818 and BD and DD in 1831. He was ordained deacon in 1822 and priest in 1823 and became Vice-Principal of St Alban Hall, Oxford 1827-1831 and then chaplain to the Archbishop of Dublin 1831-1833. He was Vicar of Yardley in Hertfordshire and rural dean from 1834-1843 and vicar of Castle Knock and Prebend of St Patrick's Cathedral, Dublin, 1843-48 when he was appointed Dean of Carlisle 1848-1849. In October 1849 he was consecrated Bishop of Norwich and held the See until 1857 when his domestic circumstances caused him to resign. He was a man of learning who produced several substantial books. In politics he was a moderate Liberal.

JACKSON, John (1811-1885)
Bishop of Lincoln 1853-1868; Bishop of London 1868-1885

He was the son of Henry Jackson of Mansfield. He was educated privately and entered Pembroke College, Oxford, in 1829 where he graduated BA in 1833, MA in 1836 and DD in 1853. He was ordained deacon in 1835 and priest in 1836 and was curate of Henley-on-Thames 1835-1836, head-master of Islington Proprietary School 1836-1842 which he combined with the post of evening lecturer at Stoke Newington parish church, incumbent of St James, Muswell Hill, 1842-1853, and Vicar of St James, Piccadilly, 1846-1853. In 1853 he was made Canon of Bristol, and was also Boyle Lecturer at Oxford. In the same year the see of Lincoln fell vacant and Jackson was appointed. Jackson was an able diocesan administrator and succeeded in drawing together the counties of Lincolnshire and Nottinghamshire. He reorganised the ruridecanal structure of the diocese and devoted much energy to diocesan schools and the education of the clergy. During his episcopate twenty-four new churches were built and more than two hundred restored. In 1868 Jackson was translated to London. Here he actively encouraged the Bishop of London's Fund for church building, promoted parochial lay helpers and established a diocesan conference. He died on 6 January, 1885.

JACOBSON, William (1803-1884)
Bishop of Chester, 1865-1884

He was born at Great Yarmouth on 18 July 1803, the son of William and Judith Clarke. He was educated at a private school in Norwich, Homerton (nonconformist) College, Glasgow University and Lincoln College, Oxford where he graduated BA in 1827, MA in 1829 andd DD in 1848. He was ordained deacon in 1830 and priest in 1831 and appointed Curate of St. Mary Magdalen, Oxford, and then perpetual curate of Iffley. In 1831 he was elected Vice-Principal of Magdalen Hall, a position which he held for 16 years. From 1842 to 1848 he was Public Orator in the University and in 1849 became Regius Professor of Divinity with a canonry at Christ Church. He was also Select Preacher in the university in 1832, 1842 and 1869. In 1869 he was one of the Royal Commissioners appointed to consider the terms of clerical subscription. As Bishop of Chester he proved a competent administrator and a wise pastor. He improved clergy stipends, promoted church building and encouraged education and the training colleges at Warrington and Chester in particular. He was a high churchman but severely orthodox and had little sympathy with ritualistic innovations. He established a Chester Diocesan Conference in 1870. In 1865 he published *Clerical Duties* which ran into a third printing, and edited the works of Clement, Ignatius and Polycarp. He died at his home in Deeside on 13 July 1884.

JEUNE, Francis (1806-1868)
Bishop of Peterborough, 1864-1868

He was born at St. Brelade, Jersey, 22 May 1806, the eldest son of Francis Jeune. He was educated at St. Servan's College, Rennes and Pembroke College, Oxford, where he graduated BA in 1827, MA in 1830, BCL and DCL both in 1834. He was a fellow from 1830-1837. He was ordained deacon in 1832 and priest in 1833. In 1834 he also became Headmaster of King Edward's School, Birmingham, where he remodelled the curriculum, introducing English and Modern Science. In 1839 he was appointed Dean of Jersey and Rector of St. Helier. In 1843 he was called back to Oxford as Master of Pembroke College, which carried with it a canonry at Gloucester Cathedral. He used his influence to persuade the government to set up a Commission of Inquiry at Oxford. He was Vice-Chancellor of the University from 1858-1862. In 1863 he was appointed Dean of Lincoln but removed to Peterborough the following year on his Consecration as bishop. As a diocesan he advocated more frequent Communion services, increased the number of Confirmations and urged the proper inspection of church schools. His convictions were strongly protestant and evangelical and he attacked ritualistic excesses. Jeune died at Whitby on 21 August 1868.

LEE, James Prince (1804-1869)
Bishop of Manchester 1847-1861

He was the son of Stephen Lee, secretary and librarian of the Royal Society. He was educated at St Paul's School in London and entered Trinity College, Cambridge, in 1824 where he graduated BA in 1828 and MA in 1831. He was ordained deacon in 1830 and priest in 1831. He was a fellow of Trinity College 1829-1830, a master at Rugby School 1830-1838 and head-master of King Edward's School, Birmingham, 1838-1847. He was elected honorary Canon of Worcester on 6 September, 1847 and nominated the following month to the newly constituted see of Manchester. As a bishop James Lee was felt, with some justification to be somewhat overbearing and despotic. Many of his clergy distrusted him in consequence. He did however prove to be a gifted organiser who devoted much time to encouraging the development of both Sunday and Day Schools within the diocese. He also actively promoted the founding of the Manchester Free Library. He died at Mauldeth Hall near Manchester on 24 December, 1869.

LONGLEY, Charles Thomas (1794-1868)
Bishop of Ripon, 1836-1856; Bishop of Durham, 1856-1860;
Archbishop of York, 1860-1862, Archbishop of Canterbury 1862-1868

He was the fifth son of John Longley, a political writer and a magistrate of the London police court. He was educated at Westminster and at Christ Church, Oxford where he graduated BA in 1815, MA in 1818 and BD and DD in 1829. Longley was ordained deacon in 1818 and priest in 1819. He became curate in 1818, then incumbent in 1823 of Cowley. In 1827 he became Rector of West Tytherley, Hampshire, but held the position for only two years, as he became Headmaster of Harrow on 21 March 1829. In 1836 he was nominated as first Bishop of Ripon, which position he held until 1856 when he was translated to Durham. While at Ripon he strongly denounced the ritualistic practices at Leeds parish church whose incumbent and five assistant clergy then went over to the church of Rome. He also established Bishop Longley's Fund to promote new church building. He was translated to York in 1860 and Canterbury in 1862. Longley was a high churchman who upheld the creedal faith and attacked *Essays and Reviews*. In concert with Archbishop Thomson who memorialised his northern province, Longley issued a pastoral letter to the province of Canterbury in 1864 in which he affirmed both the inspiration of Scripture and eternal punishment. He died on 27 October 1868.

LONSDALE, John, (1788-1867)
Bishop of Lichfield 1843-1867

He was the eldest son of John Lonsdale, Vicar of Darfield and Elizabeth Steer. He was educated at Eton and entered Kings College, Cambridge, in 1806 where he graduated BA in 1811, MA in 1814, BD in 1824 and DD in 1844. Lonsdale entered Lincoln's Inn in 1811 to read law but forsook the Bar for the Church in 1815. He was ordained deacon and priest in 1815. He was chaplain to Archbishop Manners-Sutton 1816, rector of Mersham in Kent 1822-1827, Prebendary of Lincoln 1827-1828, Precentor of Lichfield 1828-1831, Rector of St George's, Bloomsbury 1828-1834, Rector of Southfleet near Gravesend 1836-1843, Principal of King's College, London 1839-1842, Archdeacon of Middlesex 1842-1843. He was consecrated Bishop of Lichfield on 3 December, 1843. Lonsdale proved himself to be a very able bishop with a wide knowledge of ecclesiastical law. His sympathies were with the old High Church School but he often displayed liberal views, protesting over the removal of F.D. Maurice from office and condemning the law that forbade marriage with a deceased wife's sister. He died on 19 October, 1867.

MUSGRAVE, Thomas (1788-1860)
Bishop of Hereford 1837-1847; Archbishop of York 1847-1860

He was born on 30 March, 1788, the son of W. Peet Musgrave, a tailor and draper of Cambridge, and Sarah, his wife. He was educated at Richmond Grammar School in Yorkshire and entered Trinity College, Cambridge, in 1804 graduating BA in 1810, MA in 1813 and DD in 1837. He was ordained deacon in 1823 and priest in 1824. He was Rector of Over, 1823-25, Vicar of Great St Mary's, Cambridge, 1823-1833 and Bottisham 1837. Musgrave was an active county magistrate and convinced Liberal in politics. In 1837 he was appointed Dean of Bristol but held that office for only a few months before being consecrated Bishop of Hereford on 1 October 1837. In 1847 he was translated to York. Musgrave was retiring by nature. His episcopate was not marked by reform. He was a man of strong evangelical views who always made himself accessible to his clergy. He died in London on 4 May 1860.

PELHAM, John Thomas (1811-1894)
Bishop of Norwich, 1857-1893

He was born on 21 June 1811, the third son of Thomas, the second Earl of Chichester and Lady Mary Henrietta Juliana, daughter of the fifth Duke of Leeds. John Thomas was educated at Westminster School and Christ Church, Oxford, where he graduated BA in 1832 and MA and DD in 1857. He was ordained deacon in 1834 and priest in 1835 and placed in sole charge of the parish of Eastergate in the diocese of Chichester. He became Rector of Bergh Apton, Norfolk, in 1837, Christ Church, Hampstead, in 1852, St. Marylebone in 1855 and Bishop of Norwich in 1857. As a bishop he was an able administrator and a thoroughgoing pastor who visited many of his clergy in their parishes. He made education a priority and gave particular attention to the erection of new buildings for the Diocesan Training College for teachers. Although decidedly evangelical he was conciliatory in his attitude to high churchmen. He urged the reform of Convocation and the division of large dioceses into smaller more manageable units. He was not given to the habit of writing and apart his Charges published very little. The text of his sermon to the Church Missionary Society in 1852 was printed, and he edited a small collection of hymns for public worship in 1855. Pelham resigned the see in 1893 and died at Thorpe, a suburb of Norwich on 1 May 1894.

PEPYS, Henry (1783-1860)
Bishop of Sodor and Man 1840-1841; Bishop of Worcester 1841-1860

He was the third son of Sir Williams Weller of London. He was educated at Harpers School and entered Trinity College, Cambridge where he graduated BA in 1804 and then was fellow of St John's College where was awarded an MA in 1807, BD in 1814 and DD in 1840. He was ordained deacon in 1807 and priest in 1808 and was Curate of Swaffham Prior, Cambridge, in 1808 and then Rector of Aspeden, Hertfordshire, 1818-1827 together with Moreton, Essex, 1822-1840. In 1826 he was made Prebendary of Wells and Rector of Westmill in Hertfordshire 1827-1840. On 1 March, 1840 Pepys was consecrated Bishop of Sodor and Man, but in the following year was translated to the see of Worcester. He was a popular and conscientious diocesan bishop and was a generous patron of the triennial Three Choirs Festival. He aligned himself with the Liberals in the House of Lords where he rarely spoke. He died at Hartlebury Castle, Stourport on 13 November, 1860.

PHILLPOTTS, Henry, (1778-1869)
Bishop of Exeter 1831-1869

He was the second son of John Phillpotts, the proprietor of a pottery and brick factory at Bridgewater and his wife, Sybella. He was educated at the Gloucester College School and entered Corpus Christi College in 1791 where he graduated BA in 1795, MA in 1798 and BD and DD in 1821. He was ordained deacon in 1802 and priest in 1804. He was Vicar of Kilmersdon near Bath 1804-1806, incumbent of two Durham parishes, Stainton-le-Street and Bishop Middleham 1805-1808, Gateshead 1808 and St Margaret, Durham, 1810. He was also chaplain to the Bishop of Durham 1806-1826 and a Prebend of Durham Cathedral 1810-1820. He resigned his stall when in 1820 the bishop collated him to the rectory of Stanhope-on-the-Wear, one of the richest livings in England. Phillpotts was a staunch Tory who made a name for himself as a controversialist. He published a pamphlet in support of the Government's dealings with the demonstrators at Peterloo in 1819. In 1825 he expressed strongly anti-Roman Catholic views but then changed his opinion voting in favour of the 1829 Roman Catholic Relief Act. On 2 January 1831 he was consecrated Bishop of Exeter. He was outspoken against the 1832 Reform Bill which led to an attack by a mob on his palace. His episcopate continued to be marked by controversy. He opposed Hampden's appointment to the See of Hereford; he contracted a lawsuit against the Rev. John Shore for holding services in an unlicensed building and refused to institute George Gorham to the living of Brampford Speke because he did not subscribe to the doctrine of baptismal regeneration. He is estimated to have spent between £20,000-30,000 on legal costs. Phillpotts was a High Churchman of the old school but did not identify with the Oxford Movement. He founded Exeter Theological College, restored the cathedral and supported the Devonport sisterhood. He died at Bishopstowe, Torquay on 18 September 1869.

PHILPOTT, Henry (1807-1892)
Bishop of Worcester, 1861-1890

He was born on 17 November 1807, the son of Richard Philpott of Chichester. He was educated at Chichester Cathedral School and St. Catherine's Hall, Cambridge where he graduated BA in 1829, MA in 1832, BD in 1839 and DD in 1847. He was ordained deacon in 1831 and priest in 1833. He was elected Master of St. Catherine's with a canonry at Norwich in 1845, and Vice-Chancellor of the University in 1846, 1856 and 1857. Philpott's episcopate was for the most part uneventful except for his confrontation with R.W. Enraght, the ritualistic Vicar of Holy Trinity, Birmingham, in 1879. Philpott refused to call a diocesan conference until they had legal status because he had 'a horror of irresponsible talk'. He rarely attended the House of Lords and only once, when Archbishop Tait summoned him, appeared in the Upper House of Convocation. He was singularly generous to his clergy during the years of agricultural depression. He was a high churchman of the old school who sought to uphold the principles of the Reformation. He retired in 1890 and died at Cambridge on 10 February 1892.

SUMNER, Charles Richard (1790-1874)
Bishop of Llandaff, 1826-1827; Bishop of Winchester 1827-1869

He was the younger brother of John Bird (*cf infra*). Charles was educated privately by his father until 1802 and then at Eton. He entered Trinity College, Cambridge, in 1810 where he graduated BA in 1814, MA in 1817 and DD in 1825. He was ordained deacon in 1814 and priest in 1817 and was curate of Highclere 1816-1821. In 1821 Charles was introduced to the King which resulted in a succession of appointments including the vicarage of St Helen's, Abingdon, 1821-1822, Chaplain in ordinary to the King 1823, Canon of Worcester 1822-1825 and Canon of Canterbury 1827. On 21 May 1826 Sumner was consecrated Bishop of Llandaff which he held together with the Deanery of St Paul's. The following year he was translated to the See of Winchester. He was a strong Tory and opposed the 1832 Reform Bill, although he had supported the Roman Catholic Relief Act of 1829. As a bishop he showed particular concern for education and providing schools for the poor. He was a great churchbuilder, and formed a Diocesan Building Society in 1837. During his episcopate 201 new churches were built and 119 restored or rebuilt. Charles was a pronounced evangelical who rigorously contended against the Oxford Movement. He died at Farnham Castle on 3 September 1874.

SUMNER, John Bird (1780-1862)
Bishop of Chester 1828-1848; Archbishop of Canterbury 1848-1862

He was the eldest son of the Rev. Robert Sumner, vicar of Kenilworth and Stoneleigh, Warwickshire, and Hannah, daughter of John Bird, a London Alderman. He was educated at Eton and entered King's College, Cambridge in 1789 where he graduated BA in 1803, MA in 1807 and DD in 1828. He was ordained deacon in 1803 and priest in 1805. He was assistant master at Eton College 1802-1817 and fellow of Eton College 1817-1821 and Vicar of Mapledurham in Berkshire 1818-1828. His scholarly writings brought him to the notice of Bishop Shute Barrington who appointed him to a prebendal stall in Durham Cathedral in 1820. Partly through the influence of his younger brother he was consecrated Bishop of Chester on 14 September, 1828. In Chester he worked strenuously encouraging the clergy, advocating lay visitors, fostering education and promoting church building. During his Chester episcopate a total of 244 new churches were built. Sumner played a major role in the foundation of Chester Training College in 1839. In 1848 Sumner was translated to the archiepiscopal see of Canterbury. Here he continued his work of church building and education. His time at Canterbury was marked by a series of crises which included the Gorham Case, the publication of Darwin's *Origin of Species*, the *Essays and Reviews* controversy and the revival of the convocations. Sumner dealt with these issues with statesmanlike graciousness and authority. He was a pronounced protestant evangelical who was steadfast in his opposition to the theological views and ritual practices of the Oxford movement. He died on 6 September, 1862 at Addington.

TAIT Archibald Campbell (1811-1882)
Bishop of London, 1856-1868; **Archbishop of Canterbury 1868-1882**

He was born in Edinburgh on 21 December 1811, the son of Crauford Tait, who owned estates in Argyllshire. He was educated at Edinburgh High School, Glasgow University 1827-1830 and Balliol College, Oxford, graduating BA in 1833, MA in 1836, DCL in 1842 and DD in 1869. He was appointed Tutor at his college in 1835, ordained deacon in 1836 and priest in 1838 and was Curate of March Baldon on the outskirts of the city. In 1841 he was one of the signatories who protested against Newman's Tract 90. He was appointed Headmaster of Rugby in 1842 and Dean of Carlisle in 1849. In 1856 he was consecrated Bishop of London where he gave himself totally to the work of church building and home missions. He preached in Exeter Hall, at Ragged schools and at Convent Garden market. His episcopate was marked by conflict over the use of the Confessional and with ritualists at St. George's-in-the-East and elsewhere. In 1869 Tait became Archbishop of Canterbury. As primate Tait carried forward the Public Worship Regulation Act of 1874, presided over the second Lambeth Conference in 1878 and initiated two Royal Commissions, The Cathedrals Commission, and the Ecclesiastical Courts Commission, both in 1880. Although categorised by Lord Shaftesbury as the 'mildest of broad churchmen', Tait supported evangelical societies including CMS, preached in the open air and spoke on more occasions in the House of Lords than any other bishop of his generation. He died on 1 December 1882.

THOMSON, William (1819-1890)
Bishop of Gloucester, 1861-1862; Archbishop of York, 1862-1890

He was born on 11 February 1819, the eldest son of John Thomson of Kelswick, Cumberland, who was a director of a local bank and chairman of an iron company. He was educated at Shrewsbury and Queen's College, Oxford, where he graduated BA in 1840, MA in 1844 and BD and DD in 1856. He published *Outlines of the Laws of Thought*, a treatise on logic, in 1842, which was highly regarded. He was ordained deacon in 1842 and priest in 1843 and was appointed Curate of St. Nicholas, Guildford, in 1844 and at Cuddesdon in 1846. From 1847 he was appointed to several successive posts at Queen's College. He was chosen as Select Preacher in 1848 and gave the Bampton Lectures on 'the Atoning work of Christ' in 1849. In 1855 Thomson married and surrendered his Fellowship for the Rectory of All Souls, Langham Place, but was then elected Provost of Queens'. In 1861 he edited *Aids to Faith* which was a counterblast to *Essays and Reviews*. He was consecrated Bishop of Gloucester and Bristol in 1861 and translated to York in 1862. Thomson was above all the 'people's bishop' and he won the hearts of the Yorkshire working classes among whom he preached and moved with ease and confidence. He was a strict disciplinarian and supported Archbishop Tait in his introduction of the *Public Worship Regulation Bill* of 1874. He was a strong evangelical and in 1864 took proceedings against the Rev. Charles Voysey, Rector of Helaugh, for his unorthodox preaching and teaching. Thomson was occupied with the business of his diocese to the end and died on Christmas Day 1890.

TURTON, Thomas, (1780-1864)
Bishop of Ely 1845-1864.

He was the son of Thomas Turton of Hatfield, Yorkshire and Ann, daughter of Francis Harn of Denby. He first entered Queens College and then Catharine Hall, Cambridge, where he graduated BA in 1805, MA in 1808, BD in 1816 and DD in 1827. He was ordained deacon in June 1813 and priest in December 1813. He was a tutor of his college from 1807 and in 1822 was appointed Lucasian Professor of Mathematics 1822-1826. He was Rector of Gimingham-cum-Trunch, Norfolk, 1826-1833, of Somersham with Pidley and Colne, Hunts 1827-1842, Regius Professor of Divinity 1827-1830, Dean of Peterborough 1830-1842 and Dean of Westminster 1842-1845. In March 1845 he was consecrated Bishop of Ely. His episcopate was uneventful and he occupied a good deal of his time in theological writing, some controversial in nature. He opposed the abolition of religious tests at the universities in a published pamphlet. He composed several acclaimed pieces of church music. He died unmarried in London on 7 January 1864.

VILLIERS, Henry, Montagu (1813-1861)
Bishop of Carlisle, 1856-1860; Bishop of Durham, 1860-1861.

He was born in London on 4 January 1813, the fifth son of George Villiers (1759-1827), third Earl of Clarendon. He graduated from Christ Church, Oxford, BA in 1830, MA in 1837 and DD in 1856. He was ordained deacon in 1836 and priest in 1837 and was appointed Curate of Deane, Lancashire in 1836 and Rector of Kenilworth in 1837. In 1841 he was appointed Rector of St. George's, Bloomsbury, where his preaching and good relationships with Dissenters greatly endeared him to the working classes. He was made a Canon of St. Paul's Cathedral in 1847 and Bishop of Carlisle in 1856. As a bishop he was a strong pastor who worked hard to raise clerical incomes. He was a vigorous opponent of the Oxford Movement and attacked the use of the Confessional. He was a decidedly low churchman who actively supported evangelical societies. He revived the office of rural dean and created eighteen new rural deaneries within his archdeaconries of Carlisle and Westmorland. Villiers was translated from Carlisle to Durham where he was enthroned on 5 September 1860. Just as he was beginning to prepare for his Primary Visitation he was taken seriously ill and died on 9 August 1861.

WALDEGRAVE, Samuel (1817-1869)
Bishop of Carlisle, 1860-1869

He was born at Cardington, Bedfordshire, on 13 September 1817, the second son of William, Eighth Earl Waldegrave and Elizabeth, the daughter of Samuel Whitbread. He was educated at a private school in Cheam and at Balliol College, Oxford, where he graduated BA in 1839, MA in 1842 and DD in 1860. He was elected to a fellowship of All Souls' College in 1839 and held the position until his marriage in 1845. He was ordained deacon in 1842 and priest in 1843 and became Curate at St. Ebbe's, Oxford, in 1842 and Rector of Barford St. Martin, near Salisbury in 1844. He was Select Preacher at Oxford in 1845 and gave the Bampton Lectures in 1854 in which he argued for the post-millennial eschatological scheme. He was a Residentiary Canon at Salisbury Cathedral from 1857-1860 where he was on friendly terms with the Tractarian Bishop, Walter Kerr Hamilton. He was consecrated Bishop of Carlisle in York Minster in 1860. He was an able administrator and formed the Carlisle Diocesan Church and Parsonage Building and Benefice Augmentation Society. He gave particular attention to his Confirmation services, encouraged his clergy in study and preaching and vigorously denounced *Essays and Reviews.* He was a strong opponent of ritualism which he attacked in his Charges and other writings. He made forthright speeches in the Lords in 1867 and 1868 during Lord Shaftesbury's anti-ritual bills. He suffered severe ill-health and died on 1 October 1869.

WIGRAM, Joseph Cotton (1798-1867)
Bishop of Rochester, 1860-1867

He was born at Walthamstow, on 26 December 1798, the fifteenth child of Sir Robert Wigram (1744-1830), an eminent Irish merchant and ship owner of London and Co. Wexford, by his second wife, Eleanor, daughter of John Watts, Esq., of London. Joseph Cotton was educated privately and at Trinity College, Cambridge, where he graduated BA in 1820, MA in 1823 and DD in 1860. He was ordained deacon in 1822 and priest in 1823. He became Curate of Leytonstone in 1822 and of St. James's, Westminster in 1827 where he was in charge of the district church of St. Luke's, Berwick Street. During this time he was in addition secretary of the National Society. He was appointed Rector of East Tisted in 1839 and collated Archdeacon of Winchester in 1847. He was appointed rector of St. Mary's, Southampton and Canon of Winchester in 1850 and consecrated Bishop of Rochester in 1860. He was a conscientious bishop who worked hard to raise his clergy's salaries and encouraged them to use lay helpers in their parishes. He held strong evangelical views and once rashly denounced his clergy for wearing moustaches and playing cricket on village greens. Wigram was essentially a pastor rather than a scholar and the bulk of his writing was on ministerial topics. These included *Practical Hints on the Formation and Management of Sunday Schools* (1833) and *The Cottager's Daily Family Prayers* (1866). Wigram died in London on 6 April 1867 and was buried at Latton parish church in Essex.

WILBERFORCE, Samuel (1805-1873) Bishop of Oxford 1845-1869;
Bishop of Winchester 1869-1873.

He was the third son of William Wilberforce and Barbara Anne, eldest daughter of Isaac Spooner of Elmdon Hall, Warwickshire. He was educated privately and entered Oriel College, Oxford in 1823 where he graduated BA 1826, MA in 1829 and DD in 1845. He was ordained deacon in 1828 and priest in 1829 and was Curate of Checkendon, Oxfordshire, 1828-1830, Rector of Brighstone, Isle of Wight, 1830-1840, Alverstoke, Hampshire 1840-1845 and Dean of Westminster 1845. He remained at Westminster for only a few months, being consecrated as Bishop of Oxford later in the same year. Wilberforce's episcopate was marked by many reforms and his influence extended well beyond his own diocese. He ordered that rural deans convene their clergy in regular chapters, and he founded diocesan societies for church building and for augmenting poorer livings. He himself founded Cuddesdon Theological College for training ordinands and Culham College for the instruction of teachers. Wilberforce was a fluent speaker who made strong contributions in the House of Lords on ecclesiastical issues. He was the protagonist in the revival of Convocation, winning over Archbishop Sumner to his cause in 1858. Wilberforce's public persona marked him out for further honours and in 1869 he was translated to the See of Winchester. He held this office for only three years and was killed when he was thrown from his horse. He was a High churchman of conservative views who attacked the authors of *Essays and Reviews* and condemned Charles Darwin's theory of evolution.

NOTES

Notes to Chapter I

1. Carpenter, S.C., *Church and People 1789-1889* (SPCK, 1933), p. 90
2. *ibid.*, p. 55
3. Soloway, R., *Prelates and People* (London, Routledge & Kegan Paul, 1967), p. 5
4. Chadwick, O., *The Victorian Church* (A & C Black, 1970) Part 1, p. 34
5. Carpenter, S.C., *op. cit.*, p. 56
6. *ibid.*, p. 57
7. Abbey C.J., *The English Church and its History, 1700-1800* (London, Longmans, Green & Co, 1887) Volume 2, p. 215
8. *ibid.*, p. 225
9. Varley, E., *The Last of the Prince Bishops* (CUP, 1992), p. 108
10. *ibid.*, p. 112
11. Soloway, R., *op. cit.*, p. 412
12. Overton, J.H., *The English Church in the Nineteenth Century 1800-1833* (Longmans, Green & Co., 1894) p. 6
13. *ibid.*, p. 7
14 Overton, J.H., *op. cit.*, pp. 7-8
15. Soloway, R., *op. cit.*, p. 209
16. Carpenter, S.C., *op. cit.*, p. 55
17. Bowen, D., *The Idea of the Victorian Church* (McGill Queens University Press,1968), p.30
18. Soloway, R., *op. cit.*, p. 176
19. Bowen, D., *op. cit.*, p. 17
20. Stoughton, J., *History of Religion in England* (London, Hodder & Stoughton, 1901) Volume 8 'The Church of the First Half of the Nineteenth Century', p. 4
21. Chadwick, O., *op. cit.*, Part 1, p. 32
22. Stoughton, J., *op. cit.*, p. 4
23. Sumner, C.P., *A Charge Delivered to the Clergy of the Diocese of Winchester in September and August 1829* (1829) pp. 48-49 cited Soloway, R., *op. cit.*, p. 210
24. Musgrave, T., *A Charge Delivered to the Clergy of the Diocese of York, June and July 1853*) (1853), pp.12-13 cited Soloway, R., *op. cit.*, p. 211
25. Musgrave, T., *A Charge Delivered to the Clergy of the Diocese of Hereford, June 1845* (1845) pp. 21-22 cited Soloway, R., *op. cit.*, p. 212
26. *ibid.*, pp. 21-22
27. Wilberforce, S., *A Charge Delivered to the Clergy of the Diocese of Oxford 1848* (1848) pp. 13-14 cited Soloway, R., *op. cit.*, p. 211
28. Carpenter, S.C., *op. cit.*, p. 98
29. Soloway, R., *op. cit.*, p. 302
30. *Eccles. Duties and Rev. Comm., Report* (1836), p. 60 in *ibid.*, p. 302
31. Blomfield, A., *A Memoir of Charles James Blomfield* (1863) Volume 1, pp. 225-226
32. See Bowen, D., *op. cit.*, p. 22
33. Blomfield, A., *op. cit.*, Volume 2, p. 243
34. See Scotland, N.A.D., *John Bird Sumner Evangelical Archbishop* (Gracewing, 1995), pp. 32-35

35. *ibid.*, p. 50
36. *ibid.*, p. 155
37. *ibid.*, p. 155
38. *ibid.*, p. 50
39. See Ashwell, A., and Wilberforce, R.G., *The Life of Samuel Wilberforce* (London, John Murray, 1881) Volume 1, p. 276
40. *ibid.*, Volume 3, p. 95
41. *ibid.*, Volume 1, pp. 318-321
42. Scotland, N.A.D., *op. cit.*, p. 52
43. Carpenter, S.C., *op. cit.*, p. 264
44. Overton, J.H., *The English Church in the Nineteenth Century 1800-1833* (London, Longmans, Green and Co., 1894), p. 115
45. Arnold, F., *Our Bishops and Deans* (London, Hurst and Blackett, 1875) Volume 1, p. 212
46. See *ibid.*, pp. 349-357
47. Prince Lee, J., *A Charge Delivered at His Primary Visitation in November 1851 to the Clergy of the Diocese of Manchester* (London, B. Fellowes 1851), pp. 21-27
48. See Arnold, *op. cit.*, pp. 213-216
49. *Hansard* 11 April 1832, pp. 278-279
50. Raven, C., *The Christian Socialists 1848-1854* (Frank Cass, 1920), p. 24
51. Norman, E.R., *Church and Society in England 1770-1970* (Oxford, Clarendon Press, 1976), p. 163
52. Ashwell A., & Wilberforce R.G., *op. cit.*, Volume 2, p. 279

Notes to Chapter II

1. Trollope, A., *Barchester Towers* (1857)
2. Chamberlain, M.E., *Lord Palmerston* (G.P.C. Books, 1987), p. 31
3. Cited Best, G.F.A., *Shaftesbury* (B.T. Batsford Ltd, 1964,) p. 25
4. ibid., p. 30
5. *ibid.*, p. 30
6. Hodder, E., *The Life of the Seventh Earl of Shaftesbury K.G.* (Cassell & Company Ltd, 1886) Volume 1, p. 285
7. *ibid.*, p. 285
8. *ibid.*, Volume 3, pp. 190-191
9. *ibid.*, p. 191
10. *ibid.*, p. 191
11. See Ridley, J., *Lord Palmerston* (Constable, London, 1970) p. 501
12. Shaftesbury to Evelyn Ashley in Hodder, E, *Op.Cit.*, Volume 2, p. 505
13. *ibid.*, Volume 3, p. 191
14. Ridley, J., *O p. .Cit.*, p. 500
15. Hodder, E., *Op.Cit.*, Volume 3, p. 196
16. *ibid.*, p. 194
17. Bell, H.F.C., *Lord Palmerston* (Longmans, Green & Co., London, 1836) Volume 2, p 157
18. Palmerston to Queen Victoria, 2 December, 1860 in Berson A.C., *The Letters of Queen Victoria* (London, John Murray, 1907) Volume 3
19. Hodder, E., *Op.Cit.*, Volume 3, p. 198
20. Palmerston to Queen Victoria, 2 December, 1860 in Benson A.C. *Op.Cit.*
21. *ibid.*

22. *ibid.*
23. *ibid.*
24. Bell, H.F.C., *Op.Cit.*, Volume 2, p303.
25. Birrell, C.M., *The Life of William Brock DD* (1878) pp182-183 cited by Munden A., 'The First Palmerstonian Bishop: Henry Montagu Villiers, Bishop of Carlisle 1856-60 and Bishop of Durham 1860-61', *Northern History* Volume 26, p. 187
26. Kitchin, G.W., *Edward Browne DD: A Memoir* (London, John Murray, 1895) p. 113
27. Davidson, R.T. & Benham W., *Life of Archibald Campell Tait Archbishop of Canterbury*, (London, Macmillan & Co., 1891) Volume 1, pp 36-37
28. Burgon, J.W. *Lives of Twelve Good Men* (New York, Scribner & Welford, 1888) Volume 2, pp. 238-239
29. Palmerston to Queen Victoria, 2 December, 1860 in Benson A.C., *Op.Cit.*
30. *ibid.*
31. Cited in Hodder, E., *Op.Cit.*, Volume 3, pp 192-193
32. *ibid.*, p. 193
33. *ibid.*, p. 193
34. *ibid.*, p. 199
35. *ibid.*, p. 200
36. *Memorandum On Bishops*, *Broadlands Papers* (Southampton University Library MS HA/H/3/1)
37. *ibid.*, folios 5 & 6
38. Hodder, E., *Op.Cit.*, Volume 3, p. 196
39. *ibid.*, p. 197
40. Shaftesbury to Palmerston 18 November, 1862, *Broadlands Papers* Southampton University Library, MS GC/SH/50
41. See entry for Tait, Catherine, in Lewis, D, editor *Dictionary of Evangelical Biography* (Blackwell, 1995), pp. 1078-1079
42. Hodder, E., *Op.Cit.*, Volume 3, p. 199
43. 7th Earl of Shaftesbury to Palmerston, Nov 1862, *Broadlands Papers*, GC/SH/50
44. 7th Earl of Shaftesbury to Palmerston, 20 Dec 1856, Broadlands Papers, GC/SH/23-46
45. *ibid.*
46. Shaftesbury, *Diary*, Volume 6, 29 June 1856 Broadlands Papers, SHA/PD/7
47. *ibid.*, 20 August, 1856
48. *ibid.*, 14 October, 1856
49. *ibid.*, 22 November, 1856
50. *ibid.*, 23 November, 1856
51. *ibid.*, 27 November, 1857
52. Memoradum on bishoprics, p. 1, Broadlands Papers, HA/H/5
53. *ibid.*, pp. 2-3
54. Shaftesbury to Palmerston, 9 Jan, 1864, Broadlands papers, GC/SH/61
55. Shaftesbury to Palmerston, 24 Jan, 1864, Broadlands Papers, GC/SH/62
56. Shaftesbury to Palmerston, 21 June, 1865, Broadlands Papers, GC/SH/66
57. Shaftesbury to Palmerston, 12 Dec, 1863, Broadlands Papers, GC/SH/59
58. Shaftesbury to Palmerston, 17 Dec, 1863, Broadlands Papers, GC/SH/60
59. Shaftesbury to Palmerston, 29 April, 1864, Broadlands Papers, GC/SH/64/2
60. *The Record*, 8 November, 1865
61. Hodder, E., *op.cit.*, Volume 3, p. 197 (The exception was Canon Blakesley of Canterbury)

62. Shaftesbury to Palmerston, 9 November, 1860, Broadlands Papers, GC/SH/42
63. Thomson, E., *The Life and Letters of William Thomson Archbishop of York*, (London, John Lane Company, 1919) p. 59
64. Shaftesbury to Palmerston, 1 October, 1862, Broadlands Papers, GC/SH/49
65. Thomson, E., *Op.Cit.*, p. 59
66. *ibid.*, p. 58
67. *The Record*, 8 November, 1865
68. Hodder, E., *Op.Cit.*, Volume 3, p. 192
69. The Christian Observer, October, 1856, p. 724
70. Kirk-Smith, H., *William Thomson Archbishop of York His Life and Times* 1819-90, (London, SPCK, 1958), p. 15
71. *The Record*, 8 November, 1865

Notes to Chapter III

1. See *DNB* entry
2. See *DNB* entries
3. See DNB entries for John Thomas Pelham (1811-1894) and Henry Thomas Pelham (1804-1866)
4. See *DNB* entry for Samuel Waldegrave (1817-1869)
5. Davidson, R.T. and Benham W., *Life of Archibald Campbell Tait* (London, MacMillan & Co, 1891), Volume 1, pp. 1-9 and 47-49
6. Information taken from Wigram R.S., *Biographical Notes relating to Certain Members of the Wigram Family,* (Privately printed at the Aberdeen University Press, 1912) in the possession of Canon Sir Clifford Wigram
7. Arnold, F., *Our Bishops and Deans*, (London, Hurst and Blackett Publishers, 1875), p. 111
8. *ibid.*, p. 111. See also Benson, A.C., *The Letters of Queen Victoria* (London, John Murray, 1907) Volume 3, p. 276
9. Kirk-Smith, H., *William Thomson Archbishop of York His Life and Times 1819-1890*, (London, SPCK, 1958) p. 1 and DNB entry for William Thomson
10. See *DNB* entry for Charles Thomas Longley
11. See his obituary *TheTimes* 8 June, 1880
12. See *The Times* 19 December, 1891
13. Leach, J.C.H., *Sparks of Reform* (JHC Leach, 1994). pp. 1-2
14. Bickersteth, M.C., *A Sketch of the Life and Episcopate of the Right Reverend Robert Bickersteth, Bishop of Ripon 1857-1884*, (Rivingtons, London, 1887), p. 21. See also Hempton, D., 'Bickersteth, Bishop of Ripon', *Northern History* Vol 17, 1981
15. See their entries in the *DNB*
16. Kirk-Smith, H., *op. cit.*, p. 2
17. Thomson, E.H., *The Life and Letters of William Thomson Archbishop of York*, (London, John Lane Company, 1918), p. 5
18. Kitchin, G.W., *Edward Harold Browne DD Lord Bishop of Winchester, A Memoir*, (London, John Murray, 1895), p. 19
19. *ibid.*, p. 19
20. *ibid.*, p. 19
21. *ibid.*, pp. 22-23
22. See Balleine, G.R., *History of the Evangelical Party in the Church of England*, p. 267

23. Bickersteth, M.C., *op. cit.*, p. 169

24. Pelham, J.T., *A Charge Delivered to the Clergy and Church wardens of the Diocese of Norwich by John Thomas Lord Bishop of Norwich at His Visitation in 1856,* (London, Rivingtons, 1865) p. 9

25. Munden, A.F., 'The First Palmerston Bishop: Henry Montagu Villiers, Bishop of Carlisle, 1856-1860 and Bishop of Durham 1860-1861, *Northern History*, Volume 2, 1990, pp. 194-195

26. Davidson, R.T and Benham, W., *op. cit.*, Volume 1, pp. 49-50

27. Kirk-Smith, H., *op. cit.*, p3

28. Thomson, E.H., *op. cit.*, pp. 9-10

29. *ibid.*, pp. 38-39

30. Arnold, F., *Our Bishops and Deans* (London, Hurst and Blackett Publishers, 1875), Volume 2, p. 33

31. Kitchin, G.W., *op. cit.*, p. 22

32. *ibid.*, p. 32

33. *ibid.*, p. 122

34. *ibid.*, p. 217

35. Burgon, J.W., *Lives of Twelve Good Men* (New York, Scribner & Welford, 1888), Volume 2, p. 249

36. *ibid.*, p. 258

37. *ibid.*, p. 271

38. Hodder, E., *The Life and Work of the Seventh Lord Shaftesbury*, (London, Cassell & Company Ltd, 1886), Volume 3, p. 199

39. *The Times* 10 August, 1861

40. *ibid.*

41. Villiers, H.M., *On the Necessity and Value of Lay Agency in the Church*, (London, Sampson, Low & Son, 1852), p. 83

42. *The Gentleman's Magazine*, 1861, p. 325

43. Davidson, R.T and Benham, W., *op. cit.*, p. 60

44. *ibid.*, p. 60 citing Tait, A.C., *A Charge 1858*, p. 83

45. Bickersteth, M.C., *op. cit..*, p. 45

46. Brenn, W and Kennedy, *History of Leyton*, (Hand-written, undated), Volume 6, p. 55

47. See *Baptism Register St. James Westminster*, 1828 Volume 12 in Westminster City Archives

48. Wigram, J.C., *Ministerial Watchfulness: A Sermon Preached at the Visitation of the Rt Rev. the Lord Bishop of Winchester in the Parish Church of Alton on Friday October 17, 1845*, (London, Francis and John Rivington, 1845), p. 28

49. *ibid.*, p. 27

50. *ibid.*, p. 28

51. *ibid.*, p. 29

52. *Post Office Directory for Hampshire 1855*

53. See *East Tisted Burial Register* and *East Tisted Marriage Register* (Winchester Country Records Office)

54. See *DNB* entry for Samuel Waldegrave

55. Leach, J.H.C., *Sparks of Reform*, (Oxford, Pembroke College, 1994), p. 4

56. *ibid.*, p. 9

57. *ibid.*, p. 8

58. *The Times* 22 August, 1868

59. See DNB entry for Francis Jeune

60. Kirk-Smith, H., *op. cit.*, p. 6

61. *ibid.*, p. 15
62. Kitchin, G.W., *op. cit.*, p. 121
63. *ibid.*, p. 12
64. *ibid.*, p. 159
65. See Ellicott, C.J., *The Church and the Rural Poor being an Address delivered in the parish church of Stow-on-the-Wold at the Triennial Visitation, October 29, 1873,* (Longman & Co. 1873) and *The Spiritual Needs of the Country Parishes* (SPCK, London, 188?)
66. Burgon, J.W., *op. cit.*, Volume 2, p. 260
67. *Crockford's Clerical Directory* 1892 entry for Philpott, Henry
68. *The Times* 11 January, 1892
69. See for example Waldegrave,S., *The Cattle Plague a Warning Voice to Britain from the King of Nations: A Sermon preached in the Cathedral Church of Carlisle on Friday 12th January, 1866 by the Hon and Right Rev Samuel Waldegrave DD, Lord Bishop of Carlisle,* (London, William Hunt and Company, 1866); Wigram, J.C., *The Advent of the Lord the Present Glory of the Church* in Wilson, W (editor), *The Blessing of the Lord's Second Advent: Six Lectures During Lent,* (London and Winchester, 1851) and Bickersteth, R., *The Universal and Perpetual Obligation of the Lord's Day,* (London, The Religious Tract Society, 1887)
70. *Annual Register* 1861 cited by Bell, H.C.F., *Lord Palmerston,* (Longmans, Green & Co. London, 1936), p. 303
71. *The Times* 19 August, 1861
72. *ibid.*
73. *The Christian Observer* May, 1857, p. 356
74. *The Church of England Monthly Review*, January-June, 1857, p. 383
75. *ibid.*, p. 305
76. *Evangelical Christendom* 2 September, 1861, p. 550
77. *ibid.*, p. 551
78. Baring, C., *A Charge Delivered to the Clergy of the Diocese of Gloucester and Bristol at His Primary Visitation in October, 1857,* (Seeley, Jackson & Halliday, London, 1857), p. 35
79. Bickersteth, M.C., *op. cit..*, p. 27
80. *ibid.*, p. 193
81. *ibid.*, Introduction, p. vi
82. An account of the conversion of G.V. Wigram, a loose paper in Wigram, R.S., *op. cit.*, (in the possession of Canon Sir Clifford Wigram)
83. Martin, M.C., 'Women and Philanthropy in Walthamstow and Leyton 1740-1870' *London Journal* 1995, Volume 2, part 19, p. 127
84. *Hampshire Advertiser* 6 April, 1850
85. *The Saturday Review* 29 December, 1860
86. *The Pall Mall Gazette* 7 January, 1867, p. 221
87. *ibid.*, p. 221
88. *The Saturday Review* 8 December, 1860, p. 729
89. *ibid.*, p. 729
90. For the distinction between the 'Recordites' and the 'Moderates' see Hilton, B., *The Age of Atonement,* (Clarendon, 1988) pp. 3-35
91. Thomson, E.H., *op. cit.*, p. 9
92. *Evangelical Christendom* 2 September 1861, p. 551
93. Arnold, F., *op. cit.*, Volume 1, p. 321
94. *ibid.*, p. 321
95. *ibid.*, p. 317

96. Baring-Gould, S., *The Church Revival* (1914) p. 203

97. *ibid.*, p. 182

98. Kirk-Smith, H., *op. cit.*, p. 15

99. Davidson, R.T and Benham W., *op. cit.*, Volume 1, pp. 36-37

100. *ibid.*, p. 37

101. *ibid.*, p. 43

102. *ibid.*, p. 122

103. *The Church of England Quarterly Review*, Volume XL, 1856, p. 459

104. See Shaftesbury to Palmerston 18, November, 1862 Broadlands Papers, (Southampton University Archives) MS GC/SH/50. Shaftesbury's judgement, it should be noted, was not always correct. In the same letter he mistakenly categorised Wigram as 'moderate High Church'

105. Kitchin, G.W., *op. cit.*, p. 19

106. *ibid.*, p. 21

107. *ibid.*, p. 398

108. *ibid.*, p. 136

109. See Edwards D.L., *Leaders of the Church of England* (OUP, 1971) p. 83 and Marsh, P.T., *The Victorian Church in Decline* (Routledge and Kegan Paul, London, 1969), p. 17 and 28

110. Chadwick, O., *The Victorian Church*, (London, A and C Black, 1971) p. 102

111. Crowther, M.A., *Church Embattled: Religious Controversy in mid-Victorian England*, (David and Charles, Newton Abbot, 1970), p. 210

112. Shaftesbury to Palmerston 18 November, 1862, Broadlands Papers, Southampton University, MS GC/SH/50

113. Balleine, G.R., *A History of the Evangelical Party in the Church of England*, (London, Church Book Room Press, 1851), p. 211

114. Ellicott, C.J., *Some Present Dangers of the Church of England*, (Cassell, Petker & Galpin, London, 1878), pp. vi-vii

115. *ibid.*

116. Ellicott, C.J., *Sermons at Gloucester* (1905), p. 235

117. See Wilberforce, R.G., *Life of the Right Reverend Samuel Wilberforce, DD*, (John Murray, London, 1882), Volume 3, pp. 33-34

118. Longley, C.T., *A Charge Addressed to the Clergy of the Diocese of Durham at His Primary Visitation by Charles Longley DD, Lord Bishop of Durham,* (Durham, George Andrews, 1857), pp. 11-12

119. *ibid.*, pp. 19-20

120. *ibid.*, p. 26

121. Carpenter, E., *Cantuar The Archbishops in their Office*, (Mowbray, 1987), p. 333

122. Shaftesbury to Palmerston 18 November, 1862, Broadlands Papers, Southampton University, MS GC/SH/50

123. Shaftesbury to Palmerston 21 June, 1865, Broadlands Papers, Southampton University, MS GC/SH/66

124. *ibid.*

125. See *DNB* entry for Jacobson, William

126. Burgon, J.W., *op. cit.*, Volume 2, p. 27

127. Jacobson, W., *A Charge 1868*, pp. 39-44

128. Burgon, J.W., *op. cit.*, Volume 2, p. 283

129. Shaftesbury to Palmerston 20 December, 1856, Broadlands Papers, Southampton University, MS GC/SH/34/1

Notes to Chapter IV

1. Longley, C.T., *A Charge addressed to the Clergy of the Diocese of Durham at His Primary Visitation by Charles Thomas Longley DD. Lord Bishop of Durham*, (Durham, George Andrews, 1857), p. 8
2. Tait, A.C., *The Spiritual Wants of the Metropolis and its Suburbs. A letter to the laity of the diocese of London by the Right Hon. and Right Rev. Archibald Campbell, Lord Bishop of London*, (London, Rivingtons, 1863), p. 12
3. Inglis, K.S., *Churches and the Working Classes in Victorian England*, (London, Routledge & Kegan Paul, 1963), p. 25
4. Tait, A.C., *op. cit..*, p. 5
5. Kirk-Smith, M., *William Thomson Archbishop of York*, (London, SPCK, 1958), p. 18
6. Tait, A.C., *A Charge to the Clergy of the Diocese of London at His Visitation in December, 1866*, (Rivingtons, London, Oxford and Cambridge, 1866), pp. 74-75
7. Waldegrave, S., *The Charge Delivered in October, 1861 at His Primary Visitation by the Hon and Right Rev Samuel Waldegrave DD, Lord Bishop of Carlisle*, (London, Wertheim, Macintosh and Hunt; T.W. Arthur, Carlisle, 1861), p. 7
8. Thomson, W., *A Charge to the Clergy of the Diocese of York, delivered at His Primary Visitation in October, 1865 by the Most Reverend William, Lord Archbishop of York, Primate of England and Metropolitan*, (London, John Murray, 1865), p. 13
9. 'Royal Commission on the Employment of Children, Young Persons and Women in Agriculture', *Parliamentary Papers*, Volume 17, Report of the Revd James Fraser
10. *The Stamford Mercury*, 6 September, 1876
11. Thomson, A.M., *Op. Cit.*, p. 11
12. *ibid.*, p. 12
13. Browne, E.H., *A Charge Delivered to the Clergy and Churchwardens of the Diocese of Ely at his primary Visitation in October and November 1865 by Edward Harold Browne Lord Bishop of Ely*, (London, Longman, Green & Co., 1865), p. 6
14. *ibid.*, p. 7
15. Waldegrave, S., *The Charge Delivered in July and August 1864 at His Second Episcopal Visitation by the Hon and Right Rev Samuel Waldegrave DD Lord Bishop of Carlisle*, (London, Hunt and Company, 1864), p. 3
16. Sumner, J.B., *A Charge Addressed to the Clergy of the Diocese of Chester*, (Hatchard & Son, London, 1841), p. 5. For a more detailed examination of Sumner's policy on Church Building in Chester diocese see Gill, R., *The Myth of the Empty Church*, (SPCK, 1993), p. 114f
17. *Hansard* LXVIII, 5 May, 1843
18. Baring, C., *A Charge Delivered to the Clergy of the Diocese of Gloucester and Bristol at His Primary Visitation in October, 1857*, (Seeley, Jackson and Halliday, London, 1857), pp. 10-11
19. Waldegrave, S., *The charge Delivered in October, 1861 at his Primary Visitation by the Hon and Right Rev Samuel Waldegrave DD Lord Bishop of Carlisle*, (London, Wertheim, Macintosh and Hunt; T.W. Arthur Carlisle, 1861), p. 14
20. *ibid.*, p. 15
21. Thomson, W., *A Charge 1865*, p. 10

22. Baring, C., *A Charge 1857*, p. 14
23. Arnold, F., *Our Bishops and Deans*, (London, Hurst and Blackett Publishers, 1875), Volume 1, p. 165
24. Bickersteth , R., *A Charge delivered to the Clergy of the Diocese of Ripon at his Triennial Visitation, October 1861, by Robert Lord Bishop of Ripon*, (London, James Nisbet & Co., 1861), p. 22
25. Bickersteth, R., *A Charge delivered to the Clergy of the Diocese of Ripon at His Triennial Visitation, April 1864 by Robert, Lord Bishop of Ripon*, (James Nisbet, London, 1864), p. 24
26. Bickersteth, R., *A Charge delivered to the Clergy of the Diocese of Ripon at his Seventh Triennial Visitation*, (London, James Nisbet & Co., 1876), p. 27
27. *Chelmsford Chronicle*, 13 March, 1863
28. Philpott, H., *A Charge delivered to the Clergy and Churchwardens of the Diocese of Worcester by Henry, Lord Bishop of Worcester at his Visitation in June 1865*, (London, Rivingtons, 1865), pp. 10-11
29. Philpott, H., *A Charge delivered to the Clergy and Churchwardens of the Diocese of Winchester at His Visitation in June, 1874*, (London, Rivingtons, 1874), p. 8
30. *The Record*, 17 September, 1879, *Durham County Advertiser*, 19 September, 1879.
31. Tait, A.C., *A Charge 1866*, p. 69
32. Bickersteth, M.R., *A Sketch of the Life and Episcopate of the Right Reverend Robert Bickersteth, Bishop of Ripon 1857-1884*, (Rivingtons, London, 1887), p. 145
33. Bickersteth, M.R., *A Charge delivered to the Clergy of the Diocese of Ripon at his Triennial Visitation, October, 1861, by Robert Lord Bishop of Ripon*, (London, James Nisbet & Co., 1861), p. 9
34. Waldegrave, S., *Ministering Kings or Our Established Church a favour from God A Sermon on Isaiah LXV10 preached in His Cathedral on Sunday, August 2nd, 1868* (London, William Hunt & Company, 1868), p. 19
35. Philpott, H., *A Charge delivered to the Clergy and Churchwardens of the Diocese of Worcester by Henry, Lord Bishop of Worcester at his Visitation in June 1865*, (London, Rivingtons, 1865), p. 14
36. Kirk-Smith, H., *Op. Cit.*, p. 67
37. Jacobson, W., *A Charge delivered to the Clergy of the Diocese at his Second Visitation October 1871 by William Jacobson DD Bishop of Chester* (Chester, Phillipson & Golder, 1871), p. 2
38. *ibid.*, p. 3
39. Jeune, F.C., *A Charge delivered to the Clergy and Churchwardens of the Diocese of Peterborough at His primary Visitation in October 1867 by Francis Lord Bishop of Peterborough*, (Oxford and London, James Parker & Co., 1867), p. 4
40. Villiers, H.M., *A Charge delivered to the Clergy of the Diocese of Carlisle, 1858*, p. 21
41. *ibid.*, p. 57
42. See Munden, A., 'The First Palmerston Bishop: Henry Montagu Villiers, Bishop of Carlisle, 1856-1860 and Bishop of Durham', *Northern History*, Volume 26, 1990, p. 201
43. See *The Christian Observer*, February, 1857
44. Longley, C.T., *A Charge, intended for delivery to the Clergy of the Diocese of Canterbury, at His Second Visitation, 1868, by the Most Reverend Charles Thomas, Late Lord Archbishop of Canterbury*, (Rivingtons, London, 1868), p. 7

45. Bickersteth, R., *A Charge 1864*, p. 15
46. Bickersteth, M.C., *op. cit..*, p. 231
47. Waldegrave, S., *A Charge 1861*, pp. 18-22
48. Waldegrave, S., *A Charge 1864*, p. 22
49. Jeune, F.C., *A Charge 1867*, p. 11
50. *ibid.*, p. 11
51. *ibid.*, p. 11
52. Wigram, J.C., *A Charge 1864*, p. 11
53. *ibid.*, p. 12
54. Longley, C.T., *A Charge 1864*, p. 12
55. *ibid.*, p. 11
56. Pelham, J.T., *A Charge 1865*, p. 17
57. Waldegrave, S., *A Charge 1861*, p. 5
58. Wigram, J.C., *A Charge 1864*, p. 12
59. Jeune, F., *A Charge 1867*, p. 12
60. *ibid.*, p. 14
61. Philpott, H., *A Charge 1874*, p. 11
62. *ibid.*, p. 10
63. Bickersteth, M.C., *op. cit..*, p. 223
64. *The Times* 22 October, 1870, Kirk-Smith, H., *op. cit..*, p. 135
65. Jacobson, W., *A Charge 1871*, p. 25
66. Longley, C.T., *A Charge 1857*, p. 14
67. Pelham, J.T., *A Charge 1865*, p. 19
68. Bickersteth, M.C., *op. cit..*, p. 218
69. Bickersteth, M.C., *A Charge 1864*, pp. 25-26
70. Bickersteth, M.C., *Op. Cit.*, p. 219
71. Wigram, J.C., *A Charge 1864*, p. 12
72. *ibid.*, p. 12
73. Jacobson, W., *A Charge 1871*, p. 14
74. Bickersteth, M.C., *op. cit..*, p. 230
75. Jeune, F.C., *A Charge 1867*, p. 11
76. Villiers, M.C., *A Charge 1858*, pp. 23 and 26
77. Longley, C.T., *A Charge 1857*, p. 17
78. Pelham, J.T., *A Charge 1865*, p. 18
79. Bickersteth, M.C., *op. cit..*, p. 227
80. Waldegrave, S., *A Charge 1861*, pp. 22 and 25
81. Philpott, H., *A Charge 1874*, p. 13
82. Thomson, W., *A Charge 1865*, p. 13
83. Jacobson, W., *A Charge 1871*, p. 29
84. *ibid.*, p. 29
85. Villiers, M., *A Charge 1858*, p. 27
86. Bickersteth, R., *A Charge 1876*, p. 23
87. *ibid.*, p. 24
88. Tait, A.C., *A Charge 1865*, p. 82
89. Jacobson, W., *A Charge 1868*, p. 19
90. Longley, C.T., *A Charge 1857*, p. 29
91. Longley, C.T., *A Charge 1864*, p. 22
92. Kirk-Smith, H., *op. cit..*, p. 103
93. See Scotland, N.A.D., *Agricultural Trade Unionism in Gloucestershire 1872-1950*,(Cheltenham, C.G.C.H.E., 1991), p. 23
94. *ibid.*, p. 24

95. Ellicott, C.J., *A Charge 1873*, p. 9.

96. *ibid.*, pp. 14-15

97. Kitchin, G.W., *Edward Harold Browne, Lord Bishop of Winchester, A Memoir*,(London, John Murray, 1895), p. 339

98. *ibid.*, pp. 341-343

99. Davidson, R.T. and Benham, W., *Life of Archibald Campbell Tait Archbishop of Canterbury*, (London, Macmillan & Co., 1891), Volume 1, p. 470

100. *ibid.*, p. 471

101. *The Chelmsford Chronicle*, 29 November, 1861

102. *Essex Weekly News*, 25 January, 1867

103. Kitchin, G.W., *op. cit..*, p. 339

104. Browne, E.H., *The Clergyman in Social Life. A Charge Addressed to Candidates in Ely Cathedral at Trinity Ordination, 1864 by Edward Harold, Bishop of Ely*, (Cambridge, Deighton, Bell & Co.,1864), p. 12

105. *Essex Weekly News*, 25 January, 1867

106. Wigram, J.C., *A Charge 1864*, p. 22

107. *ibid.*, p. 3

108. Kitchin, G.W., *op. cit..*, p. 278

109. *ibid.*, p. 278

110. Browne, E.H., *A Charge 1865*, p. 27

111. Longley, C.T., *A Charge 1857*, pp. 18-20

112. *ibid.*, p. 20

113. See Villiers, M.C., *On the Necessity and Value of Lay Agency in the Church*, (London, Sampson, Low & Son, 1852)

114. *ibid.*, p. 60

115. *ibid.*, p. 83

116. *ibid.*, p. 84

117. Munden, A.F., *op. cit..*, p. 200

118 .Tait, A.C., *A Charge 1865*, p. 66

119. *ibid.*, p. 70

120. *ibid.*, p. 70

121. Bickersteth, R., *A Charge 1867*, p. 11

122. Bickersteth, R., *A Charge 1864*, p. 26

123. *ibid.*, p. 27

124. Kitchin, G.W., *op. cit..*, p. 357

125. Browne, E.H., *A Charge 1865*, p. 27

126. Jacobson, W., *A Charge 1868*, p. 7

127. Burgon, J.W., *op. cit..*, Volume 2, p. 281

128. *The Chelmsford Chronicle*, 23 November, 1860

129. Tait, A.C., *A Charge 1874*, p. 85

130. For a discussion of Tait's disagreements with Sisterhoods in the London diocese see Davidson, R.T., and Benham, W., *op. cit..*, Volume 1, pp. 449-464

131. *ibid.*, p. 468

132. *ibid.*, p. 464

133. *Kitchin*, G.W., *op. cit..*, p. 259

134. *ibid.*, p. 358

135. *ibid.*, p. 359

136. *ibid.*, p. 359

137. *ibid.*, p. 360

138. *ibid.*, p. 366

139. *ibid.*, p. 362

140. Wigram, J.C., *A Charge 1864*, p. 19

141. *ibid.*, p. 19

142. Jacobson, W., *A Charge 1871*, p. 45

143. *ibid.*, p. 146

144. *Carlisle Journal*, 30 July, 1858 cited by Munden A.F., *op. cit..*, p. 197

145. *Evangelical Christendom*, 2 September, 1861, p. 551

146. Baring, C., *A Charge*, p. 10

147. Davidson, R.T., and Benham, W., *op. cit..*, Volume 2, p. 503

148. *Church of England Monthly Review*, Volume 3 July-December, 1857, p. 305

149. Bickersteth, M.C., *op. cit..*, p. 118

150. Bickersteth, R., *A Charge 1876*, p. 36

151. Kirk-Smith, H., *op. cit..*, pp. 126-127

152. *ibid.*, p. 127

153. *The Eagle*, December, 1905, Volume 138, p. 103

154. Munden, A.F., *op. cit..*, p. 197

155. Bickersteth, R., *A Charge 1861*, p. 11

156. Bickersteth, R., *A Charge 1864*, p. 17

157. Kirk-Smith, H., *op. cit..*, p. 54

158. *ibid.*, p. 56

159. *ibid.*, p. 57

160. Ellicott, C.J., *Church Work Past and Present an Address in the Cathedral, Gloucester at the Triennial Visitation, 23 October, 1873*, (London, Longman & Co., 1873), p. 12

161. Browne, H.E., *A Charge 1865*, p. 116

162. Jeune, F., *A Charge 1867*, p. 15

163. Pelham, J.T., *A Charge 1865*, pp. 8-9

164. Philpott, H., *A Charge 1874*, p. 5

165. See Scotland, N.A.D., *John Bird Sumner: Evangelical Archbishop*, (Gracewing, 1995), pp. 45-62

Notes to Chapter V

1. In the 1851 *Census of Religion*, Horace Mann had calculated that 58% of the population worshipped somewhere on census Sunday which was the last Sunday in March 1851

2. Wilson, H.B. (editor), *Essays and Reviews*, (J.W. Parker & Son, Oxford, 1860), p. 47

3. Ellis, I., *Seven Against Christ: A Study of Essays and Reviews,* (Leidon, E.J. Brill, 1980), p. 12

4. *ibid.*, p. 30

5. Vidler, A.R., *The Church in an Age of Revolution,* (Pelican, Harmondsworth, 1961, edition), p. 124

6. Wilson, H.B., *op. cit..*, p. 47

7. *ibid.*, p. 78

8. *ibid.*, p. 109f

9. *ibid.*, p. 175

10. *ibid.*, p. 175

11. *ibid.*, p. 253

12. *ibid.*,

13. *ibid.*, p. 328

14. *The Freeman*, 27 June, 1860
15. *ibid.*, 27 June, 1860
16. *The Christian Observer*, June, 1860
17. See Reardon, B.M.G., *From Coleridge to Gore*, (Longman, London, 1971), p. 340
18. *The Christian Observer*, May, 1862, p. 372
19. Thomson, W., *Aids to Faith*, (London, John Murray, 1861), preface
20. *ibid.*, p. 317
21. *ibid.*, p. 314
22. *ibid.*, p. 314
23. *ibid.*, p. 314
24. *ibid.*, p. 311
25. *ibid.*, p. 320
26. *ibid.*, p. 386
27. *ibid.*, p. 387
28. *ibid.*, p. 391
29. *ibid.*, p. 411
30. *ibid.*, p. 404
31. *ibid.*, p. 413
32. *ibid.*, p. 406
33. *ibid.*, p. 408
34. *ibid.*, pp. 409-410
35. *ibid.*, p 414
36. *ibid.*, p. 415
37. *ibid.*, p. 418
38. *ibid.*, p. 428
39. *ibid.*, p. 430
40. *ibid.*, p. 433
41. *ibid.*, p. 432
42. *ibid.*, p. 447
43. *ibid.*, p. 469
44. *ibid.*, pp. 327-328
45. *ibid.*, pp. 330-331
46. *ibid.*, p. 332
47. *ibid.*, p. 334
48. *ibid.*, p. 337
49. *ibid.*, p. 345
50. *ibid.*, p. 345
51. *ibid.*, p. 352
52. *ibid.*, p. 364
53. *ibid.*, p. 364
54. *ibid.*, p. 365
55. *ibid.*, p. 365
56. *ibid.*, pp. 365-366
57. Ellis, I., *op. cit.*., p. 247
58. *ibid.*, p. 168
59. Kirk Smith, H., *William Thomson Archibishop of York*, (London, SPCK, 1958), p. 11
60. *ibid.*, p. 157
61. *Evangelical Christendom,* 2 September, 1861, p. 551
62. Cited from *The Eagle*, (Magazine supported by members of St. John's College), December, 1905, Volume 138, p. 89

63. Kitchin, G.W., *Edward Harold Browne DD., Lord Bishop of Winchester, A Memoir*, (London, John Murray, 1895), p. 207

64. See *DNB* entry for Browne, Edward Harold (1811-1891)

65. Ellis, I., *op. cit..*, p. 159

66. Wilberforce, S., *A Charge to the Clergy of the Diocese of Oxford*, November 1860, p. 67 cited Ellis, I., *op. cit..*, p. 159

67. Wilberforce, S., *Quarterly Review*, January, 1861, Volume 109, No. 217, p. 250 and p. 278

68. Waldegrave, S., *The Charge Delivered in October, 1861 at His Primary Visitation by the Hon and Right Revd Samuel Waldegrave DD., Lord Bishop of Carlisle*, (London, Wertheim, Macintosh & Hunt; T.W. Arthur, Carlisle, 1861), p. 33

69. *ibid.*, p. 32

70. *ibid.*, p. 34

71. *ibid.*, p. 35

72. Bickersteth, M.C., *A Sketch of the Life and Episcopate of the Right Reverend Robert Bickersteth DD., Bishop of Ripon 1857-1884*, (London, Rivingtons, 1887), p. 195

73. *ibid.*, p. 41

74. Wigram, J.C., *A Charge Delivered to the Clergy and Churchwardens of the Diocese of Rochester at His Second Visitation in November, 1864*, (London, Rivingstons, 1864), p. 50

75. Philpott, H., *A Charge Delivered to the Clergy and Churchwardens of the Diocese of Worcester by Henry, Lord Bishop of Worcester at His Visitation in June, 1865*, London, Rivingtons, 1865), pp. 42-43

76. *ibid.*, p. 43

77. *ibid.*, p. 44

78. Wilberforce, R.G., *Life of the Rt Revd Samuel Wilberforce*, (London, John Murray 1883), Volume 3, pp. 2-4

79. Davidson, R.T., & Benham, W., *Life of the Archibald Campbell Tait*, (London, Macmillan, 1891), Volume 1, p. 281

80. *ibid.*, p. 282

81. *ibid.*, p. 282

82. *ibid.*, p. 284

83. *ibid.*, p. 284

84. *ibid.*, p. 285

85. *ibid.*, p. 285

86. *ibid.*, p. 285

87. *ibid.*, p. 288

88. *ibid.*, p. 291

89. *ibid.*, p. 293

90. *ibid.*, p. 307

91. *ibid.*, p. 307

92. Wilberforce, R.G., *op. cit..*, Volume 3, p. 6

93. Ellis, I, *op. cit..*, p. 189

94. Vidler, A.R., *The Church in an Age of Revolution*, (Pelican, 1961), p 128

95. Longley, C.T., *A Pastoral Letter Addressed to the Clergy and Laity of His Province by Charles Thomas Longley, Archbishop of Canterbury*, (London, Rivingtons, 1864), p. 7

96. *ibid.*, p. 14

97. *ibid.*, p. 13

98. Thomson, W., *A Pastoral Letter to the Clergy and Laity of the Province of York*

by William Lord Archbishop of York, Primate of England and Metropolitan, (London, W. Clowes Sons, 1864), p. 7 and 9

99. *ibid.*, p. 8
100. *ibid.*, p. 10
101. *ibid.*, p. 13
102. *ibid.*, p. 15
103. *ibid.*, p. 16
104. *Chronicle of Convocation*, 1864, p 1666 cited by Ellis, I, *op. cit..*, p. 190
105. Ellis, I., *op. cit..*, p. 190
106. Davidson, R.T., and Benham, W., *op. cit..*, Volume 1, p. 317
107. *ibid.*, p. 318
108. *ibid.*, p. 318
109. Davidson, R.T., and Benham, W., *op. cit..*, Volume 1, p. 322
110. *Chronicle of Convocation*, pp. 1683 and 1830 in *ibid.*, p. 322
111. Davidson, R.T., and Benham, W., *op. cit..*, Volume 1, p. 325
112. Kitchin, G.W., *op. cit..*, p. 326
113. *ibid.*, p. 322
114. *ibid.*, p. 323

Notes to chapter VI

1. Knight, F,. *The Nineteenth Century Church and English Society* (Cambridge University Press, 1995) p. 153
2. Trollope, A., *The Last Chronicle of Barset* (OUP, 1980 edition) p. 890
3. Munden, A.F., 'The First Palmerston Bishop: Henry Montagu Villiers, Bishop of Carlisle, 1856-60 and Bishop of Durham 1860-1861,' *Northern History* Volume 26, 1990, p. 189
4. Villiers, M., *A Charge delivered to the Clergy of the Diocese of Carlisle at the First Visitation of the Hon. H. Montagu Villiers, DD., Lord Bishop of Carlisle 1858* (London, James Nisbet & Co.) p. 4
5. *ibid.*, p. 5
6. Munden, A.F., *op. cit.*, p. 197
7. Waldegrave, S., *The Charge Delivered in July and August 1864 at His Second Episcopal Visitation by the Hon. and Right Revd. Samuel Waldegrave DD, Lord Bishop of Carlisle* (London, Hunt & Co., 1864), p. 23
8. *ibid.*, p. 8
9. *ibid.*, p. 9
10. Waldegrave, S., *The Christian Ministry not Sacerdotal but Evangelistic. The Charge delivered in September 1867 at his Third Episcopal Visitation by the Hon. and Right Rev. Samuel Waldegrave DD* (London, Hunt & Co., 1867), p. 10
11. Baring, C., *A Charge delivered to the Clergy of the Diocese of Gloucester and Bristol at His Primary Visitation in October 1857* (Seeley, Jackson, & Halliday, London, 1858), p. 11
12. Thomson, W., *A Charge to the Clergy of the Diocese of York delivered at his Primary Visitation in October 1865 by the Most Reverend William Lord Archbishop of York, Primate of England and Metropolitan* (London, John Murray, 1865), p. 4
13. *ibid.*, p. 4
14. *ibid.*, p. 6
15. Kirk-Smith, H., *William Thomson Archbishop of York* (London, SPCK, 1958), p. 69

16. *Diocesan Year Book*, 1890, p. 187 cited *ibid.*, p. 69
17. Kirk-Smith, H., *op. cit.*, p. 70
18. *ibid.*, p. 70
19. Wigram, J.C., *A Charge Delivered to the Clergy and Churchwardens of the Diocese of Rochester at his Second General Visitation in November 1864* (London, Rivingtons, 1864), p. 26
20. *ibid.*, p. 26
21. *ibid.*, p. 30
22. *ibid.*, p. 37
23. Browne, H.E., *A Charge Delivered to the Clergy and Churchwardens of the Diocese of Ely at His Primary Visitation in October and November 1865 by Harold Edward, Lord Bishop of Ely* (London, Longman, Green & Co. 1865)
24. Jacobson, W., *A Charge Delivered to the Clergy of the Diocese at His Primary Visitation, October 1868* (Chester, Phillipson & Golder, 1868), p. 25
25. Burgon, J.W. *Lives of Twelve Good Men* (New York, Scribner & Welford, 1888) Volume 2, p. 280
26. Longley, C.T., *A Charge addressed to the Clergy of the Diocese of Durham at His Primary Visitation by Charles Thomas Longley DD, Lord Bishop of Durham* (George Andrews, Durham, 1857), p. 8
27. Waldegrave, S., *The Charge delivered in October 1861 at His Primary Visitation by the Hon. and Right Rev. Samuel Waldegrave DD, Lord Bishop of Carlisle* (London, Wertheim, Macintosh & Hunt; T.W. Arthur, Carlisle, 1861) p. 43
28. *ibid.*, p. 43
29. *The Times* Wednesday 2 May, 1894
30. Pelham, J.T., *A Charge Delivered to the Clergy and Churchwardens of the Diocese of Norwich by John Thomas, Lord Bishop of Norwich at His Visitation in 1865* (London, Rivingtons, 1865), p. 7
31. *ibid.*, p. 7
32. *Durham County Advertiser*, 19 September, 1879
33. *The Christian Observer* January 1859, p. 45
34. Bickersteth, M.C., *A Sketch of the Life and Episcopate of the Right Reverend Robert Bickersteth DD, Bishop of Ripon 1857-1884* (London, Rivingtons, 1887), p. 110
35. *ibid.*, p. 110
36. Arnold, F., *Our Bishops and Deans* (London, Hurst & Blackett, 1875) Volume 2, p. 31
37. *Chester Courant* 16 July, 1884
38. Burgon, J.W., *Lives of Twelve Good Men* (New York, Scribner & Welford, 1888) Volume 2, p. 293
39. *ibid.*, p. 279
40. *The Times* 11 January 1892
41. *Chelmsford Chronicle* 3 February 1865
42. Longley, C.T., *A Charge addressed to the Clergy of the Diocese of Durham at His Primary Visitation by Charles Thomas Longley DD, Lord Bishop of Durham*, (Durham, George Andrews, 1857) p. 12
43. Ellicott, C.J., *The Church and the Rural Poor being an Address delivered in the Parish Church of Stow on the Wold at the Triennial Visitation, October 29, 1873* (Longman & Co.,), p. 4
44. *The Eagle* December 1905, Volume 138, p. 84
45. Knight, F., *The Nineteenth Century Church and English Society* (C.U.P., 1995), p. 177

46. Burns, A., *Legitimating Church Reform in Early Nineteenth Century England* (Unpublished paper read at London University, 3 June 1996)
47. Dansey, W., *Horae Decanicae Rurales* (London, 1835) 2 Volumes
48. Trollope, J., *op. cit.*, Chapter 61 pp. 658-671
49. Munden, A.F. *op. cit.*, p. 194
50. Villiers, H.M., *op. cit.*, Chapter 61, pp. 658-671
51. Bickersteth, M.C., *op. cit.*, p. 267
52. Baring, C., *op. cit.*, p. 4
53. Baring, C., *A Charge Delivered at the Triennial Visitation of the Diocese, September and October 1860 by Charles, Lord Bishop of Gloucester and Bristol* (Seeley, Jackson & Halliday, 1860), pp. 25-26
54. Longley, C.T., *A Charge 1857* p. 12
55. *ibid.*, p. 12
56. Longley, C.T., *A Charge addressed to the Clergy of his Diocese by Charles Thomas Longley, Archbishop of Canterbury* (London, Rivingtons, 1864), p. 8
57. *ibid.*, p. 8
58. *The Times* 2 May 1894
59. Pelham, J.T., *A Charge Delivered to the Clergy and Churchwardens of the Diocese of Norwich by John Thomas, Lord Bishop of Norwich at His Visitation in 1865* (London, Rivingtonss, 1865), p. 5
60. *ibid.*, p. 5
61. *The Christian Observer* January 1861, p. 29
62. Kirk-Smith, H., *op. cit.*, p. 147
63. Ellicott, C.J., *The Spiritual Needs in Country Parishes: Seven Addresses* (London, S.P.C.K., 1887), p. 46
64. Burgon, J.W., *Lives of Twelve Good Men* (New York, Scribner & Welford, 1888) Volume 2, p. 280
65. Jacobson, W., *A Charge Delivered to the Clergy of the Diocese at His Primary Visitation, October 1868* (Chester, Phillipson & Golder, 1868), p. 6
66. *ibid.*, p. 7
67. Jacobson, W., *A Charge delivered to the Clergy of the Diocese at His Second Visitation, October 1871 by William Jacobson DD, Bishop of Chester* (Chester, Phillipson & Golder, 1871), p. 22
68. *Chelmsford Chronicle* 11 January 1861
69. Browne, H.E., *A Charge delivered to the Clergy 1865*, p. 32
70. *ibid.*, p. 32
71. Kitchin, G.W., *Edward Harold Browne DD, Lord Bishop of Winchester, A Memoir* (London, John Murray, 1895), p. 272
72. *ibid.*, p. 269.
73. Kirk-Smith, H., *op. cit.*, p. 71
74. Kitchin, *op. cit.*, p. 273
75. Kirk-Smith, H., *op. cit.*, p. 71
76. Bickersteth, M.C., *A Sketch*, pp. 262-263
77. Burgon, J.W., *Lives of Twelve Good Men*, p. 279
78. *ibid.*, p. 280
79. Villiers, H.M., *A Charge 1858*, p. 31
80. Pelham, J.T., *A Charge 1865,* p. 11
81. Ellicott, C.J., *Approaching Dangers Being an Address Delivered in the Cathedral, Bristol, at the Triennial Visitation October 22nd 1874* (London, Longman & Co., 1874), p. 5
82. Villiers, H.M., *A Charge 1858*, pp. 31-32

83. *ibid.*, p. 32
84. Baring, C., *A Charge 1860*, p. 23
85. Longley, C.T., *A Charge 1857*, p. 28
86. Longley, C.T., *A Charge 1864*, p. 15
87. Pelham, J.T., *A Charge 1865*, p. 14
88. Bickersteth, R., *A Charge 1861*, p. 14
89. Bickersteth, R., *A Charge 1864*, pp. 13-14
90. Thomson, W., *A Charge 1865*, p. 24
91. *ibid.*, p. 24
92. *The Eagle* Volume 138, p. 99
93. Ellicott, C.J., *Church Work Past and Present being an Address Delivered at Gloucester Cathedral at the Triennial Visitation 23 October 1873* (London, Longman & Co., 1873), p. 9
94. Jeune, F., *A Charge delivered to the Clergy and Churchwardens of the Diocese of Peterborough At His Primary Visitation in October 1967 by Francis, Lord Bishop of Peterborough* (James Parker & Co., 1867), p. 7
95. *ibid.*, p. 7
96. *ibid.*, p. 8
97. Philpott, H., *A Charge Delivered to the Clergy and Churchwardens of the Diocese of Worcester by Henry, Lord Bishop of Worcester at his Visitation in June 1865* (London, Rivingtons, 1865), p. 10
98. Philpott, H., *A Charge Delivered to the Clergy and Churchwardens of the Diocese of Worcester by Henry, Lord Bishop of Worcester at his Visitation in June 1874* (London, Rivingtons, 1874), pp. 35-36
99. Jacobson, W., *A Charge Delivered to the Clergy of the Diocese at His Primary Visitation in October 1868* (Chester, Phillipson & Golder, 1868), p. 15
100. Jacobson, W., *A Charge Delivered to the Clergy of the Diocese at His Second Visitation, October 1871, by William Jacobson DD, Bishop of Chester* (Chester, Phillipson & Golder, 1871), p. 9
101. Longley, C.T., *A Charge 1864*, p. 17
102. *ibid.*, p. 18
103. Pelham, J.T., *A Charge 1865*, p. 14
104. *ibid.*, pp. 14-15
105. Bickersteth, R., *A Charge 1864*, p. 9
106. *ibid.*, p. 9
107. Bickersteth, R., *A Charge 1876*, p. 16
108. Wigram, J.C., *A Charge*, p. 8
109. *ibid.*, p8
110. Ellicott, C.J., *Church Work Past and Present being an Address Delivered in the Cathedral, Gloucester at the Triennial Visitation 23 October 1873 by Charles John Ellicott* (London, Longman & Co., 1873), p. 9
111. Jacobson, W., *A Charge 1868*, p. 11
112. Longley, C.T., *A Charge 1864*, p. 28
113. *ibid.*, p. 34
114. Baring, C., *A Charge 1860*, p. 18
115. *ibid.*, p. 118
116. *ibid.*, p. 118
117. *The Christian Observer* June 1860, p. 438
118. *ibid.*, p. 438
119. Longley, C.T., *A Charge 1864*, p. 34
120. Longley, C.T., *A Charge 1867*, p. 12

121. *ibid.*, p15
122. Bickersteth, R., *A Charge 1861*, p. 39
123. *ibid.*, p. 41
124. *ibid.*, p. 41
125. Ellicott, C.J. *Revision and the Rubrics being an Address Delivered at the Parish Church of Cirencester at the Triennial Visitation 23 October 1874* (London, Longman & Co., 1874), p. 11
126. Carpenter, S.C., *Church and People 1789-1881* (SPCK, 1933), p. 252
127. Knight , F., *Op. Cit.*, p 94
128. *Life of A.W. Thorold*, p. 201 cited by Carpenter, S.C., *Op. Cit.*, p. 253
129. See Obelkevich, J., *Religion and Rural Society* (Oxford, Clarendon, 1976) p. 273
130. Knight, F., *op. cit.*, p. 92
131. *ibid.*, p. 92
132. Obelkevich, J., *op. cit.*, p. 273
133. Knight, F., *op. cit.*, p. 92
134. Baring, C., *A Charge 1857*, p. 22
135. *ibid.*, p. 23
136. *Durham County Advertiser*, 19 September, 1879
137. Munden, A., *op. cit.*, p. 198
138. Longley, C.T., *A Charge 1857*, p. 25
139. *ibid.*, p. 25
140. *ibid.*, p. 127
141. Pelham, J.T., *A Charge 1865*, p. 15
142. Bickersteth, M.C., *op. cit.*, p. 270
143. *ibid.*, p. 272
144. Thomson, E.H., *op. cit.*, p. 394 note 1
145. Kirk-Smith, H., *op. cit.*, p. 62
146. Thomson, *A Charge 1865*, p. 18
147. *ibid.*, p. 19
148. Browne, H.E., *A Charge 1865*, pp. 10-11
149. Jeune, F., *A Charge 1867*, p. 11
150. Jacobson, W., *A Charge 1868*, p. 26
151. Longley, C.T., *A Charge 1857*, p. 24
152. Bickersteth, M.C., *A Charge 1864*, p. 13, Pelham, J.T., *A Charge 1865*, p. 16, Jacobson, W., *A Charge 1868*, p. 27
153. Carpenter, S.C., *Church and People 1789-1889* (SPCK, 1933), pp. 251f
154. Pelham, J.T., *A Charge 1865*, p. 15
155. Bickersteth, M.C., *op. cit.*, p. 145
156. Bickersteth, R., *A Charge 1861*, p. 18
157. Bickersteth, M.C., *op. cit.*, p. 15
158. Kirk-Smith, H., *op. cit.*, p. 64
159. Kitchin, G.W., *op. cit.*, p. 420
160. Jacobson, W., *A Charge 1871*, pp. 4-5
161. Abbot, E., and Campbell, L., *The Life and Letters of Benjamin Jowett* (1897) Volume 2, p. 225 cited Kirk-Smith, H., *op. cit.*, p. 53
162. Munden, A.F., *op. cit.*, pp. 199-200
163. *The Eagle* December 1905, Volume 138, p. 255
164. Villiers, H.M., *A Charge 1858*, pp. 36-37
165. Baring, C., *A Charge 1857*, pp. 29-32
166. Waldegrave, S., *The Charge 1864*, p. 57
167. Thomson, W. *The Charge 1865*, p. 21

168. Kitchin, G.W., *op. cit.*, p. 339

169. *ibid.*, p. 125

170. *ibid.*, p. 125

171. Villiers, M., *A Charge 1858*, p. 32

172. Bickersteth, M.C., *op. cit.*, p. 87

173. *ibid.*, p. 250

174. *ibid.*, p. 47

175. Kirk-Smith, H., *op. cit.*, p. 107

176. *ibid.*, p. 107

177. Ellicott, C.J., *Revision of the Rubrics being an Address Delivered at the Parish Church of Cirencester at the Triennial Visitation 23 October 1874* (London, Longman & Co. 1874), p. 11

178. Pelham, J.T., *A Charge 1865*, p. 44

179. *ibid.*, p. 44

180. Bickersteth, *A Charge 1864*, p. 45

181. Bickersteth, *A Charge 1876*, p. 240

182. Philpott, H., *A Charge 1874*, p. 60

183. Browne, T.H., *The Clergyman in Social Life: A Charge Addressed to Candidates in Ely Cathedral at Trinity Ordination, 1864 by Edward Harold, Bishop of Ely* (Cambridge, Deighton, Bell & Co., 1864), p. 8

184. Wigram, J.C., *The Cottager's Family Prayers by Joseph Cotton Wigram DD, Bishop of Rochester* (Chelmsford, T.B. Arthy, 1863), p. 1

185. *Loc.Cit.*

186. *ibid.*, pp. 15, 17 & 19

187. Williams, C.P., 'British Religion and the Wider World: Mission and Empire, 1800-1940' in Gilley, S., and Sheils, W.J., *A History of Religion in Britain* (Blackwell, 1994), p. 389

188. Villiers, H.M. *A Charge 1858*, p. 28

189. Longley, C.T., *A Charge 1857*, p. 20

190. Longley, C.T., *A Charge 1864*, p. 17

191. Davidson, R.T. and Benham, W., *Life* Volume 1, p. 100

192. Pelham, J.T., *A Charge 1865*, p. 21

193. *ibid.*, p. 21

194. Bickersteth, J.T., *A Charge 1864*, p 28

195. Waldegrave, S., *A Charge 1861*, p. 8

196. See for example *Chelmsford Chronicle* 13 March 1863

Notes to Chapter VII

1. See Toon, P., *Evangelical Theology 1833-1856* (London, Marshall Morgan & Scott, 1979), p. 172f

2. Newman, J.H., *Parochial Sermons* Volume 3, pp. 268-270

3. See chapter 4

4. Colenso, J.W., *The Pentateuch and Book of Joshua Critically Examined* (Longman, 1863), p. xx

5. Bickersteth, R., *A Charge 1861*, p. 43

6. *ibid.*, p. 43

7. *A Charge 1864*, p. 34

8. *ibid.*, p. 34

9. *ibid.*, p. 35

10. *ibid.*, p. 36
11. *ibid.*, p. 36
12. Waldegrave, S., *The Charge 1864*, p. 35
13. *ibid.*, p. 51
14. Waldegrave, S., *The Christian Ministry not Sacredotal but Evangelistic* 1867 (London, Hunt and Company, Carlisle, 1867), p. 32
15. Philpott, H., *A Charge 1865*, p. 44
16. *ibid.*, p. 46
17. Smith, K.S., *William Thomson Archbishop of York His Life and Times* (London, SPCK, 1958), p. 7
18. Ellicott, C.J., *Church Work Past and Present, 23 October 1873* (London, Longman and Co. 1873), p. 20
19. Ellicott, C.J., *The Present Dangers of the Church of England: A Sermon preached at the Re-opening of Holy Trinity Church, Clifton, 8 January 1874* (London, Longman and Co., 1874), p. 4
20. Ellicott, C.J., *Christus Comprobatur or the Testimony of Christ to the Old Testament* (London, SPCK, 1891), pp.17-18
21. *ibid.*, p. 177
22. Ellicott, C.J., *Address on the Revised Verson* (1901) p. 126 cited in *The Eagle* Volume 138, p. 94
23. *ibid.*, p. 95
24. Kitchin, G.W., *Edward Browne DD Lord Bishop of Winchester, A Memoir* (London, John Murray, 1895), p. 347
25. *ibid.*, p. 470
26. Jeune, F., *A Charge 1867*, p. 31
27. *ibid.*, p. 31
28. *ibid.*, pp. 39-40
29. Jeune, F.C., *The Studies of Oxford Vindicated in a Sermon preached before the University on Act Sunday, June 29, 1845 by Francis Jeune DCL Master of Pembroke College, and late Dean of Jersey* (London, Matchard and Son, Piccadilly, 1845), p. 8
30. *ibid.*, pp. 8-9
31. *ibid.*, p. 11
32. Longley, C.T., *A Pastoral Letter Addressed to the Clergy and Laity of His Province by Charles Thomas Longley, Archbishop of Canterbury* (London, Rivingtons, 1864), p. 14
33. *ibid.*, p. 14
34. *ibid.*, p. 14
35. Ibid., p/4
36. Philpott, H., *A Charge 1865*, p. 44
37. *ibid.*, p. 46
38. *ibid.*, p. 52
39. Waldegrave, S., *The Cattle Plague a Warning Voice to Britain from the King of Nations: A Sermon preached in the Cathedral Church of Carlisle on Friday 12 January 1866, by the Hon. and Right Rev. Samuel Waldegrave DD Lord Bishop of Carlisle* (London, William Hunt and Company, 1866)
40. *ibid.*, p. 6
41. *ibid.*, p. 10
42. *ibid.*, pp. 11-13
43. *ibid.*, p. 13

44. *ibid.*, p. 16

45. *ibid.*, p. 17

46. *Rochester and Chatham and Strood Gazette* 2 October 1860

47. Colenso, J.W. *The Pentateuch and Book of Joshua Critically Examined (Longman, 1863)*, p. 35

48. *ibid.*, p. 37

49. *ibid.*, p. 33

50. *ibid.*, p. 34

51. *ibid.*, p. 128

52. *ibid.*, p. xx

53. See Brooke, A., *Robert Gray First Bishop of Cape Town* (OUP, 1947), pp. 111f

54. See DNB entry for Charles Longley

55. Longley, C.R. *A Charge 1864*, p. 48

56. Davidson, R.T. and Benham, W., *Life of Archbishop Campbell Tait* (London, Macmillan, 1891) Volume 1, pp. 342-343

57. *ibid.*, Volume 1, p. 361

58. *ibid.*, Volume 1, p. 361

59. Kirk-Smith, H., *op. cit.*, p. 36

60. Thomson, E.H., *The Life and Letters of William Thomson Archbishop of York* (London, The Bodley Head, 1919), p. 224

61. Kirk-Smith, H., *op. cit.*, p. 37. See also Thomson, E.H., *op. cit.*, p. 224

62 Pelham, J.T. *A Charge 1865*, p. 32

63. *ibid.*, p. 33

64. *ibid.*, p. 33

65. Waldegrave, S., *The Charge 1864*, p. 35

66. *ibid.*, p. 37

67. Kitchin, G.W., *Edward Harold Browne DD, Lord Bishop of Winchester, A Memoir* (London, John Murray, 1895), p. 419

68. *ibid.*, p. 218

69. *The Christian World* cited by *The Chelmsford Chronicle* 2 January 1863.

70. *The Chelmsford Chronicle* 16 January 1863

71. Bickersteth, M.C., *op. cit.*, p. vii

72. Bickersteth, R., *Romanism in its Relation to the Second Coming of Christ. A lecture by the Rev. R. Bickersteth* (London, James Nisbet and Co., 1854), p. 28

73. Wolfe, J., *The Protestant Crusade in Great Britain 1829-60* (Clarendon Press, 1991), p. 133 citing *The British Protestant* (1858), p. 155 *Durham County Advertiser* 19 September, 1879

74. Waldegrave, S., *Cattle Plague 1866*, p. 17

75. Waldegrave, S., *The Faithful Word and the Duty of Holding it Fast. A Sermon preached before the Church Missionary Society at St. Bride's Church, Fleet Street, London by Samuel Waldegrave Lord Bishop of Carlisle on Monday Evening Monday 4, 1868* (London, William Harcourt and Company, 1868)

76. Philpott, H., *A Charge 1865*, p. 23

77. Thomson, W., *Martin Luther, His Mission and His Work*, pp. 9 and 30 cited by Kirk-Smith, H., *op. cit.*, p. 122

78. *ibid.*, p. 32

79. Ellicott, C.J., *Revision of the Rubrics being an Address Delivered at the Parish Church of Cirencester at the Triennial Visitation 23 October 1874* (London, Longman and Co.), p. 11

80. *ibid.*, p. 12

81. Ellicott, C.J., *Some Present Dangers of the Church of England* (Cassell, Petter and Galpin, London, 1878), p. vi
82. Kitchin, G.W., *op. cit.*, p. 57
83. Jeune, F., *A Charge 1867*, p. 41
84. Jeune, F., *The Throne of Grace: Not a Confessional. A Sermon Preached before the University of Oxford, on Sunday, October 18, 1846* (London, Hatchard and Son, 1846), p. 3
85. *ibid.*, p. 5
86. Bebbington, D.W., *Evangelicals and Modern Britain* (Heinemann, 199), pp 1-19
87. Villiers, M.C., *A Charge 1858*, p. 35
88. *ibid.*, p. 32
89. Baring, C. *A Charge 1857*, p. 35
90. Pelham, J.T., *A Charge 1865*, p. 43
91. Bickersteth, R., *A Charge 1861*, p. 44
92. Waldegrave, S., *A Charge 1861*, p. 30
93. Kirk-Smith, H., *op. cit.*, pp. 10-11
94. *ibid.*, p. 35
95. *ibid.*, p. 168 citing *The Yorkshire Herald*
96. Tait, A.C., *A Charge 1865*, p. 47
97. Ellicott, C.J., *Revision of the Rubrics*, p. 11
98. Kitchin, G.W., *op. cit.*, p. 125
99. *ibid.*, p 130
100. Munden, A.F. *op. cit.*, p. 188
101. Bickersteth, R., *Romanism in its Relation to the Second Coming of Christ. A lecture by the Rev. R. Bickersteth* (London, James Nibbet and Co., 1854), pp. 4-6
102. Kirk-Smith, H., *op. cit.*, p. 169
103. Kitchin, G.W., *op. cit.*, p. 169
104. Wigram, J.C., 'The Advent of the Lord the present Glory of the Church' in Wilson, W., (ed) *The Blessing of the Lord's Second Advent: Six Lectures During Lent* (London, 1850), p. 35
105. *ibid.*, p. 53
106. Wigram, J.C., *The Jews, The Appointed Witnesses for God in the Successive Ages of the World* (1855), p. 15
107. Waldegrave, S., *New Testament Millennarianism: or the Kingdom and Coming of Christ as Taught by Himself and His Apostles by the Rt. Hon. and Right Rev. Samuel Waldegrave DD, Lord Bisop of Carlisle* (London, William Hunt and Company, 1866), p. 13
108. *ibid.*, p. 83
109. *ibid.*, p. 136
110. *ibid.*, p. 137
111. *ibid.*, p. 252
112. Shipley, O., *The Church and the World* cited by Rowell, G., *Hell and the Victorians* (Clarendon, Oxford, 1974), p. 1
113. *ibid.*, p. 94
114. *ibid.*, p. 163
115. Waldegrave, S., *A Charge 1864*, p. 59
116. *ibid.*, p. 60
117. Longley, C.T., *A Pastoral Letter to Clergy and Laity of the Province of Canter-*

bury by the Lord Archbishop of Canterbury, Primate of All England and Metropolitan (London, W. Clowes and Sons, 1864), p. 7

118. Thomson, W., *A Pastoral Letter to the Clergy and Laity of the Province of York by William Lord Archbishop of York, Primate of England and Metropolitan* (W. Clowes and Sons, London, 1864), p. 13

Notes to Chapter VIII

1. Rowell, G., *The Vision Glorious* (Oxford, OUP, 1983), p. 117

2. Moorman, J.R.M., *History of the Church of England* (A and C Black, 1963), p. 367

3. Butterfield was one of the first to advocate the Gothic style of church architecture in nineteenth-century England

4. Chadwick, O., *The Victorian Church* (A and C Black, 1967) Part 2, p. 310

5. *ibid.*, p. 319

6. *The Annual Register* cited by Bell, H.C.F., *Lord Palmerston* (Longmans, Green and Co., London, 1936), p. 303

7. *Carlisle Journal* 24 October, 1856, cited by Munden, A.F., 'The First Palmerston Bishop: Montagu Villiers,' *Northern History* Volume 26, 1990, p. 192

8. Villiers, M.C., *A Charge 1858*, p. 11

9. Baring, C., *A Charge 1857*, pp. 28-29

10. *Durham County Advertiser* 19 September, 1879

11. Pelham, J.T., *A Charge 1865*, p. 38

12. Bickersteth, R., *Papal Aggression: A Sermon preached in St. John's Church, Clapham Rise by the Rev. Robert Bickersteth MA, incumbent of St. John's Clapham Rise* (London, D. Batten, 1985), p. 8

13. *ibid.*, pp. 8-10

14. *ibid.*, pp. 42-43

15. Waldegrave, S., *A Charge 1861*, p. 30

16. *ibid.*, p. 30

17. Waldegrave, S., *A Charge 1867*, p. 49

18. Kirk-Smith, H., *William Thomson Archbishop of York* (London, SPCK, 1958), p. 43

19. *ibid.*, p. 43

20. *ibid.*, p. 44

21. *ibid.*, p. 45

22. *ibid.*, p. 50

23. Thomson, D., *The Life and Letters of William Thomson Archbishop of York* (London, John Lane Company, 1919), p. 211

24. Jeune, F.C., *The Studies of Oxford Vindicated in a Sermon preached before the University on Act Sunday, June 29th 1845* (London, J. Hatchard and Son, 1845), p. 9

25. *ibid.*, p. 9

26. *ibid.*, p. 27

27. Jeune, F.C., *The Throne of Grace: Not the Confessional. A Sermon Preached Before the University of Oxford, on Sunday October 18th 1846* (London, Hatchard and Son, Piccadilly, 1846), p. 29

28. Jeune, F.C., *A Charge 1867*, p. 49

29. Longley, C.T., *A Letter to the Parishioners of St. Saviour's Leeds, by the Right*

Rev. The Lord Bishop of Ripon with an Appendix of Documents (London, Francis and John Rivington, 1851), p. 50 et passim

30. *ibid.*, p. 5
31. *ibid.*, p. 11
32. Longley, C.T., *A Charge 1857*, p. 41
33. Longley, C.T., *A Charge 1858*, p. 17
34. *ibid.*, p. 17
35. *ibid.*, p. 19
36. *ibid.*, p. 18
37. Davidson, R., and Benham, W., *Life of Archibald Campbell Tait* (London, MacMillan and Co., 1891) Volume 1, pp. 215-219
38. The Bishop of London to the Rev. E. Stuart in *ibid.*, p. 220
39. *ibid.*, p. 220
40. *ibid.*, p. 221
41. *ibid.*, p. 222
42. The Bishop of London to the Rev. E. Stuart in *ibid.*, p. 222
43. *ibid.*, p. 233
44. *ibid.*, p. 235
45. *ibid.*, p. 236
46. *ibid.*, p. 236
47. King, B., *Sacrilege and its Encouragement* cited *ibid.*, p. 245
48. *ibid.*, p. 245
49. *ibid.*, p. 421
50. *ibid.*, p. 433
51. *ibid.*, p. 437
52. *ibid.*, p. 439
53. Tait, A.C., *A Charge 1866*, p. 15
54. *ibid.*, p. 16
55. Queen Victoria to Archbishop Tait 15 January 1874 in Benson, A.C., *The Letters of Queen Victoria* (London, John Murray, second series, 1926) Volume 2, p. 300
56. *ibid.*, p. 300
57. Archbishop Tait to Queen Victoria 16 January 1874 in *ibid.*, Volume 2, p. 300
58. *The Record*, 8 December 1882
59. Arnold, F., *Our Bishops and Deans* (London, Hurst and Blackett, 1875) Volume 1, p. 35
60. Ellicott, C.J., *Church Work Past and Present* (London, Longman and Co., 1873), p. 18
61. Ellicott, C.J., *The Present Dangers of the Church of England* (London, Longman and Co. 1874), p. 7
62. Morris, W., Swindon (London, Tabara Press, 1970) cited by Knight, *B., Bishop Ellicott A Victorian Bishop in a Changing World* (Unpublished MA thesis, Cheltenham and Gloucester College of HE, 1995), p. 27
63. Knight, B., *op. cit.*, p. 26
64. *ibid.*, p. 26
65. *Cheltenham Examiner* 10 December, 1873
66. Ellicott, C.J., *The Present Dangers of the Church of England 1874*, p. 5
67. Briscoe, J.F., and Mackay, H.F.B., *A Tractarian at Work, A Memorial of Dean Randall* (Mowbray, London,1932), Cobb,P., *The Oxford Movement in Bristol* (Bristol Historical Association,1988), pp. 26-28

68. Kitchin, H., *op. cit.*, p. 346

69. *ibid.*, p. 285

70. Browne, E.H., *A Charge 1865*, p. 50

71. *ibid.*, p. 50

72. Burgon, J.W., *Lives of Twelve Good Men* (New York, Scribner and Welford, 1888) Volume 2., p. 272

73. Villiers, M.C., *A Charge 1858*, p. 31

74. Longley, C.T., *A Charge 1857*, p. 40

75. Longley, C.T., *A Charge 1868*, p. 22

76. *ibid.*, p. 22

77. Bickersteth, M.C., *op. cit.*, p. 211

78. Philpott, H., *A Charge 1874*, p. 49

79. *ibid.*, p. 5

80. Kirk Smith, H., *op. cit.*, p. 33

81. *ibid.*, p. 33

82. Thomson, W., *The Atoning Work of Christ* (Bampton Lectures 1853), p. 227 cited *ibid.*, p. 33

83. Browne, E.H., *The Altar and the Lights on the Altar being a Correspondence between The Lord Bishop of Ely and the Rev. John W.H. Molyneux BA* (London, Longman, Green, Roberts and Green, 1865), p. 15

84. *ibid.*, p. 15

85. *ibid.*, p. 21

86. Longley, C.T., *A Charge 1868*, p. 13

87. *ibid.*, p. 24

88. *ibid.*, p. 12

89. Proby, W.H.B., *Annals of the Low Church Party* (London, J.T. Hayes, 1888) Volume 2, p. 230

90. Tait, A.C., *A Charge 1866*, p. 15

91. *ibid.*, p.16

92. *ibid.*, p. 17

93. Davidson, R.T., and Benham W., *op. cit.*, Volume 1, p. 234

94. *ibid.*, p. 241

95. Bickersteth, M.C., *A Sketch* (1887), p. 214

96. Ellicott, C.J., *Vestments and the Position of the Celebrant* (London, Longman and Co., 1874), p. 6

97. *ibid.*, p. 10

98. *The Guardian* 18 October 1891

99. *The Eagle* December 1905 Volume 138, p. 104

100. *ibid.*, p. 92

101. Wilberforce, R.G., *Life of the Right Reverend Samuel Wilberforce* (John Murray, London, 1883) Volume 3, p. 216

102. Villiers, M.C., *A Charge 1858*, p. 12

103. Bickersteth, R., *Papal Aggression 1850*, p. 9

104. Waldegrave, S., *The Apostolic Commission on Auricular Confession and Priestly Absolution* (London, William Hunt, 1867), p. 20

105. Waldegrave, S., *A Charge 1867*, p. 49

106. *ibid.*, p. 49

107. *The York Journal of Convocation 1878*, p. 101 in Smith K.S. *op. cit.*, p. 33. For a further explanation of Thomson's view on confession see his letter to a fellow bishop in 1878 in Thomson, E.H., *The Life and Letters of William Thomson of*

York (London, John Lowe, 1919), pp. 186-188

108. Jeune, F., *The Throne of Grace: Not the Confessional. A Sermon Preached Before the University of Oxford on Sunday 18th October 1846*, p. 46

109. *ibid.*, p. 66

110. Ellicott, C.J., *The Present Dangers of the Church of England. A sermon preached at the Re-opening of Holy Trinity Church, Clifton, 8 January 1874* (London, Longman and Co., 1874), p. 8

111. Philpott, H., *A Charge 1874*, p. 23

112. *ibid.*, p. 25

113. Longley, C.T., *A Letter to the Parishioners of St. Saviour's, Leeds, by the Right Rev., The Lord Bishop of Ripon with an Appendix of Documents* (London, Francis and John Rivington, 1851), p. 31

114. *ibid.*, p. 40

115. *The Christian Observer* April 1859, pp. 254-255

116. Davidson, R.T., and Benham, W., *op. cit.*, Volume 1, p. 223

117. See Scotland, N.A.D., *John Bird Sumner Evangelical Archbishop* (Gracewing, 1995), p. 117

118. 'Utterances of the Episcopal Bench on Confession', *Church Association Tract No. 128*, p. 1

119. Longley, C.T., *A Letter.*, p. 27

120. Kitchin, G.W., *op. cit.*, p. 370

121. Browne, H.E., *The Position of the Parties of the English Church. A Pastoral Letter to the Clergy of the Diocese of Winchester by Edward Harold, Bishop of Winchester* (London, Longman, Green and Co., 1875), p. 39

122. Kitchin, G.W., *op. cit.*, p. 368

123. David, R.T. and Benham, W., *op. cit.*, Volume 1, p. 217

124. Burgon, J.W., *Lives of Twelve Good Men* (New York, Scribner and Welford, 1888 Volume 2 p 285.

125. Jacobson, W., *A Charge 1868*, p. 31

126. Longley, C.T., *A Letter to the Parishioners of St. Saviour's, Leeds*, p. 9

127. Longley, C.T., *A Charge 1868*, pp. 25-26

Notes to Chapter IX

1. See chapter 1 notes 31-33

2. Cited by Hodder, E,; *The Life and Work of the Seventh Earl of Shaftesbury, K.G.* (Cassell and Co. Ltd. 1886) Volume 3, p. 192

3. Chadwick, O., *The Victorian Church* (A and C Black, 1967) Volume 1, p. 472

4. *ibid.*, p. 472

5. *Sir Robert Fitswygram, Bart* (A private paper in the possession of Canon Sir Clifford Wigram), p. 1

6. See DNB entry for James Wigram

7. See *Hansard*, Vol. CLXVII

8. See *DNB* entry for Philpott, Henry

9. Davidson, R.T. and Benham W., *Life of Archibald Campbell Tait* (London, MacMillan and Co. 1891) Volume 1, p. 45

10. See entry for Parnell, Sir Henry Brooke, *The Concise Dictionary of National Biography* (OUP, 1992) Volume 3, p. 2305

11. See DNB entry for Thomas Pelham (1756-1826)

12. 'The Late Hon. and Right Rev. Samuel Waldegrave, D.D., 57th Bishop of Car-

lisle', *Carlisle Diocesan Calendar*, 1870

13. Bickersteth, M.C. *A Sketch* (London, 1887), p. 189

14. See Chapter 1, notes 34 and 35

15. Arnold, F., *Our Bishops and Deans* (London, Hurst and Blackett Publishers, 1875) Volume 1, p. 167

16. This figure is computed from a complete examination of *Hansard*

17. 'The Late Hon. and Right Rev. Samuel Waldegrave D.D., 57th Bishop of Carlisle', *Carlisle Diocesan Calendar* 1870

18. Bickersteth, M.C. *op. cit.*, Chapter 11

19. *ibid.*

20. *ibid.*

21. Burgon, J.W., *Lives of Twelve Good Men* (New York, Scribner and Welford, 1888) Volume 2, p. 291

22. *The Times* 11 January 1892

23. *Hansard* Volume 204 1871, p. 557

24. *Hansard* Volume 326, 1888 p. 1807, 1812 and 1814

25. See for example 'The Endowed Schools Bill' 9 February 1860 *Hansard* Volume 156, p. 689 and 'The University Subscription Bill' 3 July 1863 *Hansard* Volume 172, p. 158

26. *Hansard* Volume 215, 1873, p. 1468 and 1470 and Volume 217, p. 272, 282, 872 and 877

27. See for example *Hansard* Volume 170, 1863, p. 1735 his Speech on London railways, and Volume 179 1865, p. 110 his speech on Fulham Gas Works and Volume 228 1876, p. 604 his speech on Sulphurous Acid

28. *Hansard* Volume 228 1876, p. 604

29. Davidson R.T. and Benham W., *op. cit.* Volume 2, p. 561

30. *ibid.*, p. 561

31. *ibid.*, p. 561

32. *ibid.*, p. 561

33. *ibid.*, p. 584

34. *ibid.*, p. 588

35. *ibid.*, p. 562

36. *Hansard* Volume 158, April 1860, p. 207

37. *Hansard* Volume 144, March 1857, p. 1891

38. *Hansard* Volume 158, 26 April 1860, p. 115-117

39. *Hansard* Volume 159, 28 June 1860, p. 983

40. *Hansard* Volume 145, 28 May 1857

41. *ibid.*, 28 May 1857

42. *ibid.*, 28 May 1857

43. Davidson, R.T. and Benham W., *op. cit.*, Volume 1, p. 256

44. *Hansard*, 8 December 1857

45. *ibid.*, 8 December 1857

46. *Hansard*, Volume 148, 8 December 1845, p. 345

47. *ibid.*, p. 345

48. Davidson, R.T. and Benham W. *op. cit.*, Volume 1, p. 258

49. *ibid.*, pp. 259-260

50. *Hansard* Volume 156, 10 February 1860, p. 803

51. *ibid.*, 24 February 1863, p. 1692

52. *Hansard* Volume 155, 29 July 1859, p. 632

53. *ibid.*, p. 634

54. *Hansard* Volume 158, 8 May 1860, p. 836
55. *Hansard* Volume 158, p. 1082
56. *Hansard* Volume 158, 8 May 1860, p. 870
57. *Hansard* Volume 164, 22 July 1861, p. 1278
58. *ibid.*, p. 1282
59. *Hansard* 19 May 1863, p. 1933
60. *Hansard* Volume 161, 16 March 1861, p. 1946
61. *Hansard* Volume 162, 18 April 1861, p. 710
62. *Hansard* Volume 180, 23 June 1865, p. 700
63. *ibid.*, Volume 239, 26 March 1868, p. 18
64. *ibid.*,Volume 154, 4 July 1859, p. 581
65. *ibid.*, pp. 583-584
66. *ibid.*, Volume 155, 26 July 1859, p. 450
67. *ibid.*, Volume 191, p. 1123
68. *ibid.*, Volume 191, p. 1123
69. *ibid.*, Volume 191, p. 1118
70. *ibid.*, Volume 191, p. 1122
71. *ibid.*, Volume 191, p. 1130
72. *Hansard* Volume 234 17 May 1877, p. 1045
73. The Lord Chancellor to the Archbishop of Canterbury in Davidson, R.T. and Benham, W., *op. cit.*, Volume 2, p. 393
74. *ibid.*, p. 394
75. *ibid.*, p. 394
76. *Hansard* Volume 252 3 June 1880, p. 1020f
77. *ibid.*
78. *ibid.*
79. *ibid.*
80. Davidson, R.T. and Benham W. o*p. cit.*,Volume 1, p. 233
81. *Hansard* 7 February 1860
82. *Hansard* Volume 156 1860, p. 914
83. *Hansard* Volume 158 1860 22 May, p. 1599
84. Davidson, R.T. and Benham W. *op. cit.*, Volume 2 p. 197
85. *Hansard* Volume 218, 20 April 1874, p. 786
86. *Hansard* Volume 218, 20 April 1874, p. 790
87. *Hansard* Volume 218, 20 April 1874, p. 790
88. *Hansard* Volume 218, 20 April 1874, p. 806
89. *Hansard* Volume 219, 11 May 1874
90. *Hansard* Volume 234, 14 June 1877, p. 1748
91. *Hansard* Volume 234, 14 June 1877, p. 1748
92. *ibid.*
93. *ibid.*, Volume 245, 5 May 1879, p. 1703
94. *ibid.*
95. *ibid.*, Volume 156, 17 February 1860, p. 1213
96. *ibid.*, Volume 172, 3 July 1863, p. 159
97. *ibid.*, Volume 170, 15 May 1863, p. 1735
98. *ibid.*, Volume 179, 12 May 1865, p. 109
99. *ibid.*, Volume 192, June 1868, p. 1385
100. *ibid.*, Volume 216 1873, p. 1468. 1470 and Volume 217, p. 872 and 1877
101. *ibid.*, Volume 228 1876, p. 604 and Volume 231, p. 791
102. *ibid.*, Volume 248 1879, p. 1520 and Volume 258 1881, p. 873
103. *ibid.*, Volume 220 1874, p. 288 and 860

104. *ibid.*, Volume 252 1880, p. 1186, Volume 269, p. 806 and Volume 288 1884, p. 413
105. *ibid.*, Volume 197, 18 June 1869, p. 307

Notes to Chapter X

1. Letter to Thomas Hughes from Mr. J. Bryce, fellow of Oriel College written in the mid 1880s and included as an appendix in Hughes, T., *James Fraser Second Bishop of Manchester* (MacMillan & Co., London, 1887), pp. 357-362
2. Henry Ryder to Gloucester 1815-24 and Lichfield 1824-36; Charles Sumner to Winchester 1827; John Kaye to Lincoln 1827-1853; John Bird Sumner to Chester 1828-1848 and Canterbury 1848-1862; Thomas Musgrave to Hereford 1837-1847 and York 1847-1860 and Henry Pepys to Worcester 1841-1861
3. *The Church of England Quarterly Review* 1856, Volume 40, p. 459
4. In addition to those filled by Palmerston, Canterbury was held by John Bird Sumner, Winchester by Charles Richard Sumner and Worcester by Henry Pepys
5. Villiers, M., *A Charge 1858*, p. 195
6. Davidson, R.T., and Benham, W., *Life of Archibald Campbell Tait* (London, MacMillan & Co., 1891) Volume 1, p. 180
7. *ibid.*, Volume 2, p. 319
8. *ibid.*, Volume 1, pp. 135-136
9. *The Times*, 2 May 1894
10. Bickersteth, M.C., *A Sketch of the Life and Episcopate of the Right Reverend Robert Bickersteth, D.D., Bishop of Ripon*, (Rivingtons, London, 1887), pp. 126-127
11. *ibid.*, p. 272
12. Thomson, W., *A Charge 1865*, pp. 25-26
13. Kirk-Smith, H., *William Thomson His Life and Times 1819-1890*, (SPCK, London 1958), p. 170
14. *ibid.*, p. 170
15. *The Pall Mall Gazette*, 19 January 1867
16. *The Saturday Review*, 8 December 1860
17. See entry for Robert Bickersteth, *DNB*
18. *The Times*, 10 August 1861
19. Kirk-Smith, H., *op. cit.*, pp. 170-171
20. Hodder, E., *Life of the Seventh Earl of Shaftesbury* (Cassel and Company Limited, 1886) Volume 3, p. 197
21. Overton, J.H., *The English Church in the Nineteenth Century*, (London, Longmans, Green & Co, 1864), p. 45
22. *ibid.*, p. 114
23. See Soloway, R., *op. cit.*, p. 348. See also Bowen, D., *The Idea of the Victorian Church*, p. 30
24. Hervey, J.F.A., *A Memoir of Lord Arthur Hervey D.D. Bishop of Bath and Wells* (Printed for Private Circulation, 1896), p. 53
25. *DNB*, entry p. 840
26. Entry for William Magee, *DNB*, p. 761
27. Chadwick, O., *The Victoran Church*, Part 2, p. 337
28. Benson, A.C., *The Life of Edward White Benson* (Macmillan & Co. Ltd., 1901), p. 265
29. *ibid.*, p. 321
30. *ibid.*, p. 345

31. *ibid.*, p. 345

32. Arnold, F., *Our Bishops and Deans*, (London, Hurst and Blacket, 1875) Volume 1, p. 229

33. Mackarness, C.C., *Memorials of the Episcopate of John Fielder Mackarness D.D., Bishop of Oxford from 1870 to 1888*, (James Parker and Co., 1892), p. 149

34. *ibid.*, p. 147

35. Eden, G.R., and Macdonald, F.C., *Lightfoot of Durham* (Cambridge Univeristy Press, 1932), p. 86

36. Sumner, J.B., *A Charge delivered to the Clergy of the Diocese of Chester at the Visitation in 1841*, (London, J. Hatchard & Son, 1848), p. 42

37. Sumner, J.B., *The Charge of John Bird Lord Archbishop of Canterbury to the Clergy of the Diocese at his Visitation 1853*, (London, J. Hatchard & Son, 1853), p. 33

38. Tucker, H.W., *Memoir of the Life and Episcopate of George Augustus Selwyn D.D.*, (London, William Wells Gardenr, 1879), p. 335

39. *ibid.*, p. 339

40. *ibid.*, pp. 345-346

41. *ibid.*, p. 347

42. *ibid.*, p. 334

43. Hughes, T., *James Fraser Second Bishop of Manchester A Memoir 1818-1885*, (MacMillan & Co., 1887), p. 283

44. *ibid.*, pp. 272-284

45. Hinchcliff, P., *Frederick Temple Archbishop of Canterbury*, (Clarendon Press 1998), p. 216

46. *ibid.*, p. 218

47. *ibid.*, p. 219

48. *ibid.*, p. 202

49. Chadwick, O., *op. cit.*, Part 2, p. 349

50. *ibid.*, p. 79

51. *ibid.*, p. 81

52. Diggle, J., *The Lancashire Life of Bishop Fraser*, (London, Sampson Low, Marston, Searle & Rivington, 1891), p. 309

53. Benson, A.C., *op. cit.*, p. 348

54. *ibid.*, p. 349

55. *ibid.*, p. 348

56. Tucker, H.W., *op. cit.*, Volume 2, p. 332

57. Arnold, F., *op. cit.*, p. 278

58. Hervey, J.F.A., *op. cit.*, p. 53

59. Ignotus, C., *A Golden Decade of A Favoured Town*, 1884, p. 17

60. Kitson Clark, G., *Churchmen and the Condition of England*, Methuen and Co. Ltd., 1973, p. 57

61. Chadwick, *op. cit.*, Volume 1, pp. 250-269

62. See Scotland, N.A.D., *John Bird Sumner Evangelical Archbishop* (Gracewing, 1995)

63. Balleine, G.R., *A History of the Evangelical Party in the Church of England*, (Longmans, Green & Co., 1993), p. 195

64. Sumner G.H., *Life of Charles Richard Sumner D.D.*, (London, John Murray, 1876), p. 121 and pp. 192-193

65. Carpenter, S.C., *Church and People 1789-1889*, (SPCK, London, 1933), pp. 263-264

66. *ibid.*, p. 258

67. Soloway, R., *Prelates and People*, (Routledge and Kegan Paul, London) 1969, p. 5
68. Chadwick, *op. cit.*, Volume 2, p. 34
69. Munden, A.F., 'The First Palmerstonian Bishop: Henry Montagu Villiers, Bishop of Carlisle 1856-60 and Bishop of Durham 1860-1861', *Northern History*, Volume 26, 1990, p. 199
70. Marsh, C., *Life of William Marsh D.D.*, (Hurst and Blackett, London, 1875), p. 162
71. Arnold, F., *op. cit.*, Volume 1, p. 162
72. Longley, C., *A Charge 1857*, p. 8
73. 'Biographical Sketch of the Hon. and Right Rev. Bishop Pelham', *Eastern Daily Press*, 4 February 1893
74. Bickersteth, .C., *op. cit.*, p. 250
75. *ibid.*, pp. 123-124
76. *Carlisle Diocesan Calendar*, 1870, p. v
77. Waldegrave, S., *A Charge 1861*, pp. 42-43
78. See for example the account of the Confirmation Service conducted by him at St. Peter's Church, Romford in *Chelmsford Chronicle*, 3 April 1863
79. *Essex Weekly News*, 19 April 1867
80. *Durham County Advertiser*, 19 September 1879
81. *The Times*, 11 January 1892
82. *Yorkshire Post*, 13 June 1883
83 Kirck Smith, H., *op. cit.*, pp. 63-64
84. Kitchin, G.W., *Edward Harold Browne D.D. Lord Bishop of Winchester, A Memoir* (John Murray, London, 1895), p. 256
85. *ibid.*, p. 270
86. Browne, H., *A Charge 1865*, p. 6
87. *The Chester Chronicle*, 19 July 1884
88. See entry for Thomas Claughton, *DNB*, p. 455
89. See Hughes, T., *op. cit.*, Chapters 3-7
90. See Hervey, J.F.A., *op. cit.*, pp. 1-23
91. See entry for Richard Durnford, *DNB*, pp. 595-596
92. Burns, R.A., *The Diocesan Revival in the Church of England c. 1825-1865* (unpublished D. Phil thesis, Oxford University, 1990), p. 4
93. Kirk-Smith, H., *op. cit.*, p. 164
94 *Eastern Daily Press*, 4 February 1893
95. *ibid.*
96. Bickersteth, M.D., *op. cit.*, p. 269
97. *ibid.*, p. 290
98. *Carlisle Diocesan Calendar*, 1870, p. iii
99. See entry for Francis Jeune, *DNB*
100. See for example Jeune, F.C., *A Charge 1867*, pp. 3-4
101. *The Chester Courant*, 16 July 1884
102. Kitchin, G.W., *op. cit.*, pp. 273
103. Bickersteth, *op. cit.*, pp. 263-264
104. *ibid.*, p. 264
105. Kirk-Smith, M., *op. cit.*, p. 71
106. *Eastern Daily Press*, 4 February 1893. Henry Philpott refused to call a diocesan conference during this time at Worcester having among other things 'a horror of irresponsible talk'. See *The Times*, 11 January, 1892
107. See Benson, A.C., *op. cit.*, pp. 164-165 et passim

108. See Diggle, J.W., *op. cit.*, pp. 119-128 et passim
109. Hervey, J.F.A., *op. cit.*, pp. 23-28
110. Eden, F.R., and MacDonald, F.C., *op. cit.*, chapters 7 and 8
111. Hinchcliff, P., *op. cit.*, pp. 230-231 et passim
112. Bickersteth, M.C., *op. cit.*, pp. 101-102
113. *ibid.*, p. 280
114. Villiers, M.C., *A Charge 1858*, p. 33
115 Waldegrave, S., *A Charge 1861*, p. 42
116. See entry for S. Waldegrave, *DNB*
117. *The Times*, 2 May 1894
118. Waldegrave, S., *Ministering Kings to Our Established Church a favour from God*, (William Hunt and Company, London, 1868), p. 11
119. *ibid.*, p. 12
120. Philpott, H., *A Charge 1865*, p. 23
121. *ibid.*, p. 26
122. Philpott, H., *A Charge 1874*, p. 57
123. See Thomson, W., *The National Church. A Sermon preached at the Opening of the Cathedral of St. Albans, on October 21st 1885 by William Lord Archbishop of York*, McCorquodale and Co. Ltd., Leeds 1885, pp. 1-4
124. Ellicott, C.J., *The Present Dangers of the Church of England*, (Longman & Co., London 1874), p. 4
125. *ibid.*, p. 6
126. Ellicott, C.J., *Church Work and Church Questions 1873*, p. 20
127. Ellicott, C.J., *Progress and Trials*, (Longman, London 1867), p. 29
128. Ellicott, C.J., *Some Present Dangers of the Church of England*. Cassell, Patter and Glapin, 1878, p. 95
129. Kitchin, G.W., *op. cit.*, p. 246
130. Browne, H.E., *The Position and Parties of the English Church. A Pastoral Letter to the Clergy of the Diocese of Winchester by Edward Harold Bishop of Winchester* (Longman, Green & Co., London, 1875)
131. Mackarness, C.C., *op. cit.*, p. 110
132. Diggle, J.W., *op. cit.*, p. 125
133. Bowen, D., *op. cit.*, p. 135

SELECT BIBLIOGRAPHY

Books and Articles

Abbey, C.J., *The English Church and its History 1700-1800* (London, Longmans, Green & Co., 1887) 2 Volumes.

Abbot, E., and Campbell, L., *The Life and Letters of Benjamin Jowett* (London, John Murray, 1897) 2 Volumes.

Anon., 'Utterances of the Episcopal Bench on Confession,' *Church Association Tract No.128.*

Arnold, F., *Our Bishops and Deans* (London, Hurst and Blackett, 1875) 2 Volumes.

Ashwell, A., and Wilberforce, R.G., *The Life of Samuel Wilberforce* (London, John Murray, 1881) 3 Volumes.

Balleine, G.R., *A History of the Evangelical Party in the Church of England* (London, Longmans, Green & co., 1933).

Baptism Register St. James Westminster, 1828 Volume 12 in Westminster City Archives.

Baring, C., *A Charge delivered to the Clergy of the Diocese of Gloucester and Bristol at His Primary Visitation in October 1857* (London, Seeley, Jackson & Halliday, 1858).

Baring, C., *A Charge Delivered at the Triennial Visitation of the Diocese, September and October 1860 by Charles, Lord Bishop of Gloucester and Bristol* (London, Seeley, Jackson & Halliday, 1860).

Baring-Gould, S., *The Church Revival*, (London, Methuen and Co Ltd,1914).

Bebbington, D.W., *Evangelicals and Modern Britain* (London, Unwin Hyman, 1988).

Bell, H.C.F., *Lord Palmerston* (London,Longmans, Green & Co., 1936). 2 Volumes.

Benson, A.C., *The Life of Edward White Benson* (London, Macmillan & Co., Ltd., 1901).

Benson, A.C., *The Letters of Queen Victoria* (London, John Murray, second series, 1926).

Best, G.F.A., *Shaftesbury* (London, BT. Batsford Ltd., 1964).

Bickersteth, M.C., *Romanism in its Relation to the Second Coming of Christ. A Lecture by the Rev. R. Bickersteth* (London,James Nisbet & Co., 1854).

Bickersteth, M.C., *A Sketch of the Life and Episcopate of the Right Reverend Robert Bickersteth, D.D., Bishop of Ripon 1857-1884* (London,Rivingtons, 1887).

Bickersteth, R., *A Charge Delivered to the Clergy of the Diocese of Ripon at his Triennial visitation, October 1861, by Robert Lord Bishop of Ripon* (London, James Nisbet & Co., 1861).

Bickersteth, R., *A Charge Delivered to the Clergy of the Diocese of Ripon at His Triennial Visitation, April 1864 by Robert, Lord Bishop of Ripon* (London, James Nisbet, 1864).

Bickersteth, R., *A Charge Delivered to the Clergy of the Diocese of Ripon at his Seventh Triennial Visitation* (London,James Nisbet, 1876).

Bickersteth, R., *Papal Aggression: A Sermon preached in St. John's Church, Clapham Rise by the Rev. Robert Bickersteth MA, incumbent of St. John's Clapham Rise* (London,D. Batten, 1885).

Bickersteth, R., *The Universal and Perpetual Obligation of the Lord's Day* (London,The Religious Tract Society, 1887).

Birrell, C.M., *The Life of William Brock DD* (1878).

Blomfield, A., *A Memoir of Charles James Blomfied* (London,1863) 2 Volumes.

Bowen, D., *The Idea of the Victorian Church* (Montreal, McGill Queens University Press, 1968).

Brenn, W. and Kennedy, *History of Leyton* (Hand-written, undated) Volume 6.

Briscoe, J.F., and Mackay, H.F.B., *A Tractarian at Work, A Memorial of Dean Randall* (London,Mowbray, 1932).

Broadlands Papers, (Southampton University Archives).

Brooke, A., *Robert Gray First Bishop of Cape Town* (Oxford University Press, 1947).

Browne, T.H., *The Clergyman in Social Life: a Charge Addressed to Candidates in Ely Cathedral at Trinity Ordination, 1864 by Edward Harold, Bishop of Ely* (Cambridge, Deighton, Bell & Co.,1864).

Browne, H.E., *A Charge Delivered to the Clergy and Churchwardens of the Diocese of Ely at His Primary Visitation in October and November 1865 by Harold Edward, Lord Bishop of Ely* (London, Longman, Green & Co. 1865).

Browne, H.E., *The Altar and the Lights on the Altar being a Correspondence between The Lord Bishop of Ely and the Rev. John W.H. Molyneux BA* (London,Longman, Green, Roberts and Green, 1865).

Browne, H.E., *The Position and Parties of the English Church. A Pastoral Letter to the Clergy of the Diocese of Winchester by Edward Harold Bishop of Winchester* (London,Longman, Green & Co., 1875).

Burgon, J.W., *Lives of Twelve Good Men* (New York, Scribner & Welford, 1888) 2 Volumes.

Burns, R.A., *The Diocesan Revival in the Church of England c.1825-1865* (Unpublished D.Phil thesis, Oxford University, 1990).

Burns, A., *Legitimating Church Reform in Early Nineteenth Century England* (Unpublished paper read at London University, 3 June, 1996).

Carpenter, E., *Cantuar The Archbishops in their Office*, (London, Mowbray, 1987).

Carpenter, S.C., *Church and People 1789-1889* (London, SPCK, 1933).

Chadwick, O., *The Victorian Church* (London, A & C Black, 1971) Parts 1 and 2.

Chamberlain, M.E., *Lord Palmerston* (London, G.P.C. Books, 1987).

Cobb, P., *The Oxford Movement in Bristol* (Bristol Historical Association, 1988).

Colenso, J.W., *The Pentateuch and Book of Joshua Critically Examined* (London, Longman, 1863).

Crowther, M.A., *Church Embattled: Religious Controversy in mid-Victorian England* (Newton Abbot, David and Charles,1970).

Dansey, W., *Horae Decanicae Rurales* (London, 1835) 2 Volumes.

Davidson, R.T., and Benham, W., *Life of Archibald Campbell Tait* (London, MacMillan & Co., 1891) 2 Volumes.

Diggle, J., *The Lancashire Life of Bishop Fraser*, (London, Sampson Low, Marston, Searle & Rivington, 1891).

East Tisted Burial Register and *East Tisted Marriage Register* (County Records Office, Winchester).

Eden, G.R., and Macdonald, F.C., *Lightfoot of Durham* (Cambridge University Press, 1932).

Edwards, D.L., *Leaders of the Church of England* (Oxford University Press, 1971).

Ellicott, C.J., *Church Work Past and Present, October 23rd, 1873* (Longman and Co., London, 1873).

Ellicott, C.J., *Church Work Past and Present being an Address Delivered at Gloucester Cathedral at the Triennial Visitation, October 23rd, 1873* (Longman & Co., London, 1873).

Ellicott, C.J., *The Church and the Rural Poor being an Address delivered in the Parish Church of Stow-on-the-Wold at the Triennial Visitation, October 29th, 1873* (London ,Longman & Co., 1873).

Ellicott, C.J., *Approaching Dangers Being an Address Delivered in the Cathedral, Bristol, at the Triennial Visitation, October 22nd 1874* (London, Longman & Co., 1874).

Ellicott, C.J., *The Present Dangers of the Church of England: a Sermon preached at the Re-opening of Holy Trinity Church, Clifton, January 8th, 1874* (London, Longman & Co., 1874).

Ellicott, C.J., *Revision and the Rubrics being an Address Delivered at the Parish Church of Cirencester at the Triennial Visitation October 23rd, 1874* (London,Longman & Co., 1874).

Ellicott, C.J., *Vestments and the Position of the Celebrant* (London, Longman and Co.,1874).

Ellicott, C.J., *The Present Dangers of the Church of England* (London, Longman & Co.,1874).

Ellicott, C.J., *Some Present Dangers of the Church of England* (London, Cassell, Patter and Galpin, 1878).

Ellicott, C.J., *The Spiritual Needs in Country Parishes: Seven Addresses* (London, S.P.C.K.,1887).

Ellicott, C.J., *Christus Comprobatur or the Testimony of Christ to the Old Testament* (London, SPCK,1891).

Ellicott, C.J., *Sermons at Gloucester* (1905).

Ellis, I., *Seven Against Christ: A Study of Essays and Reviews* (Leiden, E.J. Brill, 1980).

Gill, R., *The Myth of the Empty Church* (London, SPCK, 1993).

Hampshire Advertiser.

Hempton, D., 'Bickersteth, Bishop of Ripon', *Northern History*, Vol.17, 1981.

Hervey, J.F.A., *A Memoir of Lord Arthur Hervey D.D. Bishop of Bath and Wells* (Printed for Private Circulation, 1896).

Hilton, B., *The Age of Atonement* (Oxford, Clarendon Press, 1988).

Hinchcliff, P., *Frederick Temple Archbishop of Canterbury* (Oxford,Clarendon Press, 1998).

Hodder, E., *Life of the Seventh Earl of Shaftesbury* (London,Cassel and Company Limited, 1886), 3 Volumes.

Hughes, T., *James Fraser Second Bishop of Manchester A Memoir 1818-1885* (London, Macmillan & Co., 1887)

Ignotus, C., *A Golden Decade of A Favoured Town*,(No publication details, 1884.

Inglis, K.S., *Churches and the Working Classes in Victorian England* (London, Routledge & Kegan Paul,1963).

Jacobson, W., *A Charge Delivered to the Clergy of the Diocese at his Primary Visitation, October 1868* (Chester, Phillipson & Golder, 1868).

Jacobson, W., *A Charge Delivered to the Clergy of the Diocese at his Second Visitation, October 1871 by William Jacobson DD. Bishop of Chester* (Chester,Phillipson & Golder, 1871).

Jeune, F.C., *The Studies of Oxford Vindicated in a Sermon preached before the University on Act Sunday, June 29th, 1845 by Francis Jeune DCL Master of Pembroke College, and late Dean of Jersey* (London, Hatchard and Son, Piccadilly, 1845).

Jeune, F., *The Throne of Grace: Not a Confessional. A Sermon Preached before the University of Oxford on Sunday, October 18th, 1846* (London, Hatchard and Son,1846)

Jeune, F., *A Charge Delivered to the Clergy and Churchwardens of the Diocese of Peterborough at his Primary Visitation in October 1867 by Francis, Lord Bishop of Peterborough* (London, James Parker & Co., 1867).

Kirk-Smith, H., *William Thomson His Life and Times 1819-1890* (London, SPCK, 1958)

Kitchin, G.W., *Edward Harold Browne D.D. Lord Bishop of Winchester, A Memoir* (London, John Murray, 1895).

Kitson Clark, G., *Churchmen and the Condition of England* (London, Methuen and Co. Ltd., 1973).

Knight, B., *Bishop Ellicott. A Victorian Bishop in a Changing World* (Unpublished MA thesis, Cheltenham and Gloucester College of Higher Education, 1995).

Knight, F., *The Nineteenth Century Church and English Society* (Cambridge University Press, 1995).

Leach, J.C.H., *Sparks of Reform* (Oxford, Pembroke College, 1994).

Longley, C.T., *A Letter to the Parishioners of St. Saviour's Leeds, by the Right Rev. The Lord Bishop of Ripon with an Appendix of Documents* (London, Francis and John Rivington, 1851).

Longley, C.T., *A Charge addressed to the Clergy of the Diocese of Durham at His Primary Visitation by Charles Thomas Longley DD. Lord Bishop of Durham* (Durham, George Andrews, 1857).

Longley, C. T., *A Pastoral Letter Addressed to the Clergy and Laity of his Province by Charles Thomas Longley, Archbishop of Canterbury* (London, Rivingtons, 1864).

Longley, C.T., *A Pastoral Letter to Clergy and Laity of the Province of Canterbury by the Lord Archbishop of Canterbury, Primate of All England and Metropolitan* (London, W. Clowes and Sons, 1864).

Longley, C.T., *A Charge Addressed to the Clergy of his Diocese by Charles Thomas Longley, Archbishop of Canterbury* (London, Rivingtons, 1864).

Longley, C.T., *A Charge, intended for delivery to the Clergy of the Diocese of Canterbury at his Second Visitation, 1868, by the Most Reverend Charles Thomas, Late Lord Archbishop of Canterbury* (London,Rivingtons,1868).

Longley, C.T., *A Charge Addressed to the Clergy of the Diocese of Durham at...* (London, Macmillan & Co., 1891), 2 Volumes.

Mackarness, C.C., *Memorials of the Episcopate of John Fielder Mackarness D.D. Bishop of Oxford from 1870 to 1888* (London, James Parker and Co., 1892).

Marsh, C., *Life of William Marsh D.D.* (London,Hurst and Blackett, 1875).

Marsh, P.T., *The Victorian Church in Decline* (London,Routledge and Kegan Paul, 1969).

Moorman, J.R.M., *History of the Church of England* (London, A & C Black, 1963).

Morris, W., *Swindon* (Tabara Press, London, 1970).

Munden, A.F., 'The First Palmerston Bishop: Henry Montagu Villiers, Bishop of Carlisle, 1856-60 and Bishop of Durham 1860-1861,' *Northern History* Volume 26, 1990.

Newman, J.H., *Parochial Sermons* (New York, Scribner and Welford , 1879) Volume 3.

Norman, E.R., *Church and Society in England 1770-1970* (Oxford, Clarendon Press, 1976).

Obelkevich, J., *Religion and Rural Society* (Oxford,Clarendon, 1976).

Overton, J.H., *The English Church in the Nineteenth Century 1800-1833* (London, Longmans, Green and Co., 1894).

Pelham, J.T. *A Charge Delivered to the Clergy and Churchwardens of the Diocese of Norwich by John Thomas, Lord Bishop of Norwich at His Visitation in 1865* (London, Rivingtons, 1865).

Prince Lee, J., *A Charge Delivered at His Primary Visitation in November 1851 to the Clergy of the Diocese of Manchester* (London, B. Fellowes, 1851).

Philpott, H., *A Charge Delivered to the Clergy and Churchwardens of the Diocese of Worcester by Henry, Lord Bishop of Worcester at his Visitation in June 1865* (London, Rivingtons,1865).

Philpott, H., *A Charge Delivered to the Clergy and Churchwardens of the Diocese of Worcester by Henry, Lord Bishop of Worcester at his Visitation in June 1874* (London, Rivingtons,1874).

Proby, W.H.B., *Annals of the Low Church Party* (London, J.T. Hayes, 1888).

Raven, C., *The Christian Socialists 1848-1854* (London, Frank Cass, 1920).

Reardon, B.M.G., *From Coleridge to Gore*, (London,Longman,1971).

Ridley, J., *Lord Palmerston* (London, Constable, 1970).

Rowell, G., *Hell and the Victorians* (Oxford,Clarendon Press, Oxford, 1974).

Rowell, G., *The Vision Glorious* (Oxford University Press, 1983).

Scotland, N.A.D., *Agricultural Trade Unionism in Gloucestershire 1872-1950* (CGCHE, Cheltenham, 1991).

Scotland, N.A.D., *John Bird Sumner Evangelical Archbishop* (Leominster, Gracewing, 1995).

Smith, K.S., *William Thomson Archbishop of York His Life and times* (London, SPCK,1958)

Soloway, R., *Prelates and People* (London, Routledge & Kegan Paul, 1967).

Stoughton, J., *History of Religion in England* (London, Hodder & Stoughton, 1901) Volume 8.

Sumner, C.R., *A Charge Delivered to the Clergy of the Diocese of Winchester in September and August 1829* (London, 1829).

Sumner, J.B., *A Charge Delivered to the Clergy of the Diocese of Chester at the Visitation in 1841* (London, J. Hatchard & Son, 1848).

Sumner, J.B., *The Charge of John Bird Lord Archbishop of Canterbury to the Clergy of the Diocese at his Visitation 1853* (London, J. Hatchard & son, 1853).

Sumner, G.H., *Life of Charles Richard Sumner D.D.* (London, John Murray, 1876)

Tait, A.C., *The Spiritual Wants of the Metropolis and its Suburbs. A Letter to the Laity of the Diocese of London by the Right Hon. and Right Rev. Archibald Campbell, Lord Bishop of London* (Rivingtons, London, 1863).

Tait, A.C., *A Charge to the Clergy of the Diocese of London at his Visitation in December 1866* (Rivingtons, London, Oxford and Cambridge, 1866).

Thomson, D., *The Life and Letters of William Thomson Archbishop of York* (London, John Lane Company, 1919).

Thomson, E.H., *The Life and Letters of William Thomson Archbishop of York* (London, John Lowe,1919).

Thomson, W., *The Atoning Work of Christ* (Bampton Lectures, 1853).

Thomson, W., *Aids to Faith* (London, John Murray,1861).

Thomson, W., *A Pastoral Letter to the Clergy and Laity of the Province of York by William Lord Archbishop of York, Primate of England and Metropolitan* (London, W. Clowes and Sons,1864).

Thomson, W., *A Charge to the Clergy of the diocese of York Delivered at his Primary Visitation in October 1865 by the Most Reverent William Lord Archbishop of York, Primate of England and Metropolitan* (London, John Murray, 1865).

Thomson, W., *The National Church, A Sermon preached at the Opening of the Cathedral of St. Albans on October 21st, 1885 by William Lord Archbishop of York* (Leeds, McCorquodale and Co. Ltd.,1885).

Toon, P., *Evangelical Theology 1833-1856* (London,Marshall Morgan & Scott, 1979).

Trollope, A., *Barchester Towers* (London, J.M.Dent and Sons, 1912).

Trollope, A., *The Last Chronicle of Barset* (OUP, 1980 edition).

Tucker, H.W., *Memoir of the Life and Episcopate of George Augustus Selwyn D.D.* (London,William Wells Gardner, 1879).

Varley, E., *The last of the Prince Bishops* (Cambridge University Press, 1992).

Vidler, A.R., *The Church in an Age of Revolution* (Harmonsworth , Penguin Books, 1961).

Villiers, M., *On the Necessity and Value of Lay Agency in the Church*, (London, Sampson, Low & son, 1852).

Villiers, M., *A Charge Delivered to the Clergy of the Diocese of Carlisle at the first Visitation of the Hon. H. Montagu Villiers, DD., Lord Bishop of Carlisle 1858* (London,James Nisbet & Co,1858).

Waldegrave, S., *The Charge Delivered in October 1861 at His Primary Visitation by the Hon. and Right Rev. Samuel Waldegrave DD. Lord Bishop of Carlisle* (London, Wertheim, Macintosh & Hunt, 1861).

Waldegrave, S., *The Charge Delivered in July and August 1864 at His Second Episcopal Visitation by the Hon. and Right Revd. Samuel Waldegrave DD. Lord Bishop of Carlisle* (London,William Hunt & Co.,1864).

Waldergrave, S., *The Cattle Plague a Warning Voice to Britain from the King of Nations; a Sermon preached in the Cathedral Church of Carlisle on Friday January 12th, 1866, by the Hon. and Right Rev. Samuel Waldegrave DD Lord Bishop of Carlisle* (London, William Hunt & Company, 1866).

Waldegrave, S., *New Testament Millennnarianism: or the Kingdom and Coming of Christ as taught by Himself and His Apostles by the Rt. Hon. and Right Rev. Samuel Waldegrave DD. Lord Bishop of Carlisle* (William Hunt & Co., London, 1866).

Waldegrave, S., *The Apostolic Commission on Auricular Confession and Priestly Absolution* (London, William Hunt,1867).

Waldegrave, S., *The Christian Ministry not Sacerdotal but Evangelistic. The Charge Delivered in September 1867 at his Third Episcopal Visitation by the Hon. and Right Rev. Samuel Waldegrave DD.* (London, Hunt & Co.,1867).

Waldergrave, S., *Ministering Kings to Our Established Church a favour from God A Sermon preached in his Cathedral on Sunday, August 2nd, 1868*, (William Hunt and Company, London, 1868).

Waldegrave, S., *The Faithful Word and the Duty of Holding it Fast. A Sermon preached before the Church Missionary Society at St. Bride's Church, Fleet Street, London, by Samuel Waldegrave Lord Bishop of Carlisle 1868* (London, William Harcourt and Company,1868).

Wigram, J.C., 'The Advent of the Lord the present Glory of the Church' in Wilson, W., (ed) *The Blessing of the Lord's Second Advent: Six Lectures During Lent* (London, 1850).

Wigram, J.C., *The Jews, The Appointed Witnesses for God in the Successive Ages of the World* (London,1855).

Wigram, J.C., *The Cottager's Family Prayers by Joseph Cotton Wigram DD Bishop of Rochester* (Chelmsford,T.B. Arthy,1863).

Wigram, J.C., *A Charge Delivered to the Clergy and Churchwardens of the Diocese of Rochester at his Second General Visitation in November 1864*

(London,Rivingtons,1864).

Wigram, J.C., *Ministerial Watchfulness: A Sermon Preached at the Visitation of the Rt. Rev. the Lord Bishop of Winchester in the Parish Church of Alton on Friday, October 17th, 1845* (London, Francis and John Rivington, 1845).

Wilberforce, S., *A Charge Delivered to the Clergy of the Diocese of Oxford 1848* (London, 1848).

Wilberforce, R.G., *Life of the Right Reverend Samuel Wilberforce* (London, John Murray,1883) 3 Volumes.

Williams, C.P., 'British Religion and the Wider World: Mission and Empire, 1800-1940' in Gilley, S., and Sheils, W.J., *A History of Religion in Britain* (Oxford, Blackwell, 1994).

Wilson, H.B. (editor), *Essays and Reviews* (Oxford, J.W. Parker & Son, 1860).

Wolfe, J., *The Protestant Crusade in Great Britain 1829-60* (Oxford, Clarendon Press, 1991).

Journals, Periodicals and Newspapers

Carlisle Journal
Chelmsford Chronicle
Cheltenham Examiner
Chester Chronicle
Chester Courant
Christian World
Church of England Monthly Review
Church of England Quarterly Review
Christian Observer
Chronicle of Convocation
Durham County Advertiser
Eastern Daily Press
Essex Weekly News
Evangelical Christendom
Freeman
Gentleman's Magazine
Guardian
Hampshire Advertiser
Hansard.
Martin, M.C. 'Women and Philanthropy in Walthamstow and Leyton 1740-1870' *London Journal* 1995, Volume 2 part 19.
Pall Mall Gazette
Post Office Directory for Hampshire 1855.
Quarterly Review
Record
Rochester and Chatham and Strood Gazette
Saturday Review
The Times
York Journal of Convocation
Yorkshire Herald
Yorkshire Post

Index